the complete book of
spirits

ALSO BY **ANTHONY DIAS BLUE**

The Complete Book of Mixed Drinks
American Wine
Thanksgiving Dinner *(with Kathryn K. Blue)*
Buyer's Guide to American Wines
America's Kitchen

the complete book of

spirits

A Guide to Their History, Production, and Enjoyment

ANTHONY DIAS BLUE

HarperCollins*Publishers*

HarperCollins books may be purchased for educational,
business, or sales promotional use. For information,
please write: Special Markets Department,
HarperCollins Publishers Inc., 10 East 53rd Street,
New York, NY 10022.

FIRST EDITION

Designed by Mia Risberg

Printed on acid-free paper

Library of Congress Cataloging-in-Publication Data

Dias Blue, Anthony.
    The complete book of spirits / Anthony Dias Blue.— 1st ed.
       p. cm.
    Includes bibliographical references and index.
    ISBN 0-06-054218-7
    1. Vodka.   I. Title.

TP607.V6D53 2004
641.2'5—dc22   2004042895

04 05 06 07 08 ❖/RRD 10 9 8 7 6 5 4 3 2 1

This book is dedicated, with gratitude and admiration,
to the entire spirits industry, from the distillers to marketers,
merchants to bartenders, who have brought this category from
the ignominy of Prohibition and bathtub gin to the exquisite
golden age we are experiencing today.

acknowledgments

Writing about something you love can be an extremely pleasant undertaking, but managing so much material —technical information, history, lore, company intelligence, tasting notes—can be a daunting endeavor nevertheless. Luckily I have been blessed with a superlative team that has provided a sturdy safety net.

The mortar that holds this book together was provided by David Gadd, whose editorial skills and intimate grasp of the material forged it into a coherent whole. In addition he willingly slogged through the manuscript several times to expunge errors, contradictions, and flights of fancy.

Significant contributions were made to the project by Tanya Ward-Goodman as well as Janet Dulin Jones and Lisa King. Gayle Marsh and Cecilia Loschin, from the Blue Lifestyle offices, were also very helpful.

In 2000 I started the San Francisco World Spirits Competition, the only comprehensive judging of its type in the United States. At the 2004 competition more than 450 different products from around the world were submitted. The opportunity to taste so many spirits in a serious judging environment has expanded my knowledge and my palate considerably. The judging has been particularly significant for me since I have been able to taste with and learn from such famed tasters as: Stephen Beal, Julio Bermejo, Katie Ballou Calhoun, Dale DeGroff, Janet Dyer, Michael Feil, Doug Frost, Richard Carlton Hacker, Mendel Kohn, Meridith May, Ken McDonald, Tim McDonald, Frank Melis, Steve Olson, F. Paul Pacult, Kevin M. Vogt, and David Wondrich. I also owe much gratitude to Carol Seibert, the competition's managing director; Chandler Moore, its assistant director; and all the dedicated volunteers who make the judging run so smoothly.

My thanks also go to Susan Friedland, my long-suffering HarperCollins editor, and her able assistant, Califia Suntree.

I am also appreciative of the long-standing support of *Bon Appétit* magazine and its editor, Barbara Fairchild (also her predecessors, Bill Garry and Marilu Vaughn), as well as Lynn Heiler and Amy Foster Devore in the New York office. Thanks also to the other publications that have encouraged my interest in this fascinating subject, particularly *American Way*, *Orient-Express*, and *Robb Report*.

Finally I want to thank my family support team—my wife, Kathy; and my children, Caitlin, Toby, Jessica, and Amanda—for putting up with and understanding this hedonistic lifestyle I have chosen.

contents

Introduction   1

CHAPTER ONE   **Vodka**   9

CHAPTER TWO   **Aquavit**   42

CHAPTER THREE   **Gin**   47

CHAPTER FOUR   **Rum**   69

CHAPTER FIVE   **Tequila**   104

CHAPTER SIX   **Scotch and Irish Whiskey** 137

CHAPTER SEVEN   **North American Whiskey**   181

CHAPTER EIGHT   **Brandy**   210

CHAPTER NINE   **Liqueur and Bitters**   256

CHAPTER TEN   **The Well-Stocked Bar**   301

                   Bibliography   309

                   Index   313

the complete book of
spirits

introduction

I t's not by accident that distilled products are referred to as spirits, since they very much represent the essence of the substances from which they're made. A great brandy captures the very spirit of the grapes from which it originated, just as a great whiskey captures the spirit of its original grain. In spirits, the humble products of the earth—grapes, corn, wheat, barley, potatoes, sugarcane— are transformed into rarefied quintessences.

The early alchemists who perfected the art of distillation in the Middle Ages were searching for ways to capture living spirits, extracting them from their raw materials. The techniques that have been handed down to us from these medieval practitioners have become considerably more commercialized, of course. But, at its heart, distillation even today retains a residual element of the inexplicable. Since the earliest days of distillation, the suggestion of a "spiritual" element has always been at play in the appreciation of spirits. It is this that makes spirits an endlessly fascinating pursuit and perhaps even a near-mystical experience.

And it should be clear that I am not talking about the abuse of spirits here. Spirits are adult pleasures and should be used with thought and moderation. As people in all parts of the world have learned over the course of thousands of years, spirits can provide humankind with relaxation, refreshment, and joy when used responsibly. Spirits can be used to promote conviviality, to cement friendships, to celebrate special occasions and rites of passage, and to aid in meditation and contemplation. We all ponder the meaning of life on occasion, but pondering the meaning of life over a glass of sublime cognac makes the task of philosophy less daunting and, I find, considerably more enlightening.

✳ DISTILLATION AND ITS HISTORY ✳

The process has changed very little over time. Distillation is actually quite a simple procedure, made possible by the differing boiling points of alcohol and water. Whereas water boils at 212 degrees Fahrenheit, alcohol boils at the lower temperature of 173. To separate alcohol from water, then, all that is required is to heat an alcoholic liquid (such as wine or beer) in a still to a temperature greater than 173 but less than 212 degrees. As the alcohol boils, its vapors rise to the top of the still, where they are collected and then cooled. Cooling returns the alcohol vapor to a condensed (liquid) state. The condensed liquid can be redistilled one or more times to increase the alcohol content of the end product.

✳ A BRIEF HISTORY OF DISTILLATION ✳

Distillation has been around since ancient times. "Sea water can be rendered potable by distillation," wrote the Greek philosopher Aristotle. His discovery was allegedly based on the simple observation that steam from hot food condenses on the inner surface of the cover placed over the dish. Archaeological and historical research shows that the science of distillation was known to ancient Egyptian, Chinese, and Near Eastern societies.

Early civilizations learned how to create medicines, perfumes, and flavorings using simple distillation. Following the process, the resulting concentrated versions of herbs, spices, and plants were easy to use and store. The ancient Chinese created a unique spirit from rice and beer, and in the East Indies as long ago as 800 B.C. arrack was made with fermented sugarcane and rice.

Despite the long-standing awareness of the distillation effect, it was not until the early Middle Ages that the distillation of alcohol became a widespread practice and the modern history of this remarkable process began. The practice of distilling spirits was really instituted by Arab alchemists in the tenth century A.D. The very word "alcohol" is in fact an Arabic word, as is "alambic," or still. For centuries the Arabs had been (and, in fact, still are) making eye makeup using black powder that was liquefied, vaporized, and solidified again. They called it kohl. When wine was first distilled, the name of this cosmetic was used to describe the result—*al koh'l*—since the procedure was so similar. From the Arab masters, the knowledge of distillation was eventually passed to Western experimenters during the Middle Ages, who used it to create spirits.

In the Latin-speaking regions of medieval Europe, the newly discovered spirit was called aqua vitae (water of life). The reason for this rather grandiose name was the fact that, at first, distilled spirits were used mostly by alchemists, and many of these scientists thought that they had finally found the elusive "elixir of life." In the thirteenth century, for example, the Majorcan chemist and philosopher Raymond Lully wrote that aqua vitae was "an emanation of the divinity, an element newly revealed to men, but hid from antiquity, because the human race was then too young to need this beverage destined to revive the energies of modern decrepitude."

Wherever this knowledge of distillation spread, the Latin name was translated into the local language. In France it became known as eau-de-vie, while on the Irish peat bogs it was gaelicized into *uisige beatha,* which eventually was corrupted into the word "whiskey." In Russia "water of life" evolved into vodka, from the Russian word for water, *voda.* In Denmark, Sweden, and Norway, the original Latin name took a Scandinavian turn to become aquavit.

Fifteenth-century Europe saw the popularity of distillation take hold and spread like wildfire. It was completely unregulated, and anyone who understood how the process worked could build a primitive still and produce his own aquavit. For raw materials these cottage distillers used whatever was inexpensive and in good, constant supply. In Ireland and Scotland whiskey got its distinctive character from barley and a dose of smoky peat. In France, Spain, and Italy wine was plentiful, and it formed the basis for locally made brandies. Barley, corn, and rye were the backbone of gin in Holland. Later, Caribbean sugarcane was made into rum and the Mexican agave, or "century plant," was used in tequila. In Scandinavia the potato eventually became the spirits-making staple.

✳ A CAVEAT ✳

At this point I feel compelled to add the standard warning: *Don't try this at home!* First of all, as any backwoods moonshiner knows, distilling is strictly controlled by the federal government. Making your own backyard whiskey will draw the "revenuers" down on you like hawks on a chipmunk, leading to some very unpleasant consequences. Secondly, while the process of making alcohol is fairly simple, the process of making *drinkable* alcohol is a bit trickier. The first and last parts of the distillate (the so-called heads and tails) contain impure substances known as congeners. These include acids, esters, aldehydes, fusel oils, and salts. Some of these substances are desirable, giving each type of spirit its distinct taste—absolutely pure alcohol would be characterless—while other congeners are undesirable or even poisonous. Master distillers know when and how to eliminate these impurities, winding up with alcohol that is not only potable but tasty. Making distinctive spirits also involves many postdistillation processes, such as flavoring (as in the case of gin), aging (as in the case of bourbon and Scotch), and filtration (as in the case of vodka). Unlike beer brewing and wine making, the making of spirits is something always to be left to professionals.

✳ THE WORLD OF SPIRITS ✳

There has never before been a greater wealth of spirits available to a wider base of consumers than there is today. Admittedly, many local or regional spirits have fallen by the wayside. This is particularly true of whiskeys, for example. After the vast consolidation and corporate assimilation that took place in the mid- and late-twentieth century, many once-revered Scotch and Irish distilleries are now silent or, worse, have been razed altogether. It's tempting to lament the days when there were some two thousand distilleries in Ireland alone, until one realizes that those myriad local whiskeys had very small distribution by today's standards. Today there are only three distilleries in Ireland, producing just a handful of whiskey brands, but thanks to globalization their products are available to a very wide and appreciative audience worldwide.

By and large, today's world spirits industry is in high gear. New vodkas appear almost weekly. Scotch distillers are releasing rare, old stores that have been aging quietly in bond ʼfor decades. Tequila aficionados have access to new silver tequilas, as well as more and more upscale "sipping" tequilas. Adventuresome spirits importers are seeking out hidden stores of Caribbean rum like pirate treasure. The once-overshadowed Armagnac is making great strides in its long-standing rivalry with nearby Cognac. Rare single-batch bourbons, crafted on the model of single-malt Scotches, have become favorite drams for whiskey lovers seeking the heights of rarefaction. Grappas, those once rustic spirits made from the dregs of wine making, are now being styled from single-vineyard or single-varietal pomace and are finding top-shelf space at trendy bars. Old-style American whiskeys, such as malted rye, have been successfully revived and brought to the attention of an entirely new public.

Although the lion's share of the spirits market is now dominated by just a handful of conglomerates, their individual brands are, for the most, kept jealously distinct and still enjoy a prestige equal to or better than the reputations they've had in the past. Pernod-Ricard's handling of the historic and quite excellent Bushmills whiskeys comes to mind, as does Suntory's marketing of the exquisite Bowmore single malts.

Meanwhile, at the grassroots level, new small-scale distillers are making waves. The United States, especially, has seen the advent of several extraordinary craft distillers (some of whom were originally craft brewers). Traditional American free enterprise is still hard at work, thanks to which there are now brandies from Mendocino that rival the best spirits from Cognac. Scads of new American gins, vodkas, flavored vodkas, rums, and whiskeys made by time-honored hands-on methods are perking up palates across the country. In short, there's never been a more exciting time to explore the world of spirits.

✳ HOW SPIRITS SHOULD BE TASTED ✳

As executive director of the San Francisco World Spirits Competition, the largest professional spirits judging in North America, I have occasion to sample the well over five hundred brands of spirits entered each year. The competition has been invaluable in introducing new spirits products to the public. Many of the members of our judging panels are journalists and spirits industry veterans who help spread the news, both within the industry and to consumers, about the products they have discovered.

Of course, not all brands of spirits are entered into the yearly judging in San Francisco. This is why I maintain a rigorous schedule of weekly spirits tastings independent of the World Spirits

Competition. These tastings include not only new products submitted for evaluation by their manufacturers or importers, but also older products, which I like to revisit frequently. During a typical tasting session, I might sample ten to twelve vodkas, single-malt Scotches, or cognacs. Various types of spirits are never mixed during a tasting, allowing me to focus on the qualities that are unique to each category. The characteristics of gin, for example, are entirely different from those of brandy. If one is to judge each spirit fairly and reach any sort of objective conclusion, the two should never be tasted side by side.

For novices who wish to conduct their own spirits tastings at home, I highly recommend tasting products in "flights" of no more than six similar products. Unlike wine or beer tasting, spirits tasting is extremely fatiguing to the palate, mainly due to the high alcohol content of these products. Keep bottled water handy for refreshing the palate between tastes. A plate of good, unsalted crackers also helps to neutralize the harsh effects of alcohol. Spitting between tastes is recommended and, in fact, requisite among professional tasters, although in a nonprofessional setting you may want to allow yourself a swallow or two.

Of course, the evaluation of spirits, like the evaluation of wine or food, has a large element of subjectivity. While the science of distillation provides certain objective measures that can be applied to spirits (alcohol content being one measure quite often used), no one has yet managed to invent a machine that would provide an entirely objective and impartial evaluation of alcoholic beverages in terms of color, smell, flavor, and finish. Even if such a machine existed, its use would be questionable at best. Could a machine that rated one spirit more highly than another be said to "enjoy" the first more than the second? The answer is obviously no. The joy of spirits lies precisely in that interface between the mystical beverage and the subjective human palate, and it is something that cannot be quantified.

Although all spirits are similar in that they involve a distillation process, the variety of end products is as wide as one can imagine. In comparison with the amazing diversity of spirits, the vast numbers of wines (and beers) on the market seem relatively similar to one another. The purpose of this book is to provide a background for each spirit type, placing each spirit in its proper historical context. Afterward, I suggest a wide variety of particular brands that the reader might want to try. Except for a few instances I have avoided including mixed drink recipes, preferring to focus attention on the spirits themselves. Readers interested in how spirits are used in cocktails may want to look into this book's companion volume, my *Complete Book of Mixed Drinks,* or one of the several other excellent books available on the subject of mixology.

✳ A NOTE ON THE RATING SYSTEM ✳

Spirits evaluation is necessarily subjective, and even two experts may have radically differing opinions about the merits of a particular product. Rather than assign a fixed numerical score for each spirit listed in this book, I have chosen instead to indicate relative merit by means of a system of one to four stars. Buyers should evaluate the quality-to-price ratio to determine which individual spirits may best suit their needs.

★★★★   A world-class spirit representing the pinnacle of its type.
   ★★★   An exceptional spirit worth a special search.
      ★★   A fine spirit of its type, although not exceptional.
         ★   A decent spirit of average quality.

✳ A WORD ABOUT PRICING ✳

Spirit prices will vary considerably across the country, and not every spirit mentioned here will be available in every market. A general price range for each product is indicated by the following symbols.

$$$$ Over $200.
  $$$ $50 to $200.
   $$ $20 to $50.
    $ Under $20.

vodka

In the past several years vodka has become the best-selling spirit in the world, and its popularity is still growing. In the United States sales have reached beyond the forty-million-case mark and show no signs of abating. There are more than three hundred brands of vodka currently sold in the United States. What makes vodka so popular? Perhaps its versatility is a factor. Vodka can be infused with flavors, mixed in cocktails, appreciated neat or over ice. It can be sipped or slugged. It is famous as an accompaniment to caviar, and complements rich and spicy food. It can be made from almost any agricultural ingredient; grain, vegetable, even fruit. It has a mysterious history and inspires great affection; its name even means "dear little water" in Russian, shortened from *zhizennia voda,* "water of life." To some, it seems, vodka is as necessary as water.

✳ WHAT IS VODKA? ✳

In Russia and Poland vodka has many nicknames, such as "Hot Water," "the Monopolka," "the Bubble," "Crankshaft," "the Bitter

Stuff," "the White Stuff." The United States Alcohol and Tobacco Tax and Trade Bureau, though, defines vodka as "neutral spirits distilled from any material at or above 190 degrees of proof, reduced to not more than 110 nor less than 80 degrees of proof, and after such reduction in proof treated by one of the three methods set forth therein so that the resulting product would be without distinctive character, aroma, or taste." Federal regulations also require that the distillate, after treatment, be stored only in metal, porcelain, or glass containers or paraffin-lined tanks.

Vodka is made from a fermented mash, water, and ethyl alcohol. Unlike other spirits, which are defined by how and where they're made (brandy has to be made from fruit, rum from sugar beets or cane, tequila from the juice of the blue agave; Scotch has to come from Scotland and cognac comes only from France) vodka can be made anywhere from any raw carbohydrates that will ferment. Grains such as rye, corn, or wheat, or produce such as potatoes, beets, or sugar beets, can be the mash base for vodka. There is even a classy French grape vodka. The organic congeners that give character to Scotch, bourbon, tequila, and brandy are filtered out of vodka by a charcoal filtration process. Fuller's earth, quartz sand, and even diamond dust have also been used in the filtering process, in the effort to create a mystically "pure" vodka. In fact, there is no such thing as absolutely pure vodka. The trace elements that remain after the filtration help give each vodka brand its unique character.

✳ PURE, CLEAN WATER ✳

Water is the single most important ingredient in vodka and the one that lends this refined spirit most of its character. The Russians claim that "living water" from their rivers and lakes is what makes their vodkas stand apart from those produced elsewhere. The quest for pure water has taken the Finns to underground streams, inspired the Americans to invent more elaborate water softeners and filtration systems, and even led one producer to melt chunks of ancient icebergs with the theory that the older the water, the purer it will be. One company in Poland uses a water-softening system to create its unique "water."

Standard U.S. production of vodka often includes the purchase of neutral grain spirits at a high proof (190 or above), which are then filtered, diluted to bottle strength, labeled, and shipped. Producers of imported vodkas and smaller-batch vodkas make their neutral grain spirit from scratch so they have complete control over the process from the beginning to end. Some of the new small-batch vodkas include Teton Glacier Potato Vodka from Idaho and Tito's Handmade Vodka from Texas. The field is being redefined again by larger brands such as Grey Goose, from France, and Chopin and Belvedere, both from Poland. There are also currently vodkas from many places with no traditional history of vodka production, including Scotland (Brilliant and Hendricks), Denmark (Frïs, Danzka, and Danaka), and Ireland (Boru). Add recently arrived Mor and Stön from Estonia and Zyr and Charodei from Russia, and you have an enormous selection of premium spirits to explore.

✳ FLAVORED VODKAS ✳

While gin and aquavits can be considered a form of flavored vodka, it wasn't until 1996, when Stolichnaya introduced Stoli Limon, that distillers began to add everything from peppermint to pineapple to their vodkas. The trend created a whole new rainbow era of mixed drinks such as the blood orange vodkatini and the key lime vodka gimlet. In the fifteenth and sixteenth centuries Russians mixed vodka with sweet syrup for women (men were supposedly macho enough to drink theirs straight up), and they have also infused vodkas with spices and fruits for centuries. However, it would take another four hundred years for the practice of flavoring to catch up with the West.

Now flavored vodkas have become very popular on the cocktail circuit. Distillers all over the world are adding natural flavoring materials to their spirits, with and without sugar. It's clear that flavored vodkas are here to stay. When vodka is flavored, the name of the flavoring must appear on the label. Almost any spice, flavoring, or fruit can be infused into vodka. Some of the more popular flavorings are bilberry, blood orange, butterscotch, capsicum pepper, cherry, chocolate, cinnamon, clove, cranberry, currant, grapefruit, jalapeño, lime, lemon, Madagascar vanilla, mandarin orange, nutmeg, and raspberry. Depending on the brand and the sugar added, these flavors can range from too sweet to subtle. Some will prove delightful for sipping, while others are best served with mixers.

✳ A RUSSIAN HISTORY OF VODKA ✳

Vodka, an original eastern European beverage, appeared in either Russia or Poland around the thirteenth century. Much like its nearest relation, gin, this white spirit was originally used medicinally. But, as vodka is a step in the process on the way to gin, it is

How to Flavor Vodka at Home

Making your own flavored vodkas is very easy and requires nothing more than a few common kitchen utensils, vodka, a bottle, and flavorings. Use fresh ingredients, preferably organic. If you are not sure a plant is safe for consumption, do not use it. A number of books and websites can help you to identify edible plants. Search out ingredients at your local farmers market or specialty herb shop.

When creating flavored vodka at home, do not use plastic utensils or jars and bottles with rubber rings or plastic-lined lids. Instead, use a clean vodka bottle with a cork. Wash the fresh ingredients and let them dry completely. After they are dry, cut or crush your herbs. When peeling citrus fruits, use only the colored peel (the zest), not the white membrane. Berries can be put in whole. Place the prepared flavorings into the bottle. Add the vodka and seal the bottle. Let it sit for a week in a cool dark place. After the curing process, line a strainer with layers of cheesecloth and place it over a large glass container. Strain the vodka into the container (remember, no plastic). Use a wooden spoon to press lightly on the flavorings in the strainer, as you want the flavorings, not the whole herbs and peels, in the spirit.

If you want to make a sweet version, mix 1 cup of sugar and ½ cup of water in a saucepan, heat the mixture, and boil for several minutes to make simple syrup. Allow the mixture to cool to room temperature. When the syrup is cooled you may add it to the strained vodka. Decant the vodka into a bottle with a cork. Seal, label, and refrigerate.

Sample Recipe
Lemon Rosemary Flavoring

1 tablespoon fresh rosemary leaves
   (rub together to release their aroma)
2 three-inch-long strips of lemon peel (no white membrane)
4 coriander seeds (crush with the flat side of a chef's knife)
1 bottle of vodka

Simple Syrup
1 cup sugar
½ cup water

easier to distill. The word "vodka" is primarily attributed to the Russians. Originally called *zhizennia voda,* which translates to "water of life," the name was shortened to voda and eventually to the diminutive vodka, which literally means "dear little water." This link to water is appropriate for a spirit that stakes its reputation on purity.

Within Russia, opinions differ about who created the first distilled Russian vodka. Some credit the twelfth-century monks in the Russian monastery-fort of Viatka creating vodka as early as 1174, while others believe it was the fourteenth-century monks at the Chudov Monastery in the Kremlinand.

It is generally thought that the Chudov monks learned the art of distillation from their brothers in the Italian monasteries during the Ecumenical Council of the Roman Catholic Church in 1430. Isidor the Greek, imprisoned by Czar Vassily III in the Chudov Monastery for siding incorrectly on the schism between the Roman and Russian orthodoxy, is said to have spent a year in the monastery teaching the distillation process to the monks. As there were not abundant grapes available, as in Italy, he used grain. And for this he was allowed to escape. *Chudov,* by the way, means "miracle."

The early "distillation" process practiced by the Italian monks originated in Arabia and came to Europe in the thirteenth century with a traveler, Raymond Lully. It is believed that Lully happened upon what he termed a "water spirit" while on the Arab-ruled island of Majorca. Genoan merchants who sold it as a medicinal balsam, and may have sparked the interest of the Italian monks, capitalized upon this elixir. Early distillation used freezing, aging, and seasoning, as well as using precipitation with isinglass, a gelatin from the air bladder of the sturgeon. Pot distillation was first used in Russia in the fifteenth century.

Most of the documents relating to vodka's "birth" were destroyed in the seventeenth century when the Russian Orthodox Church deemed vodka an invention of the devil and obliterated any documentation that related to the drink's development. Interestingly, in 1697 Peter the Great commissioned a study to find the origins of vodka, and almost executed the man who could find him no answer. An anonymous note in the hand of a monk pointed him to the Chudov Monastery. Peter was attempting to establish the drink as invented by the monarchy, and therefore under its control and jurisdiction. It is said, "He who controls vodka, controls Russia." The church may have been acting against the drink as an instrument of the devil, or against the monarchy's attempt to capitalize on its creation.

Wherever it got its official start, it's clear that by 1505 vodka had definitely taken root in Russia. Swedes on an expedition to

Moscow wrote of tasting the "burnt wine" during their stay. A few decades later, this "bread wine" (vodka) became hugely popular among the Russian peasants. Vodka became customary at festive dinners to toast the health of the sovereign, the sovereign's spouse, the patriarch, famous dignitaries; basically anyone and everyone was deemed worthy of the raising of a glass. It was considered disrespectful not to participate in this binge drinking. These toasts gradually became a traditional element of any celebratory occasion. Vodka was shared at weddings, naming days, baptisms, and funerals.

Within twenty years Russians were in love with the new spirit. Drinking helped combat the inclement weather and softened the end of a hard workday. Vodka also served as a balm to the peasants living as serfs at the mercy of wealthy landowners. Over time as the czar enforced stricter restrictions and the peasants found themselves virtually enslaved, the ritual of drinking provided some consolation.

Sadly, the very conditions that drove the populace to vodka were worsened by increased public drunkenness. Rampant poverty and the ruin of the family structure eventually convinced Prince Ivan III to forbid the preparation of strong drink, but not before creating the first state vodka monopoly, which lasted until 1605. For a time spirits were lawful only on certain holidays. Of course people still drank. In 1552 Ivan IV, known as Ivan the Terrible, built a government-controlled *kabak* (tavern) for his palace guards. Here the men could drink as much as they wanted, but only during Holy Week and Christmas. Most communities in Russia adopted the idea of the tavern. By the early 1600s the *kabaks* were so prolific that Patriarch Nikon created a council to regulate taverns in order to generate revenue by taxation.

By 1648 a third of Russian males were in debt to the *kabaks* and public drunkenness was uncontrollable. Tavern owners in Moscow started calling in the debts, and a violent revolt broke out. The Great Tavern Revolt of 1648 soon spread to other, more rural towns. Peasants in the hinterlands were so besotted on vodka that they weren't cultivating the land, and hence had no money to pay their bills.

In response, the clever and determined Russians began distilling a vodkalike drink at home. These home brews, made from any and all varieties of grain, were potent enough to strip the beard off a Cossack. Czar Aleksey came to power, and correctly suspecting that home brew was dangerous at best, lethal at worst, he permitted the purchase of "take-away" liquor. He ordered a *kabak* to be constructed in every town. Slowly but surely, the *kabaks* multiplied beyond measure. This pattern of abrogating the state monopoly on the control of liquor and then reinstating it would continue throughout Russia's tumultuous history.

Aleksey's son, Peter the Great, assumed power in 1682, bringing Russia into the modern age. Standing six feet, eight inches tall, he was said to be able to drink up to twenty glasses or two liters of vodka a day. He is also rumored to have forced latecomers to his parties to drink entire bowls of vodka and encourage everyone else to watch the effects for entertainment. Vodka, though, was still by law only to be imbibed on weekends or holidays.

From this time on, a system of licensing rights to sell alcohol existed, whereby those who held licenses to produce could sell as much alcohol as the market would bear to recoup the license fee. Vodka was produced by both state-owned distilleries and landowning aristocrats. By 1759 sales from liquor made up 20 percent of the Russian government's income.

In 1765 Catherine the Great made it illegal for anyone but the aristocracy to produce vodka. All other distilleries were destroyed. Most of the vodka the aristocrats produced was flavored. The vodka was made with high-quality ingredients, including filtered water. The flavor was added after the third run, and the vodka was then distilled a fourth time. This flavored spirit was of the highest quality. Landowners even prided themselves on having flavors for every letter of the Russian alphabet, from acorn to dill to sage.

The next big change in vodka's development came in the early 1860s. Charcoal began to be used as a filter because it would absorb the flavors of the cogeners. Cogeners are organic compounds from the highly aromatic and flavorful substances present in wine and liquors. Found naturally in grapes and other fruit used to make wine, cogeners are also by-products of yeast fermentation, distillation processes, and the period of aging in wood. Charcoal filtration removed these particles from the vodka and rendered it not only virtually tasteless, but also clean and clear. The first person to use the charcoal filtration process was Piotr Arsenyevitch Smirnov.

By 1860 Alexander I could not ignore the fact that 40 percent of the government's income came from the sale of liquor. He set up a savvy dual-taxation system that would tax distillers according to output and retailers according to sales. In spite of the new taxes, legal vodka consumption increased, and taverns and liquor shops proliferated. Bootlegging boomed, too. Simply put, drinking was more popular than ever.

By 1894 drunkenness was (again) a serious issue in Russia. Czar Alexander III launched a program to improve the quality of vodka in hopes of getting the peasants to buy state vodka and give up their inferior home brew. The theory was this: If government vodka was better and less expensive, peasants would gladly stop distilling at home. With this in mind, Dmitry Mendeleyev (the god of Russian chemistry and inventor of the periodic table of the elements) developed a new process to distill vodka. Since the time of the monks, processing equal volumes of alcohol and water with trace additives was the widely accepted recipe for vodka. Mendeleyev altered the process and changed the proportion of alcohol to water by calculating the weight of the liquids, not the amounts. This process resulted in an optimum alcohol level of 40 percent, giving the spirit more kick and at the same time making it more efficient to produce.

While Mendeleyev's discovery improved the quality of vodka, it did nothing to make the peasants more docile. In fact, hostilities between the people and the czar were nearing a breaking point. Spurred on by harsh state rules, which confined liquor sales to state liquor stores and prohibited alcohol in restaurants, the people turned to bootlegging in unprecedented numbers. Flouting these laws, the populace drank their purchased state vodka on the street and smuggled it into cheap eating establishments. While the monopoly was intended to separate drinking from eating, all this vodka on an empty stomach did nothing to abate public displays of drunkenness.

It's estimated that by 1913, half of all peasant liquor sales were from bootlegging. For every ten households there was a bootlegging establishment. As in the past, great loss of income, property, and life can be attributed to alcoholism in the final days of the czarist era. By the time of the accession of Nicholas II, the country was teetering on the brink of revolution. Many people blamed the government for their woes. Though Czar Nicholas II was a proponent of prohibition, he was known to drink socially, so he was considered a hypocrite. Many felt his greed was poisoning the people with alcohol while the wealthy hid behind their gated homes enjoying all sorts of vices.

With the seeds of dissent firmly sown, it was just a matter of time before a Bolshevik revolution set Russia on fire, as it did in 1917. At the onset of the revolution, vodka production was banned. Many of the families who had manufactured it fled the country rather than have their throats slit by angry hordes bent on doing away with the aristocracy. Ironically, the incredible success of vodka in the West has its roots in the exile of Russian distillers. Before the momentous events of 1917, this clear, fiery spirit was essentially a regional drink, confined mainly to Russia and Poland.

For a hundred years before the revolution, the Smirnov family had been Russia's leading distillers. They garnered extreme wealth, and developed a close relationship with the czar and the rest of the royal household. But the violent upheaval of 1917 changed all that. Only one of Piotr Smirnov's three sons managed to escape the onslaught. His name was Vladimir and, after fleeing through Turkey and Poland, he eventually settled in Paris.

✳ A POLISH HISTORY OF VODKA ✳

The Poles claim that their vodka, originally called *gorzalka,* was developed somewhere between the eighth and the twelfth centuries. This early spirit was derived from frozen wine. Because alcohol has a higher freezing point, what wine was left unfrozen was greatly concentrated. Once the ice was cast off, the fermented liquid was, in the most rudimentary sense, distilled. More advanced distillation techniques weren't discovered until the 1400s. Initially the Poles used the spirit medicinally, but Polish historians claim that by 1405 Poles were incorporating the new distillation techniques to make a beverage-quality spirit. They also claim that around this time, vodka reached Russia via Poland.

The story of vodka in Poland has a similar plot to that in Russia. In 1550 all Poles were allowed to produce and sell alcohol by their king, Jan Olbracht. When he noticed that the business had become surprisingly lucrative, the king rescinded his permission and turned exclusive rights of production to the gentry. In 1648, the same year as the Russian Tavern Revolt, Polish peasants in the Ukraine rebelled against landowners and wreaked their vengeance on tax collectors and rural tavern keepers. Though the revolt was quashed, the Polish infrastructure was weakened and the impoverished country seemed an easy target to its invading neighbors. In 1772 Poland ceased to exist and was partitioned off to Russia, Prussia, and Austria-Hungary.

During the next 150 years, while Poland was under foreign rule, Polish distillers continued to develop flavored and specialty vodkas. Most importantly, they turned their attention to the potato. Remember that, at this time, vodka was mainly made from grain. But that great American tuber, the potato, was just being introduced into the European marketplace. It soon became an attractive raw material for the production of vodka in Poland. Potatoes were much more expensive than their grain counterparts, but the resulting spirit was incomparably smoother. Johann Joachim Becher had developed the method of producing spirits from potatoes in 1669, but it wasn't until 1798 that the first instructions for a "practical new way of distilling vodka from potatoes" was published. The Poles' techniques for distilling vodka advanced in the scientific climate of the day, and eventually resulted in triple distillation.

Today a number of the Polish distilleries established in the 1800s are still making vodka, and Polish brands are becoming more and more common on shelves in the United States and elsewhere. Since the 1820s potatoes have been the dominant base of Polish vodka, even though it is five to six times more expensive to use potato as a raw material than grain.

✳ VODKA EMIGRATES WEST ✳

Vladimir Smirnov had been stripped of his fortune, but he still had the ability to make great vodka. With the help of other Russian exiles, he started a small distillery in France. As he set up his shop, Vladimir changed the family name to Smirnoff, the French spelling. In the 1920s he sold the American rights to Smirnoff to Rudolph Kunnett, a Ukranian. Kunnett struggled to get Smirnoff into the marketplace. There was little awareness of vodka in the West, and public reluctance to try something new resulted in sluggish sales. At this time advertising efforts were rudimentary, and channels for publicizing a new product were few and far between. Kunnett had to figure out a way to sell a tasteless, odorless spirit, better known for what it didn't taste like than for what it did. As his financial hardships worsened, he luckily partnered with one John G. Martin of Hartford, Connecticut. Martin was president of beverage giant Heublein, and he believed he could turn vodka into gold.

Vodka didn't take the world by storm quite yet, but modest quantities of Smirnoff trickled into various markets. In the 1920s Paris began to embrace vodka, and it was here that one of the most popular vodka drinks, the Bloody Mary, was born. Created by American expatriate Fernand "Pete" Petiot, head bartender at the Ritz Hotel in the 8th arrondissement, the concoction was equal parts tomato juice and vodka. Originally administered to hungover hotel patrons (the Ritz being a full-service establishment!), the cocktail was christened Bloody Mary by a patron who said it reminded him of the Bucket of Blood club in Chicago, and he knew a woman there named Mary. The sanguine drink became an instant favorite in European circles. When Petiot moved back to New York in 1934 to run the legendary King Cole Bar in the St.

Regis Hotel, he introduced the Bloody Mary to savvy New Yorkers. They asked him to spice up the drink, so the inventive mixologist added jalapeños, Worcestershire, lemon, cayenne, and Tabasco sauce. The hard-to-please Manhattanites were pleased indeed. Petiot had created a drink that in time would become an American classic.

Heublein executives expected vodka sales to improve after Prohibition ended in 1933, but sales of vodka languished at about six thousand cases a year. The suits, spin doctors, and bean counters were at a loss on how to raise vodka's profile. According to Heublein lore, credit for the transformation of vodka from a fringe spirit enjoyed by a few sophisticates to a drink preferred by millions goes to an enterprising salesman in South Carolina named Ed Wooten. Wooten is credited with introducing the transparent spirit in an unusual manner that caught the consumer's imagination. It all came about by a lucky accident. After Heublein bought Smirnoff's, extra vodka was being bottled in the Connecticut plant in advance of moving the works to Hartford. Things were going along smoothly when the plant ran out of vodka-labeled corks. The company also made whiskey, and the only corks in the plant were printed with the words "Smirnoff Whiskey." The corks went into the bottles. Wooten started advertising the clear drink as "Smirnoff's White Whiskey: No Taste, No Smell." Consumers liked the fact that this curiously adaptable white "whiskey," unlike the more over-powering brown spirits they knew, seemed to mix with just about anything short of castor oil. Whether the Heublein tale is true or not, vodka started to click. The "no taste, no smell" slogan eventually evolved into the classic "It will leave you breathless."

Meanwhile, back in Mother Russia, vodka was still in the fore-front. In the 1920s, during a financial crisis, vodka labels had served in place of cash. On the literal front, vodka was doing hard service for the Russian military in their fight against the invading Nazi forces. During the war, every Russian soldier at the front was given a daily ration of a hundred grams of vodka to bolster troop spirits. It was believed to be an essential element in keeping the men in the trenches.

From the beginning America had been a whiskey-drinking nation, but in the late 1940s, after the end of World War II, the popularity of brown goods began to fade drastically. Brown spirits had a strongly defined taste and didn't mix well with certain juices and mixers. And vast popular experience seemed to indicate that they left the drinker with a hangover. Vodka, on the other hand, was easy to mix, and the low congener content seemed to reduce the number of morning-after sick calls to the office.

This was the golden age of the big screen, and vodka began to take hold among the influential trendsetters of that little village known as Hollywood. The French-born cocktail, the Bloody Mary, became the best friend of all-night revelers in Hollywood clubs, and remains a much-prescribed "hangover cure" to this day. The other cocktail that contributed to vodka's popularity among celebrities was the Moscow Mule. This mix of vodka, Schweppes Ginger Beer, and lime was created in 1946 by Jack Morgan, owner of the legendary bar and restaurant Cock 'n' Bull, on the Sunset Strip. He was, however, aided and abetted by his friend John Martin, the president of Heublein. Morgan had a large surplus of ginger beer; Martin was seeking a way to spice up vodka. So they put their heads together and concocted the Moscow Mule. Served in a copper mug with a kicking mule on the side, the drink was pitched as "the drink with a kick like a mule." This motto appealed to the party-hard Hollywood crowd. For decades, rows of copper mugs hung over the Cock 'n' Bull bar bearing the names of the kings and queens of Hollywood, including Clark Gable, Carole Lombard, William Powell, Bette Davis, and Cary Grant.

By the early 1950s the booming popularity of such concoctions as the screwdriver, the vodka martini, and, most beloved of all, the Bloody Mary brought vodka into the mainstream. It seemed as if the party would never end, but it eventually did . . . and a different kind of party started: the sixties. Instead of sitting around boomerang-shaped bars in suburban homes having martinis, people were "tuning in, turning on, and dropping out." The flip side of sixties drug culture was the health trend that swept the nation. Suddenly, taking care of yourself with a handful of vitamins in the morning and a little yoga in the evening was in. The Moscow Mule and other fifties cocktails seemed as old fashioned as sarsaparilla. That staple of 1950s business culture, the three-martini lunch, became an iced tea and mineral water nibble. The neon glow of cocktail culture started to flicker out. Vodka, like gin and other spirits, went into decline for nearly two decades.

It wasn't until the early 1980s, when Absolut entered the market with sexy, eye-catching ads, that vodka became attractive to the younger generation. The introduction of Absolut from Sweden announced a new age of premium imported vodka. Since then the popularity of the vodka martini, or "vodkatini," and the cosmopolitan have helped to solidify vodka's place at the top of the spirit world with no challenger in sight.

Vodka's 1980s popularity coincided with the demise of Communism. With markets now open, Eastern European countries could begin to flex their capitalist muscle and export their "authentic" vodkas to the United States. But the only Eastern European vodka with a foothold in America at this time was Stolichnaya (thanks to a reciprocal deal negotiated in the 1970s with Pepsi-Cola: In return for an exclusive shot at the vast Russian market, Pepsi agreed to distribute Stoli in the United States). The other two hugely successful imports came from Scandinavia—Absolut from Sweden and Finlandia from (where else?) Finland. Poland and Russia did finally, and aggressively, enter the American market in the late eighties and early nineties.

✳ VODKA TODAY ✳

Today sales of vodka have reached beyond the forty-million-case mark in the United States and show no sign of abating. Seven brands, headed by Smirnoff, account for nearly 50 percent of American vodka sales, but there are an additional three hundred brands jostling for position in this lucrative market.

An important submarket that has developed over the past ten years or so is the "premium" or "ultra-premium" vodka business. Marked by glorious packaging efforts and rather high prices, these vodkas are in sales overdrive. The category was up more than 40 percent in sales in 2002, and the increase has bred nothing but hope for fresh faces. Perhaps we can attribute this surge of interest in high-end brands to the indulgent nineties, which left affluent Americans with a distinct taste for massaged beef, four-dollar cups of coffee, and luxury spirits. Proving that the old marketing line about vodka having "no taste" is not really true, many of these premium vodka imports are distinctively flavored and therefore less likely to be used in mixed drinks. Instead, they're popular with people who drink them straight or on the rocks, and treat them with the same respect one might lavish on fine brandy or single malt Scotch whisky.

The true vodka enthusiast feels that the choice of vodka as one's drink affirms certain qualities. In the spirits world, vodka stands for purity, clarity, and the ability to be a good mixer, and we might say that vodka drinkers feel at home amid bright lights in the big city. At least for today's Americans, vodka is an urban drink, consumed where there is movement and progress. (A lover of whiskey or tequila could be said to celebrate the virtues of village life and the ideals of tradition and familiarity.) Certainly, with its long and varied history, vodka will continue to evolve and fascinate well into the new millennium.

✳ TASTING VODKA ✳

A Vodka Tasting

Vodka has become so popular because many mixology mavens consider it the perfect base for cocktails. But to appreciate the beauty of vodka, one must drink it straight. One of the best ways to explore the surprisingly vivid flavor differences is to set up a tasting with friends.

If you have friends who are seasoned vodka drinkers you might want to select your vodkas by base ingredients. For example, set up a comparison between potato vodkas and those made from rye or wheat. Taste the potato vodka Spudka against Skyy, a corn-based vodka, and Absolut, a wheat vodka. You may want to select only brands from one country; choose three or four Russian vodkas, such as Stolichnaya, Cristall, and Charodei to taste their differences. Or make it a country versus country challenge: Russian vodkas versus Polish vodkas such as Wyborowa or Chopin. There are four subgroups that experts often use to make tasting categories: Russian, Polish, American, and Western European. These four subgroups alone could supply enough basic combinations to conduct tastings into the next millennium. Have fun with creating a theme for your tasting.

To prepare a tasting, vodka should be placed in the freezer overnight. This brings the liquor to its proper viscosity and flavor. To experience vodka completely, serve the spirit straight up in a glass.

Chimney-style glasses, such as a cognac glass between five and six ounces, are good for spirits, as they focus the nose. If they aren't available, a brandy snifter or a six-ounce wineglass will work. Wash and dry glasses in nonchlorinated water before and between tastings or use a different glass for each spirit. Do not use plastic glasses! They're petroleum-based and can greatly affect the aromas and tastes (and besides, they're just plain inelegant).

You can place your glasses in the freezer an hour before the tasting. Once you pour the vodka in the glass, allow the vodka to warm up very slightly in your hands. This takes the freeze off. In addition to glasses you'll want bottled spring water on hand for the cleansing of the palate and to add water to the spirits to see how their aromas change when mixed. Water will make the by-products of distillation more pronounced, enabling you to discern the good and the bad (and any ugly) aromas.

Have food on hand that is spicy, salty, and fun to eat. Nibbling on food helps clear the palate from earlier tastings. The classic vodka food is caviar with blinis. Anchovies, herring, and spicy foods

such as Thai, Szechwan, Mexican, or Indian are also great complements to vodka. The foods should be easy to handle and available
to munch on between drinks. Keep the competing tastes from the
food to a minimum so your taste buds don't have to work overtime.

What to Look for While Tasting

Once the vodka is poured, you can begin your tasting. It's a good
idea to have notepads out so you and your friends can write down
notes as you go to make it easier to recollect the experience of each
spirit. There are three senses involved in tasting of vodka: sight,
smell, and taste.

Appearance. Hold the vodka glass up to the light and look at
the liquid's clarity, texture, and luminescence. Note whether there
are any unusual characteristics. For example, some vodkas have
bluish, yellow, or green tints. Fine vodka has a thick and creamy
texture when frozen. You can observe the "legs," the trails the
spirit leaves as it washes against the inside of the glass. Look for
clarity and luster.

Aroma or "nose." As you swirl the vodka in your glass, smell
the vodka. A good vodka will have a creamy, sweet, or grainy fragrance. Bad vodka will smell medicinal or aggressive with a harsh
odor of ethyl spirits.

Taste. Sip the drink gently and examine the taste and any
other sensations, such as the characteristic "burn" of alcohol. Let
the vodka rest on your palate while exhaling through your nose.
Then swallow and note the aftertaste. There are a number of characteristics to look for in the taste. Is the sensation sweet or dry,
complex or simple? Is the texture oily, chewy, or clean? Note
whether the flavor and sensation fill the whole mouth or only parts
of it; practicing does train your senses to discern more and more
intricate qualities of vodkas and of all spirits. *Note:* It is advisable
to provide spit buckets and encourage participants to spit rather
than swallow, especially if you are tasting six or more vodkas.

Consider the aftertaste. Each brand will have a surprisingly
unique second life after you swallow (or spit). Is the aftertaste long
or short? The finish or aftertaste should linger, perhaps for several
seconds. A lower-quality vodka will have a short aftertaste.
Second, cleanse your palate with room-temperature spring water,
then down a sip of the spirit without letting it linger in your
mouth. Compare the two experiences and their aftertastes.

Finally, taste the vodka again, this time with food. This helps
round out the taste experience and gives you a full impression of
the vodka.

✳ HOW TO ENJOY VODKA ✳

There are three ways to enjoy vodka: straight up, on the rocks, or in mixed drinks. The practice of drinking vodka straight up and icy cold came from the origins of the drink. Originally called "wine," vodkas were stored in cellars in casks. Because of its alcohol content, the spirit didn't freeze solid and was drinkable even in the dead of winter. The drink was poured straight and enjoyed with meals all day long. Some people prefer their vodka to be refrigerator cold, not freezer cold. It's all a matter of taste. While vodka purists will not water down their vodka with ice, it is perfectly acceptable to have vodka on the rocks in a highball glass. As a mixed drink base, vodka has no peer. The popularity of vodka as a base for mixed drinks is legendary, from the classic Bloody Mary to the trendy blood orange vodkatini. Try one of the recipes below.

French Martini

1¼ ounces vodka
4 ounces Chambord
1 ounce pineapple juice

Combine all ingredients in a cocktail shaker over a scoop of crushed ice. Stir carefully. Strain into a chilled martini glass. Garnish with a pineapple wedge.

Sake to Me

1 ounce vodka
1 ounce chilled plum wine
1 ounce cranberry juice
½ ounce lemon juice
½ ounce pineapple juice

Combine all ingredients in a cocktail shaker over a scoop of crushed ice. Shake to blend. Strain cocktail into a chilled martini glass. Garnish with a lemon wedge.

✳ BRAND PROFILES ✳

ABSOLUT. Made in Åhus, Sweden, this is the world's third largest premium spirits brand. The name comes from the phrase "Absolut renat Brännvin," which means "absolutely pure vodka." It is sold in 125 markets with worldwide sales of more than 7 million cases, 4.5 million of which are in the United States. Since beginning exports of Absolut in 1979, the brand has been the number one imported vodka in America. The award-winning marketing campaign for Absolut, first conceived by spirits guru Michel Roux, was groundbreaking. A first-rate advertising campaign featuring artwork by more than 350 gallery luminaries, including Andy Warhol, Keith Haring, and Edward Ruscha, helped Absolut become the best selling of all imports. The two decades of clever and visually stunning ads inspired a coffee-table book titled *The Absolut Vodka Advertising Story.* Today the ads continue to break new ground in communicating the brand's image of clarity, sophistication, and style. Made from winter wheat, the vodka has a smooth malt essence with a hint of dried fruit. The classic bottle shape, which has become an unmistakable icon over the past twenty years, was inspired by the design of a traditional Swedish medicine bottle.

BELVEDERE. Created from hand-selected Polish rye, Belvedere is made in a tiny distillery in Poland in the region of Masovia, where the Poles believe the first vodka was produced. Named for Belvedere House, the Polish equivalent of the White House, the spirit is quadruple-distilled and filtered through a natural filter of diatomaceous earth and charcoal. It has a faint vanilla nose, a slight taste of rye, and a creamy sensation on the palate. A crisp, clear spirit with a bright aroma of spice, citrus, caraway, herbs, and vanilla, Belvedere is considered one of the finest distilled vodkas.

KETEL ONE. This Dutch vodka is the original ultra-premium vodka. Privately owned, the company has been in the same family for ten generations. The vodka is made using traditional family methods created by the distillery founder, Joannes Nolet, who first created this vodka in 1691. A wheat-based spirit, Ketel One is hand-distilled using the original copper pot stills, with hand-stoked fires, the same method set forth four hundred years ago. The brand was first exported to America as far back as 1867, but failed to catch on. Ketel was not exported to America again until the 1980s. Every batch of Ketel One is tasted by a member of the Nolet family for approval. Carl Nolet, Sr., the chairman of the company in Holland, is the only person to have the distilling recipe. In 1982 Ketel One sold just seventy-six hundred cases, but the product was selling over a million cases by 1992. The company also produces Ketel One Citroen.

SKYY. In 1992 inventor Maurice Kanbar, the founder of Skyy Vodka, was looking for a way to enjoy drinks without the resulting morning-after headache. He knew that the brown spirits definitely caused the dreaded hangover because of the high level of congeners in the spirits. While a fan of vodka, he felt that there was another level of purity to reach with vodka spirits. He came up with a process of distillation that became the basis for creating Skyy vodka. When the spirit turned out to be smoother than any vodka he'd ever tried, he knew he had to come up with a name that fit. Kanbar wanted a name that conveyed the quality of the spirit. He first thought of giving it a Russian name like "Prince Romanoff," but it didn't really fit. In a quandary he let the question ruminate in his mind.

A few days later he was looking out the window of his office at San Francisco Bay. It was one of those truly gorgeous, blue-sky afternoons where everything shimmers. He noted the blue of the sky and he knew he'd found his name! Calling his patent attorney, Kanbar told him that he wanted to patent the name Sky for his vodka. The attorney was set against it: The word was too universal, he'd have to find another name. Not to be deterred, Mr. Kanbar came up with the clever solution of adding the extra "y," and thus Skyy was born. Skyy, a corn-based vodka made in Illinois and bottled in Northern California, is the fastest growing spirit globally and the leading domestic super-premium vodka in the United States. Skyy's state-of-the-art process of quadruple distillation and triple filtration yields dependably pure and ultimately smooth vodka. In addition to 80 proof Skyy Vodka, Skyy produces Skyy Cosmo Mix, a nonalcoholic cosmopolitan mixer, and Skyy Blue, a flavored malt beverage jointly marketed with Miller Brewing Company.

STOLICHNAYA. The original Stolichnaya distillery is located in the tiny town of Irkutsk in the depths of the Siberia, where Stoli has been made for more than ninety-five years using the waters of nearby Lake Baikal, one of the great natural wonders of the world. The water that comes from Lake Baikal is absolutely pure and has left scientists baffled for decades: There's no known reason for the lake's purity. Locals don't question why; they just know the water makes Stolichnaya superior. Using only the purest natural ingredients, the vodka undergoes a double charcoal filtration process, followed by a third filtration process they call mirror filtration (named so for the almost reflective quality the final filtering process gives the vodka). The bottles are washed inside with vodka prior to filling, ensuring that no water remaining in the bottles will dilute the proper proof. Over sixty million cases are produced annually, making Stoli the largest spirit brand in the world. Today Stolichnaya is produced at ten different distilleries in Russia, so the quality of the product may vary slightly within the label itself. But Stoli's reputation as a top vodka is unquestioned.

SMIRNOFF. As the first vodka introduced to the United States in 1934, Smirnoff was the vodka that began the slow but steady pace that would lead vodka to worldwide domination of the white spirits category. Founded in the 1860s, the Trading House of Piotr A. Smirnov was established in Moscow to produce vodka. Smirnov was the first distiller to use charcoal in the filtration process and continuous distillation to ensure a consistent quality product—two additions to the distillation technique that would revolutionize vodka manufacturing. As a result of its purity and quality, Smirnov Vodka became the most popular drink at the Russian Court. In 1886 the czar awarded Smirnov the distinction of Purveyor to the Russian Court. When the Russian Revolution broke out in 1917, all private businesses were confiscated. The Smirnov family lost their distillery and fled the country. One of Piotr's sons, Vladimir, made his way to Turkey, and then on to Paris, where he adopted the French spelling of the family name and began distilling vodka in France. In 1934 the Smirnoff company came to the United States and was the first vodka introduced to American drinkers. As the company grew, clever ad campaigns reached a public curious about this Russian spirit. By the 1960s they were one of the first spirit companies to use celebrities in their ads. Among the celebrities who appeared were Woody Allen, Harpo Marx, and Vincent Price. To this day Smirnoff is produced with the same methods established by Piotr in the 1860s. The company uses charcoal from maple, beech, and birch trees and demineralized and carbon-filtered water in the production of Smirnoff. Fifteen million cases of Smirnoff fly off shelves every year—that's a half million bottles a day.

tasting notes

3 Vodka, *USA*

$$ ★★★   Fresh and silky with dry, smooth, racy flavors and a clean, crisp finish; distilled from soy.

Absolut Vodka, *Sweden*

$$ ★★★   Smooth, clean, and peppery with lush vanilla and some toasty notes.

Armandale Vodka, *Scotland*

$$ ★★★   Smooth and silky with dry, balanced flavors with a hint of vanilla; elegant and long.

Belvedere Vodka, *Poland*

$$ ★★   Smooth and creamy with vanilla and spice; zippy but a bit simple.

Blavod Black Vodka, *England*

$$ ★★   Smooth with spice, dry flavors, and some lush vanilla; varies from dark amber to green; balanced and rich; catechu herb provides the black color.

Blue Ice Potato Vodka, *USA*

$$ ★★★   Smooth and lush with clean, slightly sweet notes and a long, soft finish.

Boru Original Irish Vodka, *Ireland*

$ ★★   Light and silky with simple, clean, balanced flavors; smooth and showing vanilla and some spice.

Brilliant Vodka, *Scotland*

$$ ★★★   Clean and edgy with brisk, dry flavors of vanilla and spice; smooth, long, and balanced.

Burnett's Vodka, *USA*

$ ★   Smooth and simple with decent flavors; short and light.

Charbay Vodka Clear and Dry, *USA*
$$ ★★★   Smooth and racy with elegant, dry, crisp, and stylish flavors.

Charodei Vodka, *Russia*
$$ ★★★   Thick and smooth with bright, sweet vanilla flavors; creamy and rich, dense and long.

Chopin Vodka, *Poland*
$$ ★★★   Racy and crisp with vanilla and clean spice; peppery, aggressive, and dry.

Christiania Extra Premium Vodka, *Norway*
$$ ★★   Smooth and silky with dry, spicy flavors and a finish of vanilla and varnish.

Cîroc Vodka, *France*
$$ ★★★   Fresh and lively with smooth, soft texture and a lovely hint of citrus and white flowers; distilled from grapes.

Citadelle Vodka, *France*
$$ ★★★   Dry and very smooth with lovely toasted vanilla flavors and a long, lush, elegant finish.

Cristall Vodka, *Russia*
$$ ★★★   Silky and racy with fresh vanilla sweetness and lively spice; balanced and long, clean, racy, and bright.

Danzka Vodka, *Denmark*
$ ★★   Smooth and soft with mellow, fleshy, lush flavors of vanilla and some spice; long and balanced.

Effen Vodka, *Netherlands*
$$ ★★★   Racy and dry with smooth texture, long, clean, and mellow flavors of vanilla and pepper.

Finlandia Vodka, *Finland*
$$ ★★★   Remarkably dense and smooth with thick texture and lush vanilla; some sweetness on the finish with elegant notes of cream and herbs.

French Alps Vodka, *France*

$$ ★★   Smooth and lush with clean, mild flavors; simple and long.

Frïs Vodka, *Denmark*

$ ★★★   Smooth and lush with thick, rich texture and lovely notes of vanilla and spice; dry and elegant with creamy, racy flavors and a long, lingering finish.

Grey Goose Vodka, *France*

$$ ★★★   Smooth and mellow with dry, mild flavors and a clean, pure finish.

Hampton's Vodka, *USA*

$$ ★★   Spicy, fleshy nose; dry, peppery, and dense with thick texture and a long finish.

Hangar One Vodka, *USA*

$$ ★★   Smooth and slightly sweet with heavy, creamy flavors.

Ikon Vodka, *Russia*

$ ★   Fresh and sweet with smooth, creamy flavors; decent.

Jazz Vodka, *Poland*

$$ ★★★   Smooth and mellow with soft, dry, luscious flavor; rich, ripe but elegant.

Jewel of Russia Vodka Ultra, *Russia*

$$$ ★★   Old-style vodka with a cereal nose and viscous texture; smooth, lush and spicy.

Ketel One Vodka, *Netherlands*

$$ ★★★   Intense and ripe; long and pure.

Krolewska Vodka, *Poland*

$$ ★★★   Smooth and clean with dry, racy flavors and medium weight, with lovely length and elegance.

Level Vodka, *Sweden*

$$ ★★★   Smooth and spicy with thick, ripe flavors and mellow, balanced, long finish.

Mezzaluna Vodka, *Italy*

$$ ★★★   Racy and silky with clean, dry, nutlike flavors; smooth, long, and balanced.

Mishka Vodka, *Israel*

$$ ★★★   Smooth, thick, and clean with soft vanilla and spice; made from molasses; kosher.

Olifant Vodka, *Netherlands*

$ ★★   Clean and light with vanilla and spice flavors; soft and decent.

Original Polish Vodka, *Poland*

$$ ★★★   Smooth and silky with vanilla and spice flavors; clean and mellow with lovely balance and length.

Pearl Vodka, *Canada*

$$ ★★★   Smooth and creamy with lush, sweet, fresh, and balanced flavors; long and lovely.

Peconika Vodka, *USA*

$$ ★★   Smooth and lush with ripe, smooth flavors and a long, sweet finish.

Players Extreme Vodka, *USA*

$ ★★   Lush and smooth nose; clean, racy, dry, and edgy with neutral alcohol notes.

Polar Ice Vodka, *Canada*

$$ ★★★   Rich, ripe, and racy.

Polska Vodka Extra, *Poland*

$ ★★★   Clean and spicy with dry flavors and a smooth, silky texture with a note of vanilla on the finish.

Pravda Vodka, *Poland*

$$ ★★   Smooth and spicy; crisp and balanced; long and dry on the finish.

Precis Vodka, *Sweden*

$$ ★★   Smooth, silky, and lush with sweet vanilla flavors and a slight cardboardy twinge on the finish.

Rain Vodka, *USA*

$$ ★★★   Silky and smooth with clean, fresh vanilla and sweet notes; spicy and racy with an elegant finish.

Reval Vodka Classic, *Estonia*

$ ★★   Smooth and mild with soft vanilla and clean, neutral flavors; balanced and lush, long and fresh.

Rodnik Vodka, *Russia*

$$ ★★★   Smooth and creamy with lovely vanilla and spice notes; long and lush.

Seagram's Extra Smooth Vodka, *USA*

$ ★★   Smooth and creamy with pronounced vanilla flavors; very smooth and lush with ripeness and body.

Shakers Original American Vodka, *USA*

$$ ★★★   Smooth and creamy with dense, rich flavors of vanilla and spice; long, balanced finish.

Shakespeare Vodka, *Poland*

$$ ★★★   Lush with vanilla notes; smooth, dense, and lovely.

Skyy Vodka, *USA*

$ ★★★   Clean, fresh, and racy with dry, spicy flavors and a long, smooth, vanilla finish with some edge.

Smirnoff Vodka, *USA*

$ ★★   Smooth and creamy textured with a long spice finish and fairly neutral flavors.

Spudka Potato Vodka, *USA*

$ ★★   Smooth and silky with simple, neutral flavors and a short finish.

Stolichnaya Vodka, *Russia*

$$ ★★★   Pure, racy, clean, and lovely; a classic.

Stolichnaya Vodka Gold, *Russia*

$$ ★★★   Soft and mild nose with thick, dense texture and fresh, spicy vanilla flavors; dry and smooth with a lingering finish; created to mark the one hundredth anniversary of the distillery.

Stön Vodka, *Estonia*

$$ ★★★   Rich, smooth flavors of citrus and vanilla and a long, dense finish.

Tanqueray Sterling Vodka, *England*

$ ★★   Soft and lush, velvety, complex, and quite elegant.

Teton Glacier Potato Vodka, *USA*

$$ ★★★   Smooth and creamy with spice, vanilla, and fresh, balanced finish; fresh and long.

Three Olives Vodka, *England*

$$ ★★★   Vanilla and spice in the nose; smooth and clean; moderately thick with dry, subtle vanilla flavor and lovely, long, balanced finish.

Tito's Handmade Vodka, *USA*

$ ★★★   Bright and fresh with notes of citrus and vanilla; balanced and silky with a charming bite of spice.

Türi Vodka, *Estonia*

$$ ★★   Clean and racy with dry, fresh flavors and a long, silky, pure finish; fresh and lively.

Vertical Vodka, *France*

$$ ★★★   Creamy and soft with marshmallow and vanilla notes; lush and smooth, rich and long.

Viking Fjord Vodka, *Norway*

$$ ★★   Silky and smooth with creamy vanilla and sweet, sugary flavors; long, smooth, and lush.

Vincent Van Gogh Vodka, *Netherlands*

$$ ★★   Clean and creamy with spice and good balance; vanilla and spice.

Vox Vodka, *Netherlands*

$$ ★★★ Racy, bright, and dry, with some vanilla flavors and a smooth texture.

Wódka Wyborowa Vodka, *Poland* ˙

$ ★★★ Racy and balanced with some sweet vanilla and spice and a wonderfully balanced flavor profile; fresh and long, classy and elegant with a terrific, long aftertaste.

Wódka Wyborowa Single Estate, *Poland*

$$ ★★★ Smooth and silky with no bite; mellow and bright with a long, elegant finish.

Zyr Vodka, *Russia*

$$ ★★★ Dry, clean, lush, and thick; long, smooth, and showing some vanilla notes.

FLAVORED VODKA

Berry/Cherry Fruit Flavors

Skyy Berry Vodka, *USA*

$ ★★ Dry and almost too subtle, with hints of raspberry, blackberry, and blueberry; clean and mellow with balance and length.

Voda Blueberry Infused Vodka, *USA*

$$ ★★ Lovely ruby color with a cooked berry flavor and some heavy sweetness; bright, racy acidity with a thick texture.

Effen Black Cherry Vodka, *Netherlands*

$$ ★★★ Spicy black cherry nose; bright, smooth, and dry with nice cherry flavors and long, balanced finish.

Three Olives Cherry Vodka, *England*

$$ ★★ Lush cherry and cinnamon nose; sweet and rich with candied cherry and spice; long and mellow.

Stolichnaya Cranberi Vodka, *Russia*

$$ ★★   Smooth cranberry nose; mellow, lush, and balanced with ripe cranberry notes.

Absolut Kurant, *Sweden*

$$ ★★★   Tart blackcurrant on the nose; dry, racy, and varietally correct; long and fresh.

Citadelle Raspberry Vodka, *France*

$$ ★★★   Gorgeous raspberry nose; dry and subtle flavors with fresh raspberry and smooth, clean finish.

Olifant Raspberry Vodka, *Netherlands*

$ ★★   Nice, fresh raspberry nose; smooth and quite sweet with raspberry, vanilla, and spice.

Seagram's Raspberry Vodka, *USA*

$ ★★   Sweet and smooth with fresh raspberry flavors and long, authentic berry notes; bright and balanced.

Smirnoff Raspberry Twist, *USA*

$ ★★   Smooth and clean with confected raspberry flavors and some vanilla notes; simple, basic, and mass-produced.

Stolichnaya Razberi Vodka, *Russia*

$$ ★★   Bright, fresh raspberry nose; soft and mellow with raspberry flavors and a long, smooth finish.

Three Olives Raspberry Vodka, *England*

$$ ★★   Smooth raspberry nose; lush vanilla and clean, raspberry fruit; mellow and long.

Vincent Van Gogh Raspberry Vodka, *Netherlands*

$$ ★★   Smooth and sweet with jammy fruit and good balance; lush and long.

Vox Raspberry Vodka, *Netherlands*

$$ ★★★   Clear with a lush raspberry aroma; smooth texture, bright fresh raspberry fruit and spice; long and dry.

Stolichnaya Strasberi Vodka, *Russia*

$$ ★★   Strawberry jam nose; smooth, dry, and mellow with lush stewed strawberry flavors.

Citrus Fruit Flavors

Belvedere Cytrus Vodka, *Poland*

$$ ★★   Lemon peel nose; oily and bitter with lemon peel and dry pepper spice.

Boru Citrus Vodka, *Ireland*

$ ★★   Fleshy citrus nose; smooth, dry, and lightly lemon flavored; lush and balanced.

Danzka Citrus Vodka, *Denmark*

$ ★★★   Clean and fresh with lively citrus and nice notes of bitter rind; long, dry, and balanced.

Seagram's Citrus Flavored Vodka, *USA*

$ ★★   Smooth and sweet with lemon and tangerine notes; lush and long.

Skyy Citrus Vodka, *USA*

$ ★★★   Dry and complex with lemon, orange, lime, and tangerine flavors; clean and elegant, fresh and long.

Charbay Ruby Red Grapefruit Vodka, *USA*

$$ ★★   Slightly golden in color with hot flavors of grapefruit and citrus; dry and aromatic, long and fresh.

Danzka Grapefruit Vodka, *Denmark*

$ ★★★   Grapefruity, fresh, and racy with good balance and a long finish.

Absolut Citron, *Sweden*

$$ ★★★   Fresh lemon in the nose; crisp and dry with a smooth background featuring vanilla and spice.

Charbay Meyer Lemon Vodka, *USA*

$$ ★★   Pale gold color; fleshy, bitter lemon nose; silky and long with tangy lemon and earthy flavors.

Grey Goose Le Citron Vodka, *France*

$$ ★★★   Aromatic lemon with a sweetness and spice; there are notes of citrus and lemon rind as well; a vanilla undertaste is present and the whole package is refreshing and smooth.

Hangar One Citron "Buddha's Hand" Vodka, *USA*

$$ ★★   Floral and sweet with sourball flavors.

Ketel One Citroen Vodka, *Netherlands*

$$ ★★★   Racy and crisp; lively, long, and balanced.

Mishka Citron Vodka, *Israel*

$$ ★★   Fragrant and lemony with smooth texture and undertones of vanilla; kosher.

Olifant Citron Vodka, *Netherlands*

$ ★★   Soft and smooth with subtle lemon and vanilla notes; clean and mellow.

Stolichnaya Citros Vodka, *Russia*

$$ ★★   Clean lemon nose; smooth and mellow with soft lemon drop and silky texture.

Vincent Van Gogh Citroen Vodka, *Netherlands*

$$ ★★★   Bright citrus nose; fresh and dry with racy, tangy lemon fruit and clean, spicy notes.

Zone Lemon Vodka, *Italy*

$ ★★   Rich and expressive with keen Italian lemon flavors.

Charbay Key Lime Vodka, *USA*

$$ ★★★   Pale yellow color; sweet lemon drop nose; racy key lime flavor, and a light, racy texture with a nice touch of bitter rind.

Frïs Lime Vodka, *Denmark*

$ ★★★   Lush and smooth with lovely notes of lime and vanilla; long, rich, and lovely.

Hangar One Kaffir Lime Vodka, *USA*

$$ ★★★   Bright, tangy lime nose; powerful lime flavors with some earthiness and silky texture; long and crisp on the finish.

Absolut Mandarin, *Sweden*

$$ ★★★   Sweet, fresh mandarin orange nose; dry and smooth with lively citrus, spice, and a clean, stylish finish.

Hangar One Mandarin Blossom Vodka, *USA*

$$ ★★   Lovely orange oil nose; flowery and smooth with soft texture and ripe flavors.

Belvedere Pomarancza Vodka, *Poland*

$$ ★★   Oily and floral with peppery spice and dry finish; orange peel and silky texture.

Boru Orange Vodka, *Ireland*

$ ★★   Lush orange nose; smooth and dry with lush orange flavors and nice notes of bitter rind.

Grey Goose L'Orange Vodka, *France*

$$ ★★★   Lovely, fresh, orange flavors with racy acidity and spice and a long, clean finish; bright and fresh with a snappy aftertaste.

Mishka Jaffa Orange Vodka, *Israel*

$$ ★★   Cloudy, bitter orange with a background of vanilla; kosher.

Olifant Orange Vodka, *Netherlands*

$ ★★   Smooth and clean with long, balanced flavors of light orange and vanilla; simple and soft.

Orange V Orange Vodka, *USA*

$$ ★★   Snappy orange flavors with a zesty finish.

Stolichnaya Ohranj Vodka, *Russia*

$$ ★★   Smooth orange Creamsicle nose; soft and mellow with mild orange flavors, dry and clean.

Vincent Van Gogh Oranje Vodka, *Netherlands*

$$ ★★★   Fresh squeezed orange juice nose; lush, dry, and thick with lovely fresh orange flavor.

Zone Tangerine Vodka, *Italy*

$ ★★★   Tangy, inviting tangerine flavors and a hint of spice; quite nice.

Tropical Fruit Flavors

Wokka Sake, Vodka & Sake Infused with Asian Fruits, *England*
$$ ★★★   Citrus and spice nose; dry and spicy with soft fruit notes and subtle, complex flavors; elegant and long.

Hampton's Banana Vodka, *USA*
$$ ★★★   Ripe banana nose; powerful and lush banana flavor with a long finish and lovely clean flavors.

Zone Banana Vodka, *Italy*
$ ★★   Ripe, tropical banana flavors with a rounded mouth feel.

Zone Melon Vodka, *Italy*
$ ★★★   Lush, summery melon tones; low proof allows fruit flavors to shine through.

Vincent Van Gogh Pineapple Vodka, *Netherlands*
$$ ★★   Lush and smooth with stewed pineapple flavor; clean and racy with sweet fruit and a fresh finish.

White Fruit Flavors

Citadelle Apple Vodka, *France*
$$ ★★★   Green apple flavor with spice and vanilla flavors; smooth, clean, and subtle.

Fris Apple Vodka, *Denmark*
$ ★★★   Smooth and spicy with fresh apple fruit and vanilla notes; long and balanced.

Seagram's Apple Flavored Vodka, *USA*
$ ★★   Crisp and bright with sweet apple cider and spice flavors; creamy and lush with sweetness and balance.

Smirnoff Green Apple Twist, *USA*
$ ★★   Sweet and smooth with bright, clean vanilla and faint apple fruit.

Vincent Van Gogh Wild Apple Vodka, *Netherlands*
$$ ★★   Spicy, crab apple flavors with sweet, ripe finish.

Stolichnaya Persik Vodka, *Russia*
$$ ★★★   Stunning nose with ripe, sweet peach flavors and a dry finish.

Zone Peach Vodka, *Italy*
$ ★★   Delicious, ripe, soft peach flavors; much better than the amateurish-looking packaging would suggest.

Zygo Peach Vodka, *USA*
$$ ★★   Smooth and sweet with soft peach fruit and ripe flavors; long and candied.

Vanilla-Flavored Vodkas

Absolut Vanilia, *Sweden*
$$ ★★★   Lush vanilla nose; dry and peppery with lovely, smooth vanilla flavor; thick texture and long finish.

Grey Goose La Vanille Vodka, *France*
$$ ★★   Smooth and moderately lush with creamy vanilla notes and a dry, spicy finish.

Olifant Vanilla Vodka, *Netherlands*
$ ★★★   Smooth and mellow with marshmallow vanilla flavors; lush and long.

Seagram's Vanilla Flavored Vodka, *USA*
$ ★★   Sweet, fragrant, and lacking any finesse; fat, ripe, sweet, almost cloying vanilla.

Skyy Vanilla Vodka, *USA*
$ ★★★   Smooth and mellow with lush vanilla and a relatively dry finish; elegant, lush, and balanced with long persistent flavors.

Smirnoff Vanilla Twist, *USA*
$ ★★★   Lush and smooth with rich vanilla and nice spice; long and ripe, intense.

Stolichnaya Vanil Vodka, *Russia*

$$ ★★   Ripe vanilla nose; smooth and creamy with lovely vanilla and crisp, dry finish.

Vincent Van Gogh Vanilla Vodka, *Netherlands*

$$ ★★★   Creamy, lush, and lovely with smooth vanilla flavor and a long, balanced finish.

Spice, Herb, and Miscellaneous Flavors

Absolut Peppar, *Sweden*

$$ ★★★   Green pepper nose; dry, edgy, and hot with capsicum flavors.

Shaker's Rose Vodka, *USA*

$$ ★★★   Lovely rose-pink tinge, sweet rose perfume; spicy, smooth and lush with sweet, creamy rose petal flavors.

Skyy Spiced Vodka, *USA*

$ ★★★   Lush, smooth Christmas pudding flavors of cinnamon, nutmeg, and clove with a rich, creamy vanilla component; charming and unusual, pure and nicely balanced.

Vincent Van Gogh Dutch Chocolate Vodka, *Netherlands*

$$ ★★   Chocolate and coffee flavors, sweet, lush, and smooth; clean and long.

Zhitomirska Herb Flavored Vodka, *Ukraine*

$ ★★★   Smooth and clean with subtle herbs and vanilla notes; fresh and racy, long and balanced.

Zubrówka Bison Brand Vodka, *Poland*

$ ★★   Aromatized with Polish bison grass; delicate, clean, and herbal.

aquavit

A group of people are clustered around a table for a typical lunch that will include several courses and a clear, fiery drink. The host pours the ice-cold liquid into frosty conical glasses with long stems. He raises his glass, at which point the diners turn to one another and make eye contact, making certain not to leave anyone out. "*Skål!*" calls out the host, and everyone take a sip. Again there is eye contact, and then the glasses are set on the table, not to be lifted again until the host raises his. The liquid is aquavit. The ritual is virtually the same throughout Scandinavia.

Aquavit is a distilled spirit similar to vodka. The name is the Scandinavian version of the Latin *aqua vitae,* meaning water of life. Aquavit differs from vodka in that extracts of herbs and spices are added to the final product, giving the spirit a distinct flavor. Aquavit may taste of cinnamon, Madeira, coriander, lemon, dill, and—most popular of all—caraway. Scandinavians also frequently refer to their aquavits as snaps or schnaps. These are not to be confused with the sugary, syrupy schnapps (with two "p's") found in American bars.

The manufacture of aquavit is simple and straightforward.

Potatoes are cleaned and then boiled. The resulting starch mass is combined with a grain malt, which helps the starch convert to sugar. Yeast is added, and the sugar is fermented into alcohol. The resulting spirit is rectified and distilled, after which a flavoring is added.

✳ THE EARLY HISTORY OF AQUAVIT ✳

In Sweden the first aquavit (sometimes spelled "akvavit" or "akevit") was made by distilling wine. The problem was that all the fruit had to be imported from more temperate countries because no grapes are grown in Sweden. This made the aquavit so expensive that it could only be consumed sparingly. Its use was limited almost entirely to medicinal purposes. Later, when the Swedes discovered how to produce the spirit from grain, aquavit became less costly and easier to obtain. But grain was not the ideal raw ingredient either. Because of the country's harsh weather, the crop was often cut short by the early arrival of winter. To avoid a grain shortage, the government occasionally had to prohibit the distilling of aquavit.

By the 1700s grain was scarce, but people were not yet convinced that the potato could be a staple. In 1763 Norwegian minister Peder Harboe Hertzberg took up the cause of the tuber. Eager to turn public opinion, he spoke passionately about the many uses for the potato. Hertzberg eventually took this passion to the page and wrote a book on the cultivation and practical use of the potato. The book became immensely popular and eventually went through three printings. The lowly potato was well on its way to making a permanent contribution to life in Scandinavia.

The Swedes had grown accustomed to their aquavit, so frequent interruptions in its supply were quite unacceptable. Distillers experimented with myriad substitutes for grain, but nothing seemed to yield satisfactory results until they tried the potato. To their surprise they found it was ideal for the purpose. The tuber was plentiful, inexpensive, relatively unaffected by variations in weather, and consistent in quality. Most aquavit has been made from potatoes ever since.

✳ A LIVELY DISPUTE ✳

The Swedes and the Danes like to dispute which country was the first to produce aquavit. Both countries have a good case; in fact, it is quite possible that distillation began independently in both places at about the same time. The first Swedish license to sell aquavit was granted in Stockholm in 1498. Danish distilling can be traced back to sometime around 1400, and in 1555 King Christian III of Denmark established a royal distillery.

The Danes love their aquavit. In 1800 there were more than 2,500 independent distilleries in Denmark, 273 of them in Copenhagen alone. By 1923 the large Danish Distillers conglomerate, founded in 1881, had gobbled them all up and held a monopoly on the production of aquavit in Denmark. Production is centered in Aalborg, a town of 160,000 in Northern Jutland. The Danish Distillers company was (somewhat ironically) acquired by the Swedish government–owned Vin & Sprit AB, makers of Absolut Vodka, in 1999. It now produces half of the world's supply of aquavit. The portfolio includes about a dozen versions with various flavor profiles, but only two are currently imported into the States: the dill-flavored Aalborg Jubilaeums and the caraway-flavored version, Aalborg Akvavit, which is the unofficial national drink of Denmark.

Most Swedish distilleries are located in the Southern province of Skåne. The best-known Swedish brand is O. P. Anderson, also produced by the state-operated company Vin & Sprit AB. Named after famed spirits manufacturer Olof Peter Anderson, this excellent aquavit is flavored with caraway seed, fennel seed, and aniseed. It was first released at the Gothenburg (Göteborg) Exposition in 1891.

There is also a small industry in Norway, where the Arcus distillery in Oslo produces Linie, an aquavit with a very interesting history. In 1805 the Norwegian Lysholm family accidentally sent a shipment of their aquavit to Australia. When the misdirected cargo finally got back to Norway, the Lysholms found that the stuff had developed smoother, richer flavors after crossing the equator twice. They named their new aged aquavit Linie (Norwegian for equator) and kept the process a secret for many years. Today's Linie still uses the original Lysholm recipe, right down to the sea voyage. The barrels spend four and a half months rolling with the waves, docking in thirty-five countries, and crossing the equator twice. Linie, a potato-distilled spirit, is flavored with caraway and herbs grown in the Norwegian countryside, then stored in casks previously used in the production of oloroso sherry, which add notes of vanilla and oak. At any given time, a thousand casks full of Linie are maturing as deck cargo on Norwegian freighters on the open sea. The name of the ship and the date of the voyage are marked on the back side of the front label, legible through the bottle.

✳ DRINKING AQUAVIT ✳

Aquavit is generally consumed straight up and very cold. In Scandinavia a beer chaser often accompanies aquavit. It is not unusual for a Dane or a Swede to drink three or four shots of this icy 90-proof liquor during the course of a meal. Using this spirit in mixed drinks requires some experience. Aquavit in a martini or combined with tonic might not be too well received, but a Bloody Mary made with either a dill, lemon, or caraway version is quite delicious. There is also no law that says that aquavit cannot be served over ice. In fact, people who drink vodka on the rocks may find this an exciting new alternative to their usual. Scandinavians also consume aquavit in a heady spiced wine and fruit punch called glogg, which is served warm.

Everything considered, aquavit, no matter how you choose to drink it, is surely one of the most delightful of all distilled spirits. It goes especially well with food. Scandinavians famously accompany aquavit with a hearty meal. Aquavit makes a delicious companion to gravlax, caviar, and Asian-spiced food.

Try aquavit mixed into one of the delightful recipes below.

Danish Mary

1½ ounces aquavit
2 ounces tomato juice
1 teaspoon grated onion
Dash hot sauce (such as Tabasco)
Fresh ground pepper
Sprig of dill

Fill a rocks glass with ice. Add aquavit, tomato juice, onion, and hot sauce; stir to combine. Sprinkle pepper over cocktail and garnish with the sprig of dill.

Sugarplum Cherry

1½ ounces aquavit
¼ ounce kirsch
½ ounce lime juice
1 ounce champagne

Fill a cocktail shaker with ice. Add aquavit, kirsch, and lime juice. Shake vigorously. Strain into chilled martini glass rimmed with sugar. Float champagne over cocktail.

Skål

Skål (pronounced "SKOAL") is one of the world's most recognized toasts, the Scandinavian equivalent of "Cheers!" in English or "Prosit!" in Germany. The word actually means bowl, harking back to the days when the modern Scandinavians' ancestors, the Vikings, shared a ceremonial bowl on special occasions.

tasting notes

Aalborg Akvavit, *Denmark*
$$ ★★★   Smooth, clean, and racy, with assertive caraway flavors; lush and slightly sweet.

O. P. Anderson Aquavit, *Sweden*
$ ★★   Smooth and lush with sweet flavors of caraway; creamy vanilla and spice.

Linie Aquavit, *Norway*
$$ ★★★   Amber color; smooth and dry with licorice and caraway; long and snappy.

gin

Although gin is often considered a quintessentially English drink—the kind of spirit imbibed at Mayfair cocktail parties or tippled by naughty spinster aunts at remote country houses in Sussex—you may be surprised to find that the first gin was made in Holland. Originally created as a medicinal tonic, the spirit made its way into the hearts of the common folk and the nobility and eventually became the basis for one of the most enduring cocktails of all time: the martini.

✳ THE THREE TYPES OF GIN ✳

London dry gin or British dry. These gins are usually made with a grain formula that contains more corn than barley (75 percent corn and 25 percent barley), as the manufacturers believe this produces a smoother spirit. The English distill their gin at a high alcohol content (190 proof), then redistill it in the presence of juniper berries and other botanicals. While originally produced in and around London, London dry gins can be produced all over the world including the United States, France, Scotland, Ireland, Germany, Belgium (which also makes Dutch-style genever), and Spain.

The most unusual of the London dry gins is Plymouth Gin, which is made with soft water and wheat. Distilled in Plymouth, England, this gin began production in the late 1700s and was preferred by the Royal Navy. First used in the gin and tonic cocktail, Plymouth was also often mixed with lime juice. The older, more traditional London gins, such as Tanqueray, have a stronger presence of juniper. True genevers from Holland have a bold taste due to a heavier concentration of juniper in the botanical mix, and the liquor is often straw-colored.

Genever, Holland gin, or Dutch gin. Staying true to the original spirit formulated by its inventor, Dr. Sylvius, true Dutch gin is derived from "malt wine" (fermented malt). The spirit is then redistilled with juniper berries, resulting in a very full-bodied gin with a malty aroma and flavor. Genever can take some getting used to but has a charm all its own. Genever comes in two classifications, *jonge* (young), an unaged spirit, and *oude* (old), which is stored at least one year in oak barrels. Because of its heaviness, genever usually does not work well as a cocktail mixer. Instead it is most often drunk cold and straight, sometimes with a dash of bitters.

German or Steinhäger gin. According to law, German gin must be produced solely from triple-distilled spirit, juniper berries, and water. The distillate is so powerful that the manufacturer in Westphalia adds pure spring water to the spirit before it is bottled in stone crocks. Steinhäger gin is rarely seen in the States.

✳ MAKING GIN ✳

Unlike Scotch whisky, which is only produced in Scotland, gin can be made anywhere there is a still, some grain, and the requisite flavoring ingredients.

Gin is made by redistilling grain mash with juniper berries (sourced from a plant in the evergreen cypress family). Other flavoring agents, such as dried fruit, spices, and herbs, give each version of the spirit a pronounced taste. Although juniper berries always play a role, there are dozens of other possible ingredients, including but not limited to lemon and orange peel, cardamom, anise, licorice, coriander, and orris root, which is the powdered root of the Florentina iris. The choice and proportion of these flavoring agents gives each gin its own distinct flavor profile. Gin is similar to aquavit, the national beverage of Scandinavian countries, which is flavored with caraway, and to mastikha, the Greek spirit flavored with anise.

One can't help but be impressed with the cleanliness and order of the big gin distilleries. Unlike a winery, there are no wooden barrels and no damp cellars, just rows and rows of pipes and ranks of shiny stills. There is no season for gin—it is made throughout the year—nor is it aged for any appreciable amount of time. Clean water flows into the distillery from artesian wells, and two weeks later it leaves, transformed, bottled and ready for market. Another characteristic of a gin distillery is the seductive aroma of juniper and herbs that perfumes the air.

While each manufacturer might choose a different combination of flavoring ingredients, they all approach the art of making gin using one of three basic processes: the compounding (or cold compounding) technique, the essential oils method, or gin head distillation.

The Cold Compounding Technique

There are three versions of cold compounding. In the first type, predetermined amounts of spices and botanicals are crushed to release all their aromatic properties. These botanicals are then placed in a set quantity of alcoholic spirit and left for a fixed amount of time—usually around one week. This allows for the flavor and aromas to blend in harmony. After this the spirit is filtered, bottled, and shipped.

In the second form of cold compounding, proper amounts of botanicals are crushed to suit the individual gin recipe. They are then placed in a fine mesh cloth bag and submerged into a proper quantity of alcohol until the flavors and aromas have been transfused into the alcohol. The bag is removed, the spirit "rests" and, in time, is diluted to bottle strength, bottled, and shipped.

The third approach is commonly called the circulatory method. Of the three cold compounding methods it is the least used for gin production, and is more often used in the making of cordials and liqueurs. In this method, alcohol is stored in a large tank where a fine mesh tray filled with crushed botanicals is suspended above the liquid. The alcohol is pumped over the botanicals until all the flavors and aromas have been absorbed. The gin rests for a week before being filtered, diluted, and bottled.

Mass-produced gins are almost always made by the first two methods of the cold compounding process. Compounded gin is considered to be of a lower quality than gin produced by means of the essential oils method or by gin head distillation. Of these two processes, the latter is considered to produce the finest gin.

The Essential Oils Method

This distillation process begins when the botanicals are crushed and cooked to remove all their essential oils and components. These oils are then combined with alcohol and concentrated into a clear liquid. A measured amount of these oils is then added to the main tank of neutral grain spirit and allowed to mix. After a week of rest, the product is filtered and bottled. During Prohibition, bathtub gin was often made using this method.

Gin Head Distillation

Gin head distillation is the original method of making gin and the most expensive. In addition, it is the only method that allows the producer to label the gin "distilled." Using a pot still, the neutral grain spirit is diluted with water so the alcohol vaporizes and the steam moves through a gin head, which is a separate basket positioned above the distillation column. The basket houses the finely crushed botanicals so the neutral spirit vapors pass through the botanicals and are infused with their essence. The flavored steam is collected back into a water outlet column that leads into a water condenser. At this point more water is added through the water inlet. The diluted liquid passes into a "spirit safe" connected to a large receiving tank. The tank is hooked directly into the bottling feed line so the gin is delivered directly into the bottles. Because no solid material is physically placed in the alcohol, filtration is unnecessary with gin head distilled gin.

✳ GRAINS AND BOTANICALS ✳

No matter which process is used, each gin distillery has its own private, top secret formula that's guarded as dearly as the gold at Fort Knox. While some of the compounds used by each of the three types of gin—London dry, Dutch, or German—are known, the recipe in its entirety is never divulged.

London dry gins such as Tanqueray, Beefeater, Gordon's, and Gilbey's start with a grain formula that is three-quarters corn and one-quarter barley malt and other grains. By crushing the grains before mixing with the water, the starch is broken down for better fermentation of the grains. The grain mixture is then combined with water and is called mash. The mash is then cooked and finally fermented. This procedure is virtually identical to the early stages of the production of whiskey. The initial use of large quantities of corn more than likely resulted from the Act for the Encouraging of the Distillation of Brandy and Spirits from Corn, passed by Parliament in 1690.

The resulting liquid is distilled to 180 proof (90 percent alcohol) in the column still. The result is a strong and pure spirit that retains a hint of malty, whiskeylike flavor. It is then cut to 120 proof by the addition of distilled water. This slightly diluted spirit is then placed in a modified pot still called, appropriately, a gin still and redistilled in the presence of flavorings, primarily juniper berries. The gin still was developed by James Burroughs, founder of the Beefeater distillery, in the late nineteenth century.

First cousins to the London dry gins are the American dry gins. American gins are distilled or compounded and use similar grain mixtures to their English counterparts. In the United States, laws require that gin be made from 100 percent neutral spirits. This means that the best domestic gins are crisper and cleaner tasting, but lack the extra complexity and slight hint of malt character that can be found in true London gins.

Dutch or Holland gin uses barley and ages the spirit to give it that rich, malt flavor. Scheidam Holland gin is made in the Dutch town of the same name and is distilled from a grain mash made from equal parts barley malt, corn, and rye. The mash is turned into a "beer" that is then distilled at a much lower proof than London gin. This leaves the gin with an intense, whiskeylike flavor.

✳ FLAVOR ENHANCERS ✳

Of all the botanicals used in gin production, there are two that are most frequently used.

Juniper berries. From a tree in the cypress family, these small, purplish berries (technically a small type of cone) are the predominant flavoring for all gin. Not surprisingly they have an evergreen smell and taste. German gins, for example Schlichte Steinhäger, use only juniper for flavor.

Coriander seed. This second most commonly used botanical is from the parsley family. Coriander is the seed of the cilantro plant, a pungent herb most of us know from Mexican or Thai cooking. Most coriander is harvested in Czechoslovakia and Morocco.

Other botanicals used in gin production include almonds and almond powder, angelica root, aniseed, caraway, cinnamon, ginger, lemon and orange peel, cumin, and the lyrically named grains of paradise. These peppery berries from West Africa can be used to intensify the flavoring of all the other botanicals in gin.

Let's Make Some Gin

The basic recipe for gin is simple. To 2,000 liters of 100-proof alcohol (be sure to use potable alcohol and not denatured or wood alcohol), add 100 pounds of juniper berries, 50 pounds of coriander seed, 10 pounds of cinnamon bark, 10 pounds of angelica root, 1 pound of lemon peel, 1 pound of cardamom. Use any of the methods mentioned above, let your brew rest for a week, and you will have made gin.

✷ THE HISTORY OF GIN ✷

A Dutch Beginning

Gin was originally concocted around 1650 by Franciscus De Le Boë Sylvius, a respected Dutch physician and scientist. Dr. Sylvius conducted chemical experiments and lectured at the University of Leyden. In hopes of finding a cure for stomach and kidney ailments, Dr. Sylvius turned to using juniper berry oil as a treatment. He found that the berries were a powerful diuretic and would indeed rid the body of "bad humors." But, to his dismay, he also discovered that juniper oil's acrid taste made the tonic nearly impossible to administer. To make the medicine more palatable to his patients Dr. Sylvius added the oil of juniper to a base of neutral distilled spirits. Gin was born.

Dr. Sylvius dubbed his tonic "genever," a name derived from the French word for juniper, *genièvre.* Within a few months the good doctor's medicine was the rage of Holland. Word spread that this new cure was a miracle. Suddenly people throughout the country were complaining of stomach and kidney ailments in hopes of taking the newfound cure. Demand for genever was so great that the enterprising Bols firm in Amsterdam began marketing a commercial version. This new spirit was much more aromatic than either the London or American versions of gin so prevalent today.

The English Discover "Dutch Courage"

Genever's popularity spread to England as a result of British military forays into the Netherlands. English soldiers discovered that their Dutch allies (or enemies, depending on who was in power) had a reputation for great bravery on the battlefield. The English attributed this to the Dutch habit of sipping genever from small bottles before going out and fighting like men possessed. The English dubbed the drink "Dutch courage" and triumphantly transported it back home, where it soon became known as "geneva" (mistaking it as a Swiss product). Geneva was shortened to "gen" and finally mutated to "gin."

In 1689 Prince William of Orange, a Dutch grandson of the Stuart kings, assumed the English throne and codified the British infatuation with gin in a royal decree. To protect English farmers, encourage the distillation of English grains, and counter the smuggling of contraband French brandy, King William III passed an Act for Encouraging the Consumption of Malted Corn and for the Better Preventing of French and Foreign Brandy. The populace responded enthusiastically to a law that practically required them to drink, and soon England became a land of patriotic drunks. English distillers began to make their own version of gin with a corn base, which was lighter and sweeter than the Dutch version.

The popularity of gin spread rapidly. It is estimated that in just one year's time, the English consumed five hundred thousand gallons of the stuff. By 1690 the toast of port cities such as Bristol, Plymouth, and Portsmouth, gin had become the spirit of the masses. Gin's meteoric rise in favor was due not only to King William III's new legislation, but also to the fact that beer and ales were highly taxed, raw milk was hazardous to your health, and the water in London was too polluted to drink. Legend has it that during this gin boom, one in four storefronts in London was a gin shop. Along the docks of the seedy Limehouse neighborhood there was even a Gin Alley. Suddenly the poor could afford to be as drunk as the gentry, who, until this time, had heavily indulged in expensive ports and brandies.

Queen Anne brought further accessibility to gin when her ministers canceled the privilege of the Distiller's Company. This cancellation removed strict control over English distilleries and opened the craft to the common man. Soon anyone could make or sell gin with no supervision or government regulation. The spirit made at this time was sweetened with sugar after distillation and popularly called "Old Tom."

The public embraced this sweet spirit, and by 1727 gin consumption had risen to five million gallons a year—a shocking figure when you observe that the country's total population numbered only six and a half million. Eventually the party had to come to an end. Public drunkenness among the lower classes threw the aristocrats into a panic, and they began passing laws to control the common man's drinking habits.

Controlling Gin Consumption

The Gin Act of 1736 was one such law. The Gin Act placed a high tax on the spirit and prohibited its sale in small quantities. The passage of this act sparked riots all over the country and, in the end, probably contributed to the increase in illegal distillation. Despite the strict regulations stipulated by the Gin Act, excise receipts show that in 1742 twenty million gallons of gin were distilled. The passion for gin at this time was compared to an epidemic.

In 1750 lawmakers passed the "Tippling Act." Under this new law, gin shops were outlawed, and the rights to manufacture and distribute gin were granted only to large retailers and distillers. With gin no longer as affordable to the lower and middle classes, gin consumption decreased to two million gallons a year. In 1756 the distillation of corn in England was prohibited because of crop failures and also to encourage the importation of rum from the American colonies. Despite its lowly beginnings, gin had become a drink for the elite, and they demanded quality.

The First Premium Gins

Their prayers for better tasting gin weren't answered until 1830, when two engineers, Robert Stein of Scotland and Aeneas Coffey of Ireland, invented the continuous action column still. This change brought about a significant shift in gin production. The new still allowed manufacturers to produce larger quantities of alcohol from the same amount of base materials. With improved filtration, the column still produced a purer alcohol that created a drier gin with more aroma and a cleaner taste.

The well-known manufacturer Tanqueray started making gin around this time, joining a cadre of competitors that included Gordon's, Boodles, Booth's, Beefeater, and Gilbey's. As a result of the Tippling Act, beer was much cheaper than gin and could be had on every streetcorner. To compete with the overwhelming number of makeshift beer pubs, purveyors of gin set up the fabulously ornate establishments that became known as gin palaces. At these establishments the variety of gin drinks was equaled only by the variety of the entertainment—dancing bears, fire eaters, and racy musicales. By 1850 there were about five thousand of these "palaces" in London. Over 150 years after its medicinal beginnings, gin had finally become a gentleman's drink.

As the British Empire grew, so did the popularity of the new and improved gin. In tropical outposts where the consumption of bitter-tasting quinine was a necessity to battle malaria, it was found that the addition of gin produced a most delightful cocktail.

Once again gin was being used medicinally just as Dr. Sylvius had planned, though no one gave that much thought in the desolate jungles of Africa or the teeming cities of India. When soldiers returned to England they brought back the gin and tonic, which was received enthusiastically by pubgoers in towns where malaria was about as common as the Bengal tiger or the puff adder. (An ounce of prevention, though, never hurts.)

Prohibition and Bathtub Gin

Gin's popularity continued to expand worldwide for several decades until the mid 1870s when the American-based temperance movement began to achieve global popularity. Started by women who saw drink as a threat to their household income, the movement focused on the closure of all saloons and the ban of liquor sales. The organization became known as the Women's Crusade. As the popularity of the movement grew, the crusade eventually became absorbed by the Women's Christian Temperance Union. The union, along with the Anti-Saloon League (founded in 1893), was becoming influential in Washington, D.C., where antidrink sentiments ran high. Finally, on August 16, 1919, Congress passed an amendment to the Constitution known as the Volstead Act, outlawing alcoholic beverages nationwide. The amendment went into effect on January 29, 1920, and ushered the country into a span of thirteen dark years known as Prohibition.

Suddenly all legal manufacturers and distributors of alcoholic beverages were closed down and all liquor licenses were revoked. Prohibition's supporters predicted that the Volstead Act would reduce crime and poverty, generally improving the quality of life in America by making it impossible for people to obtain alcohol. If Americans couldn't buy liquor, they reasoned, the country would turn "sober." How little they knew of human nature! Prohibition took the United States into a new era where, almost overnight, ordinary citizens and decent law-abiding people became flagrant criminals. Terms such as "bootlegger" and "speakeasy" were introduced into the vernacular as thirsty Americans sought creative new ways of getting their hands—and lips—on alcoholic beverages.

By definition, a bootlegger was someone who imported or made illegal spirits. The term was derived from the practice of hiding bottles of alcohol between the boot and pant leg. The most serious bootleggers were the gangsters who brought imported whiskey, spirits, and beer into the country by boats and through Canada. Al Capone of Chicago became the king of all gangsters and built an empire on the bootlegging business. The booming black market economy seemed to know no end as imported liquor poured into the States from Mexico and Ireland. Gangsters opened up illegal bars and clubs called speakeasies to serve Americans the drinks they wanted.

These private venues met a constant demand for cocktails and entertainment. F. Scott Fitzgerald wrote of this age that "The parties were bigger . . . the pace was faster . . . and the morals were looser." Though often raided by the police, the speakeasies were a strong industry and a source of great consolation during the Prohibition years. They came by their unusual name because patrons had to whisper, or "speak easy," a special password to gain entrance into these "clubs"—which ranged in location from converted apartments or basements to the back ends of auto repair garages. A door that seemingly led to a legitimate business was often the gateway to the all-night party created by Prohibition. Torch singers, jazz musicians, and vaudevillians suddenly had a new venue in which to perform. Jazz and gin seemed made for each other. Fred Astaire, Duke Ellington, and Bill "Bojangles" Robinson entertained at some of the clubs such as the infamous Cotton Club in Harlem and the Copacabana. At the high point of Prohibition, New York City alone housed more than one hundred thousand clandestine speakeasies.

Before Prohibition women were very rarely seen in saloons. In the past the glamorous high-end cafés and dinner clubs where women did socialize with men had catered only to the very rich. Misbehavior was rare, or at least relatively invisible. Now, however, clubs were filled with "flappers"—young single women with newly bobbed hair, short skirts, and even skimpier scruples. Social barriers crumbled. Women and men could socialize (or worse) all evening. The rich and working poor rubbed shoulders. As songwriter Hoagy Carmichael put it, the twenties came in "with a bang of bad booze, flappers with bare legs, jangled morals and wild weekends." Club owners soon found that women singing ballads boosted liquor sales, and the saloon singer was born. It seemed as if anything was possible . . . and the drink of choice was gin.

Gin flourished under the new laws because it was so easy to make. In spite of the fact that many bootleggers grew insanely wealthy, bootlegging alone could not provide Americans with enough liquor. Small-time entrepreneurs resorted to making their own spirits in rudimentary stills and home distilleries. Any industrious American could become a gin manufacturer or moonshiner in his or her own home. All you needed was a bathtub, any form of alcohol (some people used wood alcohol and methanol, both of which were lethal), and some botanical flavorings. After a week of maceration, the infused alcohol was ready to black market as gin. Policemen who were friendly to the private trade in gin were called "blind pigs." They'd gladly turn a blind eye to the smell of the fermenting juniper berries coming from your apartment or storefront in return for some free product or a payoff. "Bathtub gin" became the staple drink of speakeasies.

Thirteen years into the "dry" experiment, even the strongest supporters of Prohibition were forced to admit it was a dismal failure. Organized crime flourished, turf wars sprang up in every major city, and as many women as men were drinking. When Prohibition ended, the United States was in the third year of the Great Depression. Congress repealed the Volstead Act (a campaign promise made by Franklin D. Roosevelt while he was running for president) and alcoholic drinks became legal again. The newly elected President Roosevelt signaled the end of the dry era by drinking a martini made from his own recipe, which included olive brine. (Could Roosevelt have suspected that the dirty martini would later become a cocktail revival fad?)

Drinking continued to be an important part of popular culture as people turned to alcohol to soften the blow of the Great Depression, and to celebrate the fact that the dark night of Prohibition was finally over. Large, lavish nightclubs ruled the 1930s and Americans continued their love affair with gin drinks, especially the martini. Nick and Nora Charles, Dashiell Hammett sleuthing sophisticates, drank martinis in the midst of murder and mayhem, while Humphrey Bogart became the epitome of the hard-drinking man with a soft heart in numerous Hollywood films, including *The Maltese Falcon, The Big Sleep,* and *Casablanca.*

By the 1950s the cocktail hour became a standard feature in postwar American life. America's love of the gin and tonic and the martini became a rich bed of material for writers such as John Cheever, who saw the cocktail life through the eyes of an eight-year-old girl in *The Sorrows of Gin,* and A. R. Gurney, whose play *The Cocktail Hour* observes family members avoiding one another as they drink away the evening.

The sixties and seventies brought with them a more relaxed and open culture, and using drugs became an acceptable way to relax with friends. While the younger generation focused on a new kind of high, alcohol slipped into the realm of the "uncool." Gin, a spirit associated with the 1930s, seemed old-fashioned. People still drank and movie heroes still belted down a shot of liquor for quick courage, but average Americans had cut down on their consumption of spirits. As the Cold War coasted to an end in the *perestroika*-perfumed eighties, Russia was suddenly our friend. Gin was suddenly eclipsed by the enormous popularity of vodka. A renaissance in fine dining and drinking began in earnest in the mid-1980s. By late in the decade, vodka overtook gin as the most popular American spirit. The coup de grâce came when vodka actually replaced gin in the classic dry martini (or the vodkatini).

The future was looking bleak for gin when the cocktail life reemerged in the late 1990s. The movie *Swingers* introduced the fun of hip nightlife to a new generation, and the popular television series *Sex and the City* made mixed drinks de rigueur on an evening out on the town. A sexy drink served in a martini glass was suddenly appealing and desirable. Retro cocktails such as the dry martini and the original gimlet, both of which started out with a base of gin, were back. Younger drinkers, determined to be faithful to original recipes, began to reach for the gin bottle. The introduction of imported super-premium gins such as Bombay Sapphire and Tanqueray No. 10 has also helped boost gin's popularity.

When *New York* magazine labeled the younger generation of New Yorkers the "Cocktail Culture," it was good news for gin. Bars serving elaborate cocktails have sprung up all over Manhattan. Even the Singapore sling is being made again. Premium gins are now prominently displayed on the mirror-lined shelves. The acceptance of gin as the alternative white spirit can be partly credited to vodka distillers who introduced flavored vodkas in 1996. With vodkas being distilled with fruits and spices, the emphatic taste of gin suddenly doesn't seem quite so foreign. There are experts in the spirits business who feel that gin, in the final analysis, is basically flavored vodka. Whereas vodka manufacturers infuse their products with lime or vanilla, gin makers infuse their spirits with aromatics such as juniper, angelica, cardamom, or orris root.

With gin now front and center at the best bars and restaurants across the country and the sales of gin at their highest in two decades, it's clear gin is back and ready to join the party.

✳ GIN IN THE NEW MILLENNIUM ✳

The newest of the new gins, such as Bombay Dry Sapphire, Van Gogh, Anchor Junipero, and the Dutch-made dry gin Leyden, showcase a great range of styles. They feature more botanicals and spices in their recipes and are being distilled in smaller batches. However, the reemergence of Plymouth Gin and the continuing popularity of the original Tanqueray signal that there is room for both variety and tradition in the world of gin. With the widespread availability of better-quality product and the best selection of gins in the world at their fingertips, Americans can explore all the exciting new and old tastes of gin.

Many popular restaurants and bars around the country are turning to gin as a basis of their signature drinks. The Carlyle Hotel in Manhattan, for example, uses gin in most of their mixed drinks. Bartenders find gin has more character than vodka and adds brightness to cocktails. In Chicago, the restaurant Tru has added the Tru Blue Martini made with Bombay Sapphire, blue curaçao, fresh lime, grenadine, and tonic. Food and beverage managers everywhere are noting that patrons are looking for more flavor, and gin certainly answers that need.

MAKE MINE A MARTINI
✳ —THE GIN MARTINI ✳

It's as graceful as Fred Astaire, and as elegant as a trans-Atlantic journey on the *Queen Elizabeth*. It's simple, smooth, and icy cold. In his memoir, *My Last Sigh,* filmmaker Luis Buñuel muses, "To provoke, or sustain a reverie in a bar, you have to drink English gin, especially in the form of a Martini." But where did this reverie-inducing potion begin? Legends abound, and can be classed roughly as East Coast and West Coast theories. Some martini aficionados place the origin of the cocktail during the California Gold Rush, while others focus on the pre–World War I elegance of New York. One thing is known for certain: In New York in 1896, Thomas Stewart wrote *Stewart's Fancy Drinks and How to Mix Them.* In what seems to be the first published recipe for the classic martini the ratio was ⅔ Plymouth gin to ⅓ French vermouth.

John Doxat, a British journalist who has made an exhaustive study of martini history, asserts that the first true martini was mixed at the old Knickerbocker Hotel in New York City on an evening in 1910. The inventor was the head bartender, one Martini di Arma di Taggia, and the first to taste his concoction was none other than oil magnate John D. Rockefeller.

Soon enough, legend has it, the Knickerbocker bar became renowned for this new drink, and serious imbibers flocked there to taste Martini's cocktail. Not to be outdone, other bartenders around town began featuring the drink and adding their own modifications. And so began the evolutionary process that made the dry martini both the most satisfying and the most exasperating of cocktails.

The West Coast legend has the martini appearing at the Occidental Hotel in San Francisco in the 1860s. It is said that the bartender, one Jerry Thomas, mixed up a new drink he dubbed the Martinez for a customer who was headed to the town of that name on the other side of San Francisco Bay. This first Martinez was made from bitters, Maraschino, vermouth, ice, and the sweet gin called Old Tom.

To make matters of the martini's birth even more confounding, the first mention of a martini in American literature was made by O. Henry in his comic tale "The Gentle Grafter" in 1904—six years prior to the supposed Knickerbocker concoction! Whether it is the legendary gin and vermouth martini that O. Henry is describing is unknown, but obviously this gin-based cocktail was already in existence.

✳ THE MARTINI NOW ✳

Vodka and Specialty Martinis

The cocktail W. C. Fields referred to as "angel's milk" also prompted poetic tributes from the likes of Dorothy Parker, Ogden Nash, and Bernard De Voto and is traditionally made with gin and only gin. Aficionados are quick to point out that there is no such thing as a "vodka martini." What many would agree is an unnecessary modification of the cocktail is properly called a vodkatini. For me, there is no substitute for the exquisite synergism of the juniper berry flavor of the gin and the nutlike herbs of dry vermouth. To make a martini with vodka, while not a crime, is simply missing the point.

While there is little disagreement as to the ingredients of a martini, there is no end of discussion as to their proportions. That first martini poured at the Knickerbocker was equal parts gin and vermouth, making it an extremely "wet" martini by today's standards. A trend toward drier versions started just prior to World War II and shifted the recipe to two parts gin to one part vermouth. After the war the formula changed yet again. My father's dry martini was four to one. By the 1960s the proportions had jumped to six to one, and in the 1970s eight to one was common. Current bar trends indicate that the dry martini should be constructed in a ratio of five to one.

There are those who would choose to forget the vermouth altogether. These are hard-core types who, while mixing, lean over their drink and whisper the word "vermouth" or let the shadow of the unopened vermouth bottle fall across the glass. Winston Churchill used to simply bow in the direction of France while he poured gin straight up for his "martini." While this is all quite amusing, these individuals seem to be confusing an elegant cocktail with a straight shot of gin. True martini aficionados would never stoop to such foolishness.

Most bartenders agree that despite the predilections of one Mr. James Bond, the perfect dry martini should be stirred and not shaken. (And in any case, Bond called for vodka in his cocktail, which leaves him out of the gin discussion.) Purists will tell you that shaking "bruises the gin" and causes too much dilution from melting ice. Additionally, too much shaking can cloud the hallmark clarity of the martini. But then there are those who welcome the initial cloudiness of a shaken martini (it quickly clarifies as the ice crystals melt) and who relish the vibrant shimmer of tiny ice particles floating on top of the elegant drink.

When we speak of clarity, we should touch on the garnish. Be it an olive or a twist of lemon, it should sit neatly on the lip of the glass where it will not compromise the drink's purity. A dropped olive or spiraling twist creates a little oil slick on the surface of the drink. The dirty martini is purposely polluted with olive juice, making it sharper, saltier, and not nearly as lovely to behold.

As you learn the rules of the martini, so will you learn to break them. If we look at current trends, bartenders across the country are determined to one-up Martini di Arma di Taggia. Throwing caution to the wind, they've come up with an entirely new class of martinis. What do these crayon-colored drinks have in common with the original? Usually very little, save the shape of the glass.

There is something about the martini glass that sparks the imagination. Top heavy, yet delicate, it has the seductive wobble of Marilyn Monroe in *Some Like It Hot*. It is iconic, emblazoned on napkins and matchbooks, glowing in neon and immortalized in metal sculpture. Fill the glass with the classic martini or shock the purists and fill it with one of the newfangled cocktails. Gin may be absent, but when you hold the glass, the classic spirit of the martini remains.

✳ TASTING GIN ✳

Historically the base of the dry martini, gin is now being incorporated into racier drinks. A recent proliferation of ultra-premium gins offer delicate flavor nuances and slick packaging in exchange for a hefty price tag. Of these newcomers, I like Citadelle, a smooth, French import with layers of spicy floral flavors; Damrak, a Bolsmade product from Holland, the birthplace of gin; and, best of all, Tanqueray No. 10, the perfect martini gin. Among the standbys there are Beefeater, Gilbey's, Booth's, Boodles, and the elegant Plymouth, made with smooth, soft water. Bombay Sapphire, in its distinctive blue glass bottle and leaner style, is also a good bet. Mix these gins into your favorite cocktail or pour them over ice and let your taste buds seek out myriad flavors of licorice, pepper, lemon peel, the sweet violet whisper of orris root, and, of course, the tang of juniper.

Tasting at Home

When selecting gin for a home tasting, keep in mind that while several recent domestic brands are new creations, many brands labeled "American-made" are simply imports that have been licensed to an American distiller for production in the United States. The recipe of the original distiller is given to the American producer so the product has basically moved to an American company under license. Gilbey's, Gordon's, and Booth's all started out in England, but are now made in the United States. One way to conduct a tasting is to try a domestically distilled brand against its import equivalent.

Bear in mind that gin distilled in the traditional manner may be heavier in flavor than newer, lighter gins that are leaner, racier, and a bit easier to blend into a cocktail. It is the strong flavor of juniper in traditional gin that appeals to the traditionalists. You might want to test light gins against light, say Bombay Sapphire and Leyden, as opposed to trying to compare two very differently weighted gins such as Bombay and Gilbey's. Gilbey's is a more traditional gin while Bombay is nontraditional.

Chimney-style glasses or cognac glasses between five and six ounces are good for spirits as they focus the nose. If they aren't available a nice brandy snifter or a six-ounce wineglass will work. Wash and dry glasses in nonchlorinated water before and between tastings or use a different glass for each spirit. Don't use plastic glasses; they're petroleum-based products and can greatly affect the aromas and tastes.

In addition to glasses, be sure to have a bottle of spring water on hand. Water is necessary to cleanse the palate between tastes. When added to the gin, the water also helps clarify the flavors and aromas. By diluting the spirit a bit, it is easier to detect both the good and bad aromas and tastes.

If you'd like to serve food during the tasting, try a selection of spicy or salty foods. Asian delicacies, such as Szechwan dumplings, pair nicely with gin, as do sharp English cheeses or cheese straws. It is important to keep the competing tastes from the food to a minimum so your taste buds won't work overtime.

What to Look for While Tasting

Provide notepads so you and your friends can make notes while you taste. When tasting several gins, writing down notes as you go makes it easier to recollect the experience of each spirit.

Since all gins are made from differing recipes, you'll want to pay close attention to the flavors. There are a dizzying array of flavors and botanicals used to make gin—lemon, rose petals, cucumber, orange—the list is endless. Ultimately there is one flavor that should come through above the rest: juniper.

Three senses are involved in tasting of gin: sight, smell, and taste.

Appearance. Hold the gin glass up to the light and look at the liquid's color. Natural ingredients will impart color as well as flavor, so there may be hints of various hues in a glass of gin. A completely clear spirit tends to be artificially flavored.

Aroma or "nose." A simple sniff of gin can tell you whether it is even worth taking a sip. As you swirl the gin in your glass, smell the sample and note whether there is the aroma of juniper. A good gin, no matter what its recipe, should reveal at least some juniper in the nose. A strong chemical or overly astringent odor is a clue that you are dealing with a low-end gin. A good gin will smell soft and subtle under the high-proof alcohol. Once you are past the dryness of the alcohol, you'll want to take note of the secondary fragrances of the flavorings. High-quality natural ingredients will create pleasant aromas. A poor-quality gin will smell of perfumes, artificial flavorings, and other chemical extracts. Swirling the sample in the glass helps release the flavors. Nose the gin again to see if you pick up a deeper, rooty dryness.

Taste. Sip the drink gently and let the sip roll around the mouth before swallowing. First pay attention to the warmth of the alcohol. As you get used to it you'll start to note an array of flavors from the botanicals. Let the gin rest on your palate while exhaling through your nose. The result of the spirit should be smooth and creamy on the tongue with a long, soft taste. Then swallow and note the aftertaste.

There are a number of characteristics to look for in the taste. The first sip of gin should be a soothing, pleasant, warm sensation, with a definite, but not overpowering, floral taste of juniper. Next taste for dryness. Gin is a dry spirit due to the high proof and the natural flavor of juniper. Is the flavoring complex? Is the texture oily? Oiliness or slickness is an indication that the gin is likely flavored with extracts. It can also stem from the use of other flavors that are competing with the juniper. Note whether the flavor and sensation fill the whole mouth or only parts of it. Does the spirit feel raw in the back of your throat, or is it easy and smooth to swallow?

Great gins finish clean and fresh. The juniper shouldn't linger too long, and by the time you are ready for your next sip, the remnants of the last sip should be a memory. The best gins are smooth and subtle. Practice does train your senses to discern more and more intricate qualities of the spirits.

Second, cleanse your palate with room-temperature spring water, then sip the rest of the spirit without allowing it to linger in your mouth. Compare the two experiences and the aftertaste.

Third, taste the gin again, this time with food. A food match will help round out the taste experience and gives you a full impression of the gin.

Try gin in these delicious cocktails.

Orange Blossom

1 ounce gin
½ ounce Cointreau
¼ ounce fresh lemon juice
1 teaspoon orange marmalade

Combine all ingredients in a shaker with a scoop of ice. Shake to blend. Strain into a chilled martini glass. Garnish with a thinly sliced orange wheel.

My Precious

1½ ounces gin
¾ ounce apricot brandy
1 ounce sour mix
¼ ounce Campari

Combine all ingredients in a mixing glass with a scoop of ice. Stir well to blend. Strain into a chilled martini glass with a sugar-coated rim. Garnish with a small orange wedge.

✶ BRAND PROFILES ✶

There are dozens of brands to choose from; a few of the most prominent are listed below.

TANQUERAY. Today's Tanqueray is the result of a decision made in 1830 when, at the tender age of twenty, Charles Tanqueray left his family's traditional profession of clergyman to establish a small distillery in Bloomsbury, London. Using the spa waters from artesian wells, Tanqueray chose the highest quality grain for his famous gin, processing it with a column still and using double distillation, at the time a revolutionary distilling technique. Eventually he would triple-distill Tanqueray to ensure even higher quality. A handwritten copy of his recipe for what is now Tanqueray gin is still used and closely guarded. Today the classic emerald green bottle with the red seal is known around the world.

Tanqueray No. 10, a newer import, is crafted in the small-batch distillation process. Using only fresh, handpicked whole fruit botanicals and distilled four times in Tanqueray's swan-necked still No. 10, the spirit has a deep and complex flavor. It is wonderfully smooth and rich to the taste. Tanqueray No. 10 is highlighted by flavors of grapefruit, orange, and lime and mellowed by juniper and chamomile. Experts recommend it be served chilled and neat. This gin is a three-time winner of Double Gold, Best Gin of Show, and Best of Show White Goods awards at the San Francisco World Spirits Competition.

Tanqueray Malacca is a highly spiced gin produced in small batches. This silky and mellow gin is flavored with citrus and has the unique nuance of exotic spice. Crafted from an original 1839 recipe that Tanqueray developed following his travels through the Spice Islands of the East Indies, Malacca gin tastes great with a variety of mixers. While Malacca is no longer distributed in the United States, it remains a favorite of aficionados.

BEEFEATER. Beefeater is the last of the London gins actually to be distilled in the capital. A traditional London dry gin, this spirit was first produced in 1820 by a pharmacist, James Burroughs, in Devon. Burroughs named his quintessentially English spirit after the Yeomen of the Guard at the Tower of London. To keep up with surging demand over the past 180-plus years, the company has had to move several times, and today the distillery is in Kennington in central London, near the river Thames. Only six people know the particular combination of juniper berries, coriander, angelica, citrus peel, and other secret ingredients. Beefeater has a spicy, fruity aroma with very dry, complex flavors of mineral and juniper berry.

PLYMOUTH. Plymouth is crafted in the original copper pot stills at England's oldest working gin distillery, Blackfriars, in the historic Barbican area of the seaport town of Plymouth. Plymouth Gin began production in 1793 and is documented as the original base for the first dry martini and is the only gin consistently specified in the *Savoy Cocktail Book,* which is to mixologists what *The Joy of Cooking* is to home cooks. The unique blend of just seven botanicals, combined with the soft water from the granite hills of Dartmoor, England, create this impeccable and historic spirit. Unlike almost all other gins produced, Plymouth is the only gin that is distilled from a mash base made of 100 percent wheat. Those devoted to Plymouth swear that there is nothing as smooth as a glass of gin made from wheat.

tasting notes

Beefeater London Dry Gin, *England*
$ ★★★ Solid, clean, and masculine with firm, rich flavors and a hard edge of spice; intense, balanced, and loaded with juniper.

Beefeater Wet, *England*
$$ ★★ Smooth and simple with floral, citrus flavors and a touch of pear sweetness.

Bombay Dry Gin, *England*
$ ★★★ Orange rind and spice; slightly ripe, dense, and long.

Bombay Sapphire, *England*
$$ ★★ Lush and dry with floral spice and smooth texture; racy and light with bright flavors and a short finish.

Boodle's British Gin, *England*
$ ★★ Smooth and silky with nice complexity and finish; assertive juniper and resin notes.

Broker's London Dry Gin, *England*
$ ★★★ Smooth and floral with racy, dry flavors of spice, citrus, and white flowers; soft and fresh.

Burnett's Distilled London Dry Gin, *USA*
$ ★ Fresh and citrusy with clean, mild flavors and simple spice; smooth and mellow.

Citadelle Gin, *France*

$$ ★★★   Spicy juniper nose; smooth and mellow with pronounced juniper and angelica flavors; long and creamy with vanilla, spice, and balance.

Damrak Amsterdam Original Gin, *Netherlands*

$$ ★★★   Lean and racy with forward citrus and spice; dry and brisk.

Desert Juniper Hand Crafted American Gin, *USA*

$$ ★★   Fleshy, smooth, and spicy with juniper and simple, clean, creamy texture with vanilla and decent fruit.

Gordon's London Dry Gin, *USA*

$ ★★   Smooth and simple with decent, short flavors and velvety texture; modest and clean.

Hamptons Gin, *USA*

$$ ★★   Balanced and middle-of-the-road in flavors with good aromatics and a smooth finish.

Hendrick's Gin, *Scotland*

$$ ★★★   Spicy, clean, racy, and lovely with a long, rich finish and lovely notes of cucumber.

Junipero Gin, *USA*

$$ ★★★   Heavy and dense with sweet vanilla and smooth, lush flavors of spice; creamy texture.

Leyden Dry Gin, *Netherlands*

$ ★★★   Smooth and mellow with rich juniper and dense spice; long and racy, fresh and spicy. Distilled three times.

Magellan Gin, *France*

$$ ★★   Blue color; thin and racy with spice and edgy flavors; decent but lacking breadth and length.

Martin Miller's London Dry Gin, *England*

$$ ★★★   Lush and smooth with lovely angelica and mellow flavors of spice; long and rich, creamy.

Martin Miller's London Dry Gin Westbourne Strength, *England*
$$ ★★★   Citrus and angelica nose; spicy and lush with smooth cucumber and pear flavors; long and complex.

Mercury Gin, *England*
$$ ★★★   Thick and viscous with lush, sweet herbs and spices; dense and long.

Players Extreme Bumpy Gin, *USA*
$ ★★   Intense and powerful with herbal and pine notes; simple and dense.

Plymouth Gin, *England*
$$ ★★★   Lush and smooth with lovely, integrated flavors and a long, balanced finish of juniper and licorice.

Reval Dry Gin, *Estonia*
$ ★★★   Smooth, peppery nose; floral and lush with juniper, vanilla, creamy texture, and a long, rich finish; a great value.

Seagram's Extra Dry Gin, *USA*
$ ★★   Spicy and intriguing with a silky mouth feel; great value gin.

Tanqueray No. 10 Gin, *England*
$$ ★★★★   Smooth and aromatic with citrus and lush botanicals; fresh and gorgeous; the perfect gin.

Tanqueray Gin, *England*
$ ★★★   Spicy and long with clean, racy flavors of juniper, angelica, and licorice; long and complex; rich with intense spice and ripeness.

Van Gogh Gin, *Netherlands*
$$ ★★★   Silky and seductive with floral-herbal notes and a lingering finish.

rum

Although versions of rum have existed for centuries, the history of what we know today as rum is the history of the New World. Conquest, new lands, and new trade routes contributed to the global success of this sweet and spicy spirit. Its name conjures images of exotic locales, pirates, and colonial America. The history of rum is as exotic, exciting, and dark as the beverage itself. It's as versatile as vodka, able to be added to almost any mixer, and in some cases drunk straight for its complex, rich flavors. Rum is the drink of sailors, pirates, and the tropics. It speaks to a sense of adventure, spice, and mystery.

✳ WHAT IS RUM? ✳

Rum is made from fresh sugarcane juice, cane syrup, or molasses, which is the by-product of processing raw sugarcane into refined sugar. In some cases rum is also made from other sugarcane by-products, such as the froth (dunder) skimmed off the tops of the heating pans when processing the cane. There are deviations, as there are no regulations regarding ingredients or distillation of rum, but the majority of rums produced in the world come from fermented molasses, cane syrup, or cane juice. Molasses contains minerals and nonsugar organic compounds that give molasses-based rum special flavor and character.

Creating sugar from sugarcane is a simple though arduous process. First the stalks must be pressed. The early plantations harnessed mules or oxen to the giant mills used to crush the cane. The result was cane juice. Lime juice was often added to the juice to precipitate impurities, and then the juice was boiled. Next this cooked liquid was transferred to clay pots where the sugar would crystallize. The remaining liquid drained through a hole in the bottom of the pot and was collected in a tray. This crystallizing process took several weeks. After sufficient time had passed, the pots were broken and the dark, dried sugar was prepared for shipping. The leftover liquid was a thick, dark substance called *melaza* (from the Spanish *miel*, meaning honey), which the English pronounced "molasses." Seen as waste from the sugar-making process, the molasses was used as fertilizer or cattle feed. Today sugar is milled by machine, but the process is similar, with molasses still being the by-product of sugar refining.

The rise of rum from its lowly beginnings started when, as legend has it, a thirsty slave dipped his spoon into a tray of leftover *melaza,* which had been sitting for several weeks in the hot sun. The liquid had mixed with a little water and fermented, becoming a crude version of rum. At first mainly slaves drank the brew, but once plantation owners realized the potential of the "leftover brew"—then called *aguardiente*—they tried to refine the spirit to suit European palates. They used more sophisticated distillation techniques, but in 1651 a document from Barbados indicated there was a lot more work to do: "The chief fuddling they make in the island is Rumbullion, alias Kill-Divil, and this is made of sugar canes distilled, a hot, hellish, and terrible liquor."

To begin the fermentation process, yeast, distilled water, and nutrients are added to the raw molasses to produce a "mash." This mixture is allowed to sit and ferment anywhere from twenty-four hours to three weeks. The shorter fermentation time creates light-bodied rum, while a longer fermentation leads to darker, heavier rum. During fermentation the yeast mixes with the base product and creates compounds known as esters. The longer the mash ferments, the higher the ester yield is in the mixture. Esters add a fruity taste to the spirit. High-ester rum is one that has fermented longer, while a low-ester rum is lighter and will not have as fruity an essence.

The fermented molasses is distilled using a pot still, a continuous column still, or a two-column Coffey still. Unlike cognac, which must be processed in a pot still, there are no regulations governing the distillation of rum. Because of this, rums can be single-, double-, or triple-distilled according to the dictates of the manufacturer. Generally, light rums will be distilled in a continuous column or Coffey still, and then filtered to remove impurities. Dark rums are usually distilled in a pot still, which allows cogeners to remain. These impurities give dark, heavier rums their distinctive flavor. Caramel or molasses may also be added to give additional flavor.

When using a column still, the mash is heated and continuously passed through copper and steel distilling columns. During this process, water, alcohol, and the smallest impurities are separated. Continuous distillation column stills create an alcohol purity of up to 80 percent while a two-column Coffey still can produce a purity of up to 90 percent.

In the pot-still process, a wood fire is used to heat the mash in a kettle. Alcohol vaporizes and then is condensed in the condenser. The heat must be carefully monitored so the pot is not heated too quickly. If overheated, the fermented mash will boil over and spill out of the condenser. The first drops of condensation are called high wines or heads—they contain light alcohols, which create a fruity aroma. After this, the still begins producing mostly ethyl alcohol. Once the ethyl alcohol has been boiled the condenser slows down. The last bit of condensate produced is the low wines or tails. The heads and tails are discarded and the second (the desired condensed liquid that will make the rum) is collected and distilled again.

Rum produced from a mash that is quickly fermented will be lighter bodied than rum distilled from a mash fermented for a week or more. Longer fermentation time and lower alcohol purity yield heavier rum while shorter fermentation time and higher alcohol purity will result in a lighter-bodied rum.

Aging

In the late 1660s, when rum production began in earnest, the spirit was sometimes accidentally aged in barrels as it sat on the docks for shipping. When rum reached its destination, the aged rum was found to be superior to unaged rum. Over time distillers began to purposely age their rum to take full advantage of the flavor of the cane spirit. Spirit aged a year or less became known as light rum. Light rum may also be labeled clear, white, or silver.

Light rums exported to the United States are aged at least one year in stainless containers or oak barrels.

Dark rum is aged three years or longer. Rums labeled *añejo* are age-dated rums blended from different outstanding vintages to ensure superior quality. The age given is that of the youngest of the rums in the blend. These high-quality spirits will thrill any aficionado's taste buds. While some distillers add caramel to unaged rum to darken the color, only aged rum can be labeled dark rum. While there are deviations, it is most likely that rum labeled white or silver has been aged for one year. Those labeled amber or gold will have aged at least three years. Dark rum is generally aged five or more years.

Aging takes place in oak barrels. During the manufacture of the barrels, the staves (the wooden slats that form the barrel) are charred. This char can be kept on the barrel to neutralize any unpleasant odors in the rum and give it flavor. Some distillers use barrels previously used to age cognac, bourbon, Scotch, or sherry to give the rum additional flavor and complexity. Barrels fifteen years or older can be found in most aging rooms.

It's All in the Blend

After the aging process, blending begins. Almost all rums are blended. This means that to achieve the desired flavor, the distiller will mix rums from different stills, of different purities, or of different ages. Skillful blending is essential to the production of rum. The knowledge and intuition of the blender can make or break the brand. This was especially important before scientific controls were introduced. A stock of aged rum used for blending is a major part of a manufacturer's capital. One distillery's stock revealed 7,895 casks of under-three-years-old rum, valued at $3,000 per cask, as well as 8 casks of twenty-five-year-old rum valued at $125,000 each.

✳ THE HISTORY OF RUM ✳

Hypothetical origins of the name "rum" can be found in several cultures. The Malays concocted a cane-based drink thousands of years ago called brum, which is still known today. There are those who believe that a version of this drink was found in Barbados. Other experts claim the name originated in Barbados, not among the Malays. Dutch settlers, who farmed cane in Barbados and began producing alcohol along with sugar, would have known that Dutch seamen traveled with large drinking glasses known as rummers. The word "rummer" was a derivation of the Middle-Dutch *roemer,* from *roem,* which meant praise. Of course, the sailors filled their rummers with the brum, which influenced the evolution of the name.

The earliest mention of the tropical sugarcane drink in English writing came twenty-five years after the English first settled on the Isle of Barbados (then spelled Barbadoes) in 1651. A manuscript surviving from 1676 mentions the spiritous drink called "rumbullion," originally from the Old English Devonshire "rumbustion," meaning "a great tumult or uproar." There is also a theory that "rum" comes from *ron,* the Spanish for rum, as the Spanish were the first to distill rum in their Caribbean colonies. Other also-rans are a shortened version of *saccharum,* Latin for sugar, as well as a shortening of *arome,* French for aroma.

Whatever its derivation, rum quickly became the slang for the drink among the English settlers, while the oldest American reference was written in the act of the General Court of Massachusetts in May 1657, prohibiting the sale of strong liquors "whether knowne by the name of rumme, strong water, wine, brandy, etc., etc." The traveler Josselyn wrote of it, terming it that "cursed liquor rhum, rumbullion or kill-devil."

Lovers of rum owe much to Christopher Columbus. Charged with the task of expanding the Spanish Empire, the Italian-born Columbus landed on the island of San Salvador in the Bahamas in 1492 and claimed the land for the king and queen of Spain. A little confused in his geography, Columbus dubbed this new region "the Indies." He was more accurate in predicting that it would be ideal for the cultivation of sugarcane plants. On his second voyage to Hispaniola (now known as the Dominican Republic and Haiti), Columbus brought several hundred sugarcane shoots. These plants would begin the sugar industry in what is now known as the Caribbean. This industry would, in turn, spawn a successful rum-distilling business. In a letter written to Queen Isabella after the plants germinated Columbus respectfully informed her: "Your Majesty, the sugar canes, the few that were planted there, have taken."

Though sugar was domesticated more than ten thousand years ago, before Columbus it was primarily grown in India, China, and the Philippines. It is believed that Alexander the Great brought the cane to the Mediterranean and that the Egyptians were responsible for the early sugar milling techniques that were to become standard in medieval and Renaissance Europe. Sugar was a precious commodity, and its successful cultivation in the New World would help to ensure the success of Spain's venture.

As Columbus reported, the sugar plants took, and by the 1600s the cane plant had become the primary crop for commercial plantations on all the islands in the Caribbean. English, French, Portuguese, Spanish, and Dutch traders were establishing plantations in the Caribbean and South America to compete in the lucrative sugar market. Many of the islands—including Barbados, Antigua, and half of Tobago—became almost completely deforested to create cane fields, and were constantly fought over by the European colonists.

Rum and the Colonies

The distillation of rum went hand-in-hand with the sugar-refining business, and soon nearly every plantation was manufacturing rum as well as sugar. Both industries were labor-intensive operations, which quickly led to a shortage of workers in the Caribbean. It was at this time that hundreds of thousands of West Africans were sold into slavery by the English to work the plantations in the West Indies. This ugly link between rum and slavery would not end for more than two centuries.

The explosion of the rum business threatened the domestic spirit production of both Britain and France. As a result, these countries eventually forbade the importation of liquor from their island colonies to protect domestically distilled spirits such as gin and brandy. With no European outlet for molasses and rum, much of the product was shipped to the new English colonies in North America.

Rum took the American colonies by storm. By 1664 a distillery was set up on what is now Staten Island in New York, and three years later rum was being produced in Boston. At the peak of rum consumption in the colonies, twelve million gallons of the brew were consumed each year, almost four gallons per capita. Colonials drank as many as seven shots a day of 80-proof rum.

Many of the great figures of the War for Independence were huge rum enthusiasts, including Paul Revere, John Hancock, John Adams, and future president George Washington. In fact, twenty years before he would lead the colonial armies against Great Britain, Washington began a love affair with rum. In 1751, at the age of nineteen, he traveled with his ailing brother to Barbados. It was thought that the tropical climate would cure his brother of tuberculosis. The change of venue worked, as Washington's brother did recover. The trip was positive as well for Washington, who, despite a bout with smallpox, discovered Barbados rum. He was so taken by the island spirit that years later he imported it to serve at his inauguration. Washington's two favorite drinks were eggnog and rum punch, both of which were served at almost all social events in the colonies at the time of the War of Independence.

The colonists used rum to their advantage with the native population, trading bottles for furs, and later directly selling it. Together with brandy, rum contributed to the disorientation and defeat of the native population. Along with new European diseases to contend with, the Native Americans now had to contend with drunkenness and alcoholism. New England natives went to the colonists to ask that the commerce in alcohol with native communities be stopped. Almost every colony at one time had laws banning the trade, but without means to enforce them, the laws were short-lived. By 1800 every tribe was forced with a decision whether to allow consumption of alcohol by its members.

The New Englanders' eager embrace of rum would lead to the creation of a new center for the slave trade. New England bankers provided international currency to fill shipping vessels with slaves from the coast of West Africa. These slaves were exchanged in the West Indies for molasses, which was then brought to New England and distilled into rum. This rum would eventually be loaded onto ships returning to West Africa, where the spirit would be traded for more slaves. This business was known as the Triangle Trade or the Notorious Trade.

The sugar trade was very profitable for the colonies, especially New England. Britain saw this and, as a country in debt looking for a way to make money, attempted to levy taxes on the sugar trade through the Molasses Act of 1733. The bill was enacted to stop colonial trade with the French West Indies. New England traded lumber, fish, corn, and flour to the French West Indies in return for sugar. Because of existing restrictive British trade laws, New England was unable to trade these items to Britain. The act taxed not only six pence a gallon on any sugar or spirits produced in the colonies, but demanded that any trade of sugar or spirit go through the British, and that the colonies use only sugar from the British Indies.

Without trading with the French, Dutch, and Spanish, New England would be crippled financially. Luckily the act did not stop rum production or the sugar trade, but it did stir the ire of the colonials who despised taxation without representation—a resentment that would eventually become an important factor leading to the American Revolution. The colonists who continued to trade with the French, Dutch, and Spanish evaded the act by bribing customs officials. The act itself, though passed into law as part of the Sugar Act of 1764, was largely ignored and not enforced. If it had been enforced, it is possible it could have destroyed the nascent economy of the fledgling northern colonies. The French economy profited as well. As rum importation was forbidden in France to protect the brandy market, the French needed the colonies to purchase their sugar and molasses.

The Molasses Act was the first of several attempts at high taxation by the British (sugar and tea would be similarly taxed in 1763). These taxes did little to slow the American rum industry. By 1761 Rhode Island had twenty-two distilleries and three sugar refineries, and by 1763 Massachusetts had sixty-three distilleries in and around Boston and Salem. The Carolinas and Maryland also had a profitable, if less extensive slaving operation that played into the Triangle Trade by supplying slaves to Rhode Island and Massachusetts traders in exchange for rum.

The rum made in Rhode Island was in high demand among the Europeans living in Africa. So popular was the spirit that at one point Rhode Island rum joined gold as the accepted currency within European trading networks. Throughout the 1700s Rhode Island merchants controlled up to 90 percent of the American trade in African slaves. Rhode Island continued in the unsavory slaving business until 1807 when the state passed a law forbidding the importation of slaves.

Since Rhode Island tradesmen could no longer participate in the Triangle Trade, rum production in America began to wind down. With trade routes already disrupted by the American Revolution, the new nation's westward expansion served to further destroy the American rum routes. The Western settlers began to grow crops of corn and rye, which led to the early distillation of whiskey. As this new "American spirit" took hold, the popularity of rum and rum punch continued to wane. The center of rum production moved south, to the islands where the sugar was produced.

Coinciding with the changes in the market for rum was a change that radically affected the sugar plantations in the islands. In 1787 Franz Karl Archand developed the process to extract sugar from sucrose, and more importantly, from any plant where sugar liquids were stored in the starch. With this new process, beets were found to be an ideal substitute for sugarcane. Beets were easier to grow than sugarcane, and because they grew underground, external factors such as battles and extreme weather could not affect the crop. Suddenly Europeans did not have to wait for sugar to be produced half a world away; they could grow beets in their backyard and have as much sugar as they wanted. The importance of sugarcane in the Caribbean was measurably reduced. The discovery made cane growers even more economically reliant on rum production, as sugarcane is the necessary ingredient to its manufacture.

As the rum market in America slowed down, the Spanish territories of Cuba and Puerto Rico, the British colony of Jamaica, and the French colony of Martinique began to develop more sophisticated rum production techniques. In the 1800s Cuba and Puerto Rico would take the lead in the islands due to enterprising Catalonian wine merchants who began distilling rum. Today these areas are still responsible for the distillation of most of the world's rum.

Rum, the British Navy, and Grog

British sailors were introduced to rum when the king's fleet captured the island of Jamaica in 1655. From 1650 on, it was customary for all men serving in the fleet to receive a ration of liquor. This ration consisted of a half pint—a hefty portion by today's standards. The first rations were of beer, but soon beer was replaced by brandy, which was easier to transport. Once Britain controlled Jamaica and other islands in the Caribbean, rum became much more available, and the navy switched to rationing rum rather than imported French brandy.

As can be imagined, the custom of providing sailors with a daily half pint of rum quickly led to boatloads of drunken sailors. Seeking to restore order, naval officers talked of doing away with the ration. The sailors, accustomed to their daily dose, threatened revolt. For several decades the dilemma remained unresolved until, in 1740, the dapper and intelligent Admiral Edward Vernon (nicknamed Old Grog because he wore a heavy waterproof boatcloak made of grogram—a coarse fabric woven from silk, mohair, and wool) introduced a method of watering down the rum.

Admiral Vernon decreed that "the respective daily allowance . . . be every day mixed with the proportion of a quart of water to a half pint of rum, to be mixed in a scuttled butt kept for that purpose, and to be done upon the deck, and in the presence of the Lieutenant of the Watch who is to take particular care to see that the men are not defrauded in having their full allowance of rum . . . and let those that are good husbanders receive extra lime juice and sugar that it be made more palatable to them."

The disgruntled sailors dubbed the new rum drink "grog" as a jab at the man who watered down their rum ration. Rums from Jamaica, Trinidad, and British Guiana were blended and prepared to the admiral's specifications, then poured into oak casks known as "rumbarricoes" or "scuttlebutts" and sent to sea as naval rum. Not only did Admiral Vernon solve the navy's problem, he also created one of the first rum cocktails and started the tradition of mixing rum with fruit juice.

Sixty-five years later, grog took another admiral's name. After Admiral Horatio, Lord Nelson's death at Trafalgar in 1805, grog also became known as Nelson's Blood. According to legend, Admiral Nelson's body was preserved in a cask of rum on the journey home to England following his death in battle. Historians are at odds with this explanation, and many feel that the term Nelson's Blood was derived from the less gruesome practice of raising a glass of rum to the admiral rather than steeping him in it. Nelson's Blood is now the name of a cocktail made with port and champagne.

The navy's practice of rationing what came to be called pusser's rum ("pusser" being a corruption of "purser," the office in charge of the ship's stores) continued well into the twentieth century. Pusser's rum was made in the British Virgin Islands and was never offered for sale to the public, being manufactured exclusively for Her Majesty's ships. By 1970, however, conditions on board ship had become relatively pleasant, and the navy's sophisticated weapons systems demanded a much steadier hand than the cannons and muskets of yore. Taking these factors into consideration, the Admiralty Board decided that there was no place for the daily issue of rum in a modern navy. On July 31, 1970, the issue of rum ceased, ending one of the longest seafaring traditions of modern days. Around the world, on every ship in the Royal Navy fleet, glasses were raised in a final salute to the queen. It has been said that many a strong sailor shed a tear at the passing of grog. In 1979 Charles Tobias resurrected pusser's rum, using a recipe coaxed with much persuasion from the Admiralty, and began commercial distribution of what had been an exclusive Royal Navy spirit. The Royal Navy Sailor's Fund receives a donation for each case sold.

Rum Runners

Laws prohibiting slave trade and America's new infatuation with whiskey would reduce rum to a regional, tropical spirit that was nearly forgotten in the United States. More than a century would pass before history would conspire to reintroduce Americans to rum. Ironically, it was Prohibition that revived interest in this sultry spirit. During the 1920s steamships and charter planes in Florida would load up adventurous drinkers and take them to the tropical paradise of Cuba where they could drink freely and dance. Havana became the party capital for thirsty Americans.

Getting Americans into liquor-friendly territory was only a small part of the new rum industry. The big challenge and the big-

Rum and Coca-Cola

In a bar in 1900 a member of the U.S. Signal Corps, fighting in the Spanish-American War for Cuban independence, mixed what was destined to become a classic cocktail. Combining Coca-Cola (which was at that time a mixture of cola nut syrup and cocaine) with rum, gin, lime, and bitters, he created a new cocktail. He christened the drink the Cuba Libre, after the war in which he was fighting. After Prohibition the drink quickly caught on in the American South, due in part to rum being cheaper than whiskey. Though most think of the drink as the innocuous rum and Coke with a wedge of lime, it is actually a more complicated cocktail.

The Second World War continued to fuel America's love for rum. With thousands of American servicemen stationed in the tropics, rum became a hugely popular drink back home. The Andrews Sisters' recording of the song "Rum and Coca-Cola" was a hit and inspired a nation to mix this super-sweet cocktail in honor of the troops.

The lure of the tropics caught the imagination of Americans throughout the war. Fast on the heels of "Rum and Coca-Cola," legendary San Francisco restaurateur and raconteur Vic Bergeron created the mai tai in 1944 at his first Trader Vic's restaurant on San Pablo Avenue in Oakland, sending the desire for all things tropical into overdrive. The name is from "mai tai—roa ae," which means "out of this world—the best" in Tahitian. Soon tropical drinks were reintroduced to the public and new creations began to flood bars and restaurants across the country. Both the piña colada and the zombie were invented in the postwar years.

Cuba Libre

1½ ounces light rum
½ ounce gin
1 lime
Bitters
3 ounces Coca-Cola

Fill a rocks glass with ice. Pour rum and gin over ice. Squeeze the juice of the lime over mixture, and leave the lime in the glass. Pour Coca-Cola in glass. Top off with 2 dashes of bitters. Stir lightly and enjoy.

ger profits lay in smuggling rum up the coast as far as New Jersey. Large sailboats, steamships, and merchant boats traveled from the West Indies laden with rum. At various ports along the way, smaller contact boats met larger ships, known as mother ships. After loading up the "hooch," the contact boats returned to shore with the contraband. The only obstacle standing between the contact boats and the shore was the U.S. Coast Guard, which was unprepared for the enormous number of "rum runners" in the waters. Along with the rum runners, the influx of smugglers bringing whiskey, cognac, and brandy into the country from Canada completely overwhelmed the coast guard resources. As a result, the Atlantic shore became the main point of importation for "demon rum."

By 1922 hundreds of mother ships were anchored off the northeast, with more than sixty off the coast of New Jersey alone. In that year ten million quarts of liquor made its way into the United States, netting the rum runners a nearly 700 percent profit. In addition to smuggling, many boats were continually anchored twelve miles off shore and used to host legal liquor parties. When the supply on board ran out, they simply weighed anchor and headed back to Cuba for another load of rum. When Congress finally realized that Prohibition was a dismal failure, the legislation was repealed on December 5, 1933.

✳ RUM TODAY ✳

In the early 1960s rum production moved from a period of stability to one of appreciable growth. Competition among the distilleries was strong, and the more efficient ones increased their production markedly. By the end of the 1960s the industry was dominated by a small number of comparatively large distilleries. The demand for rum continued to grow throughout the 1970s, along with a steady increase in rum's share in the U.S. liquor market. The piña colada hit an all-time popularity high in the late 1970s, partly thanks to the Rupert Holmes hit "Escape (The Piña Colada Song)."

The turn toward ultra-premium spirits in the 1980s created a higher demand for single-malt Scotch and small-batch whiskey, and eventually led consumers to seek out premium-aged rums. To enjoy the blend of flavors and complex aroma, this high-quality spirit is best savored without the addition of juice or other mixers. Americans are learning what natives in the Caribbean have known for ages—that the type of rum you drink and where it is made make a huge difference in your experience of the spirit. Aged rums are finally being consumed in the same manner as any fine cognac. This shift in consciousness among serious drinkers is reflected in the prices major distillers are asking for their ultra-premium rums. A whole new generation of upscale rums is arriving from respected distilleries in countries such as Venezuela, Nicaragua, and Guatemala.

Rum's share of the distilled spirits market is up 3 percent in just five years. The top two rum brands in the United States, Puerto Rico's Bacardi and Captain Morgan, which is owned by the large Diageo conglomerate, are the driving forces in the market, with Bacardi leading the category overall. Recently Bacardi launched a new line of flavored rums. With flavors such as raspberry and citrus, these products are certainly aimed at cutting into the flavored vodka market, and other producers have similar lines of rums flavored with vanilla, banana, spices, and coconut. The wide range of flavors may inspire bartenders around the world to concoct what may become the next classic rum cocktail.

✳ RUM IN THE FREE MARKET ✳

Rum distillers in the world are facing a problem similar to the one that once threatened to destroy the legitimate tequila trade. Imposter products that claim to be rum yet have little or no connection to the pure spirit are flooding the market. While the tequila industry has created strict guidelines and quality controls, the rum industry has very little regulation in place. The situation is complicated by the fact that, unlike tequila or cognac, rum is distilled in many different countries. For example, while most Latin American and Caribbean countries agree that a base of cane sugar is essential to the definition of rum, there is at least one country where rum is based on plain distilled alcohol. Rum can also be sold at varying proofs. In Brazil strength is defined as 38–54 percent alcohol by volume at 20 degrees centigrade while in Chile and Venezuela the minimum is 40 percent, and in Colombia it is 50 percent. Age requirements also differ from country to country. The minimum is eight months in Mexico, one year in the Dominican Republic, and two years in Venezuela and Peru. Designations such as *añejo* (aged) can have various meanings, depending on where the rum is produced.

Making matters more complicated is the fact that the categories of rum differ according to each country's whim. In Argentina there are white, gold, light, and extra light. In Barbados there are white, overproof, and matured. In Brazil rum is classified as light, heavy, or aged. Mexican rum is called aged, reserve, or flavored, and in Peru it is either amber or white. In the United States there are rum, rum liqueur, and flavored rum. With all the variations, it will take some effort to unify the market.

It is feared that such wide differences in rum definitions and categories could be a serious nontariff barrier for rum when the Free Trade Area of the Americas (FTAA) comes into force in 2005. With no common definition in place, the way is open for imposter spirits masquerading as rum (such as the infamous German Rum-Verschnitt, which contains only 5 percent rum but is now recognized in the EU) to gain a place in the world market.

Distillers of tequila, bourbon, Canadian whisky, Tennessee whiskey, and pisco have created solid definitions of their spirits that have been adopted under the North American Free Trade Agreement (NAFTA) and the Canada-Chile FTA. Rum distillers must unite if they want to keep their product pure in the modern world. At the time of this writing, some of the countries engaged in rum production are considering passing a definition that would define rum as a uniquely sugarcane-based product, thus excluding all nonsugarcane-based products. This agreement would also preserve the sovereign right of countries that are parties to the FTAA to impose additional requirements on their domestic rums. It remains to be seen whether the rum-producing countries will rise to the challenge of preserving the integrity of their product.

✳ VARIATIONS ON A THEME ✳

French Rum

The French settled in Martinique in 1635 to produce and export coffee, cotton, and sugarcane. In 1694 they added rum distilleries to their various enterprises. Most of the French colonial manufacturers concentrated on the production of a cheap, low-quality rum made from fermented molasses called tafia, which was placed in direct competition with French brandies. To protect the French brandy industry, a royal decree banned the sale of molasses and its extracts in France.

Laws written in 1763 allowed French colonials to sell rum to countries other than France, but only in exchange for products the colonials could not import from the mother country. In the nineteenth century the French finally permitted rum to be imported into France. By 1870 some 57 percent of the island farmland was growing sugarcane, yet the growth of the sugar market had slowed. This slowing led to the emergence of *rhum agricole,* which was rum made from fresh cane instead of molasses. This is different from *rhum industriel,* which is made from fermented molasses. The aging and blending of rums for the French market is done in Bordeaux. French rums are clearly labeled either *agricole* or *industriel.*

Martinique is a protectorate of France, and the rum made there is officially recognized by the Appellation d'Origine Contrôlée (AOC) system. The fight to implement standards and gain an AOC label from the French government took fifteen years. In 1996 Martinique obtained approval to bear the AOC on their product, making it the sole French overseas region to possess this distinction. According to the terms of the AOC, rum from Martinique must follow standards in production, sugarcane cultivation, cane variety, methods of juice extraction, fermentation process, distillation process, storage, and aging.

Jamaican Rum

According to tradition, Jamaican rums are produced through double distillation in pot stills. The molasses used in Jamaican rum is left to ferment for up to three weeks, which is quite a bit longer than the fermentation time for other rums. This extra fermentation time creates a high ester rum with a very fruity flavor. Most Jamaican rum is aged for a minimum of five years and gains most of its color from molasses rather than from aging.

Cachaça—That "Crazy Cane Juice"

The Brazilians put their own twist on rum by creating what today we know as cachaça (also spelled caxaça). Cachaça is a cousin of molasses-based rum, but takes its distinctive flavor from the juice of unrefined sugarcane. This juice is allowed to ferment in wood or copper vats for three weeks before being boiled down. Three separate boiling processes create a thick concentrate.

When it was first produced on the sugar plantations, the fermented sugarcane juice (leftovers from the sugar milling process) created a potent beverage that the Indians and African slaves were given to keep them docile and cooperative. The slaves called it *garapa doida,* or "crazy cane juice." From the sixteenth century until the middle of the seventeenth century, these plantations evolved into cachaça distilleries. Cachaça, like rum in New England, became a currency for buying slaves.

Over the centuries Brazilians have coined numerous colorful slang expressions for cachaça, including *pinga* ("it drips"), *branquinha* ("the little white one"), and *engasga gato* ("cat choker"). One colorful term nicely expresses the potency of cachaça: *água que passarinho não bebe* (or "water the bird doesn't drink"). As production techniques improved, cachaça became a drink of the elite. The Brazilians bottle their own cachaça at anywhere from 100 to 140 proof—up to 70 percent alcohol. These potent cachaças rarely make their way to the United States, but there are more than four thousand different cachaças available in Brazil, which produces over a billion liters of the spirit every year. Cachaça is second only to beer in popularity in its native country.

✳ THE CLASSIC DRINKS ✳

The Daiquiri

Depending on whom you ask, numerous colorful characters are credited with the creation and perfection of the daiquiri. The three below are most often mentioned, but whatever the truth, the refreshing drink seems to have sprung from the collective consciousness of the late 1800s.

The Engineer

In 1896 Jennings S. Cox, an American engineer working in an iron mine called Daïquiri in the east of Cuba, was visited by a colleague named Pagliuchi, who was looking for ways to use deserted mines near Sanitago de Cuba. At the end of the day Pagliuchi suggested a drink, but all Cox had in his storeroom were lemons, sugar, and rum. They mixed the elements together in a shaker with ice, and the new drink was born. Cox suggested the name of rum sour, but Pagliuchi retorted that it needed a better name, and suggested daiquiri. Somehow, limes do not figure in this version of the birth of the drink.

The General

In 1898 during the Spanish-American War, American troops, under the command of American general Shafter, landed in Cuba. The obese general was too fat to ride a horse and had to be transported in a cart wherever he went. Despite this impediment Shafter, a gourmand, made certain he was introduced to local delicacies, which included partaking in libations. During his "inspection" of the various restaurants and bars of the region, he discovered a drink favored by Cuban patriots. This cocktail was a combination of rum, lemon juice, and sugar. Legend has it that, upon tasting the drink, the general claimed it needed just one thing—ice. Once again, lime didn't seem to occur to the general.

The Cantinero

Although not invented there, the daiquiri was made famous in Havana by cantinero Constantino Ribalaigua Vert, a Catalan immigrant who tended bar at (and later owned) El Floridita. What Vert called the daiquiri Floridita was the result of much experimentation. To prepare his cocktail, he imported an American ice-crushing machine to make the perfect ice. He added crushed ice and five drops of Maraschino cherry liqueur to the original recipe of Pagliuchi and Cox. After mixing the cocktail in a blender, he served it in a frosted glass. Strict observation of the mixing time and of the proportions of rum, citrus, and ice were Vert's trademark, which led to his nickname, El Grande Constante. Due to the success of Vert's daiquiri in the post–World War I era, El Floridita would eventually become referred to as La Cuna del Daiquiri, or the Cradle of the Daiquiri. In his Cuban years, Hemingway took his Floridita daiquiri as a double, without sugar, calling it Papa's Special. Some say that the Floridita daiquiri has a unique taste, unlike any other daiquiri. Perhaps it's here the lemon changed to lime.

The Original Daiquiri

2 ounces light rum
1 ounce lime juice
1 teaspoon superfine sugar
Maraschino cherry

Shake all the ingredients in a shaker with crushed ice and strain into a cocktail glass. Garnish with a Maraschino cherry.

The Caipirinha

Over the last ten years a number of tasty cachaças have been exported to the United States. This heady Brazilian spirit is the key ingredient in the Caipirinha, which is one of the hottest drinks in bars all over America. The sweetness of cachaça accents the intensity of lime zest in the Caipirinha, making it especially refreshing in the summer months. This drink, which is actually quite old, has been revived as part of the retro cocktail movement, although sophisticates might not appreciate its rustic origins. The name, roughly translated, means farmer's drink.

Traditional Caipirinha

1 lime
2 teaspoons sugar
2 ounces cachaça

Wash the lime and roll it on the board to loosen the juices. Cut the lime into pieces and place them in a glass. Sprinkle with the sugar and crush the pieces (pulp side up) with a pestle just enough to release the juice, otherwise the juice will turn bitter. Add the cachaça and stir to mix. Add ice cubes and stir again.

The Mai Tai
—Yes, Virginia, There Is a Trader Vic

The greatest rum drink inventor was born in San Francisco not long after the daiquiri was born. The charismatic Vic Bergeron opened his first bar-cum-restaurant, Hinky Dinks, in Emeryville, just across the bay from San Francisco, in 1934. Three years later he changed the name of the place to Trader Vic's and adopted the now world-famous tropical paradise theme.

One night in 1944 Vic was in the service bar of his restaurant thinking about creating a new drink. He took down a bottle of seventeen-year-old rum. It was J. Wray Nephew from Jamaica. "The flavor of this great rum wasn't meant to be overpowered with heavy additions of fruit juices and flavorings," Vic wrote in 1970. "I took a fresh lime, added some orange curaçao from Holland, a dash of rock candy syrup, and a dollop of French orgeat, for its subtle almond flavor. A generous amount of shaved ice and vigorous shaking by hand produced the marriage I was after."

Trader Vic garnished the new drink with fresh mint, left half the lime in for color, and gave a glass to a Tahitian friend who happened to be in the restaurant that night. She took one sip and said, "Mai tai—roa ae," which means "out of this world—the best." A classic was born.

The Original Mai Tai

2 ounces aged Jamaican rum
½ ounce orgeat (almond syrup)
½ ounce curaçao
¼ ounce rock candy (simple) syrup
Juice from one lime
Sprig of fresh mint

Hand shake all the liquid ingredients. Garnish with half the lime shell inside the drink and float a sprig of fresh mint at the edge of the glass.

The Mojito

From 1600 to the early 1800s slaves working in the sugarcane fields or sugar mills were allowed a glass of sugared water to renew their failing energies. Occasionally the masters would spike the sweet water with *aguardiente,* a crude cane distillate with high alcohol content. At some point some yerba buena (mint) was added to the mix, and the mojito was born. The drink's name stems from the Spanish word *mojo,* which means to blend, combine, or assemble. By the early twentieth century the mojito was a favorite drink at the bars of Playa de Marianao, a working-class beach in a borough of Havana.

Today the mojito is one of the hottest drinks on the club scene. Latin and non-Latin venues alike serve this refreshing concoction. There are a few Cuban-influenced bars that use real pressed sugarcane juice, called *guarapo,* in place of simple syrup in their mojitos. Seek these places out. The drink has even been featured in HBO's *Sex and the City,* surely a sign of its arrival on the fashion front. In one recent James Bond film, Pierce Brosnan sips (gasp!) not a martini, but a mojito.

The Mojito

8 mint leaves
1 lime
2½ ounces light rum
1 tablespoon simple syrup
5 ounces club soda

Place the mint leaves and the simple syrup in a collins glass, muddle with a wooden spoon (or whatever appropriate utensil you can find) for 20–30 seconds, until you can smell that good minty smell. Cut the lime in half, getting rid of the seeds as well as you can. Squeeze the juice out from both halves into the glass, then drop half the lime into the glass. Pour in the rum and stir. Add plenty of ice, then top off the mixture with club soda. Garnish with a sprig of mint—enjoy!

The Piña Colada

Experts agree that this fruity, zesty drink was invented in 1954 by Ramon "Monchito" Marrero, a bartender at the Caribe Hilton Hotel in San Juan, Puerto Rico. His goal was to capture all the flavors of Puerto Rico in a glass, and in my estimation he did exactly that. By the way, piña colada means "strained pineapple" in Spanish.

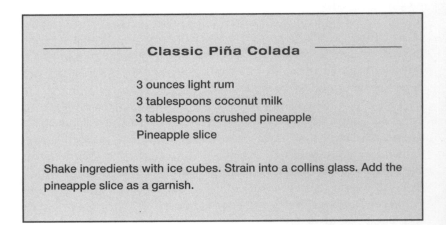

Classic Piña Colada

3 ounces light rum
3 tablespoons coconut milk
3 tablespoons crushed pineapple
Pineapple slice

Shake ingredients with ice cubes. Strain into a collins glass. Add the pineapple slice as a garnish.

✳ BRAND PROFILES ✳

BACARDI. Though Bacardi is produced in Puerto Rico, it has roots in the heart of Cuba. In 1843 Catalonian Don Facundo Bacardi Massó emigrated from Spain to Santiago de Cuba. At that time rum was a strong unblended drink, usually rudimentarily distilled, and completely unlike the refined and double-distilled spirits of Europe. The local rum was considered a drink for the working poor.

Determined to create superior rum, Don Facundo started experimenting with various distillation techniques. First he introduced the idea of charcoal mellowing. He then aged the rum in American white oak barrels that were charred inside to enhance flavor as the spirit aged. The new batches of rum turned out to be surprisingly clean, smooth, and full-bodied.

Convinced he had a created a spirit that would delight and surprise connoisseurs, he decided to become a commercial rum distiller. ·Don Facundo bought a small distillery with a corrugated metal roof and distilling flasks made of copper and wrought iron. He and his wife, Doña Amalia Lucía Victoria Moreau, worked side-by-side establishing their empire. Looking over the property, Amalia noticed a colony of fruit bats living in the rafters of the distillery. Local superstitions held that bats bring good health, fortunes, and unity, so she believed they were a good omen. Inspired, she told Don Facundo they should brand their bottles with the image of the bat. He agreed, and she designed the bat logo for their Bacardi products. To this day the bat appears on every label of every product carrying the Bacardi name.

On February 4, 1862, Bacardi y Compañia was founded. The first light rum ever made was called Los Maestros del Ron. Don Facundo revolutionized rum distillation. In addition to his practice of charcoal mellowing and aging the spirits in charred white oak barrels, he also created a natural yeast that could be added directly to the molasses during fermentation. Prior to this, molasses was left out to ferment spontaneously as it mixed with yeast elements in the air. This more organic fermentation process yielded a host of nasty bacterial impurities. Don Facundo was able to create a method that would ensure perfect fermentation without the danger of contamination. The same form of yeast continues to be cultivated today and still lends its distinctive character to rum.

The Bacardi family produced their rum through the first war of independence in 1890, which created the Republic of Cuba. Don Facundo's son, Emilio Bacardi, eventually became mayor of

Santiago and expanded the company's production by opening a bottling plant in New York. Emilio's participation in the company was short-lived, as he was exiled from Cuba for anticolonial activities. Despite his exile, the family continued to run the company with the same passion as their patriarch.

The onset of Prohibition in America saw the closing of the New York plant, and for a moment it seemed that the business could not recover from the blow. Soon, however, Americans flocked to Cuba in droves. Facundito Bacardi, Facundo's grandson, soon invited liquor-deprived Americans to "Come to Cuba and bathe in Bacardi rum." The call was heeded and Bacardi continued to prosper.

But the revolution of 1958 brought Bacardi's days in Cuba to an end. With Fidel Castro's rise to power, the Bacardi family's entire property was nationalized. With the patent for their famed rum in hand, the third- and fourth-generation members of the family fled to Puerto Rico, where they started all over again. The Cuban government confiscated the original Bacardi factories and began producing a rum known as Havana Club.

Despite great adversity, the Cuban-born Bacardi would make a home in Puerto Rico. The hard work paid off eventually, as Bacardi is both the number one producer of rum in the world and the largest distiller of alcohol in the world. The great-grandson of Don Facundo took over running the company in 1980. As of this writing, Bacardi is the only major privately held spirits company in the world. Bacardi now has bottling plants in the Bahamas, Canada, and Brazil and sells more than twenty million cases a year worldwide of quality rums in a variety of styles.

RON RICO. Rum production in Puerto Rico goes back to well before 1898 and the end of the Spanish-American War when the island was handed over to the United States by Spain. Historians believe that Ponce de León brought the precursor to rum to the island in the 1500s. By 1747 the Spanish government prohibited the production of rum to protect the sales of Spanish liquor. When rum production was finally permitted again it was heavily taxed. To get around these taxes, the distillers began to shift their focus from local consumption to exportation to the United States.

The true foundations of modern rum production in Puerto Rico were laid in the middle of the nineteenth century. In 1859, just prior to the Spanish-American War, a Spaniard named Don Sebastian Serrallés emigrated from Catalonia to settle in Puerto Rico and run a sugar plantation. After his death, his son Juan expanded the family estate and built a sugar factory. In 1865 he bought a French pot still and began producing Puerto Rico's first commercial rum. He named it Don Q, after his favorite figure in Spanish literature, Cervantes' Don Quixote.

Today only two distilleries are operating on the island of Puerto Rico: Bacardi, which operates in San Juan, and Serrallés, which is established in Ponce. In 1985 Serrallés acquired the Ron Rico brand, which had been produced in Puerto Rico since 1860. Besides the popular Ron Rico (sometimes spelled as a single word, Ronrico), the Serrallés distillery also oversees production of several other rums, including the Captain Morgan brand for the liquor conglomerate Diageo.

MOUNT GAY. Rum was probably being produced on the Mount Gay rum estate on the island of Barbados as early as 1663. A surviving legal deed dated February 20, 1703, lists the equipment necessary for the production of rum, including: "Two stone windmills . . . one boiling house with seven coppers, one curing house and one still house." This document suggests that Mount Gay is the oldest rum in Barbados, and the world's oldest rum in continual production.

The Mount Gay estate is located in northern Barbados on a ridge in St. Lucy. In the 1600s this spot was known as Mount Gilboa and was divided into several small, separately owned sugar plantations. Sometime in the early 1700s an Englishman, William Sandiford, bought 280 acres of the small estates and consolidated them into one large plantation. The land was passed on to Sandiford's son, who sold it in 1747 to another Englishman called (ironically) John Sober.

Sober and his son, who had the equally unlikely first name of Cumberbatch, were dyed-in-the-wool Englishmen who spent most of their time in England. They hired a good friend, Sir John Gay Alleyne, to manage the estate in 1787. When Sir John died in 1810, Cumberbatch Sober renamed the plantation Mount Gay in his honor. The Sober family continued to run the property until 1860. The family sold the plantation, but rum continued to be produced, and demand increased.

In the early 1900s prominent businessman Aubrey Ward saw potential in the estate. He completely updated the plantation to meet the increasing demand for Mount Gay rum. Though the production techniques were more automated, Ward was determined that Mount Gay's product would maintain its traditional character.

To this day the Ward family continues to be involved with Mount Gay Rum distilleries, but the French Rémy Cointreau Group acquired a major interest in the company in 1989. Using the highest-quality molasses, the rum is produced using both the continuous Coffey still and traditional pot stills. Mount Gay rums are all aged several years before blending.

MATUSALEM. In 1872 brothers Benjamin and Eduardo Camp, along with their partner Evaristo Álvarez, established the Matusalem brand in Santiago de Cuba. They used the blending and distilling process of the solera system, developed to create Spain's sherries and solera brandies. (A description of this system may be found in the brandy chapter.)

The name Matusalem is derived from the Spanish proverb "*Esto es mas viejo que Matusalem*," meaning "It's older than Methuselah." Biblical Methusaleh is said to have lived for 969 years, and his name was chosen to give a sense of the aging process integral to the flavors and distinction of the brand.

By the early part of the twentieth century Claudio Álvarez LeFebre, son of Evaristo Álvarez, had joined the company. Keeping things in the family, Claudio's sister married the son of Eduardo Camp. Claudio had great knowledge and expertise about rum production, and managed the company into an era of great growth. Cuban rum began catching on in world markets. The popularity only increased with American Prohibition.

Claudio's son, Claudio Álvarez Soriano, joined the company and kept it flourishing until 1956 when both father and son died within six months of each other. That same year Fidel Castro renewed his guerrilla war against President Fulgencio Batista, and by 1959 Castro had taken control of Cuba and confiscated the Matusalem properties.

The remaining family members went into exile, eventually relocating to the United States. Unfortunately, family feuding over control of Matusalem erupted and the business foundered. The company remained in shambles until the 1990s when the fourth-generation Dr. Claudio Álvarez won control of the company in a lengthy legal battle. An out-of-court settlement in 1995 gave Dr. Álvarez both the Matusalem company and the name.

Dr. Álvarez has returned the company to its original objective of producing premium rum. Today Matusalem rum is produced in the Dominican Republic. The master blenders are all descendants of the founders, and continue to use the centuries-old technique of solera blending, in which various mature aged Caribbean rums are carefully blended to create exceptionally smooth, unique blends.

SEA WYNDE. Sea Wynde is a blend of five different pot-still rums from Jamaica and Guyana. A newcomer on the market, this rum is aged in oak barrels using the aging system employed by British Royal Navy rum brokers in the 1700s. In this sense it is a throwback to the great rums of yore, but its all pot-still nature makes it the rum world's equivalent of a malt Scotch. Sea Wynde at 46 percent alcohol is the only rum in the world blended entirely from pot stills.

✳ TASTING RUM ✳

Looking at the label can help you decide which rum to choose and whether to drink it in mixed drinks or to enjoy it on its own as you would a fine brandy. Sipping rums are generally heavier, dark rums, while clear and light rums are great combined into cocktails. Most labels will list the country of origin and the alcohol content. Look for the name of the distiller, as some rum is blended and bottled by one producer but distilled somewhere else. Rums from Jamaica and Trinidad will be marked or labeled either TDL or Jamaica liquor bottle—but remember this is only the country of origin, not the distiller. The label should also tell you whether the rum is produced from molasses or cane juice, and whether it is spiced.

Treat aged rum the way you would single-malt Scotch or fine, aged tequila. Pour the spirit into a snifter or chimneyed spirits glass, which will focus the aroma.

Swirl the spirit in the glass and judge the color and clarity. Remember, the longer a rum ages, the darker it will be.

After observing the color of the spirit, take in the aroma. Be warned that while mellowed, aged rum will be a pleasure to inhale, a young, raw rum could burn your nasal passages. Keep your nose above the rim of the glass. Look for hints of vanilla, caramel, butterscotch, tobacco, and leather.

Sip the rum and allow yourself to savor the flavors. Just as your nose may have picked up a wide variety of scents, your tongue will discover a plethora of flavors. Seek out caramel, brown sugar, tobacco, molasses, and leather.

When you are drinking an overproof rum, a little water in the mix might soften the jolt to your taste buds. Sample a wide variety of aged rums by setting up selections from one particular location or distillery or compare rums from different countries. No matter how you decide to set up your tasting, I'm certain you will find the quality of aged rums comparable to other premium spirits.

Storage

Much like vodka and gin, rum is very stable, handles changes in temperature well, and can last indefinitely. Make sure the cap is sealed tightly when storing previously opened rum.

Flavored Rum

Taking a cue from the success of flavored vodka, rum distillers are now adding flavors to their rum. Not only does this move expand their market share, it also offers some new taste delights to the consumer. The refreshing bite of lemon, the tang of raspberry, or the smooth sweetness of peach can be found in some light rums on the market today. Enjoy these flavored rums in your favorite cocktail or mixed with tonic as you would a flavored vodka.

tasting notes

Angostura Rum Aged 3 Years, *Trinidad and Tobago*
$ ★★   Smooth vanilla and spice, fresh and balanced; aged in American oak but filtered for clarity.

Angostura Rum Aged 5 Years, *Trinidad and Tobago*
$ ★   Dry and edgy with simple flavors and a short finish; less impressive than the other rums from this house.

Angostura 1919 Rum Aged 8 Years, *Trinidad and Tobago*
$$ ★★   Light amber color; spicy, grassy, smooth, and sweet with lively fruit and a long finish.

Angostura 1824 Limited Reserve Rum Aged 12 Years, *Trinidad and Tobago*
$$$ ★★★   Dark amber color; spicy with toasty wood and a smooth, lively, slightly sweet flavor; long and complex.

Appleton Estate V/X Rum, *Jamaica*

$ ★★★   Light amber color; smooth, lush, and showing vanilla, brown sugar, and spice; mellow and long.

Appleton Estate Rum 21 Years Old, *Jamaica*

$$ ★★★   Medium dark amber color; toasty, buttery, popcorn, and spice; vanilla and orange peel; long and balanced.

Appleton Estate Extra Rum, *Jamaica*

$ ★★★   Dark reddish amber; lush nose of honey, banana, and spice; smooth and toasty with lovely sweet vanilla and brown sugar.

Bacardi Superior White Rum, *Puerto Rico*

$ ★★   Clean, smooth, and creamy with soft vanilla and spice; long and fresh.

Bacardi Reserva Rum Superior 8 Years Old, *Puerto Rico*

$$ ★★★   Light medium amber color; soft, caramel nose; lush, silky, and elegant with creamy, subtle flavors of wood, spice, and sweetness; long and balanced.

Bacardi Select Rum, *Puerto Rico*

$ ★★   Medium amber color; smooth and lush with sweet, balanced brown sugar and spice flavors; long and mellow.

Bacardi Gold Rum, *Puerto Rico*

$ ★★★   Light amber color; smooth and mellow with toasty wood; fresh, spicy, and elegant; balanced and long.

British Royal Navy Imperial Rum, *British Virgin Islands and South America*

$$$$ ★★★★   The world's priciest rum, sourced from rare unused British navy reserves; dusky, rich flavors with sublime notes of rancio.

Brugal White Label Rum, *Dominican Republic*

$ ★★   Racy and dry with hot, vodkalike flavors; clean, pure, and smooth.

Brugal Gold Label Rum, *Dominican Republic*

$ ★★   Light amber color; smooth, honey nose; dry and mellow with elegant, toasty, clean flavors.

Brugal Añejo Rum, *Dominican Republic*

$ ★★   Medium amber color; dry and racy with some nice toasty, caramel notes; smooth and clean.

Canne Royale Extra Old Rum, *Grenada*

$$ ★★   Sweet and enticing; dusky oak and spice tones and a balanced finish.

Captain Morgan Private Stock Rum, *USA*

$$ ★★   Dark amber color; sweet and lush with vanilla, spice, and creamy texture; woody, rich, and balanced but a trifle short.

Charbay Rum, *USA*

$$ ★★★   Soft vanilla-honey aroma; fresh and sweet with smooth texture and good length; clean, bright and nicely balanced.

Clarkes Court Superior Light Rum, *Grenada*

$ ★★★   Creamy, sweet, smooth, clean, and mellow, with a long, ripe finish.

Clarkes Court Special Dark Rum, *Grenada*

$ ★★   Coppery to the eye and smooth on the palate, with nice oak tones.

Clarkes Court Old Grog Rum, *Grenada*

$$ ★★   Coppery and deep with assured poise and balanced on the palate.

Cruzan 2 Year Old Rum, *Virgin Islands*

$ ★★★   Lush and spicy with vanilla, oak, and long, rich flavors of caramel.

Cruzan 5 Year Old Rum, *Virgin Islands*

$ ★★   Toasty, rich flavors of molasses and herbs layered with sweet oak.

Cruzan Single Barrel Estate Rum, *Virgin Islands*

$$ ★★★   The flagship of the Cruzan line, blended from rums up to twelve years old and then reaged in a

single oak cask; medium amber in color with smooth, elegant, spicy flavors of toasted honey and a dry, lush and complex finish.

Diplomatico Reserva Exclusiva, *Venezuela*
$$ ★★★   Medium amber color; smooth and balanced with elegant, rich flavors of caramel, vanilla, and spice.

Don Q White Rum, *Puerto Rico*
$ ★★   Smooth, clean, short, and simple.

Doorly's XO, *Barbados*
$$ ★★   Polished and silky with intriguing sherry notes.

Flor de Caña Extra Dry 4 Year Old White Rum, *Nicaragua*
$ ★★   Touted to be the only white rum currently available that's aged four years; smooth and creamy with sweet, lush flavors and excellent balance; filtered for clarity.

Flor de Caña Gold Rum 4 Year Old, *Nicaragua*
$ ★★   Bright amber hue with medium weight and clean delineate flavors.

Flor de Caña Black Label 5 Year Old, *Nicaragua*
$ ★★   Intriguing floral-spice nose and dry and crisp on the palate.

Flor de Caña Grand Reserve 7 Year Old, *Nicaragua*
$$ ★   Sultry and seductive with caramel and white fruit notes.

Flor de Caña Centenario 12 Year Old, *Nicaragua*
$$ ★★   Creamy and smooth with dark molasses and oak tones.

Gosling's Black Seal Rum, *Bermuda*
$ ★   Rich and intense; nice flavors of spice, cane, and sweet oak.

Gran Blason Añejo Especial Reserva, *Costa Rica*
$$ ★★★   Medium amber color; citrus, orange nose; creamy texture with lovely fruit and spice; rich, dense and long.

Grand Havana Reserva Excelencia, *Grenada*
$$ ★★   Smooth and elegant with nutlike flavors.

Inner Circle Green Dot, *Australia*
$$ ★★★   Lush and dense molasses and spice; intense and pruny.

Inner Circle Red Dot, *Australia*
$$ ★★   A revived nineteenth-century rum from Australia; intense and peppery with nice depth.

Matusalem Platino, *Dominican Republic*
$ ★★★   Sweet, creamy, lush, and ripe, with a long and lovely finish.

Matusalem Clásio, *Dominican Republic*
$$ ★★★   Smooth and lush with caramel, spice, and lovely honey flavors; snappy and deep.

Matusalem Gran Reserva, *Dominican Republic*
$$ ★★★   Smooth and spicy with creamy, silky flavors and a long, spicy finish.

Montecristo Rum, *Guatemala*
$$ ★★★   Smooth and rich; lively and bright with a long, fruity finish.

Mount Gay Eclipse, *Barbados*
$ ★★   Amber color and deep, dusky, smoky flavors.

Mount Gay Extra Old Rum, *Barbados*
$$ ★★★   Spicy, dense, and long with lively fruit and a long, toasty, sweet finish.

Myers's Legend Rum Aged 10 Years, *Jamaica*
$$ ★★★   Dark amber color; clove, chocolate, and allspice in the nose; molasses, spice, prune, and toasty oak on the palate; complex and long.

New Orleans Crystal Rum, *USA*
$$ ★★   Soft and mild with vanilla, sweet flavors and a kick of raw alcohol on the finish.

New Orleans Amber Rum, *USA*

$$ ★   Smooth and mellow with modest flavors of caramel; decent and balanced.

Players Extreme Rum, *West Indies*

$ ★★   Smooth and sweet with some raw alcohol and basic flavors; clean and creamy.

Pusser's Rum, *Virgin Islands*

$$ ★★★   Agressive and almost Scotch-like nose with intense flavors of molasses and wood.

Pyrat XO Reserve Planter's Gold Rum, *Anguilla*

$$ ★★★   Medium amber color; orange nose, silky texture, and loaded with tropical fruit; citrus, sweet mango, orange rind; toasty and smooth.

R. L. Seale's Rum Aged 10 Years, *Barbados*

$$ ★★★   Medium amber color; fruity and lush with butter-scotch and toasted almonds plus smooth vanilla.

Rhum Barbancourt Estate Reserve, *Haiti*

$$ ★★★   Medium amber color; creamy, smooth, and lush with caramel, spice, toasty oak, and a long, rich finish.

Rhum Negrita Rum, *Guadeloupe, West Indies*

$ ★★★   Dark amber color; fruity nose with thick, dense texture; intense tropical fruit and tamarind; long and smooth.

Ron Llave, *Puerto Rico*

$ ★★   Pale amber color; smooth and balanced, clean and quite decent.

Ron Viejo de Caldas, *Colombia*

$ ★★   Spicy and lively with vibrant flavors.

Ron Zacapa Centenario 23 Years Old, *Guatemala*

$$ ★★   Burnished and deep with oak, tobacco, and leather notes.

Ronrico Silver Label, *Puerto Rico*

$ ★   Clean, simple, and fresh-tasting; fine rum for mixing.

Ronrico Gold Label Rum, *Puerto Rico*
$ ★★   Coppery color with zippy, spicy notes on the nose; satisfying and rich.

Santa Teresa Ron Antiguo de Solera 1796, *Venezuela*
$$ ★★★   Orange and caramel with smooth, racy, and elegant flavors; long and spicy with lovely flavors and length.

Sea Wynde Pot-Still Rum, *Jamaica/Guyana*
$$ ★★★   Deep amber color; racy and ethery with orange rind and spice; hot and intense, complex and woody with cognaclike characteristics.

Whaler's Original Dark Rum, *USA*
$ ★★   Dark amber color; toasty and dense with caramel and spice.

Whaler's Rare Reserve Dark Rum with Natural Flavors, *USA*
$ ★★   Medium dark reddish amber; rich and fragrant, smooth and thick with spice and caramel; long and balanced.

XM Royal Demerara Rum Extra Mature Aged 10 years, *Guyana*
$$ ★★   Light amber color; smooth and fruity with sweet caramel and lovely oak; long and lovely.

Zaya 12 Year Old, *Guatemala*
$$ ★★★   Layered and sophisticated, with integrated oak and amazing length.

FLAVORED RUM

Bacardi Coco Original Coconut Rum, *Puerto Rico*
$ ★★★   Fresh cut coconut and vanilla, spice and smooth texture; ripe rum flavors and a long finish.

Bacardi Vaníla Original Vanilla Rum, *Puerto Rico*
$ ★★★   Smooth and lush vanilla with creamy texture and rich, balanced rum flavors.

Bacardi Razz Original Raspberry Rum, *Puerto Rico*
$ ★★★   Fresh, bright raspberry fruit and smooth, vanilla rum with a tangy, bright finish.

Bacardi Limón Original Citrus Rum, *Puerto Rico*
$ ★★★   Bracing lemon and lemon zest aromas; fresh and forward with a long, lingering lemon and lemon zest flavor; smooth with a backdrop of vanilla.

Bacardi "O" Original Orange Rum, *Puerto Rico*
$ ★★   Candied orange and sweet vanilla; smooth and long.

Captain Morgan Original Spiced Rum, *USA*
$ ★★   Round and mellow with zippy spice flavors.

Captain Morgan Parrot Bay Coconut Rum, *USA*
$ ★   Sweet and syrupy with simple, clean white rum and a candied coconut finish; very sweet.

Charbay Tahitian Vanilla Bean Rum, *USA*
$$ ★★★   Smooth tropical fruit nose; spicy, sweet, and tropical with notes of almond, spice, and vanilla; long and mellow.

Ciclón, *USA*
$ ★★   Bacardi Gold Rum infused with tequila and lime; citrusy with sweet, spicy flavors, racy acidity and caramel finish; interesting but weird.

Clarkes Court Spicy Rum, *Grenada*
$ ★   Feisty and snappy flavors play through to a long finish.

Cruzan Pineapple Rum, *Virgin Islands*
$ ★   Clear and sticky sweet with flavors of cooked pineapple and sugar.

Cruzan Coconut Rum, *Virgin Islands*
$ ★   Sweet and lush with decent but slightly confected flavors.

Cruzan Banana Rum, *Virgin Islands*
$ ★★   Sticky sweet with bubble gum and banana flavoring and sugary, creamy notes.

Cruzan Vanilla Rum, *Virgin Islands*
$ ★★★   Smooth and creamy with sweet, clean vanilla flavors and a thick, lush finish.

Flor de Caña Limón Lemon Flavored Rum, *Nicaragua*
$ ★   Citrusy and vibrant with tangy lemon flavors.

Foursquare Spiced Rum, *Barbados*
$ ★★   Light amber color; clean, racy, and fairly simple rum with nice allspice, cinnamon, and pepper notes; bright and balanced, fresh and long.

Malibu Carribean Rum Coconut Flavor, *Barbados*
$ ★   Creamy and sweet with modest coconut flavors.

Marimba Lemon Squeeze Rum, *Virgin Islands*
$ ★★   Lush and very sweet with lemon candy flavor and smooth texture.

Marimba Orange S'Cream Rum, *Virgin Islands*
$ ★★   Lush and sweet vanilla and orange peel with silky texture and good flavor intensity.

Marimba Tropical Tease Rum, *Virgin Islands*
$ ★★   Clear and smooth with sweet, confected tropical fruit punch flavors.

Marimba Spiced Breeze Rum, *Virgin Islands*
$ ★★   Light amber in color; thick and creamy texture with dry, spicy flavors; clove, pepper, and vanilla.

Martí Autentico Mojito Cuban-Style Rum, *USA*
$ ★★   Cuban-style rum with natural lime and mint; lush and sweet with racy lime fruit and mint flavors; long and intense.

Mojito Club Caribbean-Style Rum Cocktail, *USA*
$ ★   Synthetic-tasting cocktail with cooked lemon and spicy finish.

Players Extreme Banana Rum, *West Indies*

$ ★★★   Smooth and creamy, sweet and very true ripe banana flavor; lush and intense.

Players Extreme Coconut Rum, *USA*

$ ★★   Very sweet and syrupy with natural coconut flavors and a rich, balanced finish.

Ronrico Pineapple Coconut Rum, *Puerto Rico*

$ ★   Nicely balanced tropical fruit-punch flavors with a moderate finish.

Ronrico Vanilla Rum, *Puerto Rico*

$ ★   Modest vanilla flavors and medium body.

Ronrico Citrus Rum, *Puerto Rico*

$ ★   Clean and direct but a bit one-dimensional.

Sailor Jerry Spiced Navy Rum, *Virgin Islands*

$ ★★   Smooth and lively with caramel and peppery spice; clean, balanced, and mellow.

Whaler's Vanille Rum, *Barbados*

$ ★★   Medium dark amber; thick, smooth, and sweet with vanilla and spice; lush and long.

Whaler's Killer Coconut Rum with Natural Flavor, *USA*

$ ★   Sweet and perfumy with coconut and floral notes; fat and thick.

Whaler's Pineapple Paradise Rum with Natural Pineapple Flavor, *USA*

$ ★   Thick and sweet with light pineapple flavor.

Whaler's Big Island Banana Rum with Natural Banana Flavor, *USA*

$ ★★   Smooth and thick with sweet, rich, ripe banana flavor; long and lush.

tequila

✳ AN AZTEC BEGINNING ✳

The year is A.D. 1000. In the Aztec Empire, *metl* plants fill the horizon as far as the eye can see. A storm rages overhead. Suddenly a lightning bolt tears through the sky and strikes a plant. The air fills with a sweet, smoky aroma as the heat cooks the heart of the plant. After the storm the native Aztecs notice juice oozing from the center of the plant. One by one the people drink the nectar and thank the gods for sending them this delicious and mysterious drink. They call the drink pulque.

This is how Aztec legend describes the birth of tequila's earliest ancestor. Seen as a gift from the gods, pulque, or fermented agave juice, was generally reserved for priests, nobility, and the very ill. Priests in the Chichimecasn, Otomie, Toltecan, and Nahuatl Indian tribes used the spirit in religious ceremonies, as it was thought that the intoxicated state reached by drinking pulque enabled them to speak with the gods. The spirit was so highly valued that human sacrifices were made to guarantee the steady supply of the drink. Though much of the magic and mysticism infusing this ancient spirit has trickled down into what we know as tequila today, blood need not be spilled to ensure the availability of your next margarita.

✳ WHAT IS TEQUILA? ✳

Scientifically speaking, the blue agave plant is known by its full Latin name: *Agave tequilana* Weber *var. azul.* It is also called the Blue Weber agave. Dr. Weber "discovered" the difference between this agave and others, and named it after himself. This bluish-green succulent takes eight to twelve years to mature and can grow to a height of seven feet. While many people mistakenly believe that tequila is a drink made from cactus, the agave is part of the lily and amaryllis family of flowering plants. The plant consists of *pencas* (tightly bound sharp leaves) that shoot up into the sky, and looks a little like the top of a yucca plant.

In the production of tequila, the growing plant is referred to as the *madre* or mother. During the growing period, the leaves are continually pruned at the base to allow the heart to grow as large as possible. The *madre* produces tiny new plants called *mecuates.* The growers refer to these sprouts as *hijuelos* or children. These smaller plants spring up at the base of the *madre.* When the larger agave is between three and six years old, the children are harvested. The baby plants are dug up with a tool called the *barreton* and trimmed with a *machete corto.* Once the grower is assured of the quality of the baby plant, it is added to a row, eventually to become one in the next generation of mature agaves. Each *madre* produces between six and ten baby plants per year. The timing of taking the baby plants from the mother is important. If picked too early the plants are too immature to produce prime agave plants; if harvested too late they are too tired to produce a healthy, mature plant. This birth and death cycle of the agave plants differs greatly from that of the grains and starches that are used in most liquor production. There is no need to replant from seed; the agave reproduces itself over and over again.

If the *madre* plant is left untended, a *quiote* (stem or cane) can grow as high as thirty feet. This stem bears flowers carrying between three thousand and five thousand fertile seeds. The *quiote* will deplete the sugar from the heart of the plant and dry it out. As a result the distillers always cut off the spike the minute it starts to grow. This allows the plant to keep maturing and the juice to continue to accumulate.

The unfermented juice of the agave is called *agua miel,* or honey water. There is a regional drink by the same name that is obtained from a flowered agave plant. To make this traditional

Jalisco drink, the spike is cut off and the heart of the plant fills with its juice. This liquid is drained from the plant and sold.

✳ HOME OF THE BLUE AGAVE ✳

The two regions where blue agave is harvested are both in the state of Jalisco. The largest distillers of tequila, Cuervo and Sauza, are in the town of Tequila. When you drive toward Tequila from Guadalajara, there are miles and miles of blue agave plants on both sides of the highway, crowding between roads and walls, and even surrounding private residences. Just so you know whose agave you're viewing, the Sauza distillery has placed signs along the road reading: "*Todo en éste lado es Sauza, y el otro lado tambien*" ("Everything on this side is Sauza, and the other side too"). In the town of Tequila, streets are lined with brick houses surrounded by the rolling mountains, but in case you weren't certain where you were, you'd only have to look at the hundreds of tequila advertisements posted everywhere. About the only building not plastered with ads is the local cathedral. About forty miles east of Guadalajara, in an area known as Los Altos, or the Highlands, is the other blue agave-growing region. The towns of Arandas, Atotonlico el Alto, and Zapotlanejo are home to about twenty other distillers. The land, rich with volcanic ash, combined with the even climate make these regions perfect for growing the blue agave.

✳ LA COSECHA—THE HARVEST ✳

Technology has changed some aspects of tequila distillation, but tradition still guides the *jimadores,* the harvesters, through the harvest as they cut and prepare the agave using the same hand-made tools they've been using for more than one hundred years.

The *coa de jima* is a sharp half-moon blade attached to a long handle. The blade is used to chop the plant off at its roots. The *pencas* (leaves) are cut with the *machete de barbeo.* A stub of only an inch or two is all that is left of the giant leaves. The plant is then severed from the back. After the attentions of the *jimadores,* the large spiky plant is reduced to a rounded ball called the heart or *piña,* so named because it resembles a gigantic pineapple. The *piña* can weigh anywhere from 60 to 120 pounds, though there have been recorded hearts that tipped the scales at 200 in the region of Los Altos in Jalisco.

✳ LA FÁBRICA—THE FACTORY ✳

Cooking and Milling

The first step in the process of distilling tequila is the cooking of the heart. Because the *piñas* are so large they are usually cut in halves or quarters, which allows them to cook faster. Once cut, the *piñas* are piled into large concrete *hornos* or ovens that hold, on average, fifty tons of agave. Workers hand pack the oven until it is virtually overflowing with agaves. This packing creates a pressure cooker effect and steams the agave. After at least twenty-four hours (and sometimes up to forty-eight hours) spent in a 140-degree oven, the agaves release their *agua miel*. This liquid is collected in the bottom of the ovens and put into a large container to await the next step. In recent years some *fábricas* have begun to use large stainless autoclaves to cook the agave because they are capable of doing the same job as the oven in just seven hours.

Milling is an additional step used to extract as much juice from the cooked agave as possible. Depending on the factory, milling is done either in a juicing machine or in a hand mill. Modern juicing machines have a series of grinding blades that chop the cooked fibers. As the fibers are being chopped, water is sprayed over them to wash off the sugars. In the hand-mill process, a giant stone wheel called a *tahona* sits in a cobblestone pit. The agave is put into the pit and the wheel crushes the cooked *piña*. Today almost all *fábricas* use machines. The water used in this process is important, and most distillers use their own wells, ionization systems, and other purifying processes for the water that washes the cooked plants. Everything in the *fábricas* is washed down with the purified water. Following the milling process, the *agua miel* is collected and transported to the next step.

It's worth noting that one distiller, Tapatío, is the only tequila *fábrica* that still uses the pulp in the fermentation process. To do this a man called the *batidor* gets inside the tank with the crushed agave pulp. He adds fiber that he separates by hand from the *piñas* in the tank, until the sugar reading is at the proper level. His task completed, the *batidor* emerges from the tank, covered in *agua miel*.

Fermentation

There are two ways of preparing the agave juice for fermentation. If the distiller is making 100 percent blue agave tequila, only the blue agave juice and natural yeast will be put into the tank. If the distiller is making *mixto,* the agave juice is blended with additional sugar. This sugar, called *piloncillo,* is often diluted molasses or sugarcane. In the fermentation stage the sugars are eaten by the yeasts and convert into alcohol. The *mixtos* are usually combined with commercial yeasts and other catalysts designed to speed the fermentation process. In 100 percent agave production the yeast used is all-natural—meaning the labs of the *fábricas* create yeast from the plant itself.

The fermentation tanks themselves are either wooden (in the older *fábricas*) or steel. The traditional wooden tanks hold eight thousand to ten thousand liters, while the modern steel tanks can hold up to seventy-five thousand liters of liquid. Once mixed with the *agua miel,* the yeast causes the brew to bubble. Often the tanks will be slightly heated to help the process along. When light brown creamy-colored foam develops on the surface of the tank, the brew, called *mosto,* is ready for distillation.

Distillation

Tequila *fábricas* use copper pot stills much like those used in the production of cognac. Heat is applied to the pot of the still, causing the liquid to transform to steam. The vapor condenses and drips down into a pot and is now referred to as *ordinario.* This liquid is between 20 and 30 percent alcohol. The heads and tails, the vapors coming off the earliest and latest part of the distillation, are discarded. What is referred to as the "heart" of the *ordinario* is distilled again. The double distillation produces tequila that is between 40 and 46 percent alcohol, or 80 to 92 proof. When distilling *mixto* tequila, the final product can be up to 55 percent alcohol. These stronger *mixtos* are diluted with water or neutral spirit before being bottled. The double-distilled unaged tequila is clear, just like newly distilled unaged brandy.

✳ AGING: YOUNG AND OLD ✳

Unlike brandy, not all tequila is aged. Those that are aged will rest anywhere from three months to four years. This doesn't sound like much time, compared to Scotch or brandy, but agave spirit, like bourbon, is kept in a much hotter environment, which speeds up the entire process of aging. There are four classifications of aged tequila.

Blanco (also called *plata* or sterling in the United States) is the original style of tequila. Clear and unaged, it is usually bottled directly following distillation. *Blanco* can be 100 percent agave or *mixto*. This spirit is used primarily as a mixer.

Joven abocado (young and smooth) or gold is aged slightly or mixed with a bit of aged tequila. The gold color comes from the addition of this aged tequila or, in lesser versions, from the addition of caramel coloring. Though seeing the word "gold" might lead one to believe that this tequila is the best available, this is untrue. Tequilas classified as *joven* or gold are always *mixtos* and never 100 percent blue agave.

The classification *reposado* (rested) is applied to tequila that is aged three to twelve months. This aging takes place in wooden tanks, French limousin oak barrels, or redwood tanks, depending on the recipe of the particular *fábrica*. By law, *reposado* must be aged over sixty days, but it is never aged more than one year. *Reposado* can be 100 percent blue agave or *mixto*.

Seeing the term *añejo* (old) on a label ensures that the tequila is aged for up to four years. This fine tequila is left to rest in Kentucky bourbon barrels for flavor. By law, these barrels can be no larger than six hundred liters and are sealed by the government. The individual distiller decides the type of oak used, whether the barrel is charred, and how many times the barrels are reused for the aged tequilas. *Añejo mixtos* are aged eight months to three years, while 100 percent blue agave spirits are aged four years.

How Old Is Old?

As with other fine spirits such as brandy or Scotch, tequila improves with age. However, four years is roughly the limit for the beneficial aging process. Unlike other aged spirits, tequila stops improving at the four-year mark and may begin to deteriorate. Holding on to a bottle of tequila while it ages is a waste of perfectly good tequila. If tequila ages over five years, it begins to lose the sweet agave character and, as the wood flavors take hold, becomes a bit more like whiskey.

Sip barrel-aged tequila as you would a fine whiskey and enjoy the mingling flavors of the agave and the oak. In *reposado* and *añejo* tequilas, the blue agave essence is moderated and enhanced by delicate vanilla and oak flavors from the wood.

Though many bars and restaurants will have you believe that top-shelf aged tequilas are best in cocktails, mixed drinks such as the margarita or tequila sunrise will taste just as nice when you use a relatively inexpensive silver *mixto* tequila. Though the older tequila may add a bit of extra depth to a mixed drink, its true flavor will be lost when blended with other ingredients. Unaged tequilas retain more of the fresh flavor of agave.

✴ THE HISTORY OF TEQUILA ✴

Of course, when agave was first discovered as potable, the Aztecs had no distillation. Pulque (or what the Spaniards would later call *vino mescal*) was created simply by extracting the juice of the plant and allowing it to ferment for a short period of time. The spirit was slightly viscous, sweet, and mildly alcoholic.

As months in the new country passed, the Spaniards began to run perilously low on brandy and other comestibles they had brought from Spain. They began to partake of the local drink. Small taverns called *pulquerias,* which specialized in pulque, began springing up in every town and neighborhood. Pulque became a popular street drink with the roving Spanish soldiers. By 1864 it is estimated that one *pulqueria* existed for every 410 residents. Today there are only a handful of *pulquerias* left, mostly in the more remote areas of Mexico.

Things took a decided turn for the better when the distillation process was brought to the Jalisco region of central Mexico by the conquistadores in 1530. The Spanish saw room for improvement in the pulque and began to apply their own distillation techniques, used at home for wine. Unfamiliar with the Aztec name for the *metl* plant, the Spaniards called it maguey, after a similar-looking plant they knew from their Caribbean journeys. The term was an altered form of the word *megistos,* which means magnificent in Greek. Maguey is used interchangeably with agave, which means illustrious in Greek. The plant is also known as the century plant, rumored to bloom once every one hundred years, and then die.

The Advent of Tequila

While the conquering Spaniards began to enjoy and refine the new drink in Jalisco during the mid-1500s, it wouldn't be until 1600 that Don Pedro Sanchez Tagle, the Marquis de Altamira, started to cultivate what he called the "mezcal" plant and distill the fermented juice in the Ticuila Indian town of Tequila. Situated in the

Amatitian Valley and surrounded by the Sierra Madre Occidental Mountains, the area seemed an ideal spot for Don Tagle to establish the distillery that would be known as Hacienda Cuisillos. He began supplying nearby Guadalajara with a simple but potent *aguardiente* (firewater) made from mezcal. This spirit was, somewhat confusingly, known as mezcal wine, and was the immediate forerunner of what we know now as tequila. The government immediately imposed taxes on the spirit and by 1636 established rules governing the distillation and manufacture of mezcal. Distilled and recognized by the government, tequila was making its way from the altars of the priests to the hands of the people.

For the next 180 years the mezcal spirit became very popular all over the country. Its popularity was due not only to its superior taste, but also to the fact that it was easily exported. Mezcal was shipped from the town of Tequila, which was ideally situated on the route leading to the newly opened port of San Blas on the Pacific Ocean. From this point mezcal spirits could be shipped as far as Mexico City.

The success of mezcal came to the attention of King Charles III. In 1781, with an eye toward the promotion of imported Spanish wines and spirits, he forbade the production of mezcal. For a time locals were forced to bake their maguey underground to avoid detection by the king's men. A form of this baking method continues to be used today.

Fortunately for the distillers, the production ban was shortlived. In 1795 the new king, Ferdinand IV, reversed the rule of Charles III, and again the mezcal distilleries were up and running. Under this new regime, the very first license to produce mezcal was given to Don José Maria Guadalupe de Cuervo. Don José set up the first registered distillery and began to cultivate maguey plants in the rich volcanic soil all around the town of Tequila, in the province of Jalisco. Dedicated to the distillation of what they termed "wine of the earth," the Cuervo family would become forever linked with the production of quality tequila.

Though the end of the production ban boosted sales of mezcal in Mexico, government licensing of distilleries did not help with the exportation of the spirit. History conspired to confine mezcal within the borders of Mexico. Mexico's eleven-year battle for independence from Spain increased the popularity of Tequila-made mezcal. This national spirit was taken into battle and lifted in toast to the revolution. At war's end the spirit that would eventually be familiarly known simply as tequila was cemented in the minds of the country as the official spirit of Mexico. Despite its national popularity, however, the spirit still lacked an international following.

Tequila Moves North

Following the war for independence came the War of Reform, then a civil war, and finally another European invasion, this time by the French (yes, the French). It wasn't until 1873 that Tequila-made mezcal finally made its U.S. debut. The first distillery to export to the United States was the *fábrica* of Don Cenobio Sauza. Rumor has it that it was Don Cenobio who deemed the variety of maguey called blue agave the plant that made the finest tequila. Today blue agave is still recognized as the base of the highest-quality tequila. Sauza's company shipped three *damajuanas,* or corked barrels, of Tequila mezcal to El Paso, Texas. In a short time his competitor, Don Cuervo, also shipped three *damajuanas* to Texas. From this moment on Americans began a love affair with tequila. To service the growing demand for the "mezcal of Tequila," Jalisco distillers transitioned from making raw *aguardiente* spirit to the more refined mezcal that we know today. An industry started to form.

The growth of the transcontinental railroads across the United States helped spread the spirit further into North America, and the "mezcal brandy," as it was now more appropriately called, was now being exported regularly to the States. The "brandy" even won an award at the Chicago World's Fair in 1893. Around this time the mezcal of Tequila came to be known simply as tequila.

We know that the spirit was named for the town, but what is the basis for the town's name? The most obvious and least imaginative theory is that the name Tequila comes from a corruption of the name of the native Indian tribe, the Tiquilos, but fascinating stories abound. There are those who claim that Tequila means "lava hill," a reasonable explanation as the town was established near a dormant volcano. Others believe the word "tequila" comes from an expression used by the ancient Nahautl tribe, which meant "place of harvest," "place where they cut," or "place of work." In a similar vein, other linguists believe the word means "rock that cuts." Still others feel that the word is a corruption of *tetilla* because the nearby volcano looks like the small breast of a woman. We may never know exactly where the name came from, but each theory seems to reflect the people, place, and mystery that gave birth to tequila.

In the early 1900s Mexican president Porfirio Díaz helped the tequila business by pushing for modernization in the country. At this time many of the *fábricas* or local factories upgraded their equipment and began producing more and better tequila. While President Díaz helped the wealthy factory owners, he simultaneously enraged the working populace. He often took the side of the hacienda owners (who held a position much like the plantation owners of the South) and in some cases helped them to expand into local villages, effectively stealing land from the people. In the election of 1910 Díaz ran against the more popular candidate Francisco Madero and won by a landslide. This obvious rigging prompted Madero to call for a revolt against Díaz. This was the beginning of the Mexican Revolution.

Tequila played a large part in the revolution. This truly Mexican spirit spurred the rebels during times of victory and consoled them in times of defeat. Many colorful characters emerged during this time, among them the heroic and colorful general of the peasant armies, Pancho Villa. Today the Los Arango Tequila distillers have commemorated this rebel leader by naming a tequila after him, which is fitting considering his real name was Doroteo Arango. As if to prove that heroes need not be human, another tequila brand is named for Pancho Villa's horse, Siete Leguas (Seven Leagues).

By the end of the revolution, the popularity of tequila both in Mexico and in the United States had surged. The upswing continued, fueled in part by Prohibition. During this dry period, tequila had an edge over other imported liquors since it could be smuggled right over the border. Easy to obtain and quite potent, tequila was the drink of choice in speakeasies all over the Southwest.

The next shift in tequila's history came during the height of the Depression. In 1930 Mexico suffered an agave shortage, and it seemed impossible that growers could keep up with demand. To help distillers meet their orders the government relaxed regulations and allowed tequila manufacturers to reduce the blue agave content from 100 percent to 51 percent. Herradura was the sole producer in Mexico that kept to the original strict guidelines and continued to produce 100 percent blue agave tequila. Unfortunately, at this time Herradura was not shipping tequila to the States. As a result of the new rules from 1930 through 1960, all tequila imported to the United States was *mixto,* blue agave mixed with other sugars for fermentation.

The 100 percent pure blue agave bottled by Herradura eventually made it to the States in 1960. Serious tequila connoisseurs owe a debt to Bing Crosby and his buddy, comedian Phil Harris. Having enjoyed Herradura south of the border, the two celebrities eventually teamed up to import it to the States. For over thirty years Herradura was the only 100 percent agave tequila that made its way north.

With the advent of WWII, whiskey imports from Europe ceased almost entirely, leaving bars wide open for a tequila takeover. In 1940 six thousand gallons of the spirit were exported to the

States. By 1945 the volume of exports had swelled to a whopping 1.2 million gallons. While sales languished right at the end of the war due to a rise in export competition from Europe, tequila was about to get a boost from the invention of a cocktail called the margarita. Though the origin of this lovely, citrus-spiked drink is unclear, it would slowly catch on, becoming tequila's calling card for generations of drinkers from the mid-forties on. In 1977 Jimmy Buffett's hit song "Margaritaville" inspired millions of Americans to go looking for that lost shaker of salt. Today the tequila-laced margarita is the most popular mixed drink in America.

The Classic Tequila Cocktail: The Margarita

While no one knows for certain who dreamed up the most popular of tequila drinks, several well-polished legends explain the origins of the margarita. According to one account, the margarita was first concocted for aspiring actress Marjorie King in 1938 by Danny Herrera, bartender at the Rancho La Gloria bar in Tijuana. The starlet claimed to be allergic to all liquors except tequila, so Herrera used it to create a new drink for Marjorie and gave it her Spanish name: margarita.

Another version holds that the margarita was invented on the Fourth of July 1942 in Tommy's Bar in Ciudad Juarez by Pancho Morales. Legend has it that a woman asked for a drink called a Magnolia. Pancho hadn't heard of this cocktail, but gamely concocted his own. He called his invention the "daisy," or margarita.

In one of the most widely accepted accounts, famed Dallas socialite Margarita Sames claims to have come up with the cocktail during a 1948 Christmas party at her vacation home in Acapulco. She served the cocktail to a group of friends that included Tommy Hilton, who eventually introduced the margarita to his hotel chain. Allegedly she got behind the poolside bar and mixed up the drink, and everyone loved it. Being a socialite, she had a fast-moving, influential crowd at her party, and the drink soon made its way to Hollywood, with her name attached.

In 1945, however, a man named Vern Under, the first importer of José Cuervo in the United States, advertised Cuervo with the tagline "Margarita: it's more than a girl's name." This beats out Margarita Sames by three years.

In the final analysis, it doesn't really matter who invented the margarita. What matters is that it was invented. One sip and you'll be in the mood to raise your salt-encrusted glass in a toast to everyone and anyone who was responsible for this refreshing and delicious tequila and citrus cocktail.

Classic Margarita Recipe

Lime wedge
Kosher salt
2 ounces tequila
1½ ounces triple sec (or Cointreau)
1½ ounces fresh lime juice
1 ounce simple syrup

Using lime wedge, wet the rim of a rocks glass. Dip wet rim on plate lightly covered with kosher salt. Fill glass with ice. Add remaining ingredients. Stir well. Garnish with lime wheel or wedge.

As tequila's popularity grew, producers in Mexico started looking for cheaper and faster methods to produce the spirit. Frustrated by the twelve-year maturation process of the source plant and the arduous extraction of sugar sap, the distillers looked for shortcuts. They turned to more modern means of processing and cut the amount of actual agave sap with cane sugar to hasten the fermentation process. These changes resulted in a glut of inferior products all labeled as tequila. In 1977 to combat the influx of cheap tequila, the Mexican government overhauled regulations set in the 1940s and established a more stringent set of norms to govern the production of tequila. Strict standards for various classifications such as *añejo* and *reposado* were also set at the time. It is important to remember that there are two types of tequila: 100 percent blue agave tequila, and *mixto* tequila, which is only 60 percent agave and 40 percent other sugars. Some purists consider *mixto* not authentic tequila, but by law as long as the spirit is 60 percent blue agave, it can be labeled tequila. Tequila *mixto* is considered a blend in the same way Scotch can be a single malt or a blend. If the label does not read "100 percent blue agave," you can be certain you have a *mixto*.

While *mixtos* are perfectly acceptable in a margarita or other cocktail, today's higher standards have contributed to the production of the remarkable 100 percent agave tequilas available now. Many of these well-crafted spirits are comparable to fine cognacs, brandies, or Scotches.

✳ WHAT MAKES TEQUILA TEQUILA? ✳

Classifications

Between 1944 and 1949 the government of Mexico passed its first series of regulations to control the production and labeling of tequila. These laws are known as the Norma Oficial Mexicana Tequila. The initial laws have been revised and expanded and include the following:

> To be a tequila of Mexico the fermented spirit must be derived from the blue agave, or *Agave tequilana* Weber *var. azul.*
>
> The blue agave used in production is cultivated only in the zones and regions that have been designated by the government.
>
> The name "tequila" appears only on the labels of those bottles that contain this product.
>
> The finished product must be 60 percent blue agave (upgraded from 51 percent in 1995).
>
> The standards of quality must be supervised and regulated by the Mexican government.

Laws are now upgraded and revised on a regular basis to control and protect the Mexican tequila industry. The laws define the distinctions among various spirits. Thanks to these laws, it is possible to tell a great deal about a product simply by looking at the bottle's label. In 1974 the Mexican government moved to protect the name "tequila" and made the name an intellectual property owned by the government of Mexico. As a result the spirit was internationally recognized as a product originating only in Mexico, and tequila was permitted an Appellation d'Origine Contrôlée (a controlled appellation of origin, an AOC) in 1977.

In 1996, prompted by competition from other countries, Mexico signed a trade accord recognizing Mexico as the sole producer of tequila. This trade accord forced a name change for a South African distillery making tequila using blue agave plants that had taken root in South Africa. The product was only 10 percent blue agave. Other distilleries in Japan and Spain also tried to make "tequila." Mexico countered these moves by opening trade offices in

Washington and Madrid to protect the tequila production market in Mexico. The distillers in South Africa, Japan, and Spain are allowed to distill the agave, but cannot by law call their products tequila.

The State of Tequila. By law there are five regions/states in Mexico that can make tequila. These states are Jalisco (home of the town Tequila), Guanajunto, Michocan, Nayarit, and Tamaulipas. In the same way that the French define a bottle of champagne as being solely a product of the Champagne region, or cognac as brandy coming only from Cognac, only agave spirits from these regions can carry the name tequila.

NOM—Norma Oficial Mexicana. In 1974 the NOM regulations governing where tequila could be produced were released. These regulations stipulated that all blue agave tequila must be aged within Mexico. Distillers must apply for permission from the regulating office to age and bottle their products. Each distiller is assigned an identification number, which is always on the bottle, along with the abbreviation NOM. This is your assurance that the tequila was made in Mexico and complies with government standards. If a bottle does not have a NOM number printed on the label, it is not true tequila under Mexican law. Though tequila must be aged in Mexico, 83 percent is shipped in bulk to the United States after aging, where it is bottled and shipped domestically and internationally.

The Consejo Regulador del Tequila, a private sector nonprofit organization, was created on December 16, 1993. Known as the CRT, it integrated the government, bottling plants, distributors, tequila producers, and blue agave peasant producers into one organization. This group conducts inventories and studies on blue agave growth and planting as well as overseeing all aspects of the tequila market inside and outside Mexico. Today the CRT represents 104 tequila manufacturers who produce at least seven hundred different brands.

✳ TEQUILA TODAY AND TOMORROW ✳

What was a relatively slow growth industry in the years between 1930 and 1960 eventually became a boom. From 1970 through 1995 tequila production increased 352 percent, from 23 million liters to 104 million liters. This period was marked by a growth in the production of bulk tequila (the blended *mixtos*).

The surge in popularity started in 1968 when the Olympics were held in Mexico City. Suddenly tequila was all the rage.

Quickly tequila took hold as a popular "shot" drink for the spring-break college set. Between 1970 and 1980 the popularity of the margarita and the tequila sunrise cocktails increased the consumption of tequila. In 1970 only 14 percent of the tequila produced was exported; by 1994 the number was around 71 percent. International beverage corporations discovered tequila by the early nineties and began to cash in on the tequila boom. According to figures from the CRT, tequila sales in the United States grew an astounding 1,500 percent between 1975 and 1995.

Two things happened in 1994 to set tequila up for another growth spurt in the export market. First, the economic markets went soft at a time when tequila was less expensive than many of its imported quality counterparts, such as cognac and whiskey. Second, for the first time since the Mexican spirit began to be exported more than a century earlier, tequila was protected as a registered brand name. Now that tequila was brand-protected, the cheap imitations that had been labeling themselves as tequila for the past forty years were no longer able to do so.

Before the AOC was given to tequila in 1994, the CRT suspects that about half of the spirits sold in Mexico as tequila, and a higher proportion outside the country, were not in any manner tequila as prescribed by law. Most of the cheap knockoffs were not made from any plant in the agave family and in most cases were watered down with cheaper spirits.

Even as the quality of tequila improved, the spirit was still cheaper than other imports. Advertisers focused on the sexy, sultry qualities of tequila, often including images of smoky cantinas and long, lazy afternoons. The demand for tequila grew. In 1997 only fifty-seven tequila companies existed. According to CRT statistics, by 2001 the number of tequila firms had increased to nearly ninety companies, a 57.9 percent increase.

There are more than one hundred thousand acres of blue agave in the states of Jalisco, Michoacan, and Nayarit. Jalisco has about 95 percent of the blue agave plantations and tequila production in the country. Around 80 percent of production is centered in the municipalities of Amatitán, Arandas, and Tequila. In spite of these acres of agave fields, distillers are currently facing a shortage. The accelerated growth in tequila's popularity—particularly for 100 percent blue agave brands—coupled with the long growth cycle of the agave plant, means that demand will eventually exceed supply. Although growers have been quick to sow more agave, fields planted today will not mature for eight to ten years.

In addition to this increase in demand, Mexico's agave growers have been battling a plant fungus known as *Fusarium oxyisporum* and a bacterium called *Erwinia carotavora*. These diseases have spread into nearly a third of the country's agave crop. The blight has created an all-time high price for agave plants; the price has risen tenfold in the past four years. A ton of agave cost around $50 in January 1999, but sold for $1,500 just eighteen months later. Tequila prices have, of course, risen dramatically as well. All agave growers have been planting frantically since the beginning of the blight, but those plants are still years away from maturity. Blue agave production increased 294 percent between 1995 and 1999. By 2000, with the effects of the agave blight, 100 percent blue agave production decreased 59 percent. Now producers are making more *mixto* tequila than 100 percent blue agave. They want to be present in the market, but the financial strain created by the shortage of agave plants, and a tax on tequila imposed by the Mexican government, have made tequila production an expensive business venture. Ironically, because of the new taxes levied on the market, tequila is more expensive to buy in Mexico than it is in the United States. Sometimes the tax surpasses the actual value of the bottle of tequila.

Despite the blue agave shortage, the increase in prices, and competition from other spirits, tequila continues to bask in increasing popularity among sophisticated drinkers. Some of this has to do with the change in image of the spirit over the past decade. While most people are introduced to tequila in their early twenties as a "shot" drink, which can result in many rocky mornings-after, the tequila industry has been working hard with more sophisticated campaigns to let the connoisseur know that tequila is a quality aged drink perfect for sipping. In fact, in Mexico, drinkers very rarely do tequila in shots—unless they are hosting gringos from north of the border.

Quality-oriented producers such as José Cuervo are trying to reposition tequila in the popular mindset as something more than just a slammer for spring-break partiers in Cabo San Lucas. They are trying to reinstill a sense of the dignity of tequila. Specialty restaurants and bars are also trying to reposition tequila as a sipping spirit and often offer a vast selection of *reposado* and *añejo* tequilas.

TEQUILA VERSUS MEZCAL—
✳ ALL AGAVES ARE NOT THE SAME ✳

Popular conception holds that tequila and mezcal are the same. They are not, and it's time to clear up any confusion. For the record, all tequila is mezcal, but not all mezcal is tequila. Like tequila, mezcal is fermented agave juice. However, mezcal growers are not required to use blue agave plants; they may blend one of the hundreds of other varieties of agave plants indigenous to Mexico to make their spirit. Tequila is a mezcal that only comes from the Weber blue agave. Tequila never has a worm in the bottle.

Since mezcal is similar in spelling to the psychedelic drug mescaline, a common misconception is that the drug and drink come from the same source. They in fact do not. Mescaline is derived from the peyote cactus. Though mezcal is often cited as a hallucinogen, this is due less to the druglike qualities of the spirit than to the drinker's habit of downing many shots. Obviously, polishing off half a bottle of mezcal will lead to an altered state.

Mezcal is made primarily in Oaxaca by moonshiners and distillers. Your local Zihuatanejo moonshiner will most likely bottle your mezcal in a plastic two-liter Coke bottle. Like tequila, the spirit is either briefly aged or colored with caramel to add a golden hue. Surprisingly, mezcal is usually less potent than tequila.

Why Does Mezcal (Sometimes) Have a Worm?

The worm, known as the *gusano,* is really no worm at all. The *gusano* is the larvae of one of two moths that live on the agave plant, and is only added to a few varieties of mezcal. Though there are many explanations for the addition of the worm, the one that makes the most sense is that it is evidence of a high-proof spirit. The logic is that the percentage of alcohol must be very high if it can effectively pickle or preserve the worm intact. Though consuming the worm may get you in with your frat brothers, it will not offer any sort of psychedelic high, nor has it been confirmed as an aphrodisiac. As a rule, top-quality mezcal does not include a worm. The mezcals sold in the United States bear little resemblance to the products made locally. Most mezcal is made from the plants called the *maguey espadin.* The *piñas* are often smoked, and the brew ferments for eight to ten days and is distilled. After this it is ready to bottle. Mezcal is strongly and distinctly flavored and is definitely an acquired taste.

✳ SOTOL—A DISTANT COUSIN ✳

Sotol is produced from the wild agavacea, a plant similar to the blue agave. The agavacea is harvested in the highlands near Chihuahua. Mexico's Tarahumara Indians first produced this spirit more than eight centuries ago. The Tarahumaras used sotol in religious rituals and ceremonies. Eventually a distilled version of sotol was adopted by the Spanish. Because the fermentation process of sotol is fairly short and the distillation simple, sotol is easily made by Mexican natives, who often bottle the stuff in plastic jugs.

Looking to upgrade the quality of the spirit, the Mexican company Vinomex has taken on the task of creating a high-quality sotol and reintroducing the spirit to the U.S. market. They created a spirit known as Sotol Hacienda de Chihuahua. Vinomex built a modern facility in Chihuahua and hired a certified oenologist (an expert in the science of making wines) to oversee production. Vinomax buys *piñas* from local *jimadores* and cook them in large ovens. The process of distillation is much like that of tequila. Following the cooking process, the *piñas* are shredded and juiced. The juice ferments for fourteen to twenty-five days and is later distilled. Sotol that has aged for six months in a white oak barrel is known as *reposado,* while *añejo* signifies at least a year of aging. The resulting spirit is fruity and not too sweet and can be used in mixed drinks or savored alone.

✳ BRAND PROFILES ✳

With so many premium tequilas flooding the market, a trip to the liquor store can be a bit confusing. A few names to keep in mind are Herradura, José Cuervo, Sauza, Patrón, El Tesoro, Casa Noble, and Cabo Wabo, a delightfully smooth tequila created by rock star Sammy Hagar. Some of my favorites are listed below.

JOSÉ CUERVO—AS THE CROW FLIES. The Cuervo distilleries have been operating since 1795 when José María Guadalupe Cuervo received a concession from King Ferdinand to distill "mezcal wine." His heirs are still involved in operating the company, which is the oldest continuously running tequila distiller in Mexico.

The mascot of the Cuervo family, Cuervo tequila, and the family estate is the crow. That's because *cuervo* is Spanish for crow, and Don José Antonio Cuervo, who got the rights to cultivate a parcel of land in Mexico in 1758, was known as Joe Crow. In 1795 his son, José María Cuervo started the tradition of stamping each barrel of Cuervo with the crow symbol. The Cuervo family motto reads, "From the agave we will get our inner strength." And indeed the motto has been true for well over two hundred years. José Cuervo is the world's biggest-selling tequila brand.

Doña Maria Magdalena de Cuervo, the only child of Don José María, inherited everything from her father. She married Don Vincente Albino Rojas, who took over running the company. He changed the name of the distillery to La Rojeña, since tradition dictated that the *taberna*'s name reflect the name of the owner. La Rojeña remains the name of the distillery to this day, but the name of the product reverted back to José Cuervo in 1901.

In 1873 Cuervo shipped its first three barrels of tequila to El Paso, the beginning of its successful export business to the United States. In 1880 Jesús Flores, who ran the distillery after Rojas, became the first man to put tequila in bottles. The first bottle of tequila was sold in 1906. By this time Cuervo had more than three million agave plants in their fields. Flores also established a second, much larger distillery to take advantage of the nearby newly laid railroad. Sadly, Flores died before he could see this come to fruition.

Flores's widow married José Cuervo Labastida, the company's administrator, and they took over production of the tequila, overseeing the growth of distribution through the railroads that led to the north. Eventually a second, larger distillery was opened to keep up with demand outside Guadalajara, but La Rojeña continues to produce Cuervo tequila today.

Today heirs of Cuervo run the company in partnership with Heublein Corporation. Like all fine distillers, the Cuervo people keep their lips sealed when it comes to the recipe. Many of the Cuervo products are *mixto* tequilas. However, in the past ten years the company has been focusing on making 100-percent aged agave products, such as the 1800 line and Cuervo Añejo. A ribbon bearing the inscription "*Abolengo, Prestigio y Tradición*" ("Heritage, Prestige, and Tradition"), is on every bottle in the Cuervo line. The Cuervo brands include 1800, Tradicional, and the stunning Reserva de la Familia, released each year in a specially designed artist's box.

SAUZA—THE FIRST TEQUILA EXPORTER. In 1873, nearly one hundred years after the Cuervo *taberna* had been founded, Don Cenobio Sauza acquired the La Antigua Cruz distillery. One of the first things he did was ship three barrels of his tequila to El

Paso, Texas, inspiring the José Cuervo *taberna* to follow suit. Don Cenobio was a brave and fearless man, had a reputation for successfully defending his plantation from banditos, and was determined to be one of the best distillers of tequila in Mexico. Over his lifetime he purchased thirteen more distilleries and fields for growing blue agave. He was convinced that blue agave was the best maguey for producing tequila, and he set high standards for himself and for his competition.

Don Cenobio's son Eladio Sauza ran the company after his father's death. Eladio expanded and upgraded La Perseverancia, his father's first distillery purchase. It remains Sauza's showplace. Eladio's son Javier broadened distribution and built Sauza into Mexico's second largest exporter of bulk tequila. Sauza owns about three hundred agave plantations to date. Javier ran the company until Domecq acquired Sauza in 1987. Sauza brands include Suaza Extra, Sauza Hornitos, and Tres Generaciones.

HERRADURA—AS LUCK WOULD HAVE IT. Founded in 1861 by Feliciano Romo in Amatitán, a town just six miles south of Tequila, Herradura came by its name in a magical way. While walking his property to pick the perfect site for his distillery, Feliciano noticed something glinting in the ground. Upon examination he discovered it was a horseshoe, the symbol of good luck. He decided that providence wanted him to build his site on that spot, thus named his *taberna* Herradura, Spanish for horseshoe.

Herradura employs a unique fermentation process that lasts ninety-six hours and uses only naturally occurring wild yeasts. The company is the number one premium tequila producer in Mexico and the largest landowners and planters of blue agave. All its products are 100 percent blue agave. The Romo family grows all its own agave on their ten thousand acres, modeled on European wine estates. All the stages from fermentation to bottling are done on the premises.

After a visit to Cognac, France, some thirty-five years ago, the Romos began to experiment with aging their tequila in wooden barrels, and in the early 1970s Herradura introduced the first-ever *reposado* (aged for eleven months) and *añejo* (aged for two years) tequilas. Their launch sparked a tequila revolution.

Five generations after its founding, Herradura remains committed to the family tradition. Today the original distillery is a beautiful museum where visitors can soak up the atmosphere of 1870 Mexico. Herradura brands include El Jimador and Hacienda del Cristero, while the sublime Herradura Selección Suprema is one of the greatest tequilas.

CHINACO—BORN OUT OF STRUGGLE. In the early 1970s, by law, all tequila had to come from the state of Jalisco, but in 1973 Mexican government officials decided to expand tequila designation. They were intent on providing enough blue agave plants to meet future demands, since tequila brought in dollars to the Mexican economy. One of the new designated areas was the northern state of Tamaulipas. Representatives of one of the large distilleries in Tequila signed an agreement with the farmers there, promising to pay high prices for the agave. The farmers planted many hectares of blue agave, but when the agaves were finally ready for harvest, the major tequila producer backed out.

The farmers now had no buyer for their agaves. Some distillers came to the farmers offering to buy the plants for far below fair value. One farmer, Guillermo Gonzalez, refused to sell his agaves for less than promised, and decided to build his own distillery in Tamaulipas. Purchasing an abandoned cotton gin factory, Guillermo bought some used distilling equipment and hired a *tequilero.* The tiny distillery named La Gonzaleña was born.

La Gonzaleña's tequila was called Chinaco, after the legendary defenders of Mexico during the Guerra de Reforma (War of Reform) in the 1850s. Chinaco has fought ever since to survive as the only tequila produced in Tamaulipas.

Chinaco entered the U.S. market in 1983 and was marketed like a fine cognac. The spirit demanded the highest prices of any tequila on the market. The rich, elegant Chinaco Añejo lived up to the promises, and almost single-handedly created the North American market for upscale tequila. But the success was short-lived. The distillery closed in the late 1980s, and the remaining supply of Chinaco was quickly exhausted. However, under the guidance of Gonzalez's four sons, La Gonzaleña distillery was opened once more, and Chinaco reappeared for sale in the United States in 1994. Today Chinaco produces three styles of tequila: unaged *blanco; reposado,* aged in barrels for up to a year; and *añejo,* aged in oak barrels for up to four years.

PATRÓN—THE BOSS INDEED. Patrón was first produced and blended at Siete Leguas for the U.S. firm St. Maarten's Spirits in 1989. Siete Leguas (named for Pancho Villa's horse, Seven Leagues) is a small family-owned and operated distillery high in the mountains of Jalisco. Lucrecia Gonzales, the owner, does not sell her Siete Leguas brand in the United States. In creating the Patrón brand, St. Maarten's owner Martin Crowley chose this distillery in Jalisco because the region is known to produce agave plants with excellent high-quality "honey" or sugar levels, which makes exceptional tequila.

Recently an additional distillery has been built in Jalisco, which will incorporate the traditional tequila manufacturing methods of the past while integrating modern techniques of quality control. To make Patrón, blue agave plants are harvested at their peak of ripeness, giving Patrón its rich tequila flavor. There are certain "bitter" sprouts, which must be carefully removed from the "pineapple" before steam baking. Few producers besides Patrón take the care and time to remove these sprouts.

At Patrón the agave "must" is double distilled in copper pot stills. The tequila is then balanced to 80 proof and fine-filtered. Patrón contains no additives, coloring, or extra sugar. It is solely created from the blue agave.

The name Patrón means boss in Spanish, with connotations of beneficence and kindness. Crowley built the amazingly successful Patrón empire based on Zen philosophy, uncommon business acumen, and an insistence on creating only the finest products possible in harmonious packaging. The Los Angeles company was established just in time to catch the growing tequila wave of the 1990s.

Crowley is a trained architect with a degree in comparative religion. His quest for purity and tradition led him to select a small artisanal factory and to seek out the best agave available. Entering the market at a time when there were few other premium tequilas available, Patrón was able to quickly achieve status as a top-of-the-line spirit. The packaging is also an important part of Patrón. The rustic, hand-blown glass bottle was designed by Crowley himself, and each bottle is hand-filled and numbered. In the production of Patrón, the most traditional and artisanal methods of production are used. The agave is still crushed in the big stone pits called *tahonas*. In fact, the new factory in Jalisco has eight *tahona* pits. Rather than use more modern autoclaves, the agave is baked in traditional stone ovens. Patrón then captures as much agave flavor as possible through triple distillation and uses white oak barrels for aging. All this care and attention to detail has paid off; sales have doubled every year since the company began.

✳ DRINKING AND TASTING TEQUILA ✳

To many of us, tequila may be synonymous with shots. The mere mention of tequila may evoke hazy memories of your misspent youth. While a shot of tequila is all very well and good if you're headed off into battle (or even off to the next frat house), the best way to truly enjoy tequila is to sip it neat. It is worthy of the attention you might pay a fine cognac or Scotch.

In Mexico tequila is generally served *completo* with a side of sangrita. Not to be confused with sangria (a fruit and wine beverage), sangrita is a mixture of orange juice, grenadine, and a hint of chile pepper, and is the perfect foil for the burn of the spirit. Alternate sips between the two glasses and savor the flavor. Another way to enjoy tequila like a native is the drink *abatangas*. This is a mix of tequila, Coke, lime, and salt. Of course, tequila is also quite enjoyable when mixed into a margarita or other cocktail. *Añejo* and *resposado* tequilas are best enjoyed on their own.

A Tequila Tasting

Setting up a tequila tasting is a great way to gather friends around the table. Set out baskets of chips and bowls of salsa and guacamole, and prepare for a delightful south-of-the-border journey. When preparing food, it's a good idea to leave the spicier entrées for after the tasting. Very spicy food, when served with tequila, can burn or confuse the palate. Put out a pitcher of spring water so that tasters may cleanse their palates between selections.

Pour tequila into clear, tulip-shaped wineglasses or chimney glasses. The narrow opening of these types of glasses will concentrate the bouquet of the spirit. It is important that the glass be clear so that you may observe the spirit's color. Do not use shot glasses.

Choose between four and six tequilas to test—any more brands than six and you will overwhelm your taste buds. You might want to choose a range of 100 percent agave tequilas or a range of *reposado* tequilas. It is easy to set up a tasting of different products offered by the same distiller. For example, try five or six of the many products from Cuervo, Sauza, or Herradura. With hundreds of brands out there, the combinations are endless and tantalizing.

What to Look For

Before you even taste the tequila, you should already be making assessments. First, look at the coloring of the spirit. Is it clear or pale yellow, golden or golden brown? A change in color signifies either more extensive aging or the use of caramel coloring.

Waft the glass beneath your nose. What do you smell? Are you getting hints of true agave, or is the delicate, almost floral scent lost in an intense alcohol burn? "Agave intensity" is the term used to describe the amount of agave aroma in the tequila. The lighter or more delicate the intensity, the less pungent is the aroma. Look for other scents in the aroma. Do you smell soil? Oak barrels? There may be hints of earth, fruit, or smoke in the aroma. You can rate these aromas as slight, moderate, and high. Look for complexity in the scents. Obviously, the more things your nose can pick up, the more complex is the aroma of the tequila.

Now that your eyes and nose have tested the tequila, it's time to let your tongue in on the fun. When tasting, see if the product delivers the same experience on the tongue as it did on the nose. An intense and focused aroma should indicate a taste that is intense, with a long finish and a nicely complex aftertaste. If the taste is short, numb, medicinal, or bitter, the tequila will not be among the best available.

Take a sip of the tequila and let it sit in your mouth. Is it sweet in your mouth? Is it very sweet, pleasantly sweet, or barely sweet? And how does it feel in your mouth? Is it oily, watery, or pleasant on the tongue? Swallow the tequila and notice the flavors you sense as it goes down your throat. Again pay the same attention to the multitude of flavors that you did to the different components of the aroma. You particularly want to get a sense of the blue agave juice. Once you sample a few tequilas, you will be able to discern the agave quality.

Sip barrel-aged tequila as you would a fine whiskey and enjoy the mingling flavors of the agave and the oak. In *reposado* and *añejo* tequilas, the blue agave essence is moderated and enhanced by delicate vanilla and oak flavors from the wood.

You now come to the finish of the spirit. Finish is the aftertaste. You'll want to note how long the aftertaste continues, whether a particular flavor is dominant after a few seconds or minutes, and whether the sensation is sweet or bitter. Alcohol or "burn" relates to the experience of the alcohol itself as you drink. Is the alcohol mildly sensed, hot, or shocking to the mouth?

After the Tasting
—Oxygen and Tequila

As with any fine spirit, once the seal is broken oxygenation begins. Agave reacts rapidly to the presence of oxygen. Blue agave left in a half-full bottle for more than a month loses much of its character. If you have half-full bottles at the end of the tasting, make sure people take them home to enjoy the 100 percent agave in a timely manner. Should your fine tequila sit for a while, it is better to use it for mixed drinks than to drink it straight.

tasting notes

1800 Reposado
$$ ★★   Sweet and soft on the palate with nice poise and balance.

1800 Añejo
$$ ★★★   Fleshy, hot, spicy, and peppery; long and racy finish.

1921 Blanco
$$ ★★★   Smooth and elegant with sweet, lush vanilla and spice; mellow and rich.

1921 Reposado
$$ ★★   Smooth and creamy with spice, sweet fruit, and a long, mellow finish.

1921 Reserva Especial
$$$ ★★★   Smooth and creamy with toast, spice, and vanilla; lush and dense, long.

Amate Silver
$$ ★★   Dry, spicy, fleshy, and ripe with smooth texture and a long finish.

Amate Reposado
$$ ★★   Pale amber color; lush and smooth with spice, toast, and notes of coffee, flesh, and agave.

Amate Añejo
$$ ★★   Medium amber; soft and aromatic with peppery spice and smooth, long finish.

Arandas Oro Tequila
$ ★★   Pale amber color; smooth and mild, simple and slightly sweet.

Asombroso El Platino
$$$ ★★★   Creamy and lush with vanilla and spice; long and rich with dense flavors and a complex finish.

Asombroso Añejo

$$$$ ★★★   Smooth and creamy with caramel and spice; long and silky, incredibly mellow and rich.

Asombroso El Carbonzado

$$$$ ★★★   Lush and smooth with caramel and vanilla spice; long and mellow with spice and luscious flavors.

Asombroso Del Porto

$$$$ ★★★★   Smooth and mellow with honey and vanilla and lovely flavors of spice and lovely port wine; long and amazing.

Cabo Wabo Reposado

$$ ★★★   Fresh, clean, and racy with clean, peppery, spicy flavors; long and fresh.

Cabrito Tequila Reposado

$$ ★★   Smooth and spicy with decent, clean flavors; simple but long and balanced.

Cabrito Blanco

$$ ★★   Smooth and fleshy with mild, sweet, spicy flavors; clean and moderately long.

Casa Noble Crystal

$$ ★★   Spicy, smooth, and balanced with clean, racy flavors and a long, snappy finish.

Casa Noble Reposado

$$$ ★★★   Pale gold; bright and racy with clean, smooth flavors of spice, oak, and agave; long and lovely.

Casa Noble Añejo

$$$ ★★   Herbal and spicy with ripe vegetal flavors and decent finish.

Casa Noble Extra Aged Añejo

$$$ ★★   Pale amber color; smooth and clean with spice, lively flavors, and dry, balanced finish.

Cazadores Reposado

$$ ★★   Exotic spice and white pepper note with a lingering finish.

Centinela Reposado

$$ ★★   Warm and smooth with lovely notes of cinnamon and herbal overtones.

Centinela Añejo

$$ ★★   Pale amber; spicy and fresh with lively, racy flavors; long and clean.

Centinela Añejo 3 Year Old

$$$ ★★★   Pale amber; spicy, peppery, dense, and long.

Cesar Monterey Gold Reserva

$ ★★   Pale gold color; leafy, spicy, and smooth with creamy, sweet flavors.

Cesar Monterey Blanco Reserva

$S   ★★   Fleshy and weedy, smooth and sweet with vanilla, spice, and length.

Cesar Monterey Reposado Reserva

$$ ★★   Pale gold color; soft, creamy vanilla nose; lush, creamy, and ripe with spice.

Chinaco Reposado

$$ ★★★   Lush and spicy with pepper, spice; racy and dense; earthy, ripe, and long.

Chinaco Blanco

$$ ★★★   Intense agave fruit, smooth, creamy texture with vanilla and pepper spice notes; mouth-filling and complex.

Chinaco Añejo

$$$ ★★★   Light amber in color; dry, assertively spicy, smooth and lush, complex and intense.

Corazon Blanco

$$ ★★   Smooth and rich with spice; creamy texture and lush vanilla notes.

Corazon Reposado

$$$ ★★★   Creamy, spicy, and dense with caramel, vanilla, and toasty notes; smooth, seamless, lovely.

Corazon Añejo

$$$ ★★★   Medium amber color; intense and smooth with creamy, toasty, caramel flavors; lush and balanced with density and ripe, rich fruit.

Corralejo Reposado

$$ ★★   Very pale gold; silky, smooth, and balanced with clean, elegant flavors of vanilla, oak, and fruit.

Don Alejo Reposado

$$ ★★   Spicy and smooth with grass and herbs; long and fresh, lively and lush.

Don Eduardo Silver

$$ ★★   Agave-forward flavors and a vibrant presence in the mouth.

Don Eduardo Añejo

$$$ ★   Silky mouth feel with pronounced wood tones and a long finish.

Don Julio Reposado

$$ ★★   Nicely defined flavors with sultry background tones.

Don Julio Blanco

$$ ★★   Juicy and bursting with agave flavors; zippy finish.

Don Julio Añejo

$$$ ★★   Oaky sherrylike tones underlying a bouquet of white fruit; very nice.

El Conquistador Reposado

$$ ★★   Lush and aromatic; peppery tones with a velvety mouth feel.

El Jimador Añejo

$$$ ★★★   Ripe, rich, and round with polish and complexity.

El Tesoro de Don Felipe Platinum

$$ ★★★   Smooth and creamy with spice, vanilla, and lush, long finish.

El Tesoro de Don Felipe Reposado

$$ ★★★   Smooth and sweet with creamy vanilla and spice; toasty, rich, and long.

El Tesoro de Don Felipe Añejo

$$$ ★★★   Smooth and spicy with fresh, lively, balanced flavors; long and fleshy.

El Tesoro de Don Felipe Paradiso Añejo

$$$ ★★★   Medium amber color; sweet and lush, ripe and smooth, rich and creamy; long, dense, and mellow.

Espolon Silver

$$ ★★   Kicky and vibrant agave flavors and a long finish.

Espolon Reposado

$$ ★★★   Smooth and spicy with clean flavors and a long, sweet, balanced flavor; rich, spicy, and lovely.

Espolon Añejo

$$ ★★★   Spice-bomb nose with citrusy overtones moderated by wood.

Gran Centenario Plata

$$$ ★★   Sophisticated and polished flavors; subtle and balanced.

Gran Centenario Reposado

$$$ ★★★   Velvety and warm with ripe, chewy flavors of spice and oak.

Gran Centenario Añejo

$$$ ★★★   Dense, layered, and sultry with a sweet roundness.

Herencia de Plata Reposado

$$ ★★   White fruit and agave with good structure and medium body.

Herencia de Plata Añejo

$$ ★   Herbal notes predominate with soft oak and a polished finish.

Herencia Historico 27 de Mayo Añejo

$$$$ ★★★   Dark and honeyed with a silky mouth feel and a spicy finish.

Herradura Silver

$$ ★★★   Zippy and stylish with loads of character; a classic silver tequila.

Herradura Reposado

$$ ★★   Smooth and creamy; light, fresh, and lively.

Herradura Selección Suprema

$$$$ ★★★★   Medium dark amber color; smooth, spicy agave nose; smooth and mellow with elegant, complex flavors of toasty oak and spice, and a lovely, clean, balanced finish.

José Cuervo Tradicional

$$ ★★★   Smooth and clean with lush, toasty flavors; balanced, toasty vanilla and a long finish.

José Cuervo Añejo Extra Aged

$$ ★★★★   Dark amber, toasty, sweet, and smoky; long, rich, and intense; spicy, lush, and rich.

José Cuervo Reserva de la Familia 2003

$$$ ★★★   Medium amber color; toasty caramel and lush, rich, sweet flavors; complex, intense, and long.

La Cava del Villano Gold

$ ★★   Pale amber color; smooth, fleshy, sweet, and creamy; soft and decent.

Leyenda del Milagro Silver

$$ ★★   Smooth and clean with creamy texture and a touch of sweetness; balanced, lush, and ripe.

Leyenda del Milagro Reposado

$$ ★★   Lush and creamy with ripe, fleshy flavors and a smooth, rich texture; long and spicy.

Leyenda del Milagro Añejo

$$ ★★   Smoky, spicy, and slightly sweet; lush, dense, and peppery.

Los Arango Reposado

$$ ★★   Luscious and layered, with smoky, earthy notes.

Los Azulejos Gold

$$ ★★   Pale amber color; minty, spicy, and dry with racy, oaky flavors.

Los Azulejos Reposado

$$ ★★   Very pale amber color; smooth and spicy with creamy notes and some composty notes; mild and balanced.

Nacional

$$ ★★★   Dry and spicy with smooth, creamy texture and notes of vanilla and pepper; intense agave flavors.

Oro Azul Blanco

$$ ★   Keen agave sensation on the palate; fresh and zesty.

Oro Azul Añejo

$$$ ★★   Smooth, delicious flavors rounded by soft oak.

Patrón Silver

$$ ★★★   Spicy and forward nose with dry, peppery, leafy flavors; ripe and long with a clean finish.

Patrón Añejo

$$$ ★★★   Pale amber color; forward and spicy nose with deep, peppery flavors and a long, smooth finish.

Penca Azul Reposado

$$$ ★★   Sexy and seductive with notes of caramel and nice complexity.

Reserva del Dueño Añejo

$$$ ★★★   Spicy, ripe, fleshy, and sweet with creamy, dense flavors with a peppery finish.

Reserva del Señor Reposado

$$$ ★★★★   Massively complex and rich with superb balance; endless finish.

Rey Sol Añejo

$$$$ ★★★   Deep, rich, and complex flavors with stunning packaging created by Sergio Bustamante.

San Matias Gran Reserva

$$ ★★   Medium amber color; smooth, spicy, and elegant with lush oak and mellow fruit.

Sauza Gold

$ ★★   Dusky and sweet; competent but ultimately unexciting.

Sauza Hornitos Reposado

$$ ★★★   Spicy white fruit and complex herbal tones; very nice.

Sauza Tres Generaciones Plata

$$ ★★   A superb tequila for margaritas, with plenty of snappy citrus and spice.

Sauza Tres Generaciones Añejo

$$ ★★   Racy and alive with bright notes of citrus and spice.

Two Fingers

$ ★★   Smooth and mild with peppery spice, sweet notes, and a clean, soft finish.

Two Fingers Gold

$ ★★   Pale amber color; sweet, mellow, and smooth with mild, balanced flavors.

XXX Siglo Treinta Gold

$$ ★★★   Pale gold color; creamy and lush with lovely, elegant, balanced flavors; complex, balanced, and delicious.

MEZCAL AND SOTOL

Del Maguey Single Village Mezcal San Luis del Rio

$$$ ★★★   Intense tobacco and cayenne with clean, racy, long flavors.

Del Maguey Single Village Mezcal Santo Domingo Albarradas
$$$ ★★★   Fleshy, smoky, and smooth with balance and a lovely, peppery finish.

Del Maguey Single Village Mezcal Chichicapa
$$$ ★★★   Delicate, elegant, and aromatic with racy, smoky flavors.

Del Maguey Single Village Mezcal Minero
$$$ ★★★   Spicy and earthy with pepper and lush agave; fleshy, intense, and long.

Del Maguey Single Village Mezcal Tobalá
$$$ ★★   Clear; edgy tobacco and spice flavors with leafy, forward flavors.

Del Maguey Single Village Mezcal Pechuga
$$$ ★★★   Minty, racy, and spicy; elegant, bright, and racy with lush, tangy flavors.

Don Amado Plata Mezcal de Oaxaca
$$ ★★   Fleshy and toasted with tobacco and earth flavors; smooth and dense, long.

Don Amado Reposado Mezcal de Oaxaca
$$ ★★   Smoky and earthy, smooth and mellow with long, fleshy flavors.

Don Amado Añejo Mezcal de Oaxaca
$$ ★★   Smoky, fleshy, and dense with complex, rich flavors and good length.

Hacienda de Chihuahua Sotol Reposado
$$ ★★★   Pale gold color; smooth and creamy with notes of mint, spice, and lovely vanilla.

Scorpion Silver Mezcal
$$ ★★   Fresh, clean and crisp with rustic, tangy agave flavors; all Scorpion products come with a (harmless) scorpion shell in the bottle.

Scorpion Añejo Three-Year-Old Mezcal
$$$ ★★   Smoky and rich with dense, earthy flavors.

6

scotch
and
irish whiskey

I t's not inappropriate to discuss Scotch whisky (without an "e") and Irish whiskey (with an "e") in the same chapter. The two spirits have been intimately related historically from the earliest days of distillation in the British Isles. Their fortunes have been further interwoven and then torn asunder by historical events, including the repeated imposition of taxation by England, the declaration of Irish independence, and American Prohibition, among many others.

This is not to say that they are identical or even similar spirits. Far from it. Recipes and distillation techniques vary widely between Scotch and Irish pot-still whiskeys. But each has its ardent enthusiasts, and to develop an appreciation of one leads to an understanding of the other. While Scotch shines in the limelight today as it never has before, Irish whiskey is just now making a comeback after years of neglect.

✴ SCOTCH WHISKY ✴

No other spirit has quite the same allure as Scotch whisky. Its unique character has made it a global success. In its blended and single-malt forms combined, Scotch outsells all other noble spirits worldwide and retains an absolutely unique appeal. Scotch speaks of the ruggedly breathtaking beauty of the place where it's made: of moody, cloud-filled skies over desolate, haunting landscapes; of storm-lashed seas slapping against the very foundations of white-washed distilleries; of freshwater streams cascading through granite glens. It also speaks of the Scottish people and of their love of freedom. "Freedom and whisky gang thegither!" wrote Robert Burns, Scotland's iconic poet.

✳ THE PROCESS ✳

There are two basic types of Scotch whisky: malt whisky (made from malted barley) and grain whisky (made from raw grain such as corn or wheat). The process for each is described below.

Making Malt Whisky

At least since Friar John Cor received his eight bales of malt in 1494, the Scots have been making spirits from malted barley. Although Friar Cor's malt spirit may have been flavored with herbs and consumed shortly after production, the process of making aged malt whisky eventually evolved from early spirits production methods and has remained relatively unchanged for several hundred years. In spite of slow modernization in the industry and some conformity of standards, each distillery is very much a unique entity and is fiercely proud of its own recipes, techniques, and equipment.

Malting

The whisky-making process begins with raw barley, a grain in the grass family. Barley was one of the earliest grains cultivated by man, and even into the sixteenth century was the principal grain used for making bread in Europe. To make the malt required for whisky, raw barley grain is screened for impurities and then soaked in water for two to three days in tanks known as steeps. The damp barley is then spread on a concrete floor, called the malting floor, where it begins to germinate over a period of eight to twelve days. During germination the barley batch, called a piece, is turned frequently to dispel heat. If the barley were left unturned, the accumulated heat would cause the germination to become too rapid. Traditionally the turning was done by hand, using flat wooden shovels known as shiels. Many maltings, however, now use a French-invented device called a Saladin box, in which the barley is turned automatically by mechanical rakes and the temperature is controlled by forced air.

The germination is terminated at an optimal point and the malted barley, or green malt, is dried in kilns on perforated metal plates until it is brown and toasty. The lower compartment of the kiln was traditionally fired by whatever material was available locally. In the Lowlands this was usually coal, coke, or anthracite. The peat used in the Highlands lends the Highlands whiskies their distinctive peat reek. Peat can also be added in greater or lesser amounts to more modern fuels, to flavor malt. The chimneys of the malting kilns, usually in the familiar pagoda shape first designed by master distillery architect Charles Doig in the 1890s, are the instantly recognizable marks of a malt distillery. But in truth most distilleries today obtain their malt from centralized maltings works, where the steeping, germination, and kilning process is carried out mechanically. Balvenie, Bowmore, Laphroiag, Springbank, and Tamdhu are among the small number of distilleries that still operate their own maltings.

Mashing

The malt is ground in a mill into grist, a coarse type of flour, and then mixed with warm water. This mixture, called the sparge, is fed into a large copper or stainless steel mash tun, where the fermentable sugars in the grist are dissolved. The resulting sugary liquid is called the wort. The solids remaining from the mashing process, called the draff, are sold as cattle feed or used as fertilizer. The water particular to each distillery is also a matter of pride and helps individualize each malt. The most prized streams (or burns, as they're called) are those containing soft water that has passed over indigenous granite. Other streams, such as those on Islay, pass through peat, which adds to the assertive peaty character of the Islay malts.

Fermentation

After mashing, the wort is cooled and transferred to the washback, a large wooden vessel of pine, Douglas fir, or larch holding from nine thousand to forty-five thousand liters, where it is fermented by the addition of yeast in a process that resembles beer making. The yeast fermentation process is quite violent and produces heat, noise, and gases. In the days before mechanization, distilleries used to employ boys with wooden whips who would thrash the foamy, billowing head of the fermenting wort to keep it under control. The fermentation process results in a mildly alcoholic liquid called the wash.

Distillation

The real alchemy of distillation begins when the wash is placed in the first of two pot stills. These gleaming, bulging copper stills with their swanlike necks are the heart of a malt distillery and, in spite of their ungainly appearance, are things of great beauty to any lover of Scotch. They are also special objects of pride for each distillery, and many of them have been given affectionate names by the distillery workers. The shapes and sizes of the stills are closely tied to the character of the individual whiskies they produce.

The first distillation takes place in a wash still, in which the wash is heated to boiling. Alcohol boils at a lower temperature than water, so the alcohol vapor rises up the neck of the still first. As the vapor reaches the top of the neck, it is diverted into a coiled copper tube called the worm. The worm is surrounded by cold water, which causes the alcohol vapor to condense into a liquid state. The result of the first distillation is known as the low wines, which contain about 25 percent alcohol and need to be redistilled before becoming whisky.

The second distillation takes place in a spirits still, smaller and more complex than the wash still. The low wines are again heated, and the alcohol vapors move up the neck of the still. Since the low wines contain several types of alcohol, each with its own distinct vaporization temperature, the neck of the spirits still is shaped so as to force the various vapors to mingle. Stills with short necks are said to produce more intensely flavored whiskies, while long-necked stills or those with a large ball shape in the neck (called a Balvenie ball) usually produce gentler, more refined spirits. The first part of the run, called the foreshots, is too impure to be used and is diverted by means of a valve into a chamber where it will be recombined with the low wines for redistillation. Likewise, the last part of the run, called the feints, is too weak to be used and is also channeled off for later redistillation. Only the central part of the run, or middle cut, is allowed to pass into the so-called spirits safe by the watchful stillman. This new make is now officially under bond, and must be kept under lock and key. Special customs locks, with an internal slot for a government excise inspection slip, were traditionally used to secure the spirits safe. Any tampering with the spirits safe could thus be easily detected.

Aging

A minimum aging period of three years is mandated for all Scotch whisky, whether malt or grain, but in actual practice the period is usually much longer. Between ten and twenty-five years is not uncommon. Well over half of any given whisky's flavor comes from the wood in which it's aged, so the types of barrels used are quite important. Depending on the quality of spirit being sought, the distillery might choose casks previously used to age sherry, those used to age bourbon, or new oak barrels. The place where the whisky ages is also important. The distilleries on the island of Islay, for example, are built right on the sea, with the waves literally slapping against the foundations. The proximity allows salt air to permeate the aging whiskies, giving them a distinct seaweedlike character.

Single Malts

Scotch single malts are the true thoroughbreds of the spirits world. They're racy, temperamental, engaging, individual, and inimitable. They've been savored and studied, analyzed and written about voluminously, but in the end they remain almost mystically enigmatic. Every great single malt, and even some of the better blends, has an irreducible quality that first seduces and then leads the drinker magically into the Scottish mist. Scotch is a lifelong pursuit.

Independent Bottlers

As was traditionally the case with the wines of Bordeaux and Burgundy, single malts are sometimes bought in barrel direct from the producer and packaged for sale by independent bottlers, who may be either merchants or societies of connoisseurs. Two of the most important today are Gordon & MacPhail, in Elgin, and the Scotch Malt Whisky Society, headquartered in Edinburgh.

Gordon & MacPhail

James Gordon and John Alexander MacPhail opened their "centrical and commodious" new shop on South Street in the city of Elgin, in Speyside, on May 24, 1895, selling groceries, wines, and spirits. The firm blended and bottled whiskies under its own label, and dealt also in mature whiskies purchased directly from Highlands distillers. Today Gordon & McPhail offers one of the largest selections of rare single malts available anywhere, with around seven hundred different bottlings in stock at any given time. Single-malt enthusiasts consider a trip to Gordon & MacPhail's historic Elgin shop a required pilgrimage.

The bulk of the flavorful malt whisky made in the process just described is used to blend with milder grain whisky, resulting in blended Scotches such as Dewar's, Chivas Regal, or Teacher's. Small amounts, however, are often held back by the distillery to be bottled as single malts. These single malts—malt whiskies produced by a single distillery—are the unique spirits that have captured the imagination of Scotch lovers worldwide. Certain distilleries, such as Glenmorangie, have gained such a following for their single malts that none of their whisky is sold for blending.

Scotch Malt Whisky Society

Founded in 1983 as a small group of whisky enthusiast friends, the Scotch Malt Whisky Society now has around sixteen thousand members in the United Kingdom, the United States, and seven other countries. Since its founding the society has bottled over 750 casks of single malts from 150 different distilleries and has offered these bottles for sale to its members. All whiskies are bottled at cask strength. The society also provides members' tastings and other educational programs. For more information, visit their informative website at www.smws.com.

Making Grain Whisky

Unlike malt whisky, grain whisky is made from raw grain, usually wheat or corn (called maize in Scotland). These cereals are cooked under pressure to break down the fermentable sugars, and are usually combined with a certain percentage of malted barley in the mash tun. The fermentation process is essentially identical to that described for malt whisky, but the distillation process is quite different.

Grain whisky is made in a two-column patent still (also known as a Coffey still, or simply a column still). The wash enters at the top of the still and cascades down the first column, called the analyzer, where it runs over a series of copper plates. Steam rising from below "strips" the alcohol from the wash in the form of vapors, which are carried into the second column, called the rectifying column, which is situated parallel to the analyzer. Whereas making malt whisky is a batch process in which the still must be cleaned thoroughly after every distillation, the patent process is continuous and the stills are self-cleaning.

Blended Scotch

It is possible occasionally to find single-grain whiskies—that is, unblended whiskies that have been bottled as the product of a single-grain distillery—but they are extremely rare outside the United Kingdom. (One brand available there comes from Invergordon, the only grain distillery in the Highlands.) Nearly all grain whisky is used in blends. In spite of the cult importance attached to single malts, blends actually account for about 95 percent of Scotch sold. Since the development of blending in the mid-nineteenth century, the art of the blender has been one of the most important factors in the global success of Scotch whisky. It's been said that distillation is a science, but blending is an art. Not only must the blender assure that his or her whisky is balanced and satisfying, but consistency is also expected from blend to blend and from year to year. This is not at all easy, considering that the ranges of available malt and grain whiskies change continually. Many years of experience with a wide range of whiskies is required to become a master blender. The logistics of producing and storing whiskies for blending must also be planned out many years in advance of the blend itself being created, a feat that involves predicting the Scotch market with spot-on accuracy.

A typical blend might be composed of a dozen to three dozen or more different malt whiskies, purchased from various malt whisky distilleries, and two or three grain whiskies. Less expensive blends will consist mostly of mild grain whisky, perked up with around 20 percent malt whisky. More expensive and complex blends, on the other hand, will contain more malt whisky than grain whisky, and the malts included in the blend will usually be older and rarer. Some popular blended brands commonly found in the U.S. market include Ballantine's, Chivas Regal, Cutty Sark, Dewar's, Famous Grouse, J&B, Johnnie Walker, and William Grant's. Most of these come in bottlings of different ages. The age on the bottle refers to the age of the youngest whisky in the blend, but all will include much older malts as well.

✳ THE REGIONS ✳

Scotch is very much a regional product, with each region's climate and natural resources contributing to the unique flavor of its malt whiskies. Historically, there are just two main regions: the Lowlands and the Highlands. They were divided in 1784 for purposes of taxation by the imaginary "Highland Line," drawn across Scotland from east to west. However, in practice, smaller areas of each have become acknowledged as separate regions in their own right. Campbeltown, located at the tip of the Kintyre peninsula in the southwest Lowlands, has just one distillery left but was historically an important subregion. Speyside, in the northeast Highlands, has long been the most concentrated and important area of Scotch production, with many distilleries grouped along the valley of the River Spey. The islands include Orkney in the far north, Skye and Mull in the west, and Jura and the justly famous Islay (pronounced "EYE-lah") in the southwest.

The Lowlands

The Lowlands have been known since the early nineteenth century for their grain whiskies and blends, which were extremely popular farther south in England. Because of the importance of blends in the whisky trade, most Lowlands malts went into the blending vat rather than being bottled as single malts, a tendency that led to their declining reputation when compared to Highlands malts. Today only Glenkinchie and Auchentoshan are still producing whisky, although previous bottlings from now-defunct distilleries such as Rosebank may still be found. Lowlands whiskies tend to be soft and smoother than other Scotch single malts, with little of the peat and brine characteristics of Highlands malts. These are good whiskies for those who are just discovering Scotch.

Campbeltown

Campbeltown was once a thriving center of distilling. Distilling may have been brought to Scotland from Ireland by way of Campbeltown, which lies quite close to the Northern Irish coast. In the early days illicit distilling was rampant in this isolated peninsula, but, by the end of the eighteenth century there were more than thirty licensed distilleries in Campbeltown. That number dwindled to twelve in 1925, and today only one distillery remains in Campbeltown. It is, however, one of the greatest of all Scotch whiskies: Springbank. The style is slightly briny but not so aggressive as the peaty malts that are made not far away on the island of Islay.

The Highlands

Much larger than the Lowlands, the Highlands have scattered distilleries in the southern and western reaches. Glengoyne, for example, lies just north of Glasgow and right on the "Highland Line," but since its water comes from north of the demarcation, it is regarded as a Highlands malt. Oban and Ben Nevis are among the westernmost of the Highlands distilleries. The various whiskies of the Highlands represent a range of styles, but generally show more peat character and more individuality than their Lowlands counterparts.

Speyside

A subregion of the Highlands, Speyside lies just below the Moray Firth in northeastern Scotland. Here, just south of the city of Elgin, "the whisky capital of the world," lies the greatest concentration of distilling activity on the planet. More than half of Scotland's single malts are produced here, including such household names as The Glenlivet, Glenfiddich, Balvenie, Glenrothes, and Macallan. Several factors contributed to Speyside's rapid growth in the nineteenth century. There was a ready source of good water, from the Spey, the Livet, and several other rivers that run through the region on their way to the sea. Unlike Campbeltown or the islands, the Speyside region was not remote and had easy access to rail transport. There was also a ready supply of local barley. The Speyside malts are sweet, delicate, and endearing. For many whisky drinkers, they are the quintessential dram of Scotch.

Islay

The island of Islay in the Hebrides produces the most assertive and masculine of all Scotch malts. The island is practically one vast peat bog, and the distinct flavor of peat is imparted to the region's whiskies not only through the malt kilning process but also because the Islay water flows through peat beds on its way to the distilleries. The seaside location also heavily influences the taste of these single malts, since the peat contains a significant portion of seaweed. With many of the distilleries built right on the sea, salt-laden ocean air also penetrates the casks during the aging process and brings yet another level of heady character to these whiskies.

Most connoisseurs move to Islay malts after cutting their whisky-drinking teeth on other Scotches. Once they discover Islay, however, many become fanatic devotees. The Islay single malts from Lagavulin, Ardbeg, and Laphroaig have achieved something approaching cult status. They are an acquired taste, but one that every lover of Scotch will want to experience at least a few times. Bowmore, which is one of the least aggressive and smoothest of the Islay malts, is a good place to start.

✳ THE HISTORY ✳

The story of how Scotch went from being the favorite quaff of hard-scrabble peasants in a remote northerly country to one of the world's most highly prized liquids is perhaps the most compelling adventure in the annals of drink. The history of this quirky beverage is as full of fire and pride as the drink itself.

The Beginnings

The first written reference to anything resembling whisky being made in Scotland occurs at the relatively late date of 1494, when the Scottish Exchequer Rolls notes "8 bolls of malt for Friar John Cor wherewith to make *aquavitae*." Far be it from me to diminish the otherwise unknown friar's share of credit as one of Scotland's pioneer distillers, but the Scots were almost certainly making spirits long before John Cor took delivery of his malt shipment. For one thing, it's been estimated that eight medieval bolls (or bales) would weigh about half a ton. That's quite a heap of malt, enough in fact to produce a good fifteen hundred bottles of whisky. Friar John was obviously no amateur dabbler making malt-based moonshine in his cell behind the abbott's back. Instead, this entry in the official record shows us that Scotch whisky was already well established at this time and, like much of medieval culture, was under the protection of the church.

The making of distilled spirits was probably first brought to Scotland from Celtic Ireland, where the practice had been established in Irish monasteries since at least the late twelfth century. The Celtic monks supposedly employed their aqua vitae, or "water of life," for medicinal purposes, a theory that doesn't sound so improbable considering that the soul needs medicine as much as the body. These aquae vitae would hardly be recognizable to a modern whisky aficionado, however, since they were not aged, and were usually flavored with herbs such as heather, roots, spices, and even honey. In fact, they were much closer to today's Scandinavian aquavit than to whisky as we know it.

In any case, the spirited monks had already been sailing for centuries on evangelical missions across the cold seventeen-mile-wide Northern Channel of the Irish Sea, from the tip of Ireland to Kintyre and to the islands of the Hebrides, where they were attempting to Christianize the recalcitrant, heathen Scots. The shared warmth of an Irish dram was probably a potent inducement to conversion. In 1534, a generation after Friar John received his historic shipment, the vast religious conflict known as the Reformation had gripped Europe. As part of the general chaos, the Irish-run Catholic monasteries were torched by straitlaced, papophobic Protestants. The friars and their stills were dispersed. Local peasants, faced with the bleak prospect of a drought of monastic spirits, began to make their own aqua vitae. In doing so, the illiterate distillers translated the monks' Latin for "water of life" into their familiar Gaelic as *uisge beatha,* which gives us the Anglicized version *fwisge* and, later, whisky.

The Dreaded Excise Tax

Whisky was a cottage industry for the next two hundred years, dispersed among many small artisanal distilleries and consumed locally. By 1644, however, the practice was at least widespread enough that the Scottish Parliament recognized an opportunity to get its hand into the lucrative pie, in the form of an excise duty. Whisky was taxed at the rate of two shillings and eight pence per Scots pint (about a third of a gallon). As if that weren't enough, the government also taxed stills, barley, mash, and wash. The Treaty of Union, signed in 1707, united England and Scotland. The two countries' superimposed flags created the new symbol of the United Kingdom, the Union Jack, which now flew like a challenge to Scottish distillers over the offices of the dreaded Scottish Excise Board. Even though the treaty specified that taxation would be distributed proportionately between England and Scotland, to take unequal national economic conditions into account, by 1713 revised legislation made the tax rate uniform on both sides of the border. The Scots were determined to resist.

Like their American counterparts in the wilds of Appalachia, the rugged Scottish distillers lived in hatred of the official excisemen, or "gaugers." Their conflicts were often bloody. The whisky smugglers, as illegal distillers were called, became quite crafty in hiding both their "bothies" (portable illegal stills) and their "make." The smoke from illicit distilling could be hidden in caves behind waterfalls, or by routing it through the family hearth. Women could conceal bootleg whisky under their ample dresses, while ministers of the Scottish Kirk shamelessly hid it in their pulpits. Even empty coffins were famously used to transport bootleg in mock funeral processions. In his humorous book on Scotch, entitled *Still Life with Bottle,* artist Ralph Steadman illustrates several more of these methods of evasion in a fanciful fashion, including a whisky still disguised as a bagpipe. Thesmugglers even developed mutual signal systems warning of gaugers in various

Highlands vicinities. The excisemen persevered, and by the 1820s nearly fourteen thousand illicit stills were being destroyed per year. But the frustrated gaugers had barely put a dent in illegal whisky.

The Rise of the Lowlands

In 1725 the prime minister, Sir Robert Walpole, pushed a malt tax bill through Parliament. It placed the tax on malt at three pence per bushel. This was actually a compromise measure on Walpole's part, meant to forestall a proposed tax on Scottish ale, which would have been unfavorable to Scottish brewers. But the measure proved extremely unpopular in Scotland nevertheless, and resulted in riots in Shawfield in which one member of Parliament's house was burned down. The malt tax also had the unfortunate side effect of encouraging distillers to include large amounts of raw grain, in place of taxed malt, in their whiskies, significantly lowering the quality of the product.

It was around this time that the Lowlands distillers, using larger stills, began to produce larger and larger quantities of whisky, generally considered inferior to that found in the Highlands. Whereas many Highland distillers relied on small portable stills that were easily concealed from the gaugers in the desolate mountain terrain, the more populous Lowlands provided far fewer hiding places. Legitimate distillers grew in size and importance in the Lowlands, and whisky making became a capitalist enterprise as opposed to an artisanal craft.

The division of Scotland into two unequal parts—the smaller and more cultured Lowlands in the south, and the larger and more rugged Highlands in the north—was effectively codified for purposes of whisky taxation by the Wash Act of 1784, which established an imaginary "Highland Line" running from Dundee on the Firth of Tay in the east, to Greenock on the Firth of Clyde, near Glasgow, in the west. The purpose of the act was to stem the growing number of illicit distillers in the Highlands by applying lower excise duties on smaller distilleries in the north. Whisky makers in the Lowlands naturally objected, so the law was soon amended to prohibit Highlands whisky from being brought into the Lowlands.

The split between higher-quality Highlands and lesser-quality Lowlands whisky became firmly established by the end of the eighteenth century. Robert Burns once referred to Lowlands whisky as "a most rascally liquor." Ironically, Burns was actually a Lowlander from Ayrshire. But he was also a major figure in the burgeoning Romantic movement, and his exalted view of the Highlands and their whisky helped to romanticize the north in the public's mind. The distinction between Highlands and Lowlands continues even today, with the south and its whisky generally getting the short end of the stick. By the end of the eighteenth century there were an estimated two thousand distilleries operating in Scotland.

Scotch in the Nineteenth Century

Much of the history of Scotch can be told in terms of attempts by the government to bring this lucrative and socially potent substance under control and taxation. As we've already seen, at various times Parliament adjusted the rate of taxation in an effort to encourage distillers, mainly in the Highlands, to go legal, while at the same time assuring the government of its share. Too high a tax rate, and distillers tended to distill illegally and smuggle their make. Too low, and the government saw a drop in revenue. The seesaw was shoved in the opposite direction once again in 1816, when the Small Stills Act lowered the minimum legal capacity for stills to forty gallons. This was an encouraging piece of legislation for small-still operators in the Highlands. Forty-five new distilleries opened (or went legal) in the north.

One man had perhaps more to do with shaping the direction of Scotch whisky in the nineteenth century than any other person: George, Fifth Duke of Gordon. The Gordons were large landowners in northeastern Scotland, where today many of the great Scotch distilleries are still found. The clan had risen to prominence in the fourteenth century under the legendary Scottish king Robert the Bruce, and had subsequently risen through the ranks of aristocracy to be granted the title of dukes. Reasoning that his tenants were dependent on revenue from their distilling, whether legal or illegal, the Fifth Duke of Gordon marshaled fellow landowners and encouraged the government in Westminster to draw up reforms to promote legal distilling. Everyone would benefit, he theorized, if distilling was legitimized. The result of Gordon's efforts was the Excise Act of 1823. Duties were reduced drastically. Gordon encouraged one of his tenants, George Smith, to take advantage of the new legislation and license a new distillery on Gordon lands in the valley of the River Livet. Smith obliged his landlord and opened the first legal distillery in 1824. It was named for its location, The Glenlivet, and it's still one of the most famous of all Scotch whiskies. Within a short time after Smith opened his operation, the number of legal distilleries in Scotland had doubled.

Meanwhile, in the Lowlands, the invention of the patent still revolutionized whisky making. In 1826 Robert Stein, a cousin of the Lowlands' premier whisky family, the Haigs, invented the patent still. This new product of the Industrial Revolution enabled distillers to meet increasing demand by making copious amounts of spirit from raw grain such as wheat or corn, rather than from more expensive malted (germinated) barley. In 1827 the Cameron-bridge Distillery in Fife became the first Scotch distillery to make grain whisky with a patent still. The patent still (later known as the Coffey still, for the former Irish exciseman Aeneas Coffey, who perfected and patented it in 1830) is a very efficient continuous-operation device in which the wash enters at the top of the column and falls through a series of hundreds of perforated copper plates, or "trays." Steam rising from the bottom captures the alcohol from the wash in the form of vapor and carries it to the top, where it is sent to the rectifying column, or condenser, and brought back to a liquid state. Whereas the pot stills used for malt whisky distillation need to be cleaned thoroughly between batches, the patent still can run indefinitely.

The end product of the patent-still process is a light whisky with little of the character of Highlands malt whisky. In fact, many patent distillers also shipped their newly made grain spirits south to England for the manufacture of gin, which was also enormously popular at this time. To give the Lowlands patent-still whisky some authentic Scotch character, some dealers began blending them with small percentages of more flavorful malt whiskies. The Edinburgh merchant firm of Andrew Usher and Company pioneered the art of blending Scotch whisky in the mid-1800s. Usher released the first vatted malt (a blend of malt whiskies of different ages) as Old Vatted Glenlivet Whisky in 1853.

Blends of malt and grain whisky soon followed, created mainly by grocers and wine merchants in cities such as Glasgow and Edinburgh. Before bottling, the grocers stored their blends in whatever barrels happened to be on hand: some had contained sherry, others port. It was soon noted that each type of barrel had a different effect on the whisky. Although the companies themselves were eventually purchased by large corporations, the names of these original grocers are still famous today as some of the world's best-known Scotch blends: Dewar's, Teacher's, Ballantine's, Johnnie Walker, and Chivas.

This was the age of the Whisky Barons, when colorful and forceful men such as Tommy Dewar, Peter Mackie (creator of White Horse), and James Buchanan (creator of Black & White), made vast fortunes in the sale of blended whiskies to markets the world over. Buchanan, the Canadian-born son of Scottish immigrants, was even raised to the peerage, as Lord Woolavington, in 1922, at the age of seventy-three. The Whisky Barons invented the art of spirits salesmanship, a combination of personal charm, publicity stunts, and glad-handing that persists behind the scenes in the industry even now.

Although we are currently witnessing a boom of specialized interest in single malts, it was actually blends that would become the Scotch of preference for most whisky drinkers throughout the nineteenth and twentieth centuries, making patent-still spirits immensely profitable. Much smoother, more agile, and cheaper than pure malt whisky, blended whisky was the perfect base for newfangled cocktails, and it found new favor among drinkers for whom pure malt was overly aggressive. At around the same time, the arrival of the devastating phylloxera vine louse in the vineyards of France in the 1870s practically put a stop to cognac production, and whisky stepped in to fill the breach. The potent United Kingdom Distillers' Association was formed to promote the interests of patent-still operators. The group became so powerful that it was known familiarly as the Whisky Parliament.

Meanwhile, much blended whisky of inferior quality was also being foisted off on unsuspecting consumers as more expensive malt by unscrupulous merchants and pub owners, leading to government crackdowns. By the end of the century Scotch production had revved up to such a pace in anticipation of demand that there was a whisky glut, with well over thirteen million gallons of Scotch in storage, much of it of decidedly inferior quality. Like an overfilled water balloon, the whisky bubble burst in 1899, and several distilleries declared bankruptcy. It seemed that the glory days of Scotch might have come and gone.

Into the New Century

In the first decade of the twentieth century the fiery members of the Scottish Malt Distillers Association got their kilts in a twist over the continued flood of inferior and immature grain spirit being sold as whisky, which they thought was diluting the image of true Scotch, not to mention cutting into their business. Only malt spirits produced in pot stills—that is, Highlands-style spirits—should be called whisky, they argued before a special royal commission set up to investigate the matter. The makers of blends, mostly Lowlands quantity producers, naturally lobbied for the term "whisky" to continue to apply to their products as well, as it had for decades. In spite of the fearsome line of Highland tartan standing in opposition, the royal commission concluded that the use of the term "whisky" should not be restricted to pot-still spirits alone. The commission also refused to establish required minimum aging requirements for whisky. It was a clear victory for the blenders. A few years later, however, the government did take a little wind out of the Lowlanders' sails when, in 1915, Parliament established a minimum aging period of two, and later three, years for whisky. (A three-year period is still the requirement.) Shortly afterward the Scotch whisky industry got an unexpected boost when Ireland declared its independence from England. Irish whiskey (with an *e*) was banned in Great Britain and throughout the British Empire, giving Scotch a perfect opportunity to fill yet another vacant niche.

The consolidation of individual distilleries under the ownership and control of large corporate umbrellas is a given in the twentieth-century whisky industry, but the corporate trend was actually set in motion as far back as 1856, when six major companies set up a trade arrangement, actually a whisky cartel. In 1877 the companies merged to form Distillers Company Limited, or DCL. Distillers Company Limited and its various production and marketing arms would become a dominant force in the Scotch industry throughout the remainder of the nineteenth and through most of the twentieth century. By 1927 DCL had assumed control of the Dewar's, Buchanan's, Johnnie Walker, and White Horse brands. By 1934 the growing conglomerate controlled dozens of malt distilleries as well, including such names as Craigellachie, Dalwhinnie, Knockdhu, Oban, Coal Isla, and Lagavulin. By the mid-century DCL had become the fourth largest company in Great Britain.

In spite of corporate growth, World War I saw a downturn in Scotch production and consumption. Pot distilling was suspended entirely in 1917, and malt distilleries were converted to wartime manufacture. Dalmore, for example, became a mine factory. The larger Lowlands grain distilleries were used to produce industrial alcohol. Even after the Armistice the news was hardly rosy for the Scotch industry. Pot distilling was permitted again in 1919, but that same year the ugly specter of Prohibition in the United States put an official halt to that important market. Fortunately for whisky drinkers, bootlegging seemed to run in the Scottish blood, and many a New York speakeasy could offer a variety of authentic smuggled Scotches (as well as a host of ersatz ones). Prohibition was lifted in 1933, but the midst of the Great Depression was hardly an opportune time for Scotch to reestablish itself in the American market. World War II likewise took its toll.

Postwar optimism finally seemed to bring a break in the gloom. Cocktail culture was reaching its peak and the demand for whisky was back, especially in the United States. Much of this demand was satisfied by Canadian blended whisky rather than Scotch. In 1958, however, work was started on the first new Highlands distillery to be built in the twentieth century: Tormore, in Speyside. Hiram Walker, a large Canadian firm, had already built a massive plant at Dumbarton as early as 1938, and now other international spirits conglomerates turned their attention to distilleries in Scotland as investments, taking advantage of British government subsidies. Seagram, another important Canadian spirits firm, bought Strathisla in 1950, and later acquired The Glenlivet single-malt and the Chivas blend. British government taxes on Scotch were increased routinely during the 1960s, and the industry responded by consolidating into ever larger and more powerful groups.

The 1970s ushered in yet another worldwide economic recession that, coupled with changing tastes and lifestyles, threw Scotch into a crisis once again. As had happened at the end of the previous century, a surplus of Scotch started to accumulate. Too much of a good thing lying around unsold in bonding warehouses meant falling prices and decreasing returns for Scotch producers. By the mid-eighties nearly thirty distilleries in Scotland had folded. But even in the midst of crisis, a new phenomenon was about to unfold.

The Single-Malt Trend

The rise of interest in single malts was foreseen with great prescience in the 1960s by William Grant & Sons, whose successful strategy for their Glenfiddich brand made it the sales leader in this category, a position it still retains today. Most malt whisky produced in Scotland is used for blending, to add flavor to more neutral grain whisky, with only about 3 percent of it being bottled and sold as single malts. And although single malts in turn account for only about 5 percent of the Scotch consumed, they enjoy a reputation that far exceeds their relatively modest market share.

Single malts, in fact, have achieved cult status over the past two decades. The affluent eighties and nineties saw an entire new generation being introduced to this not inexpensive pleasure. Knowing one Glen from another became a sign of surefire sophistication among the twenty-something crowd. In our lifestyle-conscious age, single malts are generally regarded as one of the finer things life has to offer, in the same league with fast cars, Cuban cigars, and boutique Cabernet Sauvignons. Your choice of single malt also speaks volumes about your personality: a svelte Speyside malt for the sensitive art patron; an aggressive, masculine Islay for the ruthless CEO. Trends aside, single malts are among the most complex and exciting of all spirits, and certainly deserve every bit of the attention lavished on them by both experts and wannabes.

The Future of Scotch Whisky

The interest in Scotch has never been higher, a fact of which corporate concerns are keenly aware, adding and subtracting malt distilleries to their portfolios in an effort to second-guess the public's taste for whisky. In 2002 Scotch whisky exports (malts and blends) topped the $3 billion mark for the tenth year in a row. That translates to thirty bottles of Scotch being sold overseas *per second.* It's no wonder that corporations have taken a keen interest in Scotch. South Korea and Japan are the fourth and fifth largest markets for Scotch in the world, respectively, coming just after the United States, Spain, and France. It's not uncommon in our postmodern world to spot Japanese businessmen downing shots of Chivas with their sushi.

In 1987, in a hostile takeover that rocked the spirits world, Guinness, Irish maker of Guinness Stout and many other beverage brands, acquired the once all-powerful Distillers Company Limited. The spirits division of this new leviathan was named United Distillers. Guinness and its arch-rival Grand Metropolitan later merged, in 1998, to create the world's largest drinks company, Diageo (which until recently also owned Burger King and Pillsbury). The wine and spirits arm of Diageo is known as United Distillers and Vintners (UDV). The trend of foreign ownership and consolidation continues. In 1994 the Japanese Suntory corporation acquired Morrison Bowmore, the company that operates Bowmore, Glen Garioch, and Auchentoshan.

With corporation devouring corporation like a series of increasingly larger fish, it's often difficult to keep up with who owns which brand. But from the consumer's viewpoint, ownership is not so terribly important. Corporate owners are almost always extremely careful to maintain the integrity and tradition of the Scotch whiskies under their control. After all, Scotch whiskies, whether single malts or blends, are some of the most highly revered brands in the world, and the whole point of owning them is to invest in the brand. Even if the profits are headed to Tokyo, the chance of finding a single malt that has deliberately assumed the flavor of saké is pretty slim indeed. If anything, an infusion of corporate capital has actually helped the individual malt distilleries maintain their homespun quality, spiff up their physical plants, and continue to bring whisky lovers their favorite drams. The people who make Scotch are still strongly Scots in character and fiercely passionate about their whiskies, proud to be continuing a tradition that started so many centuries ago.

✳ HOW TO ENJOY SCOTCH ✳

Scotch is a very versatile spirit. It can be used in such simple mixed drinks as the once-ubiquitous Scotch and soda, or in more complex cocktails such as the Rob Roy (Scotch and vermouth) or the Scotch sour (Scotch, citrus, and sugar syrup). Blended Scotch is fine for these purposes. But many Scotch drinkers take their favorite dram neat. This applies not only to thoroughbred single malts but also to the better blends. Drinking Scotch on its own, or perhaps over ice, allows the intriguing flavors of this unique spirit to speak clearly without being covered by other flavors.

Choose glasses that are clean and free of any dish-detergent residue. Sherry or port glasses or small dessert-wine glasses are ideal, since they allow you to swirl the spirit before nosing and tasting, to release aromas and flavors. Some glassware manufacturers, such as Riedel, have special whisky glasses designed for single malts. You may want to invest in a set of these if you share your Scotch regularly with friends.

✳ A SCOTCH TASTING ✳

One very instructive way to appreciate the differences between blends, between the malts of various regions, or between malts within one region, is to hold a side-by-side Scotch tasting. For this, choose between four and eight blended Scotches and/or single malts. (More than eight will simply induce palate fatigue.)

Hold your tasting in a room that is free of cooking odors or other smells. Don't wear perfume or cologne or heavily scented deodorant, which will interfere with the aroma of the Scotch. Set up the table with one glass per Scotch per taster, and pour one ounce of Scotch into each glass, keeping the order the same for each taster. For more accuracy and fun, your tasting can be done "blind," that is, without the tasters knowing in advance which Scotch is in which glass.

First, hold each Scotch up against a white background (a sheet of white paper will work) and examine the color and clarity. The darkness of the whisky is a clue to its age, and to the type of wood in which it's been stored. Some whiskies aged in sherry wood (the Macallan, for example) pick up much more color than whiskies stored in bourbon casks. Swirl the whisky in the glass and look for the "legs" or "tears" that form against the side of the glass. The richest whiskies have the most noticeable tears.

Next, "nose" through each of the Scotches, to get an idea of their differing aromas. Do this before tasting any of the whiskies. The nose is extremely important in any beverage tasting, and Scotch is no exception. You'll find you won't need to stick your nose far into the glass; you can get a far better sense of the whisky's aroma by simply raising the glass slowly up to your nose until you begin to get a rich but not overpowering sense of aroma. Try adding a few drops of bottled water to the glass. This will release further components of the whisky's smell. (Do not use chlorinated tap water!) Give the glass a second pass under your nose and see how the aromas have become more complex.

Finally, taste. A small sip is plenty. Let the whisky coat your tongue and note whether it feels rough or smooth, overly hot or simply warming. Is it sweet or savory? Can you guess from the

Do-It-Yourself Blending

Whisky enthusiasts may wish to try their hand at Scotch blending, comparing their own blends with those available commercially. Unfortunately, since there are currently no Scotch single-grain whiskies on the American market to use as a base, you will have to start your blend by using an already-blended Scotch. Choose a relatively neutral one, such as Cutty Sark or J&B. Then add various single malts in higher and higher proportions until you find one that suits your palate. Some blends contain upward of thirty different malts. Adding an Islay malt, for example, will bring an aggressive note to your blend, while adding a Speyside will tone it down a bit. Your other option is to create a vatted malt: that is, a mixture made only of malt whiskies, with no grain whisky in the blend.

tones of seaweed, iodine, and brine whether this might be an Islay malt? Does it have the more floral delicacy of Speyside?

Everyone's taste is different, and there are whiskies to appeal to a wide variety of preferences. Discovering which ones are right for you can be a rewarding and educating experience.

Scotch-based cocktails are a delightful way to enjoy this smoky spirit. A blended Scotch is best suited for mixing.

Cheery Cherry

⅓ ounce Maraschino cherry juice
6 mint leaves
½ ounce vanilla liqueur
1 ounce Scotch

In a mixing glass, muddle mint and liqueur until the mint is somewhat bruised. Add Scotch, cherry juice, and a scoop of ice. Shake to combine. Strain into a chilled cocktail glass. Garnish with a mint leaf.

Highland Refresher

1 ounce Scotch
½ ounce Rose's lime juice
2 dashes bitters
3 ounces club soda

Combine Scotch, Rose's lime, and bitters in a shaker with a scoop of ice. Shake to mix. Strain into an ice-filled collins glass. Top off with club soda.

A SHORT LEXICON
✳ OF SCOTCH WHISKY TERMINOLOGY ✳

Bothy—an illegal still, usually portable, used by early whisky makers.

Burn—a fresh stream, used to provide water for a distillery.

Draff—the barley solids left behind after the mashing process, usually sold as cattle feed or fertilizer.

Dram—a small sip or draught of intoxicating spirit, synonymous with "nip."

Feints—the last part of the run from the spirits still, containing impurities; the feints are drawn off and later redistilled.

Foreshots—the first part of the run from the spirits still, containing impurities; the foreshots are diverted and redistilled.

Grist—milled malt, resembling coarse flour.

Grist mill—a mill that grinds malt into grist.

Kiln—oven for drying the malt; the chimneys are often shaped like pagodas.

Low wines—result of the first distillation, about 25 percent alcohol.

Malt—germinated barley; also used to refer to the whisky resulting from malt distillation.

Maltings—a facility for producing malt from raw barley.

Malting floor—broad concrete floor on which barley is germinated, resulting in malt.

Mash—liquid containing the fermentable sugars of the malt.

Mash tun—vessel, usually stainless steel or copper, in which the fermentable sugars in the grist are dissolved.

New make—clear, freshly made whisky, before aging in barrels; new make must be aged three years in Scotland before it can legally be called Scotch.

Peat—partially decomposed vegetable matter with a high carbon content, used as fuel.

Pot still—a copper vessel with a long, swanlike neck used to distill alcohol.

Piece—a single bed of barley during the malting process.

Shiel—a flat wooden shovel used to turn barley during malting.

Single malt—a malt whisky produced by one single distillery; not blended.

Sparge—mixture of grist and hot water that is pumped into the mash tun.

Spirit still—the second, smaller still in which the product of the first distillation is reprocessed for refinement; also called the low-wines still.

Spirits safe—chamber into which the new make is transferred and kept under lock and key.

Vatted malt—a blend of two or more malt whiskies, without the addition of grain whisky.

Wash—fermented barley liquid (really a sort of beer) that is distilled to produce whisky.

Washback—a stainless steel or wooden vat in which fermentation of the wash occurs.

Wash still—the first (larger) still in which the wash is transformed into alcohol.

Worm—coiled copper tube immersed in water that serves to condense alcohol vapors into liquid alcohol.

Worm tub—wooden vat that collects the freshly made whisky at the end of the worm.

Wort—the mash after transfer to the washback, ready for fermentation.

✳ BRAND PROFILES ✳

Blends

JOHNNIE WALKER. John Walker was just fifteen years old in 1820 when he took over his family's grocery store in Kilmarnock after his father's death. He became an expert at blending tea, the life's blood of the Victorian age. By 1850 John Walker had started offering his customers something a little stronger than Darjeeling. His new product, sourced from local distillers, was sold under the brand name Walker's Kilmarnock Whisky.

Not long afterward, John's son Alexander convinced his father to go into the wholesale business, with a whole range of spirits encompassing malts from Islay, Speyside, and Campbeltown as well as grain whisky. Alexander was a savvy marketer with a good sense of timing. He saw the need for a standard, easily recognized whisky brand, and created the blend that would eventually be named Johnnie Walker Black Label. He registered the distinctive slanted black label (nearly identical to the one still used) in 1867, and took out one of Britain's first trademarks on the name.

Alexander passed the business to his three sons. One of them, Alexander Walker, Jr., would create two new blends: Old Highlands with a white label, and Special Old Highlands with a red label, both less pricy siblings to the original black-labeled Extra Special Old Highlands blend. In 1893 Alexander also purchased the Cardhu malt distillery in Speyside. The Cardhu malt whisky would become the backbone for the Johnnie Walker blends.

In 1909 the company made yet another in a long line of savvy marketing decisions. Since customers usually asked for the Walker blends by the color of the label, the whiskies were officially renamed White Label (now defunct), Red Label, and Black Label. At the same time the distinctive "striding man" logo was first created, said to be a representation of John Walker. Even though it's become stylized over the years, the logo is still a charming image that suggests a brand that is striding confidently into the future.

By 1920 Johnnie Walker was available in 120 countries across the globe. The largest export market at the time was Australia, but that would soon change. Ironically, it was Prohibition in the United States that created an opportunity for the younger Alexander Walker (who by now had been given a knighthood) to ship massive quantities of Johnnie Walker to islands off the Canadian coast, from where they could be smuggled to speakeasies below the border. Alexander dryly referred to this in board meetings as "our special trade."

In 1925 the company became part of Distillers Company Limited consortium, the most powerful force in the Scotch whisky industry. (Through subsequent mergers and acquisitions, Johnnie Walker would become, along with J&B, one of the signature Scotch brands in the portfolio of the giant spirits company Diageo.) Alexander Walker retired in 1939, leaving behind notes for several experimental blends. One of these, a sweeter blend than either the Red or Black Labels, would finally be realized in 1995, when Johnnie Walker Gold Label was first brought to market. The Blue Label, a rare and pricy jewel in the Johnnie Walker crown, was created in 1992 and aims to replicate (or at least approach) John Walker's original blend. It contains a high percentage of Islay malts made by distilleries that John Walker originally bought from in the mid-nineteenth century. The Green Label Pure Malt is a vatted malt (a blend only of single malts); it has been mainly available in duty-free shops but is being introduced now to the American market.

In spite of its enormous global success, Johnnie Walker is still blended and bottled within a short distance of John Walker's original grocery store in Kilmarnock.

CUTTY SARK. Cutty Sark is a relatively recent creation. Its official birth was on March 20, 1923, when the partners of the highly respected London wine and spirits firm Berry Brothers & Rudd agreed to create a new Scotch blend. The firm had been in business since 1698 and was holder of warrants to supply the royal family. But, looking to the future, Francis Berry, the senior partner in the firm, believed that the time was ripe for a new, naturally colored blended whisky.

The story of this blend's name is quite interesting. Scottish artist James McBey attended the Berry Brothers & Rudd meeting and suggested that the new Scotch blend be named after a famous sailing ship, the *Cutty Sark*. Built in Dumbarton, Scotland, in 1869, the *Cutty Sark* had been the last of the nineteenth-century tea clippers, ships that raced to bring the season's first tea to Britain from China. After the Suez Canal opened, the tea cargo was taken over by steamships and the *Cutty Sark* became sorely dilapidated under Portuguese ownership.

But the ship was back in the news just as Berry Brothers & Rudd were contemplating their new Scotch: The *Cutty Sark* had just been repurchased by a Cornish sailor and had undergone a major restoration in 1922. The ship's name refers to Robert Burns's poem "Tam O'Shanter," in which Tam, a simple farmer, witnesses a beautiful young witch dancing only in her "cutty sark," her "short shirt." The ship had carried a metal emblem in the shape of a shirt attached to its mast. The artist McBey would also design the Cutty Sark label, with its representation of billowing, wind-filled sails. In tribute to the ship that gave the whisky its name, the company for many years sponsored the Cutty Sark Trophy in the international Tall Ships' Races.

Cutty Sark is made principally of delicate Speyside malts, matured in Oloroso sherry casks. The final blend is aged for a further six months to allow the whiskies to "marry." Cutty Sark is a wonderfully light and refreshing Scotch that is approachable on the rocks and equally at home in cocktails.

Single Malts

THE GLENLIVET. When the Excise Act of 1823 was passed, largely due to the lobbying efforts of the Fifth Duke of Gordon, taxes on Highlands whisky were lowered to encourage legal distilling. The duke was a large landholder in Speyside, and to prove that his theory was correct and that the Excise Act was justified, he wanted to create an exemplary legal distillery in the valley of the River Livet, an area whose illegal whiskies were already renowned and were even called for by King George VI on his visit to Scotland in 1822. The duke convinced his tenant George Smith, a farmer who was also one of around two hundred illegal distillers in the Glenlivet, to go legal. Smith took out his license in 1824 and set up operations at Upper Drummin farm. It was a daring move. "I was warned before I began by my civil neighbours," Smith later wrote, "that they meant to burn my new distillery to the ground and me in the heart of it."

But Smith survived. He produced around fifty gallons of whisky a week and by 1839 was making two hundred gallons a week.

Within a decade of the Excise Act, most of the illegal distillers had been closed down. Business was so good for Smith that in 1850 he built a second distillery at Delnabo. When fire destroyed the original Glenlivet distillery in 1858, Smith consolidated his operations at a new facility at Minmore, on land donated by the Duke of Gordon.

The fame of Smith's whisky and the glen of the Livet spread far and wide. Many other distilleries in the valley, and even some that were nowhere near it, began to cash in on its reputation by using the name Glenlivet as an appellation on their products. So widespread was the practice that wits referred to the valley as "the longest glen in Scotland." To protect his whisky's reputation, John Gordon Smith, George's son and successor, brought suit in the 1880s. The court decided that, while other distillers might call their whiskies Glenlivet, only the Smiths could use the definite article in front of their brand: The Glenlivet.

John Gordon Smith was succeeded in 1901 by his nephew, George Smith Grant. The distillery merged with Glen Grant in 1952 as Glenlivet and Glen Grant Distilleries, Ltd. The Canadian drinks firm Seagram acquired the company in 1977. Through the breakup of Seagram's wine and spirits division in 2001, The Glenlivet passed to its current owners, the French Pernod-Ricard group. The modern-day Glenlivet distillery is a large and rather industrial-looking operation but is on the same picturesque site in the Banffshire hills to which George Smith moved in 1858. The Glenlivet is one of only two distilleries remaining in the glen of the Livet. (The other is Braeval, nearly all of whose malts go into blends.) The historic Josie's Well provides the pure, clean water, which flows up from granite substrate and is rich in minerals. The distillery hosts more than two hundred thousand visitors per year.

BOWMORE. The wild, oceanic Inner Hebridean island of Islay could hardly be more different from the hilly Banffshire setting of Speyside, nor could the whiskies they produce be more different. Like other Islay distilleries, Bowmore is located on the sea, situated in the town of Bowmore, capital of Islay, on the inner curve of this crescent-shaped island. Some of Bowmore's original cellars are set below sea level, and the distillery wall can be lashed by five feet of water at high tide, factors that contribute to Bowmore's typical Islay sea-wrack and brine flavors. Loch Indaal, the inlet whose moody, tempestuous waves make this one of Scotland's most romantically situated distilleries, is a constant presence. This west-facing shore, however, is not as exposed to the ocean as the southern shore that is home to Islay's more pungent malts:

Laphroaig, Lagavulin, and Ardbeg. As might be expected on an island that is one-quarter covered in peat, Bowmore has its own peat bog. It's also one of the few distilleries to maintain its own malting floor, which produces about a third of its malt requirements. The water used at Bowmore rises through Islay's famous peat and travels from River Laggan to the distillery via a nine-mile-long watercourse.

Bowmore was founded in 1779, making it the oldest surviving distillery on Islay. We know that an Islay merchant named Simpson (or Simson, as some records say) applied for permission to build structures at the foot of Hill Street in 1776, one of which was converted to distilling three years later. In the late nineteenth century the distillery was expanded by James and William Mutter, heirs of a progressive farming family that had introduced scientific agricultural methods to Islay. The Mutter family sold the distillery to Bowmore Distillery Company in 1892. During World War II the buildings were converted into a coastal patrol base.

In 1963 Bowmore was purchased by the Glasgow spirits brokering firm of Stanley P. Morrison, creating Morrison Bowmore Distilleries, Inc. The Bowmore whiskies became favorite drams in Japan, and the Japanese Suntory corporation developed a long-term trading arrangement with Morrison Bowmore. Suntory even owned a share of the company, and eventually acquired Morrison Bowmore outright in 1994.

Bowmore is central to the town's social life, and the company even donated a warehouse that was converted into a community swimming pool, heated by the distillery's heat-recovery system. The Bowmore whiskies fall into the middle ground of Islay malts, neither overly assertive nor overly refined. They retain a certain mystique all their own that has made them some of the most desirable single malts in the world.

✳ IRISH WHISKEY ✳

The Bushmills distillery, in County Antrim on the northern coast of Ireland, lies just seventeen short miles from the Kintyre peninsula in Scotland. In fact, the Scotch-producing center of Campbeltown lies closer to Bushmills than it does to the closest Scotch distilleries on Islay. Legend has it that the Giant's Causeway, a massive outcropping of basaltic columns on the Ulster coast less than two miles from Bushmills, was the southern end of a mythic bridge that linked Ireland with Fingal's Cave on the Hebridean island of Staffa. In this case legend speaks of a deep link between Ireland and Scotland, one that is also seen in their whiskeys.

The Celtic monks who preserved and passed on the art of distillation (as well as much other culture) in the Middle Ages were most likely responsible for the foundations of both Irish and Scotch spirits. These friars could have learned the craft of making spirits from wine or beer while they were away on pilgrimages in Mediterranean countries in the twelfth century. While the spirits were originally concocted for medicinal purposes, it would have been difficult to ignore or suppress their more "recreational" aspects.

A statute dating to 1450 refers to "Irish wine, ale or other liquor," which scholars take to mean distilled spirits. Archaeologists have even unearthed such implements as an ancient worm (the coiled tube for condensing distillate) in their exploration of the Irish bogs. By 1556 the making of aqua vitae was widespread enough among innkeepers and private households that a license from the lord deputy was required. As in Scotland of the same period, illegal distilling was the norm, although there was no spirits industry as such. One particularly colorful historian, writing in 1633, noted that "the Irish eat raw meat which boyleth in their stomachs with aqua vitae, which they swill in after such a surfeite by quarts and pottles."

By the reign of Charles II, in the mid-seventeenth century, distillation had become enough of an industry in Ireland that the government began not only to require a license but also to charge duties on the product based on quantity. Excise commissioners were charged with overseeing the taxation system, and were empowered to hire "gaugers" to monitor legal stills and "searchers" to seek out illegal ones. In reality, the excisemen had little power to control illicit distilling.

The Irish gentry of the early eighteenth century actually preferred brandy from the Continent (Richard Hennessy, an Irishman, was among the first to trade in the spirits of cognac), while Irish aqua vitae was a drink of the lower classes. But a distinction soon began to be made between rural spirits called poitin (sometimes spelled poteen), consumed by the peasants, and "town whiskey," branded eaux-de-vie, which were at the time often flavored with roots or herbs. Irish spirits were even appreciated in the salons of Paris. By the end of the eighteenth century it's estimated that there were two thousand stills operating in Ireland.

The powerful Act of 1779 wreaked havoc on the fledgling Irish whiskey industry by setting a minimum revenue to be collected from each still. At first the minimum prescribed had little effect, but when the amount was raised the following year, small distillers were hit hard. One-quarter of all the legal distilleries in Ireland closed down or, more likely, went underground. By the end of the century only 15 percent of the country's licensed distillers remained in business. The minimum charge was raised periodically until 1823, when sweeping reforms were made in the excise laws, the net effect of which was to concentrate whiskey production in the hands a few established urban distillers, such as Dublin's John Jameson and John Power.

It's difficult to believe today, but at the beginning of the nineteenth century Irish spirits, made in pot stills, were actually more widely appreciated and highly esteemed than their Scotch counterparts. But due to several circumstances the Irish distillers were soon to fall from their position of superiority. When Aeneas Coffey, a former Irish exciseman, perfected the patent still, Irish distillers scoffed. They considered patent-still whiskey an inferior product, beneath their contempt. Scotch manufacturers in the Lowlands, on the other hand, embraced the patent still and were soon reaping the benefits of mass production that could furnish blended Scotch to worldwide markets. Then the Great Famine of 1845–49 decimated the Irish rural population, and the amount of grain available for distilling dwindled.

World War I took another toll on Irish distillers. Unlike patent-still operators in Scotland, who could convert their operations to producing high-strength industrial alcohol, the Irish pot-still manufacturers were out of luck. Another blow came when the Irish Free State declared its independence from England, in 1922. Parliament enacted a trade embargo on Irish products in England and the entire British Empire, effectively closing those markets to all Irish whiskies except those made in the six remaining counties of Ulster, which remained under British rule. American Prohibition cut off another important market, and by the time Prohibition ended, Canadian whisky and Scotch blended whisky flooded the American market. The Irish government closed down all distillation during World War II.

The future for Irish whiskey looked bleak. By the 1960s there were just four distilleries left in operation in all of Ireland: Bushmills, Jameson, Powers, and Cork Distillers. In 1966 the latter three of these decided to unite forces against the world's indifference. Merging as Irish Distillers, they consolidated their production into a state-of-the-art new plant at Midelton. Bushmills, the final holdout, was incorporated into the group in 1973 but retained its historic distillery in County Antrim. Now all the Irish whiskey in the world was being produced by just one company. The French-owned Pernod-Ricard group acquired Irish Distillers in 1988, after winning a corporate takeover battle with another large and hungry conglomerate, Grand Metropolitan.

With its corporate ownership settled, Irish whiskey seemed to be in a holding pattern, generating modest sales but little real excitement. Then, on Easter Sunday, 1989, a new distillery was born. The Cooley Distillery was started in County Louth by a group of entrepreneurs who hoped to revive competition and breathe new life into the Irish spirits industry. It was an underfunded enterprise that just barely got off the ground. When a buyout bid by Irish Distillers was nixed by the Irish government on grounds of unfair monopoly, Cooley managed to struggle by. Today Cooley's unique range of Irish whiskeys, made under the Tyrconnell, Kilbeggan, and Connemara brands, are symbols of the renaissance taking place in Irish whiskey.

✳ BRAND PROFILES ✳

Bushmills

Bushmills is located in Northern Ireland, in the town of the same name, in County Antrim, on the rugged and mystical northern coast. Having been granted its first license in 1608 by King James I, Bushmills is far and away the oldest existing legal distillery in the world. Just to put that date in perspective, Shakespeare had just finished writing *Macbeth* the previous year. The permit was issued to Sir Thomas Phillips, a local landowner, and the license is still filed in the Public Records Office of Ireland, but it is almost certain that illegal distilling was taking place here even centuries before Phillips obtained his license.

After a succession of owners, most of whom left little trace in the record, the distillery was acquired in 1884 by the Bushmills Old Distillery Company, headed by Samuel Boyd. The company later registered its name in slightly different format as the Old Bushmills Distillery Company. The Boyd family remained in charge until after World War II, when they sold the distillery to Great Universal Stores. After several more ownership changes, the company became part of Irish Distillers in 1973 and belongs to the Pernod-Ricard Group.

In the late nineteenth century Bushmills was a whiskey consumed mainly by locals, who preferred its malt-based whiskey to the grain whiskeys coming from other Irish distillers. In fact, Bushmills whiskeys are often grouped with Scotch because of the company's commitment to malt pot-still distillation (and probably because of its region's political status as a part of the United

Kingdom). The difference, however, is that Bushmills dries its malt in closed ovens, where it is protected from contact with smoke. The rise of interest in malt whiskeys has meant that Bushmills single malts now have a wide and loyal following. The company's Black Bush bottling is a blend of single malt and a small portion of grain whiskey.

Jameson

While Bushmills has stylistic ties with Scotch whisky, Jameson has close historical ties. John Jameson was a Scotsman who arrived in Ireland in the 1770s. He was related by marriage to the Haigs, a Lowlands family that was one of the most powerful forces in the Scotch whisky industry. At the time of Jameson's arrival on the Emerald Isle, the Steins, another well-known Lowlands family of distillers, were already active in Ireland. (Two generations earlier, Robert Stein had installed the first continuous still in Scotland, a design later perfected and patented by Aeneas Coffey.) John Stein owned a small distillery in Bow Street, Dublin, and Jameson's sons became involved in the business. Jameson's son, in fact, married Stein's daughter, further cementing their connection. Jameson took over Stein's Bow Street distillery operation in 1780. By 1810 the company was operating under the name John Jameson & Sons.

The Bow Street facility was enlarged at the end of the nineteenth century to accommodate increased demand for Jameson's whiskeys. At the height of its glory it had three hundred employees and reserves of two million gallons of whiskey maturing in bond. But Jameson insisted on producing pot-still whiskey, turning its back on the growing demand for lighter-style whiskeys in the progressive twentieth century. By mid-century times were bleak for the Irish whiskey industry, and in 1966 Jameson merged with Powers and Cork Distilleries to form Irish Distillers.

In 1971 the original Bow Street facility was closed down. Production was moved for several years to the Powers facility before the opening of Irish Distillers' ultra-modern plant at Midelton, County Cork, in 1975. Irish Distillers was acquired by the Pernod-Ricard Group in 1988.

Today the Jameson brand has been rethought and restyled for the contemporary market as a clean, stylish blend of malt and grain whiskeys. It is now the world's largest-selling Irish whiskey. The original Bow Street facility was reopened in November 1997 as a visitors' center known as the Old Jameson Distillery. It lies just a few minutes' walk from the River Liffey, immortalized by James Joyce in *Finnegans Wake*.

tasting notes

SINGLE-MALT SCOTCH

Highlands

The Dalmore 12 Year Old

$$ ★★★   Complex and vibrant with spicy, dried citrus tones and a zippy finish.

The Dalmore 21 Year Old

$$$ ★★★   Spicy and lush with lovely peat and honey.

Edradour 10 Year Old

$$ ★   Medium amber color; soapy, dense and sweet with leather, cereal, and malt.

Glen Garioch Aged 10 Years

$$ ★★★   Lush and toasty with sweet, mellow flavors of vanilla, spice, and lovely honey; long and balanced.

Glen Garioch Aged 15 Years

$$ ★★★   Lush and complex with sweet oak, lively caramel, and complex raspberry fruit; long and dense, balanced and lovely.

Glen Garioch Aged 21 Years

$$$ ★★★   Spicy and smooth with spice and sweet caramel; wood, honey, and ripe fruit; long and stylish.

Glengoyne 10 Year Old

$$ ★★★   Light amber color; smooth and clean with creamy, buttery flavors with no peat smoke; lush and elegant with a long, gentle finish.

Glengoyne 17 Year Old

$$$ ★★★   Lush and clean with smooth, floral, caramel, and spice; pure and lush with toffee, apple, sweetness, and cream.

Glengoyne Limited Edition Scottish Oak Wood Finish

$$$ ★★★★   Rich and spicy with a peppery finish; lush and creamy, smooth and sweet with long, elegant flavors and a ripe cinnamon finish.

Glenmorangie 10 Year Old

$$ ★★★   Smooth and mellow with creamy, nutty, smoky, toasted flavors; rich, long, and lovely.

Glenmorangie 12-Year-Old Port Wood Finish

$$ ★★★   Firm on the palate, offering spicy, toasty flavors and a suave finish.

Glenmorangie 12-Year-Old Sherry Wood Finish

$$ ★★★   Medium amber color; smooth and soft with nuts, spice, and oloroso sherry notes; mellow and moderately long.

Glenmorangie Vintage 1977

$$$ ★★★   Pale amber color; smooth and creamy with lovely smoky notes; toffee and vanilla with creamy, dense flavors.

Glenmorangie Côte de Nuits Finish

$$$$ ★★★★   Rich and smooth with lovely spice, fruit, and oak; long, complex, and exquisite. Limited supply.

Glenmorangie 1981 Sauternes Wood Finish

$$$$ ★★★   Medium amber color; rich and toasted with dense, spicy flavors; lush, complex, and long; fleshy and intense with a woody, deep finish.

Highland Park 18 Year Old

$$$ ★★★★   Herbal, deep, and complex, with striking notes of leather and peat; a superb malt from the northernmost Scottish distillery, located in the Orkney Islands.

Isle of Jura 15 Year Old

$$ ★★★   Light amber color; smooth and delicate with light smoke and lovely length; elegant and balanced.

MacTarnahan 15 Year Old

$$ ★★   Bottled for an Oregon brewery and importer by an undisclosed Highlands distillery; malty, smoky, and rich.

Oban 14 Year Old

$$ ★★   Almost Islay-like peat and smoke, with a viscous mouth feel and long finish.

Oban 32 Year Old

$$$$ ★★★   Hot and rich; dense and woody; dry, smoky, and lush.

Talisker 10 Year Old

$$ ★★★   Medium amber color; peat smoke nose; intense, toasty, spicy with mellow fruit and a slight saltiness; from the Isle of Skye.

Talisker 20 Year Old

$$$ ★★★   Oily and peaty, with intense spice and smoke; bottled at cask strength.

Talisker 25 Year Old

$$$ ★★★★   Oak smoke and ripe honey flavors; elegant peat and spice; concentrated and lush with intensity and long, rich flavors.

Speyside

While Speyside is technically part of the Highlands, its malts are often classified independently due to the high concentration of distilleries in this region.

Aberlour 10 Year Old

$$ ★★★   Medium amber color; soft peaty nose; lush and sweet with caramel and rich toffee flavors; long and balanced.

Aberlour A'bunadh

$$$ ★★   Cask-strength malt with creamy, sherry-laced tones.

Aberlour 21 Year Old

$$$ ★★★★   Medium amber color; fresh, nutty, sweet, and peated nose; spicy, sweet, and rich with long,

complex flavors of treacle and marshmallow with walnuts and spice.

The Balvenie Double Wood 12 Year Old
$$ ★★★   Smooth and smoky with lovely, creamy flavors; dense, long, and rich with complexity and depth.

The Balvenie Founder's Reserve 10 Year Old
$$ ★★★   Medium light amber color; smooth and lush with amazing complexity and depth; clover honey nose; sweet, rich, and malty.

The Balvenie Single Barrel 15 Year Old
$$$ ★★★   Ripe and rich with sweet vanilla, hazelnuts, and spice; long and luscious with lovely notes of coffee and honey.

The Balvenie 21 Year Old Port Wood
$$$ ★★★   Medium amber color; soft, dense, and lush with peach and beeswax on the nose; sweet and dense with toffee and vanilla flavors; exquisite.

The Balvenie 25 Year Old
$$$$ ★★★★   Medium dark amber color; lush caramel, peaty nose; rich and spicy with notes of chocolate, hazelnuts, honey, and cream; complex, dense, and gorgeous.

The Balvenie Vintage Cask 1966
$$$$ ★★★★   Smoky and toasted with lovely biscuit flavors and lush oak with lively spice and smooth fruit; a lovely, long finish.

Cragganmore 12 Year Old
$$ ★★★   Amber and gold color; dried apricots, honey, and smoke in the nose; creamy, lush, and bursting with sweet toffee and peat; long and luscious, elegant and superb.

Cragganmore 29 Year Old
$$$$ ★★★   Chocolate, composty, and rich with long, spicy flavors of varnish and spice.

Dalwhinnie 29 Year Old

$$$$ ★★★   Dense and grassy with spice, honey, and racy fruit; long and ripe, intense, peaty, and rich.

Glen Moray 16 Year Old

$$ ★★   pale amber color; light, creamy, and smooth with vanilla and apple fruit.

Glendronach 15 Year Old

$$ ★★★★   Rich and mouth filling with sherry highlights and some peat.

Glendronach Vintage 1968

$$$$ ★★★   Dark, dense, sweet, and lush with smoky honey and spice.

Glenfiddich Special Reserve 12 Year Old

$$ ★★   A lovely introduction to single malts; pure, clean, and fruity with a silky mouth feel and enticing flavors.

Glenfiddich 15-Year-Old Solera Reserve

$$$ ★★★   Fresh and clean with balance and finesse; nice notes of oak and hints of sweet sherry and spice.

Glenfiddich 18-Year-Old Ancient Reserve

$$$ ★★★   Lush and smoky with deep flavors of wood and spice; dense and smoky with clean, smooth, sweet sherry finish.

The Glenlivet 12 Year Old

$$ ★★★   Gorgeous nose of spice and wood; rich and full on the palate.

The Glenlivet 12-Year-Old French Oak Finish

$$ ★★★   Medium amber gold color; peaty, earthy nose; smooth and creamy with toasty oak and lush peaty flavors with notes of butterscotch, spice, and fruit; elegant.

The Glenlivet 18 Year Old

$$$ ★★★   Deep amber color; fruity, molasses, peat nose; smooth, round, and gently peaty with lovely

notes of pear, fruit, and spice; elegant, complex, and long.

The Glenlivet 21 Year Old

$$$ ★★★   Silky, stylish, and superb, revealing layers of fruit, malt, and smoke; a definitive Speyside malt.

The Glenlivet Cellar Collection 1983 French Oak Finish

$$$ ★★★   Dark amber color; rich and complex with lovely treacle and nuttiness, sweet and smooth with elegant toasty flavors and a long, dry finish.

The Glenrothes 1989

$$$ ★★★   Rich and smoky with light peatiness and spice; nutmeg, allspice, lush toffee, and creamy texture.

The Glenrothes 1979

$$$ ★★★★   Deep and rich with dark color and lovely tobacco, spice, chocolate, honey, and mature fruit; long and luscious.

The Macallan 12 Year Old

$$ ★★★   Rich, complex, and polished, with lovely floral and fruit flavors and sherry tones.

The Macallan Cask Strength

$$$ ★★★   Luscious and ripe, with sherry-cask notes and a sublime finish.

The Macallan 1861 Replica

$$$ ★★★   Distiller's recreation of an 1861 Macallan, down to the bottle and label; gorgeous peat and sherry notes.

The Macallan 25-Year-Old Anniversary Malt

$$$$ ★★★★   Deep, rich amber color; rich, nutty with pronounced sherry notes on the nose; creamy and lush with sherry sweetness and nuts; licorice, spice, and toast.

Strathisla 12 Year Old

$$ ★★★   Medium amber color; dense hazelnuts and smooth fruit; spice, oak, and a long creamy finish.

Tomintoul 16 Year Old

$$ ★★★   Medium amber color; fleshy nose; spicy and smooth with creamy texture and mellow, fruity flavors.

Islay

Ardbeg 10 Year Old Islay

$$ ★★★   Pale and smooth; ripe and smoky; spicy, clean, and long on the finish.

Ardbeg 17 Year Old Islay

$$$ ★★★   Pale amber color; smoky nose; dense, complex, and smoky with fruit, tar, and spice; long and silky.

Ardbeg 1978 Limited Edition

$$$ ★★★   Bright medium amber color; intensely smoky nose; poweful and briny with toasty, smoky flavors; long, dense, fleshy, and complex; not for the faint of heart.

Bowmore Legend

$$ ★★★   Light amber color; pungent with smooth, rich flavors of smoke and delicate perfume; bright and full with lovely length and spicy finish.

Bowmore Dawn

$$ ★★★   Dense, smoky nose; ripe, clean, sweet, and spicy with a balanced, complex finish.

Bowmore Dusk

$$ ★★★   Smooth, sweet, spicy, ripe, and rich; fleshy, long, and racy on the finish.

Bowmore 10 Year Old

$$ ★★★   Smoky, peaty nose; toasty and rich with notes of caramel and smoke; long and briny.

Bowmore 12 Year Old

$$ ★★★   Bright amber; pungent and rich with smoke and notes of salt, iodine, and lovely peatiness; lovely floral hints of heather and a touch of chocolate.

Bowmore 15 Year Old

$$ ★★★   Smooth and peaty with flesh, spice, caramel, and lovely fruit.

Bowmore 17 Year Old

$$$ ★★★   Rich and dense; spicy, smoky, long, and intense.

Bowmore 21 Year Old

$$$ ★★★★   Medium amber color; smooth and creamy with deep, rich, toasty, fleshy, smoky flavors and a lovely touch of sweetness on the finish; long and complex with lingering flavors of chocolate, almonds, and spice.

Bowmore 25 Year Old

$$$ ★★★★   Fleshy and honeyed; flavors of smoke and caramel; rich, smoky, and long on the finish.

Bowmore 30-Year-Old Ceramic

$$$$ ★★★★   Lush and fleshy; long and ripe; smoky and dense.

Bruichladdich The 10 Year Old (The Aperitif)

$$ ★★★   Pale amber color; lush and smooth with vanilla, smoke, honey, spice, and toasty oak.

Bruichladdich The 15 Year Old (The Stimulative)

$$$ ★★★   Medium amber color; lush and dense with lovely, smooth texture and smoky, rich flavors of almonds and sweet oak.

Bruichladdich The 17 Year Old (The Contemplative)

$$$ ★★★   Pale amber color; peaty, spicy, and complex with lovely toffee and briny flavors; long and lush.

Lagavulin 12 Year Old

$$$ ★★★   Smoky and lush with vanilla, spice, and briny peat; rich and assertive, long and intense; cask

strength (115.6 proof) and hence more expensive than the sixteen-year-old.

Lagavulin 16 Year Old
$$$ ★★★   Smoky and toasted with sweet notes and spice; hay and seaweed; smooth and rich.

Laphroaig 10 Year Old
$$ ★★★   Smooth and mellow with lovely, clean, but simple flavors; lush, smoky finish.

Laphroaig 30 Year Old
$$$$ ★★★★   Smooth and long, smoky, fleshy, clean, and intense; complex, layered, and long on the finish.

Lowlands

Auchentoshan 10 Year Old
$$ ★★   Smooth and lush with spice and rich, clean flavors; long and mellow, balanced and dense; like all Auchtentoshan malts, it's unpeated.

Auchentoshan Three Wood
$$$ ★★★   Dark amber color; lush and rich with lovely toast, spice, and caramelized fruit; long and intense.

Auchentoshan 21 Year Old
$$$ ★★★   Smooth and fruity with lush wood and spice; mellow, round, and long.

Auchentoshan 1966 37 Year Old
$$$ ★★★   Smooth and mellow with intense flavors of spice, caramel, and vanilla; available through selected retailer bottling programs only.

Glenkinchie 10 Year Old
$$ ★★   Delicate malt and herb flavors with a lingering finish.

Campbeltown

Springbank 10 Year Old
$$$ ★★★   Lowlands softness with distinctive sweet-savory notes with hints of brine; lovely.

Springbank 15 Year Old

$$$ ★★★   Deep, dusky, and rich with deep, rich, complex flavors and a sherry-laced finish.

BLENDED AND VATTED SCOTCH WHISKY

Ambassador 12 Year Old

$$ ★★   Stylish and refined; malty tones and a long finish.

Ambassador 25 Year Old

$$$ ★★★   Deep, satisfying, and complex with cereal flavors and gorgeous oak tones.

Ballantine's 12 Year Old

$$ ★★★   Silky and nicely balanced with soft, rounded wood tones.

Chivas Regal 12 Year Old

$$ ★★   Light, medium amber color; smooth and toasty with grass, fruit, and a touch of vanilla.

Chivas Regal 18 Year Old

$$$ ★★★   Medium amber color; smooth and lush with smoke, spice, soft fruits, and lovely caramel; elegant and generous.

Chivas Regal Royal Salute

$$$ ★★★   Medium amber color; smooth and balanced, clean, toasty, and long with straightforward flavors and a fresh finish.

Clan MacGregor

$ ★★   Smooth and spicy, mellow and balanced with clean, appealing flavors.

Cluny

$ ★   Smoky and peaty with some edgy, toasty flavors; clean but a bit short.

Dewar's 12 Year Old

$$ ★★   A classic blended Scotch with sweet and spicy flavors; smooth finish.

Glen Salen Pure Malt Scotch Whisky

$ ★★   Smoky, dense, and dry with intensity and depth; a vatted malt.

John Barr Gold Label

$ ★   A bargain among blended Scotches; smooth, balanced, and complex.

John Barr 17-Year-Old Premium Reserve

$$ ★★★   Smooth, spicy, balanced, rich, and mellow.

Johnnie Walker Black Label

$$ ★★   Medium amber color; smooth, aromatic, peaty on the nose; smooth, creamy, and fruity with leather and spice; complex and long.

Johnnie Walker Blue Label

$$$ ★★★   Smoky, dense, and peaty with long, husky flavors.

Johnnie Walker Gold Label

$$$ ★★★   Smooth and creamy; clear and racy; short but dense.

Johnnie Walker Red Label

$ ★★   Rounded and complex with nice peaty and brine character for a blend.

The Famous Grouse 12-Year-Old Gold Reserve

$$ ★   Feisty and vibrant with hints of exotic spice.

White Horse

$ ★   A classic blend with polish and sophistication; great as a mixer or served on the rocks.

White Horse 12-Year-Old Extra Fine

$$ ★   Older sibling of the standard White Horse blend, with more intensity, depth, and oakiness.

William Grant's Family Reserve

$ ★★   Smoky, spicy, and dense with caramel and balanced flavors; long and dry.

IRISH WHISKEY

Bushmills Original
$$ ★★   Smooth and mellow with soft caramel and spice; balanced and long.

Bushmills 10-Year-Old Single Malt
$$ ★★★   Smoky with smooth toasty flavors; long and dense on the finish.

Bushmills 16-Year- Old Single Malt
$$$ ★★★   Fleshy and fruity, with clean, lively flavors of spice.

Bushmills 21-Year-Old Madeira Cask
$$$ ★★★   Smoky and rich with spice, wood, and smooth texture; warm, complex, and toasty with a long, lush finish; classic.

Connemara Peated Single Malt
$$ ★★★   Smoky, peaty, and complex with long, delicious flavors.

Jameson Irish Whiskey
$$ ★   Clean, stylish, and assured, with mellow malt and grain tones and a nice finish.

Jameson 1780 12-Year-Old Reserve
$$ ★★   Fleshy, dense, fat, and ripe.

Jameson Master Selection 18 Years Old
$$$ ★★★   Malty and sweet with charming notes of cereal and toast.

Knappogue Castle Special Reserve 1993
$$ ★★★★   Silky, smooth, buttery, and nutty with dry, spicy notes; creamy, vanilla, caramel, and wood; long, rich, and delicious.

Midleton Very Rare 1994
$$$ ★★   Orange nose; spicy and dense, ripe and lush.

Redbreast 12-Year-Old Single Malt Irish Whiskey
$$ ★★   Fleshy, dense, spicy, long, and ripe.

Tullamore Dew 12-Year-Old Blended Irish Whiskey
$$ ★★★   Orange on the nose with creamy, lush, sweet orange and spice; clean, lovely finish.

Tyrconnell Single Malt Irish Whiskey
$$ ★★   Smooth and lush with grass, caramel, and spice; racy and balanced.

north american whiskey

✳ BOURBON ✳

Officially recognized by an enthusiastic Congress in 1964 as a "distinctive product of the United States," bourbon came of age as the country matured. With roots sunk deep in rebellion, uprising, and plain old American gumption, this proud native spirit can be traced back to the early 1700s.

✳ WHAT IS BOURBON? ✳

To be considered bourbon, the whiskey must be made in the United States. It must be composed of at least 51 percent corn, though many types of bourbon contain quite a bit more. Bourbon must be aged for a minimum of two years in new, charred American white oak barrels. As no artificial coloring may be added to the spirit, this aging is responsible for the deep, amber color of bourbon.

Though bourbon takes its name from Bourbon County, Kentucky, it does not necessarily have to be made in Kentucky to be called bourbon. In fact, no bourbon is actually made in Bourbon County today.

But just as it's been said that Kentucky would not be Kentucky without bourbon, bourbon would not be bourbon without Kentucky. The Bluegrass State, a granite region, is extremely well suited to the bourbon industry. The soil is rich in phosphates, which make it suitable for growing all types of grain, and the river water is filled with calcium and is very pure. The state's hot summers and cold winters are ideal for aging whiskey in casks. And Kentucky's forests of oak provide the wood for the casks.

Once known familiarly as "red likker," bourbon was originally made either in a pot still or by "running it on the log." In the latter method, the halves of a split log would be hollowed out, bound together, and filled with fermented mash. A lid on the top of the log had a tube that would carry the vapors to the condenser. Crude, but effective. This type of still was used for primary distillation only. Before being bottled, the spirit would be redistilled using a pot still. The final product of this method was referred to as "log and copper whiskey."

After distillation the spirit is aged for a minimum of two years in charred, new oak barrels. The first person to age bourbon was Dr. James Crow, a Scot, who also perfected the sour-mash method of whiskey making. No one knows exactly why the barrels began to be charred. One theory is that when the barrel staves were toasted over a fire for bending, the cooper got a bit overzealous and charred them. Another theory postulates that the barrels were charred to rid them of the taste and smell of whatever they previously held. Whatever the reason, the charred oak barrels seemed to become the norm sometime around the mid-1800s, when we see the first references to "red liquor." As the whiskey is clear following distillation, this reddish color can only be the result of aging in charred oak. Each distiller can choose the amount of char that the cooper puts on his barrels. The rating system starts at one and ends at the highest level of four. Some distillers claim that more char means more character.

All straight bourbons are sour-mash whiskeys, which means that a portion of the residue from one batch is used to start the next. The sour-mash process is quite similar to the process used in the baking of sourdough bread. Dr. Crow began experimenting with sour mash around 1823. His whiskeys, Old Crow and Old Pepper, were very popular during the Civil War. As a scientist, Dr. Crow was very careful with his process and documented his use of sour mash, charred oak, and aging. It is possible that Dr. Crow invented bourbon sometime between 1823 and 1845, but there are enough other contenders for the title of inventor of bourbon to get you into a dozen Kentucky bar fights. Whether or not he can be credited with the first bourbon, Dr. Crow's sour-mash process is still used today by distillers who use the "center cut" of the distillate for barreling and return the "end of the run" to the barrel for the next batch.

The mash itself is a combination of corn and another grain. Though required by law to use at least 51 percent corn, most distillers use somewhere around 70 percent, with the remaining mixture (called the small grains) a combination of malted barley and, most often, rye or wheat. Whiskeys made with rye are often spicier than those made with wheat, which makes a bit smoother whiskey. Those whiskeys made with wheat rather than rye are often referred to as "wheated bottlings." Each distiller's recipe, or mash bill, varies slightly and contributes to the unique quality of the individual spirit.

Yeast also contributes to the specialized taste of each spirit. Many distillers cultivate their own strain of yeast on the premises. At the Heaven Hill, Maker's Mark, and Jim Beam distilleries, hops are added to the cooked mixture of grains in which the yeast grows. Old Forester and Wild Turkey use lactic bacteria to add a sour tang to their sweet yeast mashes.

The last component of bourbon is the water. Whether it's pure spring water filtered by the limestone below the soil of Kentucky, treated river water, or tap water, it is as important to the final taste of the red liquor as the corn.

To make bourbon, grains are cooked in a mash tub and transferred to a fermenter. The yeast is added to the mash, where it acts on the fermentable sugars and converts them into beverage alcohol, carbon dioxide, and heat. At this point the "back-set," or residue from a previous batch, is added. This contributes some of the qualities of the previous batch to the current batch and helps the distillery maintain a consistent flavor. The mash is then allowed to ferment for three or four days until the alcohol level has reached about 8 percent. At this point it is called "distiller's beer." This beer is added to a still, where it is distilled into what is referred to as "low wines" or "singlings." At this point the mixture is still low in alcohol, so it must be redistilled. This second distillation process yields what are called "high wines" or "doublings." These high wines are put in charred oak barrels and left to mature.

The aging process adds a great deal to the final taste of the whiskey. Much depends on the placement of the barrels and the conditions in the aging facility. It is possible that two barrels from the same distillate, aged in the same facility, can turn out tasting entirely different simply because they are kept in different areas of the aging house. These facilities are built from metal, brick, or wood and are completely unheated. In the warm summers the whiskey on the upper levels of these structures ages much more quickly than the whiskey on the lower levels. While some distillers rotate the barrels in their storage facilities to achieve a consistent flavor, most distillers avoid this costly proposition by simply marrying whiskeys from different areas to create their end product. In this way, different types or profiles of bourbon can be created from what started out as the same whiskey.

Following the aging process, most bourbons are filtered. The only exception to this rule is Booker's Bourbon, which is bottled unfiltered by the Jim Bean Distilleries. Various methods of filtration are used. Some bourbons are filtered through activated charcoal, others refiltered at room temperature and then chilled. The main reason for filtration is to keep the whiskey from developing what is known as a "chill haze," a cloudiness that can be offputting to the consumer.

In the early days there was simply straight whiskey, but modern drinkers demand better treatment. As a result of the popularity surge of single-malt Scotch, bourbon makers began to produce premium spirits. Today you can find bourbon labeled "single barrel," which means that it is the product of one barrel of whiskey. This barrel is carefully selected from a specific area in the aging facility, and the barrel number is generally noted on the label. This type of bourbon will vary slightly from bottle to bottle, but the distiller tries to choose barrels that have matured in similar ways so as to keep the flavor consistent.

"Small batch" is another term you will hear relating to bourbon. This does not mean that the bourbon is made in small batches, but instead refers to the distillers' practice of marrying several exceptional barrels to create a particularly delicious end result. The barrels in small-batch bourbon often come from different areas in the aging facility, each bringing slightly different qualities to the mix. In small-batch bourbon, the sum is definitely greater than its parts. "Vintage bourbon" is the term used to describe bourbon that has been marked with the date of its distillation or bottling. I encourage you to explore these specialty bourbons, savor their differences, and enjoy their quality.

✳ A TRUE AMERICAN SPIRIT ✳

As befits a spirit of the American melting pot, bourbon was the brainchild of the Scotch-Irish who emigrated from Ulster. On the run from poverty, religious persecution, and famine, these settlers sought a better life in the New World. By 1776 more than 250,000 of them had come to America from Northern Ireland. They moved first to Pennsylvania, Maryland, and Virginia, where they planted easy-to-grow crops such as corn, rye, and barley and began to distill the first truly American whiskey from these grains. In addition to grains, the early distillers also used fruits such as apples as a base for spirits.

The rough new spirits began to pass for a new frontier currency. This make-it-yourself, multipurpose whiskey was traded to the Indians for furs, land, and food. It was used by politicians to buy votes and given to soldiers as part of their rations. Carpenters who were paid in whiskey built many of the military's forts and camps.

In 1777, two years into the Revolutionary War, so great was the fledgling country's dependence on whiskey that George Washington suggested that public distilleries be built throughout the states. The nation's first president, Washington was also one of the country's first distillers. He was known for his fine rum and later for rye whiskey. After his death it was found that he had more than 150 gallons of whiskey in storage. After all, Mount Vernon can get pretty cold in the winter.

The Revolutionary War separated many of the settlers from their homes to fight against the British. In 1781, at the end of the lengthy war, those still standing returned to their farms and their stills to enjoy their newly won liberty over a dram of whiskey. Unfortunately, they were about to become the victims of new oppressors. The long war had left the treasury of the new nation nearly empty, and so, in an effort to refill the nation's coffers, treasurer Alexander Hamilton proposed an Excise Tax on Spirituous Liquors. It was deemed that these taxes would be placed on all makers of distilled spirits, whether they were for commercial or personal consumption.

✳ THE WHISKEY REBELLION ✳

Many of the Scotch-Irish had come to America to escape the punitive taxes on distilleries in their homeland, and they were outraged by these new imposts. Further, the settlers in the backwoods of Pennsylvania saw little direct government aid and reasoned that a distant government that didn't provide roads or protection from Indian raids had no right to require payments.

Whiskey was the main medium of exchange in these small communities. Residents accustomed to trading spirits for food, clothing, land, and livestock were outraged by the federal government's incursion into their daily lives. They took drastic action to express their displeasure. There were countless incidents in which tax collectors were threatened and intimidated. In 1786, for example, the unfortunate excise officer William Graham came to Washington County, Pennsylvania, to tax the distillers. Bad idea. He was tarred and feathered, had half his head shaved, and finally was forced to drink the local whiskey, which may have been the cruelest punishment of all. He returned to his superiors frightened, embarrassed, but most of all glad to be alive.

These small uprisings continued for more than six years and grew in intensity, probably often fueled by the same whiskey that was at issue. Finally the western Pennsylvanians mounted an insurrection. They marched seven thousand strong to Pittsburgh where they were met by town officials who managed to placate them by promising to get rid of the region's senior excise officer and by plying them with food and, yes, whiskey. Though this was a small victory for the government, the settlers continued to rebel.

By 1792 the government reduced the onerous taxes, and in the same year Kentucky, destined to become synonymous with American whiskey, became the fifteenth state in the Union. Despite a reduction in tariffs, distillers continued to rebel against government rule. As more tax agents were terrorized, President Washington decided to quash the rebellion once and for all. He accused the distillers of "inflicting cruel and humiliating punishments upon private citizens for . . . appearing to be friends of the law." He even accused some whiskey makers of treason. In 1794 Washington sent out over twelve thousand militiamen. It was one of the first instances of federal government overkill, but this impressive show of force did put the rebels to rout. Thankfully, the incident resulted in no bloodshed.

Following the military showdown, pardons were offered to anyone who agreed to comply with the law. Those who refused had their property plundered. Some were bullwhipped publicly before being taken to collection centers to settle their debts. Eventually all the distillers gave in to Washington. The Whiskey Rebellion was over. Surprisingly, there were only a handful of deaths in those six years of fierce unrest.

✳ THE MOVE WESTWARD ✳

Many of the rebellious farmers decided to pack their families—and their stills—into wagons and move to areas that were less accessible to the hated "revenuers." They left the friendly valleys of the Ohio, Monongahela, and Allegheny Rivers and trekked more than four hundred miles westward to settle in the virgin lands of Bourbon County. This vast and unspoiled region eventually became the north central part of Kentucky.

The migrants got land in the burgeoning Bluegrass State in exchange for the promise to build a cabin and grow corn, a deal based on previous Virginia legislation known as the "corn patch and cabin rights" law. By the mid-1790s a newly established cottage distilling industry was flourishing. All that was distilled was corn.

It was during this time that many of Kentucky's first distilleries appeared. General James Wilkinson built a distillery in Harrodsburg and is often thought of as the first distiller of bourbon. Wattie Boone, a relative of legendary woodsman Daniel Boone, began to make whiskey in Nelson County (now, appropriately, the home of country music great Willie Nelson's Whiskey River Bourbon). Evan Williams built the first commercial distillery in Louisville.

Many of the most familiar names in bourbon soon arrived on the scene: the Boehms of Jim Beam, the Samuels of Maker's Mark, the Browns of Brown-Forman, the Peppers, the Wellers, the Haydens, and the Dants. Reverend Elijah Craig, a legendary Kentucky bourbon distiller, began distilling around 1789. (Later this Baptist minister's name would be summoned in the whiskey industry's fight against the growing temperance movement and, ineffectively, against Prohibition.) In Davidson County alone, in an area with a population of just over four thousand, more than sixty-one stills were in operation. Kentucky was awash in whiskey.

✳ THE FIRST BOURBON APPEARS ✳

By the late 1700s Kentuckians were busy shipping whiskey down the Ohio and Mississippi rivers to thirsty New Orleans. The crates, shipped out of Limestone, a riverside port in Bourbon County, were stamped "Bourbon." As a result, the spirit began to be known as bourbon whiskey and, finally, simply bourbon. The name would naturally have appealed to French-speaking Louisianans.

In 1803 whiskey got a huge boost in popularity with the Louisiana Purchase. As the United States doubled in size with the stroke of Thomas Jefferson's pen, more and more people began moving west. The farther they moved from the Eastern seaboard, the more expensive it became to distill rum from imported molasses. They turned instead to the more plentiful and inexpensive local bourbons.

During his presidency from 1801 to 1809, Jefferson also contributed to an increase in bourbon production by repealing the tax that had started the Whiskey Rebellion in the first place. Though the refined Jefferson was more a wine connoisseur than a whiskey drinker, distillers of the hard stuff found a soft spot in their hearts for this openminded president. Whiskey would not be taxed again until 1862.

The onset of the Industrial Revolution made it easier to ship bourbon out of Kentucky. New markets were opened as steamboats traveled up the Mississippi River to new population centers. More than two thousand barrels were shipped out in 1820. Bourbon also traveled by rail. Railroad track length grew from fifty miles in 1830 to more than nine thousand miles in 1850, and wherever the iron horse went, there went bourbon.

✳ A DARK CLOUD LOOMS ✳

With no taxes, plentiful shipping options, little competition from other spirits, and a vast public appreciation of the spirit, it seemed whiskey distillers were poised for a lifetime of success. What they could not have anticipated was the temperance movement.

Whiskey's greatest foe, the American Temperance Society, was founded in straitlaced Boston in 1826. The society rapidly expanded, taking hold in cities and rural areas across the nation. Blaming liquor for loose morals, family dissolution, unemployment, and just about every other social ill, the society was bound and determined to banish hard alcohol. While public allegiance to the temperance movement was not yet total, the popularity of whiskey was beginning to wane. The New York branch of the society allowed its members to swear off liquor while still drinking beer and wine. Those who swore off everything were marked in the register with a "T" for total: the first teetotalers.

The beginning of the Civil War in 1861 also contributed to a decline in whiskey sales. The war tore whiskey-making states apart. Pennsylvania took an antislavery stand, while Kentucky and Maryland were proslavery states. Though Kentucky was linked politically with the Union, the bourbon industry depended on Southern demand for whiskey, and many Kentucky distillers served on the Confederate side. In 1862 President Lincoln reintroduced the excise tax on distilleries to help pay for the war. Following the war's end in 1865, there were fewer distilleries and the demand for whiskey was ebbing.

In the years between the end of the Civil War and the turn of the century, bourbon makers saw little of their early success. By the time Prohibition went into effect in 1920, brown spirits were considered completely passé. Gin rose to popularity based partly on the fact that with the right ingredients, almost anyone could make it in his own bathtub.

By the end of Prohibition in 1933, whiskey supplies were at an all-time low. Though there was quite a bit of whiskey stored during the ban, eager Americans made quick work of the stash as they celebrated their freedom to drink. As American whiskey distillers struggled to meet the new demand, the Canadians and Scots seized upon the opportunity to export their vast stores of whiskey to the United States. For a period after the end of Prohibition, all American whiskey was "blended" with neutral spirits in an effort to stretch the good stuff. By the time American distilleries had gotten back on their feet, the public had grown used to the lighter taste of blended whiskey and didn't want to go back.

After Prohibition fewer distilleries remained in business, though many of those that survived remain in operation today. The James B. Distilling Company is now Jim Beam Brands. National Distillers Products Company, formed in the 1920s, owned Wathen Distillery, which produces Old Grand-Dad, Old Taylor, and Old Crow. The Overholt Distillery continues to produce Old Overholt. The George T. Stagg Distillery went on to become Ancient Age and currently produces a number of very good single-barrel bourbons.

These steadfast distilleries continued to produce bourbon through the next several decades despite the fact that public demand was at an all-time low. With the onset of World War II the distilleries were enlisted to produce industrial alcohol, needed to manufacture rubber, antifreeze, ether, and rayon for parachutes. It took one gallon of alcohol to make sixty-four hand grenades and more than twenty-three gallons to manufacture a Jeep. With the distilleries focusing their attentions on the war effort, whiskey supplies dwindled again. Without plentiful whiskey, Americans turned to rum, a spirit that was cheaper than whiskey and, because it was made in the Caribbean, not subject to American whiskey rationing. Though the whiskey industry contributed a great deal to the war effort, the public showed little gratitude. When the war ended, the popularity of whiskey was at an all-time low. It would be another forty years before straight whiskey would return to public favor.

Following the extremely liquid decades of the sixties and seventies, the trend turned to moderation in the 1980s. Spurred by a desire to drink less, Americans began to turn to a better quality of drink. After two decades of quaffing jug wine, wine drinkers developed a taste for fine wine. This, in turn, led to an interest in high-quality spirits. In the mid-eighties a marked rise in the popularity of single-malt Scotch opened the door for high-end bourbon. American whiskey distillers met the demand and coined new terms such as "small batch" and "single barrel" in a successful effort to cash in on the snob appeal of Scotch.

Today the hard-boiled habit of drinking straight whiskey is making a definite comeback. In upscale bars it's not uncommon to find vast whiskey-tasting menus filled with any number of delicious bourbons waiting to tempt the budding connoisseur. Look at the list and you'll recognize some familiar names. Some of the very first bourbon makers continue to supply this truly American spirit. Though these new Bourbons are probably quite a bit smoother, tastier, and more complex than those original barrels that floated down the Mississippi, I like to think that when I sip a small-batch bourbon over ice, I'm still savoring a pure taste of freedom.

✳ TASTING BOURBON ✳

Just like the American people, bourbons belong to a single category of spirit but their individual characters differ greatly. The "red likker" adopts myriad styles from lean and light to bold and deep. There are certain whiskeys that are ideally suited to a brandy snifter, while others blend quite nicely into a Manhattan or mint julep. There are those bourbons that call out for ice and a bit of pure Kentucky "branch water," and others that are meant to be savored alone at room temperature. When tasting all bourbons, I recommend that you start with the spirit neat and later add water or ice to your liking. Often a bit of water or ice will open up new flavors and expand the whiskey, but it is important to make your first taste the unadulterated straight spirit.

Before we get into the particulars of setting up a tasting, you should know that while there is a lexicon of standard bourbon descriptors, you should not be afraid to make up a few of your own. The experts will tell you that bourbon tastes of banana, burnt sugar, caramel, or hazelnut. They will ask that you look for hints of leather, new-mown hay, smoke, or tar. In books, the spirit is often described as tasting of violets, vanilla, walnuts, or earth. You are of course entitled to your own opinion. If a particular bourbon tastes to you like the smell of those cork-sided coasters that belonged to your great-aunt Gertrude, by all means go ahead and say so. Tasting is, ultimately, a most personal experience.

Setting up a bourbon tasting is a delightful way to pass an evening with friends. Bourbon is a complex and interesting spirit and lends itself well to conversation. Invite a few people over to explore the nuances of a few bottles of premium spirit. When putting together a tasting, there are a few points to remember. It's nice to have a white tablecloth so that you can see the color of the bourbon, which ranges from a light amber to a deep red. You'll

want to rid the room of anything aromatic such as candles or flowers (and perhaps your dog), as these might interfere with your
ability to smell the spirit. Also encourage guests to eschew perfume or cologne. When tasting, it's good to have at least three different bottles of whiskey and generally no more than six. Set out
plates of bread or crackers to cleanse the palate between
whiskeys. A jug of chilled water can be used to dilute the bourbon,
allowing complex flavors to open up.

When selecting bottles for your tasting, you might want to
choose a set of similar bourbons such as wheated bourbons. You
could also try a few wheated bourbons against those made with
rye. Several of the larger distilleries turn out a number of premium
spirits, which differ greatly from one another. A good tasting menu
might include a selection of small-batch bourbons from the Jim
Beam Distilleries. Taste their unfiltered Booker's Bourbon against
the smoother, sweeter Knob Creek.

Begin the tasting by using your nose. Gently breathe in the
aroma of the spirit, keeping your nose above the rim of the glass.
You may find vanilla, hints of herb, and often floral qualities.
Lighter bourbons tend to tickle the nose with a drift of clover or
grass, while heavier bourbons pack a punch of caramel, intense
citrus, or berry fruit. If you are using the correct type of tasting
glass, one that is narrower at the rim than at the base, the aromas
will be concentrated and will float up to greet you.

Next, sip. Look for the same flavors on the tongue that wel-
comed your nose. You may find caramel, sugar, grass, berry fruit,
and walnut. Also pay attention to the feel of the whiskey in your
mouth. Test for weight and body or mouth feel. Feel the body of
the whiskey as it coats your palate.

When you swallow, the whiskey should not burn your throat,
but rather warm it. This last sensation, which we refer to as the
finish, is one of lingering heat. Savor any spiciness or sweetness
left in your mouth and prepare for the next sip.

While many types of bourbon are best on their own, this quintessentially American spirit finds itself easily at home in that
American invention, the cocktail. One traditional bourbon cocktail, the Manhattan, was first introduced in the 1870s at a ban-
quet hosted by Lady Jenny Churchill at New York's Manhattan
Club. There are those who believe that the Manhattan was ultimately responsible for the creation of the dry martini. More
famously, the mint julep is traditionally drunk to celebrate the
annual running of the Kentucky Derby and is also enjoyed on
June 1 by students at Oxford University, who continue to celebrate the 1874 visit of South Carolinian William Heyward Trapier.

The nineteenth-century distiller Colonel James E. Pepper brought the old-fashioned to New York. Muddle an orange slice, a cherry, sugar, bitters, and water and then add ice and bourbon to make this refreshing cocktail.

✳ THE MAJOR KENTUCKY DISTILLERIES ✳

Before Prohibition there were hundreds of distilleries in Kentucky; now there remain only a handful. They are close together and bordered by Louisville, Bardstown, and the state capital, Frankfort. Be aware that a particular bourbon brand name is not necessarily named for the distillery where it is made. In fact, several different bourbon brands are produced at the same distilleries.

Jim Beam Distilleries

The Jim Beam Distilleries, which celebrated two hundred years of bourbon production in 1995, is the maker of probably the best-known bourbon in the world. The Beams have been known in Kentucky since before the Civil War. Their first brand, Old Tub, was sold nationwide. The first of the line to set foot in the Bluegrass State was Jacob Boehm, who changed his surname to the easier-to-pronounce Beam after emigrating from Germany in 1752. He began to sell whiskey in 1795.

Jacob fathered several sons who continued in the bourbon business. One of Beam's sons, John, founded the Early Times Distillery. Another, David, eventually took over his father's distillery. David had three children, one of which was James Beauregard Beam. Known as Jim by his friends, he took over the distillery in 1892, and it became the Beam & Hart Old Tub Distillery. The company changed hands in the 1940s when Harry Blum, a Chicago liquor merchant, took over, and again in 1967 when it was purchased by American Brands. No matter who actually owns the company, the Beam family remains in charge of making whiskey. Carl Beam (Jim's nephew) and his son Baker were master distillers for Beam, and Jim's grandson, Booker Noe, is still master distiller emeritus.

The Jim Beam Distilleries' main line of bourbon includes Jim Beam, four years old, which bears Jim Beam's autograph and the slogan "None genuine without my signature." Beam's Choice is a spicy, well-priced bourbon, ideal for mixing. Beam's Black Label is aged a bit longer, resulting in a smoother, richer flavor. Jim Beam Black is an ideal sipping whiskey and also makes an elegant addition to your favorite cocktail.

In addition to the aforementioned main line of bourbons, a number of small-batch bourbons are released under the Beam label. These include Booker's, the first small-batch bourbon on the market. Released in 1989, Booker's is named for Jim Beam's grandson, master distiller emeritus Booker Noe. It is distinguished from most other bourbons by the fact that it's unfiltered and bottled at barrel proof, which means it is bottled directly from a variety of barrels without the addition of water to lower the proof, which is generally somewhere around 126. Booker's is allowed to age for six to eight years and is always selected by Booker Noe himself. Booker's, with its spicy flavor and huge body, is great over ice and especially delightful when cut with a bit of spring water.

Jim Beam Distilleries introduced three other small-batch bourbons in 1992.

Baker's, named for retired master distiller Baker Beam, is the distilled result of six generations of bourbon skill. The label suggests that the bourbon be savored over ice. It's a fruity whiskey with a nice spicy finish and is well suited to ice and even to a bit of club soda.

Basil Hayden's was named for "Old Grand-Dad" Basil Hayden, a famed Kentucky whiskey maker. Mr. Hayden was an eighteenth-century distiller whose grandson started the original Old Grand-Dad Distillery. The distillery was closed during Prohibition, but mysteriously the whiskey seemed to circulate throughout the era, and once Prohibition was ended Old Grand-Dad was almost immediately back on the market. Currently Old Grand-Dad is also bottled by the Jim Beam Distilleries, making Basil Hayden, "Old Grand-Dad" himself, lucky enough to be the namesake of two fine whiskeys.

Knob Creek is named for the site of one of Abraham Lincoln's childhood homes. This smooth and delightfully sweet whiskey is aged nine years. The label is designed to look as if it rolled off a hand press and reads "Like the Bourbon bearing its name, there's not much of Knob Creek, but what there is rewards your finding it." Savor Knob Creek over ice or let it spice up a Manhattan.

The Wild Turkey Distillery

Originally known as the Old Moore Distillery, the Wild Turkey Distillery is situated in Lawrenceburg, Kentucky. It was purchased in 1905 by the Ripy brothers, whose father, Thomas B. Ripy, was a Kentucky distiller in 1869. Following the repeal of Prohibition, the Ripy brothers reopened the plant.

In 1940 distillery executive Thomas McCarthy brought a private supply of whiskey on a wild turkey hunt. His friends liked the whiskey so much, they asked him the next year to bring along some of that "Wild Turkey" whiskey. He honored their loyalty and good taste by changing the name of the whiskey. In 1970 Austin, Nichols & Company purchased the plant, later partnering with the Pernod-Ricard Group in 1980. Jimmy Russell, the current master distiller at Wild Turkey, joined the distillery in 1954 and was trained by a member of the Ripy family. The Wild Turkey Distillery uses a mash bill that includes 75 percent corn along with 13 percent rye. It is the rye that gives Wild Turkey a complex, peppery flavor.

The Wild Turkey Distilleries bottle a number of fine bourbons. Among them are Wild Turkey Bourbon, Wild Turkey Old No. 8 Brand, Wild Turkey 12 Years Old, and the fine Wild Turkey Rare Breed, which is rich and round and ideally savored neat. Rare Breed is a "barrel-proof" whiskey. This bourbon is a marriage of the Wild Turkey six-, eight-, and twelve-year-old stocks. Wild Turkey Kentucky Spirit is the distillery's single-barrel brand and is packaged in limited quantities.

Maker's Mark Distillery

Situated in Loretto, Kentucky, Maker's Mark Distillery is home of the most popular bourbon in Kentucky. The distillery is owned by Hiram Walker & Sons, but production remains in the hands of Bill Samuels, Jr., who is descended from Robert Samuels, one of the earliest Kentucky bourbon makers. The Samuels family has been making bourbon since 1780 and established the first commercial distillery in 1844. This distillery was run by Robert's son William and later by William's son Leslie Samuels. Following Prohibition Leslie built a new plant in Deatsville and reopened as the T. W. Samuels Distillery. Eventually Leslie's son, T. William Samuels, took over the operation and ran the distillery until 1943, when the family sold the plant and dropped out of the whiskey business.

In 1953 T. William Samuels decided to get back into the bourbon business. According to family lore, he sought to create a finer, smoother product than the earlier Samuels family whiskeys. To this end he burned the original family recipe, which had a heavy percentage of rye, and began to experiment with wheat. Lacking a distillery, he ran tests by baking bread with the wheat rather than distilling it, finally coming up with the ideal flavor combination of wheat and corn. Satisfied with his new recipe, T. William Samuels bought the distillery that now houses Maker's Mark and translated his bread recipe into a terrific bourbon. After a careful restoration, the plant became a National Historic Landmark.

Originally known as the Star Hill Distillery, the Maker's Mark Distillery owes its name to T. William's wife, Margie. An avid pewter collector, she noticed that every piece in her collection bore a "maker's mark," which signified that the maker was proud enough to put his name on it. The distinctive bottles sealed with red wax were inspired by her collection of old cognac bottles.

Today the whiskey continues to be made using T. William's original 1953 recipe. Maker's Mark is made in small batches of fewer than nineteen barrels (one thousand gallons) and each bottle is hand-dipped in red wax. This smooth, wheated boubon is a lovely sipping whiskey and makes a delightful addition to the traditional mint julep or Manhattan.

The Buffalo Trace Distillery

Buffalo Trace Kentucky Straight Bourbon Whiskey was launched in 1999, but the history of what is now known as the Buffalo Trace Distillery goes back to 1865, when Harrison Blanton started distilling on what was then called Rock Hill Farm. Formerly the Leestown Distillery, the Blanton Distillery, and the Ancient Age Distillery, the current Buffalo Trace Distillery takes its current name from the trails left by buffalo across the frontier. Westward expansion led early explorers to follow these paths, or "traces," to uncharted territories. In addition to Buffalo Trace Kentucky Straight Bourbon Whiskey, the sprawling distillery produces several other excellent bourbon brands, including Eagle Rare, George T. Stagg, Elmer T. Lee, W. L. Weller, and (as of 2002) Old Rip Van Winkle. The distillery is owned by the New Orleans–based Sazerac Company and is also used to produce that firm's Rain Vodka.

Buffalo Trace contains a larger percentage of rye, which accounts for its spiciness. The distillery takes special pains with the aging process, selecting only barrels made from "center ring" wood that is seventy to eighty years old. They have the highest rejection rate of barrels in the business, preferring not to use wood with too fine or too coarse a grain. Barrels are aged in a series of wood beam and brick warehouses. Each warehouse imparts a slightly different flavor to the bourbon. Buffalo Trace Kentucky Straight Whiskey has won numerous awards and is delicious on the rocks or adds a bit of class to mixed drinks.

Four Roses Kentucky Bourbon

Four Roses brand has been around since the 1800s and by the 1940s was this country's biggest-selling bourbon brand. Today it's still one of the most recognized bourbons outside the United States, especially in the Far East. After a forty-five-year absence from the market, it was just recently reintroduced to the States by its parent company, Japan's Kirin Brewery, which acquired the brand in 2002.

The distillery was originally the brainchild of Paul Jones, who started a whiskey and tobacco business in Georgia. Around 1886 Georgia enacted a statewide prohibition, and Jones was forced to move his operations to Kentucky. He distilled variously under the names Old Joe Distillery, Old Prentice Distillery, and Four Roses Distillery. It is thought that the Four Roses name was Jones's affectionate tribute to a Southern belle with a proclivity for four-rose corsages.

Following Jones's death in 1895 the distillery changed hands a number of times before being purchased by Joseph Seagram and Sons, Ltd. in the mid-1940s. Creel Brown built the current distillery, which replaced the Old Prentice Distillery, in 1910. The huge yellow building was modeled after popular California architecture and looks very much like a Spanish mission, complete with bell tower.

The most familiar product sold under the Four Roses name is a blended bourbon. Advertisements in the 1960s depicted this spirit as so light that the bottle literally floated above the ground. Currently the distillery sells a Kentucky Straight Bourbon in the United States along with several bourbons that are distilled for export only. All Four Roses bourbons are distinguished from other bourbons by the fact that they are the end results of eleven different types of individually produced whiskeys blended together. Each of the eleven whiskeys is made according to an entirely unique recipe or mash bill. These eleven bourbons are then mingled together in different ways to create the variety of Four Roses bourbons. Each label bears handwritten numbers on the back that tell when the whiskey was barreled and when it was bottled. While the Four Roses bourbons can be tricky to track down in the States, they are well worth searching out in duty-free shops the next time you find yourself traveling abroad.

✳ TENNESSEE WHISKEY ✳

While many Scotch-Irish settlers fled to Kentucky during the Whiskey Rebellion, others found sanctuary in Tennessee, where they too set up their own distilleries. Producing whiskey from local cereal grains, they set about creating a spirit similar to bourbon whiskey. The result was officially recognized in 1941 by the federal government as "Tennessee Whiskey."

What sets this whiskey apart from bourbon or rye is the filtering process. All Tennessee whiskey is filtered through a thick layer of sugar maple charcoal. This gives the whiskey a very different flavor from that of bourbon or rye. Known as the Lincoln County process, this type of filtration was invented by Alfred Eaton around 1825. The filtration, also known as "charcoal mellowing," takes the distilled whiskey on a four-day journey through twelve feet of charcoal held in leaching vats. As the spirit passes over the charcoal, some of the larger flavor congeners are captured. This purified spirit is finally passed through a thick layer of white wool before trickling into the finished vat.

At the Jack Daniel Distillery in Tennessee, it is quite common to see large piles of locally procured maple wood burning in specially constructed ricks. These constructions assure that the wood will fall in on itself as it burns and create the perfect charcoal for the filtration process.

Tennessee whiskey, much more than bourbon, still feels the effects of Prohibition. A little over a century ago there were somewhere around seven hundred distilleries in Tennessee. When Prohibition hit the Volunteer State in 1910 it took just three years for the number of distilleries to plummet to seven. Out of these seven, only one Tennessee distillery remains today. Its name, however, is one of the most celebrated by-words in American whiskey: Jack Daniel's. (The George Dickel Distillery, in Cascade Hollow a few miles from Tullahoma, is currently not making whiskey, but production may start again in the future.)

✳ JACK DANIEL DISTILLERY ✳

Situated in Lynchburg, Tennessee ("population 361," as it says right on the label), Jack Daniel Distillery is the nation's oldest registered distillery and perhaps the most famous distillery in the world. Founded by Jasper "Jack" Newton Daniel in 1866, the distillery was built on land known as The Hollow at Cave Spring. The spring provided what Jack deemed the perfect water for his enterprise.

Young Jack learned the whiskey trade as a child working for the Lutheran minister Dan Call. Reverend Call imparted all he knew of whiskey (and, presumably, of godliness) to the lad. Finally, in 1863, Call bowed to the pressures of his pastoral duties and sold his still to the then thirteen-year-old Jack Daniel. Three years later the teenage entrepreneur registered his namesake distillery with the state. Known as a bit of a perfectionist, Jack Daniel took it upon himself to create the best whiskey possible. In 1904 his Old No. 7 took the only gold medal at the St. Louis World's Fair.

The Daniel Distillery was up and running in The Hollow until 1909, when the growing temperance movement dried up Moore County. In 1910 the entire state of Tennessee went drier than moon dust. Jack Daniel, now under the control of Jack's nephew, Lem Motlow, moved its operations to St. Louis, Missouri, where the teetotalers had less influence. A year later Jack Daniel died from gangrene infection, a complication resulting from a broken toe he got by kicking a safe that wouldn't open. (American whiskey is full of folklore, but this story is a favorite.) It wasn't until 1938, five years after the end of Prohibition, that Motlow was able to return the Jack Daniel Distillery to its home in Lynchburg. (Ironically, Moore County remains dry to this day.)

Lem Motlow, a legend in his own right, passed away in 1947, leaving his sons, Robert, Reagor, Daniel, and Clifford—known collectively as the "Shirtsleeve Brothers"—in charge. In 1956 the Kentucky-based Brown-Forman company assumed control of the Jack Daniel's brand, but production remained entirely centered in Lynchburg. Since 1988 the master distiller has been the colorful Jimmy Bedford, a Lynchburg native. Bedford is a wonderful raconteur who travels the globe spreading the gospel and legend of Jack Daniel in his deep Moore County accent.

Today the distillery continues to make Jack Daniel's Old No. 7 Tennessee Sour Mash Whiskey. Familiarly known as "Jack" or "JD," this square bottle with the black label is a constant in nearly every bar in the world and is favored by drinkers of all ages. Whether mixed with cola or ginger ale or simply savored neat or on the rocks, Jack Daniel's is a legend in a glass. The smoother, lower-proof Gentleman Jack is lighter and more debonair (and a bit more feminine). The classy Jack Daniel's Single Barrel (available for purchase by the bottle or the barrel) shows great concentration, depth, and style.

AMERICAN BLENDED WHISKEY:
✳ A PRODUCT OF PROHIBITION ✳

As you may have noticed, the history of America is very closely tied to the history of its distilled spirits. The Spanish brought the still to the New World from Europe, and its first product was probably a crude Aztec beer distilled in the sixteenth century from the agave plant in Mexico; this drink was a rudimentary precursor of tequila.

By the mid-seventeenth century commercial rum production had begun in Massachusetts. This development had a profound effect on the future of the young American nation. First of all, rum figured directly in the infamous slave triangle between Africa, the Caribbean, and New England. It was also responsible for the establishment of a network of taverns that later served as the gathering places for colonial revolutionaries. And it was the onerous English taxes in 1733 on the molasses used for making rum that began the colonists' march toward independence.

But in the late nineteenth and early twentieth centuries, while most Americans were enjoying their whiskey and other alcoholic beverages, Prohibitionist forces were gathering strength. For fifty years the temperance movement pursued a relentless campaign against alcohol and saloons. This intense effort took the form of a persuasive public relations blitz and extremely effective political manipulation. Before they knew what hit them, the majority—who favored the continued use of alcohol—were finding that a minority of rural legislators had been gradually turning state after state dry. On January 16, 1919, a resolution written by Prohibitionist congressman Volstead became the Eighteenth Amendment to the United States Constitution. President Wilson had the sense to veto the bill, but his veto was overridden by a browbeaten Congress. One year later it became the law of the land.

What followed was one of the greatest disasters in the history of social legislation. Instead of turning the United States into the righteous, churchgoing nation the temperance movement dreamed of, Prohibition created a land of speakeasies, crime, corruption, and bootleg hooch. Meanwhile, every legitimate winery and distillery was padlocked.

In 1928 a Canadian distillery executive, looking over the chaos in the United States, became convinced that Prohibition's repeal was inevitable. To back up this thinking he increased production and began stockpiling whiskey in Canada. His name was Samuel Bronfman and the name of his company was Distillers Corporation—Seagram's, Ltd.

Between 1928 and repeal on December 5, 1933, Seagram's created the largest stock of Canadian whisky in the world. While other distillers had to start from scratch after repeal, Seagram's was ready with mature, high-quality whiskey for the U.S. market.

Bronfman had another interesting idea. "When I found, following Repeal, that many U.S. distillers had decided to make straight Bourbon or rye and to sell their products as straight whiskey, it was time for a major decision," he wrote in 1971, at the time of his eightieth birthday. "Quality Canadian and Scotch whiskies generally were all blended. I appreciated that by blending we could produce a better-tasting product, the quality of which would be uniform year after year, and decided that we would produce blended whiskey in America."

American blended whiskey is a smooth and mellow mixture of straight whiskeys and grain-neutral spirits or light whiskeys. It has become a fundamental part of the U.S. distilled spirits market, yet it is a relatively new product, having been introduced here only after the repeal of Prohibition in 1933.

The idea of blended American whiskey is a natural. Taking feisty American bourbons and removing some of their aggressiveness by combining them with soft, neutral-flavored spirits is a very logical concept. Such a coalition was almost a necessity just after repeal, since most distillers had to start from scratch and had no mellow older whiskeys to bottle.

Of course, the federal government has set down guidelines for the manufacture of blended whiskey. There must be a minimum of 20 percent straight whiskeys in the blend. The rest can be grain-neutral spirits, grain spirits, or light whiskeys. Grain-neutral spirits are distilled out at a very high proof and have no noticeable flavor or aroma. Grain spirits are neutral spirits that have been aged in used oak barrels to give them a subtle, soft flavor. Light whiskeys are similar to grain spirits; they are just distilled out at a lower proof.

Most blended whiskeys are 80 proof. The finest ones are soft and balanced, mellow and smooth. The suggested way to consume blended whiskey is on the rocks or with a splash of water. People also use them extensively in cocktails and mixed drinks, most notably the Seven and Seven, a mixture of Seven Crown and Seven-Up, a combination that is, for many, the first alcoholic drink they ever taste.

A number of people who drink blends call them "rye." This is a complete misnomer; rye is a whiskey made from at least 51 percent rye. A true rye, such as Old Overholt, is an aggressive, strong drink that would probably horrify the people who normally drink blends.

American blended whiskey is a gentle and charming product that allows consumers to savor the rich taste of good bourbon whiskey without having to experience the fire and brimstone that sometimes characterizes these whiskeys. At their best, American blends are among the most refined and subtle of all distilled products.

Southern Comfort

Southern Comfort is a proprietary blend of bourbon whiskey, peach liqueur, and fresh peaches. This American product can be listed as either a liqueur or a blended whiskey. This blend is 100 proof, but is mellowed by the liqueur and fruit. The concoction was originally created in 1875, and was first known as Cuff and Buttons. Louis Herron, a bartender in St. Louis, Missouri, changed the name to Southern Comfort.

Canadian Club Whisky

Hiram Walker walked a crooked path toward his ultimate career as spirits maker. Along the way, this New England–born entrepreneur pursued a number of failed enterprises, including a grocery business and a cider vinegar distillery. Finally, in 1854, with the then princely sum of $40,000 in his pocket and the Michigan Prohibition movement nipping at his heels, he moved across the Detroit River to Canada. He purchased an old farm and surrounding property and began to build a distillery. The entire project wound up costing upward of $100,000, but Walker was saved from bankruptcy by the fact that the Bank of Montreal didn't foreclose because they could see no way of recouping their funds. Ultimately, the success of Canadian Club Whisky (as in Scotland, whisky is usually spelled without the "e" in Canada) would prove bankruptcy to be a laughable proposition.

Not content to simply distill whisky, Hiram Walker also grew the grain for his product and fed the remaining mash to his own herds of cattle and hogs. Eventually he began to build housing, which he leased exclusively to his employees. As Hiram Walker continued to build what folks began to refer to as "Walker's town," his whisky surged in popularity. At a time when whisky was sold in large, unmarked casks, Walker packaged his spirit in smaller bottles all bearing his name. These smaller, more genteel bottles became popular in hotels and gentlemen's clubs, and Walker's whisky began to be referred to as "club whisky." The first Canadian whisky, Canadian Club was marketed with such success that U.S. competitors lobbied Congress to force Hiram Walker to add "Canadian" to his whisky name. Canadian Club was born.

As the popularity of Canadian Club grew, so did Walker's town, which was incorporated in 1880 as Walkerville. Hiram Walker employed almost the entire population, and they all lived in houses he owned, walked on streets he paved, and were protected by policemen he hired. Their children were educated in schools he built and played under streetlights he paid for. The Fourth of July was declared a civic holiday not because it was American Independence Day, but because it was the birthday of Hiram Walker. Eventually Walker left Walkerville for Detroit, but built a ferry to carry him across the river to the Walkerville plant. Hiram Walker died in 1899 at the age of eighty-four, leaving the distillery and all business and land properties to his son James, who, with his brothers, continued to run the distillery until the 1920s.

In 1926 with the onset of Prohibition, James's three sons, seeking to distance themselves from what was seen as an unseemly business for the wealthy elite, sold the distillery, severing all connection between Walkerville and the Walker family. By 1933 they began to divest all land and buildings. In just seven years the grandsons liquidated what had taken their grandfather more than forty years to acquire and their father and uncles more than twenty years to build up. To the chagrin of many of its residents, Walkerville became part of the neighboring town of Windsor in 1935.

While the town has changed, the whisky has not. Though now owned by Allied Domecq, Canadian Club is still triple distilled to achieve a lightness and smoothness uncommon to straight whiskies. The distillation process includes trips through an extraction column still, a rectifying column still, and a barbet unit. What really sets Canadian Club apart from other whiskies is the fact that it is blended from three separate whiskies, one made primarily from corn and two with rye as their base. The rye "flavoring whiskies" are distilled in a copper pot still to a lower alcohol level, which produces higher grain character. Once the whiskies are blended, they're placed in used white oak barrels that previously held bourbon. The bourbon-soaked oak imparts fruitiness and a richness of flavor to the whisky. Following a period of at least six years, the product is reblended and refiltered before being tested and bottled. This bright gold spirit still pays tribute to Hiram Walker's hard work and unflinching eye to detail. It can be savored on the rocks with just a splash of soda or mixed into a variety of delightful cocktails.

Seagram's Seven Crown

Seagram's owes its success to a man called Samuel Bronfman. Foreseeing the end of Prohibition, Bronfman approached the Canadian distiller Seagram's who had been selling whisky in Canada since 1857. Relying upon the Seagram family's experience, Bronfman created the Distillers Corporation—Seagram's, Ltd. in Canada and began producing whisky in 1928. In 1934, when Prohibition officially ended, Bronfman was ready to ship whisky to the United States.

Two types of whisky were originally produced, Seagram's Five Crown and Seagram's Seven Crown. By the end of 1935, the combination of Seagram's Five and Seven were selling one million cases a year, making Seagram's the best-selling whisky in the United States. In just five years, sales increased by five hundred thousand. The company was poised to soar when America went to war. During World War II all American distilleries were ordered to shut down to produce industrial alcohol for use in the war. This might have seemed like the end for Seagram's, yet they had stored away a great deal of whisky and were able to start supplying thirsty Americans with spirits immediately after the end of the war. The only casualty of the war was Seagram's Five Crown. Production ceased in 1942 and stores of the stuff ran out by 1946, allowing Seagram's to focus on Seagram's Seven Crown.

Being the only Seagram's product helped Seagram's Seven Crown achieve greater success, but its popularity was also due to savvy marketing. Knowing that many American distilleries would resort to blending to stretch their available whiskey, a process that inevitably would change the flavor and quality, Seagram's promoted itself with ads that read "Say Seagram and be sure of prewar quality." The ads worked, and in 1946 Seven Crown sold 2.5 million cases. It was at this time that the crown appeared over the "7" on the bottle label. Just a year later sales were up to 4.5 million and by 1948 had nearly doubled to 8 million. Seagram's Seven was America's best-selling whisky and continued to head the market well into the 1970s. Today Seagram's has sold over 370 million cases. Its popularity is based on its consistency. Seagram's has not changed one bit since its debut in 1928.

Seagram's Seven Crown is made using the sour-mash method of fermentation. The mash bill is a mix of corn, rye, rye malt, and barley malt. The whisky is double distilled, which results in a smooth, light flavor and texture. Seagram's Seven ages for a minimum of four years in both new and used charred oak barrels. Following this aging process, the barrels are lab blended to achieve the ultimate consistency in flavor. Seagram's Seven is traditionally mixed with Seven-Up for the beloved Seven and Seven, and also blends nicely into other cocktails.

Other Seagram blended whiskies are also very popular. Crown Royal was first blended to celebrate the visit to Canada by King George VI and Queen Elizabeth in 1939. The whisky comes in a familiar royal purple pouch with a drawstring. Contrary to popular belief, Seagram's VO does not stand for "Very Old." Instead, it was the result of Joseph Seagram's instruction to the master distiller to create a blend for his own personal use. He labeled it "Seagram's Very Own," later shortened to VO.

tasting notes

BOURBON

Baker's Kentucky Straight Bourbon Whiskey

$$ ★★★   Medium amber color; spicy, racy, and complex with lovely sweet oak and notes of cinnamon and licorice.

Basil Hayden Kentucky Straight Bourbon Whiskey

$$ ★★   Medium amber color; smooth and spicy with soft oak and sweet, toasty flavors of toffee, spice, and balanced fruit.

Booker's Kentucky Straight Bourbon Whiskey

$$$ ★★★   Fiery and dense with spice, smoke, and a long caramel and fruit finish.

Buffalo Trace 8 Year Old

$ ★   Complex and smoky with spice and leather notes.

Eagle Rare 10 Year Old

$$ ★★★   Elegant, toasty, dry, and smoky with smooth vanilla; gorgeous.

Eagle Rare 17 Year Old

$$ ★★★   Complex honey and leather flavors with overtones of orange zest.

Elijah Craig 12 Year Old

$ ★★   Raw and racy; clean and rough with good balance.

Elijah Craig 18-Year-Old Single Barrel

$$ ★★★   Rich, dense, and smoky with power, depth, and flavors of butter and oak.

Elmer T. Lee Single Barrel Sour Mash

$$ ★★★   Smooth and dry with toasty, smooth, spicy flavors; lush and balanced.

Evan Williams 7 Years Old

$ ★★   Dry-styled with rich, smoky flavors and a lingering finish.

Evan Williams 1993 Single Barrel Vintage

$$ ★★★   Smooth with notes of lavender and vanilla in the nose; creamy, lush, and lovely.

Evan Williams 1992 Single Barrel Vintage

$$ ★★   Smooth and creamy with spice, vanilla, and toasty oak; long and mellow.

Fighting Cock Bourbon

$ ★★   Smooth and mellow with spice, sweet caramel, and good length.

Four Roses Bourbon

$ ★★★   Mellow, smooth, and golden-hued, with nice length and depth.

George T. Stagg 15 Years Old

$$ ★★★   Rich and sultry with hints of mushroom and earth; excellent.

Heaven Hill Old Style

$ ★   Simple, basic, and thin with clean, short flavors.

Henry McKenna Sour Mash Straight Bourbon Whiskey

$ ★   Smooth and dusty with simple, clean flavors; balanced and short.

Henry McKenna Single Barrel

$$ ★★   Smooth and dense with spice, caramel, and sweet oak; long and elegant.

Jim Beam Kentucky Straight Bourbon Whiskey

$$ ★★   Deep medium amber color; grassy, smooth, balanced with toffee, sweet oak, and spice.

Jim Beam Distiller's Masterpiece

$$$$ ★★★   Supple and polished with gorgeous notes of spice, wood, and yellow fruit.

Knob Creek 9 Years Old
$$ ★★★   Rich, textured, and complex with layered flavors of dried fruit and smoke.

Maker's Mark Bourbon
$$ ★★★   Mouth-filling flavors of vanilla and toast with a marvelously balanced finish; a classic.

Old Fitzgerald Kentucky Straight Bourbon Whiskey
$ ★★   Thin and edgy with sweet oak, spice, and caramel; spicy and balanced.

Old Fitzgerald 1849 Bourbon
$ ★★   Smooth and creamy with caramel and spice; balanced and long.

Old Fitzgerald Very Special 12 Year Old
$$ ★★   Leafy, dry, and dense with spice and good length.

Old Forester Bourbon
S   ★★★   Toffee and vanilla notes with a rich, intense mouth feel.

Old Forester Birthday Bourbon
$$ ★★★   Assertive and assured, with straight-ahead flavors and a toasty finish.

Old Whiskey River Bourbon
$$ ★★★   Round and mellow with dusky undercurrents; smooth, lingering finish.

Pappy Van Winkle's Family Reserve
$$$ ★★★   Sweet and luscious with toasty notes of honey and stone fruit.

Peter Jake's Private Keep Small Batch
$$ ★★★   Toasty and mellow with lovely leather and spice tones.

Virginia Gentleman Small Batch Bourbon
$$ ★★★   Smooth, sweet, lush, creamy, and long.

W. L. Weller 12 Year Old

$ ★★★   Smooth and complex with treacle, vanilla, and caramel flavors; molasses, spice, and a long finish.

Wild Turkey Russell's Reserve

$$ ★★★   Amber-hued with spicy, citrusy notes and an intense finish.

Wild Turkey Rare Breed

$$ ★★★   Dense and spicy with smoke, spice, and hot finish; toasty, rich, and long; bottled at barrel proof.

Wild Turkey 101 Proof

$$ ★★   Dark amber color; smooth, toasty, and lush with vanilla and spice; long and balanced with simple flavors.

Woodford Reserve Kentucky Straight Bourbon Whiskey

$$ ★★★   Elegant and seductive with luscious vanilla with lovely, complex flavors.

OTHER AMERICAN WHISKEY

Jack Daniel's Old No. 7 Tennessee Whiskey

$ ★★★   Deep amber color; spicy and complex with soft caramel and vanilla; dry, edgy and intense; balanced, long, and smooth.

Jack Daniel's Gentleman Jack Tennessee Whiskey

$$ ★★   Medium amber color; smooth and creamy, feminine and soft with sweet, mellow caramel and honey flavors; long and soft with spice and treacle.

Jack Daniel's Single Barrel Tennessee Whiskey

$$ ★★★   Deep amber color; dense and concentrated with spice, caramel, vanilla, and pepper; rich, long, and showing great depth and style.

Old Potrero Single Malt Straight Rye Whiskey

$$ ★★★   An early American–style whiskey from San Francisco's Anchor Distilling; potent and rich with nice grip and a long finish; barrel strength.

Rittenhouse Straight Rye Whiskey
$ ★★   Spicy, rich, tealike flavors; dense, deep, and long.

Sazerac 18 Year Old Rye Whiskey
$$ ★★★   Heady, dry, and spicy with a tight, aggressive finish.

Seagram's Seven Crown
$ ★★   Dusky and rich with nice weight and balance.

St. George Single Malt Whiskey
$$ ★   Medium amber color; banana nose; simple, smooth, and melony.

Van Winkle Family Reserve Rye Whiskey
$$ ★★   Chewy and textured with assertive flavors of toast and toffee.

CANADIAN WHISKY

Black Velvet Canadian Whisky
$ ★★   Soft and medium-bodied with balanced flavors and a wood-toned finish; good value.

Canadian Club 6 Year Old
$ ★★   Light amber toned with earthy, smoky tones and a malty finish.

Canadian Club Classic 12
$$ ★★★   Smooth and mellow, with spice and long, racy flavors.

Canadian Mist Whisky
$ ★   Pale dried-straw hue and nice zippy notes of spice and orange.

Crown Royal Canadian Whisky
$ ★★★   Medium amber color; smooth and lush with sweet vanilla and toasty oak; balanced, elegant, and long.

Crown Royal Special Reserve

$$ ★★★   Luscious tropical fruit flavors with a lengthy finish of spice and citrus.

Forty Creek Barrel Select Canadian Whisky

$$ ★★★   Rich and lush with vanilla and spice and notes of fruit; nutty, toasty, and long, complex.

Forty Creek Three-Grain Canadian Whisky

$$ ★★   Deep orange-amber color; spicy, toasty, and sweet nose; toasty oak, sweet vanilla, and notes of orange, toffee, and spice.

brandy

✳ WHAT IS BRANDY? ✳

I n Dutch it was called *brandewijn* and the Germans heralded it as *Branntwein*. Both these terms mean "burnt wine," and today we know it in its anglicized form as brandy, the definitive warming drink. Made virtually anywhere wine is produced or fruit is grown, brandy is distilled from fermented fruit juice. While grapes are the primary fruit of choice for brandy production, it is not uncommon to find fine brandies made from apples, pears, and other high-sugar fruits.

Quality wine-based brandies are produced in France, Italy, Spain, Germany, Portugal, and the United States. Most every brandy produced in these places will be quite acceptable when used in mixed drinks and as the base for liqueur production. However, if you are planning to drink brandy in the more traditional manner—without ice, water, or other additives, straight up in a snifter—you'll want to stick to the better (and more expensive) brandies. While drinking brandy used to be relegated to the after-dinner hours as a digestif, today brandy can be enjoyed anytime.

When it comes to selecting a top-quality brandy, the choice narrows. There are some excellent boutique brands being made in California. There is solera brandy from Spain. There's Calvados, an apple brandy made in Normandy. Grappa and marc are the Italian and French names for brandies made from grape pulp left over from the production of wine. The exquisite artisanal grape-based brandy made in southwestern France is called Armagnac. While all these versions can be excellent, the crème de la crème of the brandy world is cognac, a French brandy made in the region of that name. But before discussing these and other brandies in greater depth, I want to look at the basic elements of creating brandy.

✳ BRANDY BASICS ✳

Brandy begins its life as wine made from fruit. Grapes are the most common fruit base for brandy, but any fruit that can be made into wine can also be taken a step further and be turned into brandy. The wine is heated to boiling, at which point it vaporizes. As with other spirits, the alcohol vapors, which form first, are separated from the water vapors and then condensed back into liquid form. The recondensed alcohol is further distilled, ultimately resulting in brandy. The process originally took place in a simple pot still, which was heated over a wood fire. Wine imparts many of its own flavorful and aromatic qualities to brandy. This character is passed on through organic compounds called cogeners, which are found naturally in grapes and fruit. Cogeners can also be produced as by-products of yeast-induced alcohol fermentation of the original wine. They can also form during the aging process of the base wine, in the distillation process, and during the aging of the brandy in the wood casks.

In pot-still distillation these cogeners vaporize rather easily and quickly, due to the fact that they have lower boiling points than that of ethyl alcohol. In a continuous still they pass to the top of the column, where they can be removed from the main product. The bulk of the cogeners, also called acetaldehyde, are removed to keep the spirit from smelling and tasting unpleasantly hot and harsh. Other compounds called ethyl esters are also present in fermented wine. Desirable in small quantities, they add complexity to the aroma of the brandy. More than one hundred different compounds have been identified as contributing to the aroma and flavor of brandy. The challenge for a master distiller is not only to capture enough of the ethyl esters without including overwhelming quantities of the undesirable cogeners, but also to identify the wines that will best mature into rich, flavorful brandy. The distiller must also be on the lookout for acetate, which is present when wine begins to vinegarize, and the gaseous form of sulfur, which is often applied to wine grapes to prevent bacteria and mold. These substances too can unfavorably affect the taste of the brandy. As you can see, it is imperative to start the brandy-making process with good, well-made wine to achieve the highest-grade end result.

✳ AGING ✳

Brandy straight out of the still is clear as water. Its beautiful golden color comes from aging in wood. Because wood is porous, it allows air to combine with the spirit, creating a slow oxidation that creates intriguing new flavors as the brandy mellows. In addition, the brandy leeches some tannins and flavor from the wood itself. Most brandy producers prefer oak aging casks, and the variety of oak available enables them to impart slightly different flavors to the final product. Cognac is aged in Limousin oak, Armagnac in local black oak, and California brandy in oak from Arkansas and Tennessee. New oak imparts more color than a previously used cask and can also add too much wood flavor, resulting in a bitter or "woody" brandy. For this reason brandy often spends a short time in a new oak cask before being moved to an older cask for a longer period of aging. For brandy to gain its typical golden color it must be aged ten years or more. About 90 percent of the brandy sold in the world is aged less than ten years and coloring is added to compensate for the shortened aging time. Caramel syrup, which is used to lend its hue to brandy (and often to whiskey as well), is added in such minute portions that it does not significantly alter the flavor. To compensate for a shorter aging time, some brandy producers will also add sugar to create a smoother brandy. Brandy that is aged in glass or stainless steel drums will remain clear. This type of spirit will also be minimally oxidized and may be rougher in quality.

✳ BRANDIES OF THE WORLD ✳

Cognac

Location, Location, Location
What Boardwalk is to the Monopoly board, cognac is to the world of brandies. While there are several elements that make this

brandy unique, the most important is location. The most revered and celebrated cognacs are produced in the Cognac region of France. It may be called koniac, konac, or brandy, but only brandy from the Cognac region is a true cognac.

The cognac-producing region is sixty miles north and just to the east of the best vineyards of Bordeaux, within the two French administrative *départements* of Charente and Charente-Maritime. The region's growing area extends to the banks of the Gironde, a wide and well-protected estuary that is formed by the confluence of the Dordogne and Garonne rivers and opens out into the Atlantic Ocean. This unusually serene and inviting marine thoroughfare became, early on, a popular trading stop for ships from Holland, Scandinavia, and Britain. The secure Atlantic port of La Rochelle also attracted many vessels. The small towns of Cognac and Jarnac, about sixty miles north of Bordeaux, are the centers of the cognac industry. The region is divided into seven sectors, which delineate the quality of the wines produced for cognac distillation.

This fertile region originally included three ancient provinces of Angoumois, Saintogne, and Anuis, which in Roman times were already noted for their wheat and salt. The Romans loved wine and introduced vineyards to the region. For such a small town, Cognac has a remarkably rich history, made all the richer by the strong English presence in this part of France in the Middle Ages. The stark tenth-century castle, the Château de Cognac (now the seat of the Otard Cognac firm), was first erected as a rampart to protect the villagers from the Norman invaders. It was at this castle that Richard the Lionheart, King of England, married his son Philip to Amelia de Cognac in the twelfth century. The dukes of Burgundy, Philippe le Hardi and Philippe the Good, as well as the notorious English knight Edward the Black Prince, father of Richard II of England, also lived in Cognac. In 1487 Charles d'Orleans, Duke of Angoulême, married Louise de Savoie, who was barely twelve years old at the time. Together they would turn Cognac into a brilliant artistic and intellectual center of France. Their daughter Marguerite would become queen of Navarre and, more importantly, when King Louis XII died with no heir, their son would become François I, one of the most illustrious of all French kings.

History suggests that François was in large part responsible for the success of the Cognac region. As a reward for its loyalty in the wars of the era, François exempted Cognac from taxation, giving the town an economic advantage in trade. This patron of the arts (Leonardo da Vinci was his artist-in-residence) also loved good food and wine, a predilection that led to the planting of better vineyards. This, in turn, led to increased wine trade with England and

Scandinavia. The thin, acid wine of the Charentes and salt were the most important exports and were used to trade for goods such as wool and spices.

In 1619 the East India Company purchased some of the Charentes wine, called "coniak," for its ships. For preservation on long voyages, the thin wine was fortified with distilled spirits and began to be consumed on board in this high-strength state. Although this could be considered an early attempt at the cognac we know today, it was not technically a distilled brandy but rather a fortified wine. It was not until 1643 that the first commercial cognac firm, Augier, was founded. There is no record of formal brandy production in the region before that time, although the regions of Alsace, Paris, and Armagnac had been distilling wine a hundred years earlier, creating the first versions of what might be considered brandy. Eventually Cognac would make up for the lost time by creating the most famous of all these spirits.

The Birth of Cognac

The wines produced during the twelfth century in the Vignoble de Poitou, the great wine-producing area in what is now Cognac, were supported by William X, Duke of Guyenne. By the fourteenth century wines produced in this region were a popular export and transported on Dutch ships to the north. The wine trade became an important part of the development of the entire region. By the time François I assumed the throne in the sixteenth century, the vines in Champagne and Borderies areas had matured and were producing wine in great quantities. But it was the enterprising Dutch who actually invented cognac, albeit indirectly. The Dutch cashed in on the ready supply of inexpensive wine and shipped it home in bulk to turn into what they called *brandewijn,* "burnt wine." Later they realized they could save a bundle on shipping costs if they simply built distilleries in the Charentes region. The Dutch merchants could now ship the distilled wine in smaller casks to their ports far to the north. Brandy wine began to replace table wine as the local Charentais export. Not only that, but the brandies of the Cognac region were found to have none of the undesirable tastes found in other brandies, which often had to be covered up with additional flavoring.

The people of Cognac started to adopt the new Dutch distillation practice for themselves. This initially led to the creation of simple eaux-de-vie (waters of life). The brandy was produced in much the same way as it is today, but locally the spirit was consumed raw, straight from the still. Aging occurred only as the clear eau-de-vie was shipped in wooden casks for export. Eventually distillers and merchants discovered that the extra time actually improved the qualities of the eau-de-vie. In fact, long-term aging was discovered almost by accident. It happened when the Spanish War of Succession virtually stopped the brandy trade. For twelve years brandy could not reach England. The casks sat in storage, aging quietly as the war raged. In 1737 when the Treaty of Utrecht brought a cease to hostilities, the brandy was found to have a rich, golden color and to have lost a great deal of its harshness. This spirit was probably the first brandy to resemble what we know as cognac today. These brandies first made their way north with Dutch merchants, then west with the English traders. While cognac was becoming known all over the Continent and beyond, French distillers improved the technique of producing the spirit by introducing double distillation.

As the market became more established, agencies called *comptoirs* were created in the main towns of the region to collect the cognacs from various distillers and establish regular links with buyers in Holland, England, Northern Europe, and later America and the Far East. The drink became wildly popular in the British Isles. It was at this time that three enterprising men, Thomas Hine from Dorset, Jean Martell from the Channel Islands, and Richard Hennessy from Ireland set out for France, all determined to get into the cognac business. The distilleries they founded are still producing cognac today.

The influence of the British distillers in Cognac was crucial to the development of the unique style of the region's brandy. The English obsession with elegance and finesse dictated right from the beginning what cognac was to become. By the middle of the nineteenth century brandy began to be shipped in bottles rather than in casks. Suddenly a whole network of glassworks, case and cork manufacturers, and printing shops sprang up to meet the demand. In this way cognac brandy created prosperity for the entire region. By this time the vineyards covered almost 280,000 hectares (691,880 acres). Cognac production was at an all-time high, and the quality was consistently good.

But bad news was on the horizon in the form of a tiny yellow vine louse called phylloxera. Its appearance in the Charentes region in 1875 would bring Cognac, and the rest of the French wine industry, to its knees. By the time phylloxera was finally controlled in 1893 there were only 40,000 hectares (98,840 acres) of vineyards left. Over the next decades, planting slowly increased, fortified with American vine stock. A major increase in plantings during the 1970s boosted cognac production, but the vineyards have never again reached the size of those in the late 1800s. Nevertheless, thanks to modern vineyard production techniques, more wine is currently being produced in the region than during those early times. The resulting cognac is still a superior and marvelous product.

The Growths

The stony, chalky, lime-rich soil of Cognac and along the south banks of the Charente River is ideal for grapes and produces brandies of superb bouquet and great finesse. Mother Nature has generously provided a mild climate to the maritime-influenced Cognac region, where the vines are little affected by the extremes and weather patterns found further inland. Within the region, several smaller sectors have been drawn that are specifically delineated by soil content. Careful observation over the years has made it possible to define which exact area will grow grapes of the highest quality. These areas are known as *crus,* or "growths," and are the cognac equivalent of appellations—officially recognized districts that may be used on labels to indicate geographic origin.

The most desirable growths are Grande Champagne and Petite Champagne. Note that the French term *champagne* (from *champ,* "field") originally described plains, meadows, or open country and was not specific to the now well-known sparkling wine district. Surrounding the two Champagnes concentrically are the various growths known as the Bois: Fins Bois, Bons Bois, and Bois Ordinaires (formerly called Bois Communs or Bois à Terroir). The word *bois* refers to the woods or forest. Borderies, the smallest of the growths, lies north of the Charente River; the word *borderies* is the French name for the sharecropper's farms that used to cover this area.

Grande Champagne lies south of the Charente River. Its climate is mild and the soil has a high proportion of carbonate of lime. This small growth of 88,200 acres (oddly, it is actually smaller than Petite Champagne!) produces Cognac's most highly prized brandies, from 32,000 acres of cultivated vines. The eaux-de-vie of this region are elegant and often possess a violet bouquet as they age. Partly because of the higher acid content of the base wines, Grande Champagne spirits are generally aged longer than cognacs from the other subregions.

Petite Champagne is the next best area, and it forms a semicircle around Grande Champagne. At 169,000 acres, it is nearly double the area of Grande Champagne, but only 39,500 acres of the region are cultivated for cognac. While still highly desirable, the Petite Champagne eaux-de-vie are not thought to match the finesse of Grande Champagne cognacs. Blending Grande and Petite Champagne results in a cognac with an appellation of Fine

Champagne. A minimum of 50 percent of the blend must come from Grande Champagne.

The Borderies is the smallest subregion, with 33,200 acres, and lies to the north of the river and to the west of the town of Cognac. The soil here contains only half of the carbonate of lime found in Grand Champagne. Due to the quality of the soil and increased sun exposure, the grapes in this region ripen faster than the grapes of the other growths. This growth has only around 9,900 acres of planted vines; only 5 percent of the cognac produced comes from Borderies. These eaux-de-vie have a fine floral aroma.

The Fins Bois, a large growth of 875,000 acres, surrounds the first three subregions and is more subject to the changes in weather from both the east and the west. From its 81,500 acres of vines, Fin Bois produces excellent quality cognacs, which generally mature more rapidly than those from Grande and Petite Champagne.

The Bons Bois surrounds the Fins Bois like a large loop of over 955,000 acres, with around 30,000 of them under the vine. This growth produces 22 percent of all cognac distilled. Cognacs from the Bons Bois are often used in less expensive blends.

The Bois Ordinaires, with 677,500 total acres, lie mainly west of the Bons Bois, with another small section to the southeast, is the least desirable of the growths. Locals refer to these areas as the Bois à Terroir, that is, a region where the taste of the soil can readily be found in the brandy. They are also sometimes referred to as the Bois Communs. The soil here is mostly sandy and the 4,200 acres of scattered vineyards are greatly affected by the coastal climate. The growth even includes two islands in the Atlantic off the Charentais coast, Oléron and Ré. The vineyards of the Bois Ordinaires produce coarser, earthier, less complex spirits. Seaweed, which is used as a fertilizer, gives the eau-de-vie a particular iodinelike taste. It's ironic that the sandy soils of the Bois Ordinaires are considered less desirable, because in Armagnac, Cognac's great rival brandy-producing region, the best growth, Bas-Armagnac, boasts of its sandy soil.

The Grapes

When the original Cognac vineyards were planted, the Colombard varietal was the most common grape. Once the practice of distillation began, the Folle Blanche variety became more widely used. These vines were especially susceptible to the plague of phylloxera. By 1881 more than 70 percent of these original Folle Blanche vines had been lost, and the grape fell out of favor. Folle Blanche was replaced by Ugni Blanc, which is known regionally as Saint-Emilion and is the same grape as the Italian Trebbiano. Currently Ugni Blanc accounts for 95 percent of the white grape vineyards in the Charentes.

Ugni Blanc has remained the favorite blending grape not only because it is resistant to frost and rot, but also because it yields wines that are low in alcohol (about 8 percent) and high in acid. This type of wine, which is surprisingly ordinary and a bit acidic in the glass, produces the best cognac. According to a French law passed in May 1936, cognac must be made solely from white grapes, and 90 percent must be a combination of Ugni Blanc, Folle Blanche, and Colombard. The remaining 10 percent is permitted to be other white varietals, including Blanc Ramé, Jurançon, Montils, and Sémillon.

The grapes are harvested in October and November and are pressed immediately after harvest in either a traditional horizontal plate press or a pneumatic press. French law forbids the use of the more modern continuous press or Archimedes' screw press. After two to three weeks of fermentation, the grapes are ready for distillation. According to law, this distillation must take place in the copper pot stills of Charentes and must be completed by March 31 following the year of harvesting.

Although there are some fifty thousand winegrowers in the Cognac region as delineated by the French government in 1990, most of these take their grapes to one of 250 small distilleries or cooperatives. There are six thousand growers, however, who actually distill their own brandy.

Distillation

Nearly all distilled spirits and most brandies (including Armagnac) are made in a continuous or column still, which is a fast, efficient, and relatively inexpensive process. Cognac, on the other hand, is made in distinctive, onion-shaped copper pot stills with elegant swanlike necks. This design is also used in Scotland to make mash whisky. When used to make cognac, this type is called the alambic Charentais. The term "alambic" (also spelled "alembic" in English) comes from the Arabic word for still, *al-anbic,* which in turn derives from the Greek *ambix,* for the cap of a still.

The simple boiler is heated directly by a coal or wood fire, or by natural gas. Most of the distillers have *chauffe-vins* on their pot stills. The *chauffe-vin* is a warming pot that resembles Aladdin's lamp, used to prewarm the wine. As the chamber is not required by law but only suggested by tradition, it is a matter left to each distiller's taste. Martell does not use the *chauffe-vin* chambers, while Camus insists on putting the chamber on all its new stills.

The distillation procedure, known as *double chauffe,* requires that the wine be distilled twice. This method allows for greater control and because the alambic pot stills are small, also permits individual growers to distill their own brandy. The first distillation, known as *première chauffe,* results in a rather flat, milky liquid called the *brouillis,* which has an average alcohol content of 28 to 32 percent. The *brouillis* takes eight to twelve hours to distill. Approximately three *première chauffes* or first distillations are needed to produce enough *brouillis* to fill the boiler for the second distillation.

The second phase of distillation relies heavily on the skill of the distiller, who is on call twenty-four hours a day, seven days a week, tending the wood fire that keeps the still operating. This lonely task is performed day and night all through the cold weeks of the wintertime distillation period. To assure the highest quality of the final product, rigorous standards are applied to the separation of the distillate and to the heating process. The first part of the distillate is called the heads; the last is called the tails. The most important decision for the distiller is deciding exactly where to separate the heads and tails, retaining only the "heart" or *coeur* of the eau-de-vie. The procedure is known as *la coupe,* or "the cut." The heads and tails contain cogeners that could add unwanted flavors to the spirit. Following separation, the heart, which is at this point a colorless spirit, is ready for its transformation into cognac.

Aging

Before eau-de-vie can become cognac, it must spend time in quality oak casks. This aging period brings both color and bouquet to the final product. The oak casks are as important to the process as the grapes. Though there are close to three hundred cooperages in the Cognac region, some of the most important distillers operate and strictly oversee their own barrel-making operations. Although some labor-saving machines have been introduced in the newer cooperages, cognac barrels are made almost entirely by hand from staves that have been air dried for at least four years. The staves are carefully bent with the use of heat and fitted together by hand. No nails may be used in making barrels because of the disastrous effect metal has on the flavor of the brandy.

After distillation the clear, transparent eau-de-vie is put into small oak barrels made from wood from the forest of the Limousin (near Limoges) or the Tronçais, not far to the northeast of the Cognac district. This oak is highly porous and quite low in harsh wood tannins, which could add an unwelcome bitterness to a young brandy.

The raw, young brandy is put into new oak barrels and stored in a well-ventilated warehouse called a *chais.* Unlike wine cellars, the chais is situated above ground. The resulting temperature fluctuation is thought to aid the slow oxidation of the brandy. The natural humidity of the warehouse is one of the determining factors in the maturing process. Harmonious balance between humidity and dryness gives the spirit its mellowness. As the spirit ages, a remarkable natural procedure begins. The brandy extracts tannins, color, and taste from the wood while, at the same time, the alcohol gradually evaporates through the porous oak. The annual amount of evaporation, called by some "the angel's share," is equivalent to one-quarter of the annual world consumption of cognac evaporating into thin air. That's about twenty million bottles. As a result of this evaporation, the air around the city of Cognac, where many of these *chais* are located, has a persistent but delightful perfume. The vapors also promote the growth of a particular brandy-loving fungus, which blackens the roof tiles on traditional cognac *chais.*

The maturation process of cognac can last for decades. Throughout this time, the porous nature of the wood provides indirect contact between the spirit and the surrounding air. Cognac extracts substances from the wood called dry extracts, which change the appearance of the cognac by giving it color. The color ranges from golden yellow to fiery red-brown. As it ages, it is essential to rack the young spirit into older wood to prevent too much extraction of tannins and other substances. The natural characteristics of oak allow the brandy to develop what is called rancio, an oxidized quality that enhances both the bouquet and flavor of cognac. The oldest cognacs are kept in a dark cellar known, for obvious reasons, as *le paradis.* A cognac house's store of eaux-de-vie are tasted regularly during maturation. Only the cellar master, or *maître de chais,* can decide when a particular cognac has reached maturity. To stop the aging process he racks the cognac into very old oak casks, or into glass demijohns. It is at the point that the *coupage,* or blending, takes place.

Blending

Except for some rare single-vintage bottlings, cognac is always blended. The master blender is perhaps the single most important person in the cognac production process. In each cognac house the master blender, who in some cases is also the owner, will subtly blend eaux-de-vie of different ages and crus to produce a range of cognacs with defined personalities. He must decide whether to add a touch of Grande Champagne or a bit of Petite Champagne to maintain his signature blend. Once they are put in a large vat, various brandies are brought down to shipping strength by adding distilled water or diluted brandy. If it is used, caramel is added at this point to ensure uniform color in every bottle. Enormous wooden paddles inside the vats rotate from time to time, mixing or "marrying" the brandies. After several months the blend is bottled and made ready for market. Since the end result is a blend of different years, the age indicated on the label is that of the youngest brandy in the bottle.

Labeling

According to law, cognac must be aged for a minimum of two and a half years. The least expensive cognac, three-star, is a blend that actually averages closer to five years of age. Some houses call their three-star brandies VS (Very Superior or Special). The next step on the age scale is VSOP (Very Superior Old Pale), which by law must be at least four and one-half years old, but is usually closer to seven to ten years of age. Next comes XO (Extra Old), or Napoleon. By law these cognacs must contain no brandies that are less than five and one-half years old, though most average between fifteen and twenty-five years of age. Finally there are the Grande Reserves. These are not defined by law, but most average around fifty years of age. Some of the best known of this group are Hennessy Paradis, Martell Extra, Rémy Martin Louis VIII, and Delamain Reserve de la Famille. Traditionally the casks are left no more than half full at any time, so the actual age of a cognac may be much older than stated on the label.

The term "fine" on a label was authorized in 1938 as a Controlled Appellation of Origin (AOC) for cognac. A "fine champagne" cognac is one that is a blend of Grande and Petite Champagne cognacs, with a minimum of 50 percent of the blend from Grande Champagne.

The following designations may be found on cognac labels:

Cognac
Fine Cognac
Eau de vie de Cognac
Eau de vie des Charentes
Grande Champagne or 100 percent Grande Champagne
Fine Champagne (blend of Grande and Petite Champagne)
Fine Borderies—100 percent Borderies Cognac
Fine Fins Bois—100 percent Fins Bois Cognac
Fine Bons Bois—100 percent Bons Bois Cognac

Markings on the Label

C—Cognac
E—Extra
F—Fine
O—Old
P—Pale
S—Special
V—Very Special

The People Behind the Product

The last and ultimately the most important aspect of cognac production is the people. The Cognaçais take their local brandy seriously, and they are willing to expend the extra effort required to make it special. There is a vast network of growers, hard-working distillers, and, most remarkable of all, the tasters. Each of the 320 cognac houses has a head taster on staff. His taste buds are responsible for the success (or failure) of the house product. His job is to taste and judge the thousands of samples brought to him each year by local growers and distillers. From these he selects and buys sound brandies that eventually will find their way into one of the house cognacs. Each house, not unlike key champagne producers, has its own distinctive style. A consumer who enjoys a glass of a particular cognac in Paris should be able to buy the same brandy in Chicago and have the identical sensory experience. This distinctive characteristic of good cognac is the result of the master taster's talent.

Cognac has been called "the distilled quintessence of wine," and there is no more perfect finale to a succession of good wines than a few ounces of this toasty, rich, softly fruity, intensely perfumed liquid. Watching the shimmering amber swirl up the walls of a graceful glass, one can appreciate all the things that make this elegant brandy so special: the location of its vineyards, the Charentais soils, the time-honored techniques, the wood, the aging, and the people who have devoted their lives to making cognac the world's finest brandy.

Armagnac

The Other Great Brandy of France

In most serious drinking circles there are lines drawn between those who prefer cognac and those who prefer its not so distant cousin and rival, Armagnac. While one is not to be directly compared with the other, they are both first-class brandies with their own special characteristics.

The Armagnac region lies midway between Bordeaux and Toulouse and is part of Gascony. This region is, if anything, even more steeped in history than Cognac. Gascony, for example, is the birthplace of the mother of Henri IV, and a wonderful bit of folklore says that, on his birth, the future French king was given a sip of Armagnac along with a taste of garlic. It is believed that the Armagnac gave him his wisdom, while his strength is credited to the garlic. The "liquid gold of Gascony" was being distilled two centuries before anyone even thought of creating cognac. Three cultures meeting in the rich countryside of what is now France led to the creation of Armagnac. The Romans brought the vines, the Arabs contributed the still, and the Celts imported the barrel. The first eau-de-vie was produced there sometime between 1411 and 1441.

Because the region lacks easy access to the sea or a large river, Armagnac remained a local drink. Cognac, on the other hand, had access to the important port of La Rochelle and the navigable Charente River, and began to export its brandies all over Europe. The houses of Cognac prospered from their rich trade routes. The resulting abundant capital reserves enabled them to further market their spirit. Cognac gained worldwide renown while Armagnac lingered in the shadows. The distillers of Armagnac were (and still are) mostly small farmers with limited distribution, and were more easily hurt by the vagaries of the market and vine disease. Even today, only one in ten bottles of brandy consumed in France is Armagnac.

The Growths

Like Cognac, Armagnac is divided for purposes of production into growths. Three distinct subregions were established by a decree of May 25, 1909.

Bas-Armagnac, with its capital city in Eauze, is considered the most important of the three subregions. It extends from Landes and Gers and represents 57 percent of the vineyards. The soil contains high quantities of sand and silt as well as a mixture of a clay called *boulbènes*. The brandy produced here is elegant, fruity, light, and delicate.

Armagnac-Tenareze surrounds the small town of Condom (yes, that's its real name). This growth covers the northwestern part of the Gers *département* and southern sector of the Lot-et-Garonne *département*. About 40 percent of the Armagnac vineyards planted for distillation are in this region. The clay-limestone soil produces rich and full-bodied spirits. They are seldom bottled on their own, however, and usually are blended with brandy from other regions.

Haut-Armagnac is the most distant growth from the ocean and has a chalky white soil. Because of the abundance of limestone, it is called the "white" Armagnac. Haut-Armagnac includes the area east of Gers and a small part of the Lot-et-Garonne. It represents only a small percentage of the production, since the brandy from Haut-Armagnac is considered the lowest in quality. Much of the production from this region's vineyards ends up as white table wine rather than as brandy.

The Grapes

The variety of grapes used in Armagnac are controlled by France's strict Appellation d'Origine Contrôlée laws and include ten grape varieties: Ugni Blanc, Colombard, Folle Blanche, Baco Blanc, and to a lesser extent Clairette de Gascogne, Graisse, Jurançon Blanc, Mauzac white and rosé, and Meslier St. François. Like their neighbors to the north, the farmers of Armagnac also lost a huge number of vines to phylloxera. Before the arrival of the yellow bugs, the vineyards covered 250,000 acres. Today there are a total of 100,000 acres of vineyards, and only half are used for the production of Armagnac. As in Cognac, grapes are harvested and fermented, but without the addition of sulfur or chaptalization, the practice of adding sugar to the wine before fermentation to increase the alcohol level after fermentation.

Distillation

Once the grapes are picked and the wine has been fermented, distillation begins. The closing date varies a little every year, but distillation usually ends around mid-February of the year following harvest and is required by law to be completed by March 31. The most significant difference between cognac and Armagnac is in their methods of distillation. Farmers in Armagnac originally used a double-distillation process similar to that used in Cognac, but in the early 1800s several ingenious engineers and entrepreneurs in France came up with a still that operated in a single-distillation process. This device is also known as the alambic continuous still, or alambic Armagnacais, and was officially patented in 1818 by a Monsieur Tuillière. Some distillers do use the traditional pot stills used in Cognac and perform a double distillation, mainly for Armagnacs meant to be sold young, but these producers are the exception, not the rule.

The alambic Armagnacais is a squat, squarish laminated copper still with little of the flashy appeal of the domed pot stills used in Cognac. In fact, it looks rather like some kind of basement boiler. Many of them are portable devices that are taken from farm to farm, allowing each producer to make his or her own Armagnac without having to invest in a still. In the Armagnac continuous still, the process begins as the base wine is fed into a holding tank.

From there it is gravity-fed into a neighboring compartment, where it cascades down and fills several tiers of shallow trays or plates before falling into the boiler below. A gas or wood fire heats the wine. Vapor begins to rise through sets of curved metal tubes, which are positioned so that, as the vapor exits from the tubes, it bubbles back through the wine accumulated in the trays. As the vapor passes through the wine in this fashion on its way up the still, it picks up further flavors.

Finally the vapor reaches the top of the still, where it escapes through a coiled copper tube. Rather than using cold water to cool the tube and condense the vapors, as is done in Cognac, the Armagnac device simply and rather ingeniously runs the condensation tube back through the incoming cool wine in the first compartment. The vapors condense into eau-de-vie, which is collected at the bottom of the tube. The heads and tails, instead of being recycled as in Cognac, are kept. They add complexity to the finished product. Most Armagnac stills can produce between and four and six barrels of Armagnac per day. As it exits the still, the aroma of the eau-de-vie is already rich with fruity and often floral notes, among them linden, violet, or vie blossom.

Aging

The colorless eau-de-vie is put into barrels for aging and maturation. While Armagnac makers traditionally used dark oak from the regional Gascon forests of Monguilhem or Monlezun for its barrels, today the barrels are generally sourced from large barrel brokers, most of whom deal in white Limousin oak. Regional oak has become scarce today, and in any case, the difference between Armagac matured in regional and Limousin oak are very slight. The process of aging for Armagnac is practically identical to that for cognac, except that most Armagnacs wind up being aged ten years or more, which is much longer than typical cognacs. The tannins are extracted from the oak barrel, and evaporation and maturation occur over the two years the spirit evolves. Following this short period of aging, the spirit is transferred to older barrels where it continues to age. The cellar master will determine when the aging is satisfactory, and at this time the master blender will start to blend the different Armagnacs. Some of these brandies are so exceptional that there is no need to blend them. They can be sold as vintage Armagnac.

Labeling

The labeling system for Armagnac is similar to that employed for cognac. The youngest brandies are labeled as three-star, as in Cognac. Other designations you might find on Armagnac include:

VS (or three-star) is aged two years.

VSOP is aged five years.

XO or Vieil Armagnac is aged six years.

Hors d'age is aged ten years.

Vieille Réserve is aged from fifteen to twenty-five years.

Vintage refers exclusively to the harvest year. Vintage
   Armagnac remains at least ten years in oak barrels and it
   is very often sold at its natural proof (between 40 and 50
   percent alcohol).

The bottles used for Armagnac traditionally come in two designs. The most popular style is an oval bottle with flat sides and a long neck. The other is round and squat and is called a *pot gascon* and is often used for quantities of several liters. While most small vintners traditionally handle their own production, today there are fourteen cooperatives that represent eighteen thousand growers in the region. The best-known brands from the Bas-Armagnac region are Chateau Laubade, Janneau, Sempé, Marquis de Montesquieu, Dartigalongue, Cles des Ducs, Lafontan, and Larresingle.

Other Armagnac Products

There are several other Gascon specialties related to Armagnac. Blanche d'Armagnac (or simply La Blanche) is the distilled eau-de-vie, with no aging. La Blanche is usually served with heavy foods such as Gascony's famous foie gras, where it acts as a mid-meal digestif. Floc d'Armagnac is unfermented grape juice fortified with Armagnac, and is the Armagnacais equivalent of Cognac's Pineau des Charentes. Adding fruit to bottled Armagnac is very popular as well, and is sold as an artisanal product. Chestnuts and the famous prunes of Agen are the most traditional fruits to preserve in Armagnac; however, apricots, cherries, and oranges are equally delicious.

While there will always be those connoisseurs who prefer cognac over Armagnac, nine million bottles of Armagnac are sold in more than 130 countries every year. This golden spirit definitely has its fans, and its enthusiasts will swear its charms far outweigh those of cognac. Armagnac has a grapey character in the aroma and a heady flavor. Cardinal Vital Dufour, writing in the fourteenth century, sang early praises of the eaux-de-vie of Armagnac: "This water, if taken medically and soberly is said to have forty virtues . . . and when retained in the mouth, it loosens the tongue and emboldens the wit, if someone timid from time to time himself permits a taste." A different opinion comes from the renowned French wine writer André Simon, who had this to say about the difference between the two spirits: "Good Armagnac can be very good and much better than ordinary Cognac, but the best Armagnac cannot hope to approach, let alone rival, the best Cognac." I leave it to your discriminating taste buds to try both of these golden delicacies and decide for yourself.

Calvados

The versatile fruit that tempted Eve, inspired Sir Isaac Newton, served as a target for William Tell, and was the calling card for one John Chapman (a.k.a. Johnny Appleseed) took on new dimensions when the Normans decided to distill the fruit to make an apple brandy. This fiery Norman spirit would become known as Calvados. There are many apple brandies in the world, but none is better known than Calvados. The spirit, which gets its name from the Normandy region where it is produced, is a fruit brandy made from apple cider.

Centuries ago, Norman and Breton peasants made a hard cider drink from the wild apples that grew in local forests. When Charlemagne came to power in the eighth century the first rules for making cider were put into effect. Orchards were planted and stewards were assigned to tend to the crops. In 1553 the first mention of "eau-de-vie de sydre" was found in the journal of Gilles de Gouberville, a Norman who distilled cider spirit on his farm in Mesnil-au-Val. In his self-published newspaper he told of receiving a young man, a native of Touraine, as a guest in his house. The young man revealed to him a way to produce brandies from wine, a recipe that the practical Norman decided could be adapted to hard cider, the favorite tipple so common in Normandy. Gouberville's first attempt to distill brandy from apple cider was done in a still made of glass. A pear eau-de-vie was distilled around the same time.

As Normandy's new signature spirit was being concocted in farmhouses around the region, the Spanish were fighting the English off the Norman coast. Enraged by the execution of the Catholic Queen Mary of Scots, King Philippe II of Spain sent his "invincible" armada against England in 1588. One of its caravelles, the *El Calvador*, ran aground on a beach in Normandy. While the ship sank, its name lived on by being attached to the region. The name was changed from El Calvador to Calvados in 1790, when the region became an official French administrative *département*. Calvados is in the region of Basse-Normandie, bordered on the north by the Baie de Seine, on the east by the River Seine, and on the south by the Orne. The beaches of Baie de Seine were the staging area for the D-Day invasion of Normandy in June 1944. Shortly afterward, many an American GI got his first taste of Normandy's most famous product.

From its introduction in the sixteenth century, the drink steadily grew in popularity. Copper stills were introduced and Normans all over the region began to make the spirit, but it wasn't until the nineteenth century that this cider spirit was officially named Calvados. The finest apples in the region come from one privileged zone, the Pays d'Auge, and this is the only area granted the *appellation contrôlée* of Calvados du Pays d'Auge. All Calvados must be submitted to a tasting committee before a certificate of quality is granted. All aspects of the production are carefully controlled. Since 1942 the Institut National des Appellations d'Origine has recognized three types of cider-based spirits:

> Le Calvados—Pays d'Auge, which is made in Charentais-type stills of the cognac type and using only Pays d'Auge–grown fruit.
> Le Calvados, which is made in open fire still.
> Eau-de-vie de-cidre, which is produced in vapor column stills. The eau-de-vie de-cidre is young and rough, but Calvados du Pays d'Auge is much closer to cognac than to a fruit eau-de-vie.

Apples

It takes over thirty varieties of apples to make the cider that becomes Calvados. The correct blend of sweet, bittersweet, bitter, and acid apples must be used to create the perfect spirit. While most of us are familiar with the idea of apple picking, the apples of Calvados are harvested by shaking the branches of the trees. The apples fall to the ground on tarpaulins underneath, then are gathered into sacks and taken to storage. Ripeness is very important in the process as well. There are three periods of ripening for the apples: early-season apples (September); midseason apples (October to mid-November) and late-season apples (December harvest, stored until January). Early-season apples are not used for Calvados (though they are used for eau-de-vie de-cidre) because they would be mashed when temperatures are still too high for the production of good cider. The apples are crushed into a homogeneous pulp called pomace. The pomace sits for a few hours, making it easier for the distiller to extract the juice. This pomace is then conveyed to a hydraulic press, which squeezes the juice, called the *moût*. For Calvados the pomace is pressed only once. For some months the apple juice will ferment naturally and turn to cider. Once this cycle of fermentation is complete, the distillation process required to obtain "water of life" from cider begins.

From Cider to Calvados—Distillation

According to the regulations set in 1942, Calvados distillers who want to apply the highest appellation of Calvados Pays d'Auge must adhere to the following rules:

> Use only cider apples from the Pays d'Auge.
> Distill the cider by the traditional method using double distillation in a pot still.
> Obtain the approval of the Institut National des Appellations d'Origine after analysis and tasting.
> Allow fermentation of the juice to take place naturally, for at least one month.

The double distillation process is exactly like that for cognac. The first distillation produces *petites eaux*. From this, the heads and tails are put aside, as only the heart of the run qualifies for the *appellation contrôlée* product.

Aging

Most of the oak used for the aging process comes from Limousin, though a few old sherry and port casks made from the oak of the Orne valley are still used. The optimum age for an old Calvados is twenty-five to thirty years. Traditionally, Calvados is bottled at 90 proof.

Designations:

> Three stars or three apples—minimum of two years.
> Vieux or Réserve—minimum of three years.
> VO or Vieille Réserve—minimum of four years.
> VSOP or Grand Réserve—minimum of five years.
> Napoleon/Hors d'age/Age Inconnu or Extra—minimum over five years.

In the United States, the apple brandy called applejack is similarly made, but it is marketed much younger than Calvados. The apple brandies from this historic Laird and Company, whose founder fought with General George Washington in the Revolutionary War, are especially fine. Enjoy Calvados or other apple brandies the way you would any good brandy, warmed in the palm of the hand in a tulip-type glass. As a treat you might enjoy a glass of young Calvados in the traditional Norman way, as a *trou normand,* or "Norman hole." This involves downing a quick shot of heady Calvados during a break in a large and delicious meal, in order to make room for more food. This practice may have had an influence on the invention of Liquid-Plumr.

Brandy de Jerez

In Jerez, Spain, wine has been a tradition since the time of the Arab domination of the region, from the tenth through the fourteenth centuries. In fact, the term "alcohol" itself is actually an Arab word that migrated into European languages via Spanish during this time. As far back as the fourteenth century, sherry and wine were the primary exports from the region, and distilled spirits followed shortly after that. In the eighteenth century the Jerez wine merchants began making unaged eaux-de-vie that they sold to Dutch traders, who shipped it home to turn into their famous liqueurs. These spirits were known as *holandas,* or Dutch spirits. Eventually bodega owners began to age these *holandas* in their own cellars, and true aged brandy de Jerez was born.

The Jerez Brandy Regulating Council has established guidelines for the making of brandy de Jerez. The aging process must be done in American oak barrels; the base must be wines of Jerez; and the product must be aged through the traditional Jerez system of maturation known as *criaderas y solera.* The production can only be done in the three municipalities of Jerez de la Frontera, El Puerto de Santa Maria, and Sanlúcar de Barrameda.

The *ciraderas y solera* system (also known simply as the solera system) was developed in the nineteenth century to age sherry wines, and is now also applied to aging brandy de Jerez. In this rather elaborate system, the barrels are placed in tiers on top of one another. The *solera* is the row closest to the ground and is the level where the oldest brandy is stored. The *criaderas* (or "nurseries") are the levels above the *solera* and contain younger brandies. As the finished brandy is drawn off from the *solera,* brandy from the *criaderas* above is moved down one tier, and newly made brandy is added to the top *criadera.* This system has the effect of smoothing out any inconsistencies in the blend. The extractions (called sacas) and replacements (called rocios) are turned over every three to five months, or every year or two, depending on the recipe and tradition of each solera distiller. The barrels have already been used in the aging of sherry wine and have different characteristics, depending on the type of sherry that they formerly contained. Barrels previously used to age wine from the sweet Pedro Ximenez grape, for example, will impart a sweet taste to the brandy as it passes into this level of the solera system.

There are three classes of brandy de Jerez. Solera is the youngest, aged at least six months by law. Solera Reserva is aged over two years. Solera Gran Reserva is the oldest and finest, aged over three years by law, but usually much longer. Distillers of note are Sanchez Romate, Parra, and Bodegas Osborne.

Pomace Brandies: Grappa, Marc, and Pisco

Pomace brandies result from distilling the remnants of the wine-making process—skins, seeds, and stems—and are the less-polished stepsisters of the brandies mentioned above. Strong and fiery, various pomace brandies are produced in Italy, France, Germany, Spain, Peru, and Chili.

When grapes are pressed in the beginning stages of the wine-making process, the juice is put into a fermenting tank where it continues the dramatic transformation from grape juice to wine. Left behind after the pressing is a dense mass of grape skins, pulp, and seeds plus stems and leaves. In English we call this residue pomace. In Italy it is referred to as *vinacce,* in France as *marc* (pronounced "marr"), and in Germany as *Trester.* Since the grapes are not pressed so hard that all the juice is extracted, the remains still contain liquid. This pomace can be fermented and then distilled.

Grappa

Grappa is (often unaged) Italian pomace brandy. This harsh distil-late was directly descended from the medicines and digestive tonics of the Middle Ages. It was only as recently as 1933 that it was decreed that this traditional spirit must be bottled, instead of sold directly from the barrel. Initially these harsh alcoholic drinks were made for the peasants as rustic, unrefined spirits not unlike moonshine; the wealthy landowners kept the wine and left the grappa to their workers. The spirit was of such a poor quality that it inspired novelest Italo Calvino to comment, "Grappa was suitable only for defrocked priests, unemployed bookkeepers and husbands that have been cuckolded."

Despite rather rocky beginnings, pomace brandies have become smoother, more complex, and much more drinkable. Some grappas are matured in oak barrels, leaving them light brown in color. Though there is still plenty of fiery grappa around that tastes like a fermented compost heap or paint thinner, the carefully made premium versions of grappas have captured the attention of connoisseurs around the world.

The gentle process of making modern grappa begins the moment the grapes are first crushed. Both red and white grapes can be used; distillation removes the coloration. In fact, in the old days, very little attention was paid to the variety of grapes used to make grappa. Whatever residue was left after winemaking was combined and eventually processed. Pomace from various crushings was customarily distilled together. The result was a distillate that was high in alcohol but missing specific flavor and complexity.

Today a sizable number of the best grappas are made from an individual grape variety, and frequently they derive from a particular vineyard. More and more of them are being vintaged. Many of the finest versions carry some very well-known wine names. Lungarotti, Ceretto, Gaja, Marchesi de Gresy, and many other notable Italian wineries now release their own branded grappas. There are grappas made from Nebbiolo (the red grape from Barolo and Barbaresco), Sangiovese (the red grape from Tuscany), Chardonnay, Barbera, Moscato, and Prosecco (the sweet white grape that is made into sparkling wine in the Veneto). Some grappas are made from pomace that comes from specific cuvées of certain blended wines such as Chianti Classico or Rubesco Torgiano. Others are even vineyard-designated, such as Ceretto's Grappa di Brunate, which comes exclusively from the Barolo vineyard of this name.

In 1951 a decree was passed to codify the denomination "grappa." From this time on grappa had to be a distilled spirit made only from pomace. To protect the wine industry, the production of eaux-de-vie from grapes was forbidden (a rule finally overturned in 1984). Until 1970 winemakers had stills on their own property and made their own grappas. That year, however, a law was passed forbidding distillation on a winery estate. Most wineries either arranged to have their pomace turned into grappa by a reliable local distiller, or they built their own distillery off the property but nearby. The pomace is only lightly pressed, kept fresh, and quickly processed to minimize oxidation and to preserve fresh perfumes and flavors. Some grappa is aged in oak casks, but only for a year or two, in order not to obscure the character of the brandy. Older bottlings are labeled *vecchia* (old) or *stravecchia* (extra old).

Serving grappa. Grappa is traditionally served at cellar temperature (about 68 degrees) or lightly chilled, but there are many other ways to sip the stuff. Try a Correto, which is grappa floated on top of coffee. This morning pick-me-up is based on a tradition among Italian men of having a grappa before their morning coffee at the corner café. Another technique is to rinse your espresso or coffee cup with grappa before adding coffee, a tradition called a *rasentin* in Italian. According to Jacopo Poli, the quality of the coffee is of paramount importance; otherwise there would be no reason to rinse your cup. In Veneto it is common to drink a concoction of lemon sorbetto or gelato and grappa for an after-dinner treat. This is called a *sgrappino*.

There are a number of special grappas on the market that contain various kinds of fruit or herbs. After several months of steeping, the brandy will begin to pick up the flavors of whatever has been added to it. Many northern Italians like to make their own flavored grappas. They buy a good clean grappa, pour it into a wide-mouthed jar, add fresh fruit, seal it, and allow it to stand for a year or two.

As seems to be the case with many premium spirits, packaging is part of the allure. Many of these grappas are available in beautiful glass bottles, including some from hand-blown Murano glass. In some bottles, blown glass fruit or flowers may provide colorful accent to the clear liquor, while in others, the purity of the spirit is highlighted by the simplicity of the bottle's form.

There are a number of fine, high-quality versions that I have tried. Here are my favorites.

NONINO. This remarkable family has been distilling grappa in Friuli since 1897. Nonino has been a leader in the metamorphosis of the grappa industry. In the 1960s, when grappa first became widely known among consumers and sales began to increase, most distillers switched from the slow, discontinuous stills—similar in style to the pot stills used in the production of cognac—to speedy continuous column stills. They managed to produce the quantity of spirits the market demanded, but quality slipped significantly. The Noninos, on the other hand, added more costly *bagna-maria* (*bain-marie,* or double boiler) stills and decided to focus on quality.

In 1974 Nonino introduced the first varietal grappa, made from Picolit, Friuli's rarest grape. It was packaged in a graceful, hand-blown clear glass cruet designed by one of Italy's best architects. This bottle, topped with a plated stopper, has become the Nonino trademark. Elizabeth Nonino, the fifth-generation distiller, says of the bottle, "Now a lot of ordinary grappa is put in very special bottles. But back then we didn't want something beautiful to hide an inferior product. We just wanted to make a statement, so that people would understand that there is something very special inside. We want to sell what we make because you want to drink it, not because it is a beautiful bottle."

The Noninos have been fastidious in encouraging the cultivation of grape varieties that are in danger of becoming extinct. They now produce a whole line of grappas from these obscure varieties: Fragolino, Ribolla, Tacelenghe, Verduzzo di Ramandolo, Pignola, and Schiopettino. Determined to advance the evolution of grappa, Giannola and Benito Nonino, after battling notoriously bureau-cratic Italian red tape, in 1984 successfully lobbied to have the national ban on grape brandy production lifted. They became the first to distill whole grapes, in addition to pomace.

JACOPO POLI. Jacopo Poli, a fourth-generation distiller, enjoys one of the best reputations in Italy and around the world. The brandies of Poli are superb and beautifully presented in delicate crystal bottles. They are produced using fresh pomaces, and dis-tilling is done only during the six weeks of grape harvest. In addition to their standard, Sarpa di Poli, the Polis distill single-variety grappas called Amarosa using Cabernet, Merlot, Pinot, and Tocolato grapes. The distillery also produces a number of fine fruit brandies and the grape brandy L'Arzente. Jacopo Poli, a bit of a grappa iconoclast, is enthusiastic about new ways for people to enjoy grappa. Having been served his own grappa at a Las Vegas bar, he took a sip and discovered to his shock that the barten-der served the grappa warm. Not wanting to leave his drink un-touched, Poli asked for some ice and was surprised to find that he liked his grappa on the rocks. "There are no written rules as to how to drink grappa," Poli was quoted as saying in an interview with Stephen Beaumont. "Sometimes we are victims of our own pre-conceptions."

Lungarotti Rubesco is distilled from the pomace of this famous Umbrian wine. It is rich and clean with complex, refined licorice flavors.

Andrea da Ponte makes another lovely Prosecco grappa that is aged three years in wood.

Ceretto grappa is made entirely from Nebbiolo grapes grown in Piedmont for the production of Barolo and Barbaresco. This spirit is spicy and dry with an appealing herbal quality.

Ceretto Grappa Delle Brunate is also produced from Nebbiolo. The difference is that this earthy, rich, and herbal spirit is made from the fruit of one single vineyard. The Ceretto firm makes grappa in its own distillery.

Gaja Costa Rusi is a crisp and austere Nebbiolo grappa made from a single Barbaresco vineyard.

Other excellent grappas include l'Aquavite de Castello, Castello di Querceto (Tuscany); Grappa di Capezzana (Tuscany); Monte

Vertine (Tuscany); Conte di Cavour (Piedmont); Zeni (Friuli); Jermann (Friuli); Castello di Gabbiano (Tuscany); and Germain-Robin (America).

The popularity of imported grappa has inspired some American producers to make grappas of their own. The results have been quite good. In addition to Germain-Robin, Bonny Doon, Creekside, and St. George Spirits have made very attractive versions.

Marc

Produced throughout France, eau-de-vie de marc (usually shortened simply to marc) is a pomace brandy made in Aquitaine, Burgundy, Bugey Coteaux de la Loire, Champagne, Franche-Comté, Languedoc, Provence, Côtes du Rhône, Auvergne, Centre-Est, Savoie, and Alsace. The Charente-type pot still is generally used in Burgundy, while marc de Champagne is made in portable stills that are taken from village to village. Like grappa, marc has softened over the decades since it was first produced. Most distillers now removed the stems before production, and many marcs are aged a few years in small oak barrels. A favorite way to drink this pomace brandy among the French is to dip a sugar cube into the marc and suck the spirit from the cube. Two primary names in marc distillation are Jules Belin and Morin.

Pisco

The simple distilling process that creates grappa and marc is used in Peru and Chile to create the spirit known as pisco. The extracted pulp and juice from grapes, primarily the Muscatel variety, are fermented in large containers before being distilled and cooled. Pisco originated in Peru where it has been made for more than four hundred years. It is believed that the name is the Incan word for a clay vessel used to distill a kind of crude beer from corn mash. Peruvian pisco is generally of a much higher quality than its Chilean cousin, since production is government regulated in Peru. Pisco from Peru is also purer and stronger, not being blended with water or other neutral spirits. While pisco from Chile gets some of its flavor from aging in oak casks, Peruvian pisco is stored in casks lined with paraffin, which keeps the liquor clear and the flavor pure.

There are three types of Peruvian pisco. Acholado is distilled from a combination of grapes, while aromatico uses only Muscatel. Puro, the highest quality and the only one exported in any quantity, is distilled from Quebranta grapes. Puro is lovely in a traditional pisco sour or other mixed drinks, but its distinctive dry flavor and aromatic nose make it ideal for sipping alone or on the rocks. Despite the difficulty of finding a good pisco in the United States, the search is definitely worth your while. One relatively available brand is Capel.

Domestic Brandies

California produces 95 percent of the brandy produced in America. Spanish missionaries distilled the first California spirits, but by the middle of the nineteenth century a Frenchman, Jean Louis Vignes, created the first California brandy. John Sutter, who ran the settlement called Sutter's Fort, also tried his hand at brandy distillation, but it wasn't until 1867, when the Almaden Vineyards in Madera set up its brandy operation, that Californian vintners began to seriously compete in the brandy market.

By law, California brandy must meet several qualifications: It must be made from grapes grown and distilled in California. Unlike cognac, the type of grape is not specified. The grapes used for California brandy include Thompson Seedless, Flame Tokay, Colombard, Ugni Blanc, and Folle Blanche. The majority of the grapes are grown in the San Joachin Valley. California brandy must be aged for two years in white oak; otherwise the label must read "immature brandy." Some distillers age their brandies between four and eight years, but that is the exception. But, as Americans' drinking tastes become more refined, California brandies are being aged longer and longer.

It used to be that brandies made in the United States were mass-produced, distilled in tall column stills. These brandies, which continue to represent the lion's share of the domestic brandy market, are usually simple and a little sweet, pleasant in mixed drinks, and fine for flambéing a pan of crêpes Suzette. Over the past twenty years, however, a few hardy souls have attempted to reproduce the handmade, oak-aged, pot-still brandies that have made cognac so renowned, and some have also set out to make serious pomace brandies such as grappa or marc—distillates produced from the grape solids that remain after the winemaking process.

Notable American producers such as California's Germain-Robin and Oregon's Clear Creek Distillery are producing amazing spirits that can easily hold their own in the company of some of the best distilled products of Europe.

Germain-Robin

French-born Hubert Germain-Robin was hitchhiking one day in 1981 just north of San Francisco, when Ansley Coale stopped to pick him up. It was an auspicious meeting. Hubert was the son of a family that had been producing brandies in Cognac since 1782.

The family had just sold out to the large Cognac house of Martell. The nostalgic Hubert longed to return to the old ways of producing brandy. Ansley Coale convinced him that great brandy could be made in California. Hubert found an abandoned pot still in Cognac and shipped it to Mendocino County. The rest is history. Today Germain-Robin produces several superb brandies using premium varietal wines such as Pinot Noir. Brandies such as the sublime, vintage-dated Anno Domini are the equal of the finest cognacs. These brandies are made using a traditional alambic still. This type of pot still works only one batch at a time, setting these fine brandies apart from other mass-produced American brandies that are made in a continuously processing column still. Germain-Robin also makes a range of varietal grappas.

Clear Creek Distillery

The Pacific Northwest is known for its fruit. Apples and pears, especially, are big here. Former attorney Steve McCarthy is now a distiller, owner of Portland, Oregon's pacesetting Clear Creek Distillery. His apple eau-de-vie is aged for four years in Limousin oak casks from France that were previously used to store cognac. Steve also makes other excellent brandies, all from fruit grown in orchards near his grandfather's farm. He intentionally set out to duplicate the age-old procedures of Normandy's Calvados makers, but he likes to point out that his New World version of apple brandy stands out because of the tart, racy quality of the Oregon fruit. These are consistently some of the finest spirits made in America.

Eaux-de-Vie and Fruit Brandies

You've just finished a lovely meal and you're not ready for the evening to end. Continue the magic by having a glass of fruit eau-de-vie. These fruit-based brandies are clear, dry, unsweetened, and distilled at a higher alcoholic strength than most liqueurs. In the past decade American distillers are competing with their German, Italian, and French competitors to turn out exemplary products. Clear Creek (in Portland, Oregon), St. George Spirits (in Alameda, California), Germain-Robin (in Ukiah, California), and Bonny Doon (in Santa Cruz, California) are all making excellent fresh fruit eaux-de-vie. Eaux-de-vie taste best chilled but not iced, in a one- or two-ounce serving.

Basically, eau-de-vie is created from perfectly ripe fruit that has been crushed, pressed, fermented, and distilled. Outstanding spirits can be made from cherries, pears, apples, blueberries, and apricots, among other fruits. Other well-known eau-de-vie styles are poire William (from William pears), kirsch (from cherries), cassis (from currants), apricot, and plum. Alambic copper stills are used to obtain the best results. Approximately twenty to twenty-two pounds of fruit are required to make one liter of eau-de-vie. While some experts argue over whether the terms "brandy" and "eau-de-vie" are synonymous, technically, any distilled fruit wine that is unaged and has not had sugar or coloring added is an eau-de-vie. But aging an eau-de-vie, whether it's made from pears or from the wine of Cognac, makes it a brandy. The Alcohol and Tobacco Tax and Trade Bureau (to whom I defer, naturally, in all matters alcoholic) holds that any distilled spirit of a particular fruit can be labeled as brandy.

Make sure, however, not to mistake a fruit-*flavored* brandy for an eau-de-vie or an authentic fruit-based brandy. "Fruit-flavored" is just what the name implies, a fruit essence added to an inexpensive spirit. And a sweetened fruit brandy liqueur is not an eau-de-vie either. These days spirits manufacturers are stumbling over themselves to titillate the palates (and massage the pocketbooks) of consumers with sweetened blends of fruit and various spirits, so reading labels closely is a must. Some of these products are quite delicious, but they are not true fruit brandies.

✳ TASTING BRANDIES ✳

The first step in tasting brandy is to have the correct glass. The tulip-shaped glass (preferable to the now-outdated round snifter) contains the aroma of the brandy and then releases it slowly while you taste. While shape is most important, the glass should also be clear to allow appreciation of the color and body of the spirit.

Once you've poured your brandy, smell the spirit. Swirl it in your glass to reveal the true character of the bouquet. Cognac tasters (or nosers, as they are sometimes called) have their own vocabulary that can be applied to all other brandies as well. The first fragrance released from a cognac is known as the *montant,* or that which rises. Unlike nosing wine, you don't have to stick your snout far into the brandy glass to get a good smell; if you do, you'll just get an overpowering and unpleasant rush of alcohol vapors. Instead, let the *montant* meet your nose just above the rim of the glass. Hold the glass in the palm of one hand and pass the glass under the nose several times, gently inhaling as the glass passes by. This allows you to sense all the subtleties in the brandy as the vapors fan out of the glass.

Now comes the fun part, tasting. Flavors and aromas combine as the spirit is sipped and savored. Look for roundness, sweetness, smoothness, refinement, and lightness. Notice how long the first sensation tastes on the tongue and palate. Look for sweet, acidic, salty, and bitter qualities. Try to appreciate all the sensations— after all, brandy is all about pleasure. Notice whether the body is soft and smooth, or harsh and angular. How does the brandy feel as it rolls under the tongue? The finish is the sensation the brandy leaves in the mouth after you swallow, while length refers to how long the sensation lasts. The best brandies will have a finish that goes on for several minutes, and your memory of them will hopefully last much longer than that.

Brandy Now

There are a thousand ways to enjoy brandy. The conventional, straight-up style is, of course, the classic manner. Warming brandy over a flame, as is still sometimes done in pretentious restaurants, is today regarded as hopelessly old-fashioned and can serve no real purpose unless you've been storing your brandy in the icebox (which is, obviously, not recommended). Brandy can also be served with sparkling water or tonic for the perfect aperitif.

Locals who live in Cognac and work in the brandy business have actually confessed that they love their cognac on ice with a twist of lemon. Don't let anyone tell you how your brandy should be enjoyed. There are numerous recipes for American brandy drinks. In Japan cognac is served as a long, cooling summer drink with dinner. Brandy also serves a place in the kitchen as a flambé base, as an addition to sauces and gravies, as well as an addition to fruit or ice cream desserts, and, of course, in soufflés.

tasting notes

COGNAC

Alizé VS
$$ ★★   Medium amber with notes of red; lush treacle and honey; smooth and fruity with balance, sweet caramel, and fairly simple but quite charming flavors.

Alizé VSOP

$$ ★★   Medium reddish amber color; lush nose; smooth and balanced, creamy and rich with sweet treacle notes; long and mellow.

Ansac VS

$ ★   Dry, woody, and a bit rough on the finish; balanced and decent.

Brillet Très Vieille XO Réserve Grande Champagne

$$$ ★★   Auburn-hued; silky mid-palate with nice oak notes.

Camus Cuvée

$$ ★   Elegant and poised; notes of leather and spice.

Camus XO Borderies

$$$ ★★★   Seductive and enticing nose; supple on the palate, with nice fruit tones.

Courvoisier L'Esprit de Courvoisier

$$$$ ★★★★   Elegant, fruity, rich, spicy, long, and complex; notes of wood, tea, and honey; superb in every way. The greatest brandy I have ever tasted. Comes with crystal decanter.

Courvoisier Initiale Extra

$$$$ ★★★   Dark amber, dense, smoky, complex, and layered with vanilla and caramel; explosive and lustrous.

Courvoisier VSOP

$$ ★★★   Lush, complex, dense, and elegant with smoky, ripe, dried apricot tones and lovely spice.

Courvoisier XO Impérial

$$$ ★★★   Bright amber hue; mellow nose with lily and violet floral notes; toffee, prune, and chocolate on the palate.

Courvoisier VS

$$ ★   Pale golden in color; rich and spicy with very nice caramel notes; clean, balanced, and long.

Courvoisier Napoléon

$$$ ★★★   Rich amber color; fruity and dense with complex, masculine flavors of cigar box and cinnamon and some sweetness.

Delamain Réserve de la Famille

$$$$ ★★★   Fruity, spicy, and rich with dense complex flavors and a long, rich finish.

Delamain Vesper

$$$ ★★★   Smoky, dense, creamy, lush, and balanced; rich and long on the finish.

Delamain Très Vénérable

$$$$ ★★   Smoky, dense, spicy, ripe, long, and smooth.

Delamain XO Pale and Dry

$$$ ★★   Medium amber color; lush vanilla and caramel in the nose; soft and smooth with clean, balanced flavors of wood, spice, and vanilla; fruity, clean, and moderately long.

Dobbé VSOP "Dixie Band"

$$ ★★   Soft, faint nose; smooth and simple with a balanced but short finish.

Dobbé Extra "The Duke"

$$$ ★★   Medium dark amber; floral, smooth, and light nose; mellow, balanced, and toasty, dusty and moderately long.

Dobbé XO "The Count"

$$$ ★★   Medium amber color; soft caramel and vanilla in the nose; bright and smooth with wood, spice, and good balance; long and toasty.

E. & J. VS

$$ ★★   Clean and smooth with wood and good structure; balanced and complex.

Frapin VS Luxe Premier Grande Champagne

$$ ★★   Treacle and spice, racy with vanilla and citrus fruit.

Frapin Extra

$$$$ ★★★   Lush and creamy with rich, sweet, spicy flavors; long and balanced.

Frapin V.I.P. XO

$$$ ★★★   Caramel and honey, vanilla and toasty oak, smooth texture, mouth-filling flavors; long and lush.

Frapin XO Château Fontpinot Très Vieille Réserve du Château Grande Champagne

$$$ ★★★   Creamy and lush with vanilla, spice, and caramel; long and smooth.

Frapin VSOP Grande Champagne

$$ ★★★   Medium amber color; dense, toasty nose; dry and intense with clean, well-structured flavors of spice, caramel, and vanilla; long, smooth, and complex.

Gabriel & Andreu Borderies

$$ ★★★   Deep reddish amber color; toasty, lush, and rich nose; smooth and dense with lovely caramel and smooth, creamy flavors.

Gabriel & Andreu Fins Bois

$$ ★★★   Medium amber nose; smooth and fruity nose; mellow caramel and toasty oak; long and delicate with great length and sweet fruit.

Gabriel & Andreu Petite Champagne

$$$ ★★★   Medium amber color; rich and powerful nose; lush and dense with smooth, ripe fruit and caramel and treacle; long and rich.

Gabriel & Andreu Grande Champagne

$$$ ★★★   Dark, reddish amber color; dense, smooth molasses nose; rich and complex with smooth texture and lovely vanilla spice.

Hennessy Richard Hennessy

$$$$ ★★★★   Smooth and spicy with sweet fruit and rich wood; toasty, dense, and complex, rich and long.

Hennessy XO

$$$ ★★★   Smooth, ripe, bright, and long.

Hennessy Private Réserve

$$$ ★★★   Fruity and smooth; lush and floral with lovely, creamy flavors or honey and spice.

Hennessy Paradis Extra

$$$$ ★★★   Smooth and spicy with rich, toasty flavors and a long, rich, honey, caramel finish.

Hennessy VSOP Privilège

$$ ★★   Rich and suave with lovely, deep caramel and toasty flavors.

Hennessy Timeless

$$$$ ★★★★   Dark, reddish amber color; spicy vanilla and mint nose; toasty, rich, and complex with lovely spice and rancio; very long.

Hine Antique

$$$ ★★★   Warming and seductive; not showy but beautifully poised.

Hine Rare VSOP

$$ ★★★   Earthy, mushroomy flavors and a silky mouth feel.

Hine 1953

$$$$ ★★★★   Sophisticated and gorgeously balanced; lovely wood tones.

Jean Fillioux Très Vieux Grande Champagne

$$$ ★★★   Medium amber color; smooth caramel and spice in the nose; lush and rich with complex wood, spice, and toast; mellow and smoky, long and dense.

Jean Fillioux Réserve Familiale Très Vieille Grande Champagne

$$$ ★★★   Medium amber color; toasty, rich nose; complex and mature with elegant fruit, spice, and wood; long and spicy with rancio and notes of leather, vanilla, and clove.

Jean Fillioux XO Réserve Grande Champagne

$$$ ★★★   Medium amber color; lush, creamy caramel in the nose; smooth, lush, and concentrated with lovely soft fruit, sweet oak, and a long, balanced finish.

La Fontaine de la Pouyade 1er Cru Grande Champagne

$$$$ ★★★★   Medium amber color; lush and mellow with mature, soft flavors; intense and complex with wood, mature fruit, spice, and elegant notes of earth and dried fruits; long, elegant, and refined.

Landy XO No. 1

$$$ ★★   Medium amber color; smooth and fresh with soft, mild flavors; oak, fruit, and spice.

Léopold Gourmel Age du Fruit

$$$ ★★★   Pale, bright amber color; smooth, mellow nose; lively and smooth with spice, wood, and vanilla; delicate, fresh, and long.

Léopold Gourmel Age des Fleurs

$$$ ★★★   Medium, reddish amber color; lush, smooth, vanilla oak; smooth and spicy, long and balanced; rich and fresh.

Léopold Gourmel Age des Epices

$$$ ★★★   Medium, reddish amber color; smooth, spicy, and lush nose; rich and complex with ripe fruit and smooth oak; long and balanced.

Maison Surrenne Ancienne Distillerie

$$ ★★   Smooth and toasty, mellow and balanced.

Maison Surrenne Borderies

$$$ ★★★   Light medium amber color; caramel, spice nose; intense, forward, and spicy with light vanilla and oak.

Maison Surrenne Petite Champagne

$$ ★★★   Medium, reddish amber color; delicate, fruity nose; bright and lively with spicy apple fruit and lovely floral notes.

Maison Surrenne Tonneau No. 1 Petite Champagne
$$$$ ★★★   Dark, reddish amber color; fleshy, mature nose; dense and rich, toasted oak, mature fruit and a long, complex finish.

Martell VSOP
$$ ★★   Supple and likable, with nutlike tones and a dry finish.

Martell XO
$$$ ★★★   Spicy, vanilla, toasty, rich, and meaty with a long finish.

Pierre Ferrand Amber
$$ ★★★   Light amber color; smooth and light with floral, clean flavors and an elegant, slightly grassy finish.

Pierre Ferrand Réserve
$$$ ★★★   Medium amber color; ripe and fleshy with lush flavors and a long, rich finish.

Pierre Ferrand Cigare
$$$ ★★★   Dark amber color; smoky, dense nose with lovely caramel flavors; long, elegant, and lovely.

Pierre Ferrand Séléction des Anges Grande Champagne
$$$ ★★★   Dark, reddish amber color; powerful, intense nose; dry and toasty with wood and spice; clean, smooth, and a bit short.

Raynal VSOP
$ ★   Soft nose and moderate flavors; a good mixing cognac.

Raynal XO
$S   ★   Amber-gold color and decent flavors.

Rémy Martin XO Fine Champagne
$$$ ★★★   Medium amber color; rich, complex bouquet of wood, spice, and mature fruit; thick and rich flavors with ripe fruit, toasty oak, vanilla, caramel, and lots of spice; smooth and dense, complex and elegant.

Rémy Martin 1738 Accord Royal Fine Champagne

$$$ ★★   Deep, redish amber color; fresh prune and spice in the nose; smooth and lively with caramel, vanilla, and dry, toasty oak; long, balanced, and racy.

ARMAGNAC

Cerbois VSOP Bas Armagnac

$$ ★★   Bright orange color; wood and vanilla nose; smooth and mellow with caramel and wood notes; elegant and long.

Cerbois 1982 Vintage Bas Armagnac

$$$ ★★★   Medium orange/amber color; wood and spice nose; smooth and dense with toasty oak, caramel, rancio, complex flavors; long and layered.

Cerbois 1961 Vintage Bas Armagnac

$$$ ★★★   Dark orange/amber color; fruity and lush nose; intense and rich with vanilla, spice, toast, and long, lingering, modulating flavors; amazing.

Cerbois 1900 Vintage Bas Armagnac

$$$$ ★★★   Medium orange/amber color; smooth, lush, mellow nose; light and elegant with lovely caramel and spice; complex and long; intense and balanced.

Château de Laubade VSOP Bas Armagnac

$$ ★★   More angular than the XO, with a coppery tint and a long, deep finish.

Château de Laubade XO Bas Armagnac

$$$ ★★   Soft, rounded, and inviting; dusky flavors of dried fruit.

Château de Laubade 1984 Bas Armagnac

$$$ ★★★   Muscular and yet supple; gorgeous flavors of red fruit, oak, and a hint of rancio.

Château de Laubade 1963 Bas Armagnac

$$$ ★★★   Floral aroma with notes of eucalyptus; intriguingly complex and long.

Château de Ravignan 1973 Bas Armagnac

$$$ ★★★   Deep, long, and enticing, with lovely notes of rancio and oak.

Dartigalongue Hors d'Age Bas Armagnac

$$ ★★   Deep orange/amber color; toasty and lush nose; racy and bright with balance and clean, lively flavors of fruit, caramel, and oak.

De Montal 1976 Armagnac de Montal

$$$ ★★★   Medium orange/amber color; vanilla and spice nose; lush and rich with toasty oak, rich caramel, and honey; long and dense.

Laberdolive 1985 Domaine de Jaurrey

$$$ ★★★   Lush and intense, with vanilla, spice, and a long, toasty finish.

Laberdolive 1942 Domaine de Jaurrey

$$$$ ★★★★   A sublime Armagnac with multidimensional, textured flavors and a velvety finish.

Sempé VSOP Armagnac

$$ ★★   Smooth and creamy with floral, spice, vanilla flavors and a long, rich finish.

Sempé Vieil Armagnac 15 Ans

$$$ ★★★   Lush caramel and spice; rich and smooth.

Sempé Extra Grande Reserve Armagnac

$$$ ★★★   Toasty and complex with elegance and finesse; floral, spice, and rich, dense flavors; long and balanced.

Sempé 1963 Bas Armagnac

$$$ ★★★★   Lush fruit and vanilla, rancio, and nuts, leather, and spice; creamy and long, lovely.

Sempé 1942 Bas Armagnac

$$$$ ★★★   Smooth and rich with spice, flowers, and smoke; balanced and luscious, long and intense; rancio.

Sempé 1941 Bas Armagnac

$$$$ ★★★   Dry, edgy with wood and spice; rich and powerful with long, toasted finish.

Sempé 1934 Armagnac

$$$$ ★★★   Sweet oak and rancio with gorgeous dried fruit and spice; long and complex.

Sempé 1914 Armagnac

$$$$ ★★★★   Dark, lush, and loaded with sweet hazelnuts and rancio; caramel, spice, and lush honey; long and complex.

CALVADOS

Boulard Grand Solage Pays d'Auge

$$ ★   Medium orange-amber color; smooth ripe apple nose; soft and dull with mild, simple brown apple flavors.

Boulard XO Très Grande Fine Pays d'Auge

$$$ ★★   Medium orangy amber color; soft apple nose; rich and ripe with apple and toasty oak; long and smooth with caramel and spice.

Christian Drouin Coeur de Lion Hors d'Age Pays d'Auge

$$$ ★★★   Brilliant clarity and sharply drawn flavors; rich, snappy, and thrilling.

Christian Drouin Coeur de Lion 25 Year Old Pays d'Auge

$$$ ★★★★   Intense entry with layer after layer of shimmering flavors; superb.

Daron Fine Pays d'Auge

$$ ★★   Pale amber color; smooth, earthy apple nose; silky, racy, and fresh with apple fruit and vanilla.

Daron XO Pays d'Auge

$$$ ★★★   Medium orange/amber color; smooth and fruity nose; lush and mellow with fresh apple fruit and elegant, balanced flavors; long and lovely.

Le Compte Originel Pays d'Auge

$$ ★★   Nice appley-toasty tones with a lengthy finish.

Le Compte Pays d'Auge

$$$ ★★★   Explosive apple flavors and a warming finish.

Père Magloire VSOP Pays d'Auge

$$ ★★   Bright medium orangy amber color; smooth and fruity nose; bright and racy with spice, vanilla, and a clean finish, but lacking apple fruit.

AMERICAN BRANDY

Aristocrat

$ ★   Smooth and simple with caramel and a hot blast of alcohol on the finish.

Christian Brothers Amber

$ ★   Smooth and decent with caramel and spice; clean and balanced.

Christian Brothers VSOP Grand Reserve

$ ★★   Smooth and mellow with toffee, caramel, and spice; long and balanced.

Christian Brothers XO Rare Reserve

$ ★★   Smooth and toasty with wood, complex flavors and a long, lush finish.

E. & J. VS

$ ★★   Medium amber color; smooth and creamy with mild but decent flavors; clean and mellow.

E. & J. VSOP Superior Reserve

$ ★★   Smooth and lush with toffee and caramel; balanced, long, and complex.

E. & J. XO 10 Year Old

$$ ★★   Smooth and mellow with notes of oak and spice; clean, balanced, and long.

Germain-Robin Fine Alambic Brandy

$$ ★★   The entry-level brandy from this superb boutique producer; not as fine as its pricier offerings but very solid, with racy, forward flavors.

Germain-Robin Select Barrel XO

$$$ ★★★   Rich and complex with lovely caramel, spice, and ripe fruit; vanilla, toast, and good length.

Germain-Robin Anno Domini 2003
$$$$ ★★★   Smooth and leafy with rich vanilla flavors and a long finish.

Germain-Robin Anno Domini 2004
$$$$ ★★★   Medium amber color; lush vanilla and toasty nose; lush and dense with lovely wood, caramel, and spice; long, rich, and complex.

Jepson Signature Reserve Mendocino
$$$ ★★★   Lush and smooth with toast, spice, and complex flavors; mellow, lush, and long.

Jepson Rare Mendocino
$$$ ★★   Fragrant, smooth, and balanced with modest flavors but good texture and length.

Jepson Old Stock Mendocino
$$$ ★★   Smooth and mellow with spicy, dry flavors of wood, fruit, and toast; long and balanced.

Korbel Classic
$ ★   Pale medium amber color; simple, vanilla, and toasty oak nose; smooth and sweet with simple flavors of vanilla and caramel; short and balanced.

Korbel VSOP Gold Reserve Rare
$ ★★   Medium amber color; smooth and balanced with toasty oak, spice, and clean, long finish.

BRANDY DE JEREZ
AND MISCELLANEOUS BRANDY

Cardenal Mendoza Uno En Mil 10 Years Old, *Spain*
$$ ★★   Dry and precisely delineated flavors with nice sherry-cask oak notes.

Cardenal Mendoza Solera Gran Reserva 15 Years Old, *Spain*
$$ ★★   Rich, full-bodied, and massively styled; a classic solera brandy.

Conde de Osborne Solera Gran Reserva, *Spain*
$$$ ★★★   Medium, reddish amber color; toasty and complex nose; smooth, lush, and sweet with lovely molasses and toasty oak; mellow, dense, and long.

Gonzalez Byass Lepanto Gran Reserva, *Spain*

$$ ★★   Pale medium amber color; lush cream and vanilla nose; clean, smooth, and simple; dry, edgy, and balanced; long and pleasant.

Gran Duque d' Alba Gran Reserva Brandy de Luxe, *Spain*

$$ ★★   Dark chocolate brown; molasses and brown sugar nose; smooth and toasty with sweet, spicy flavors; lush and dense.

Imoya VSOP, *South Africa*

$$ ★★   Medium reddish amber color; lush brown sugar and spice nose; smooth and lush with pumpkin and honey flavors; long, balanced, and racy.

Jacopo Poli L'Arzente 10 Years Old, *Italy*

$$$ ★★★   Amber and smoky with butterscotch and spice.

Romate Cardenal Mendoza Solera Gran Reserva, *Spain*

$$$ ★★   Dark amber color; mature, spicy nose; dense and rich with lovely toasty oak and sweet caramel.

Torres Torres 20 Hors d'Age, *Spain*

$$ ★★   Medium amber color; neutral nose; smooth and balanced with sweet, lush flavors; toasty and long.

Torres Jaime I Reserva de la Familia, *Spain*

$$$ ★★   Medium amber color; caramel, spice, and wood nose; chocolate, molasses, and spice; long and smooth.

Vecchia Romagna Etichetta Nera, *Italy*

$$ ★   Pale medium amber color; smooth, mild, and simple with toasty oak and soft flavors.

Vecchia Romagna Riserva 10 Anni, *Italy*

$$ ★★★   Smooth and toasty with caramel, spice, and lush fruit; dense, complex, and elegant.

FRUIT BRANDY, EAUX-DE-VIE, AND FLAVORED BRANDY

777 Orange Flavored Brandy, *Israel*

$ ★★   Medium amber color; thick and jammy with ripe, sweet orange marmalade flavors; kosher.

Aqua Perfecta Kirsch Eau de Vie Cherry Brandy, *USA*
$$ ★★★   Dry and stylish with spicy cherry flavors and notes of toasted almond; silky and long.

Aqua Perfecta Poire Eau de Vie Williams Pear Brandy, *USA*
$$ ★★★   Rich and spicy pure pear essence with notes of honey and spice; long, intense, dry, and complex.

Aqua Perfecta Framboise Eau de Vie Raspberry Brandy, *USA*
$$ ★★★   Intense and exploding with the essence of raspberry; dry, smooth, lush, and aromatic; long and lovely.

Bonny Doon Vineyard Poire Pear Eau de Vie, *USA*
$$ ★★★   Smooth and rich with elegant pear fruit and a mellow, dry finish.

Christian Brothers Frost White Brandy with Natural Flavors, *USA*
$ ★   Clear, smooth, and slightly sweet with very modest flavors; clean and decent.

Germain-Robin Apple Brandy, *USA*
$$$ ★★★   Medium orangy amber color; vanilla and spice with long, hot flavors and clean, dry, lifted notes.

Gioiello Nonino Distillato di Miele di Castagno/Chestnut Honey Distillate, *Italy*
$$$ ★★   Snappy yet rich grappa flavors with a fiery finish.

Gioiello Nonino Distillato di Miele di Agrumi/Citrus Honey Distillate, *Italy*
$$$ ★★   Lush honeysuckle nose; smooth, floral, and dense; long and mellow.

Jacopo Poli Uva Viva Malvasia & Moscato, *Italy*
$$ ★★★   Peppery and spicy with lovely aromatics and smooth, long finish.

Jacopo Poli Chiara di Moscato, *Italy*
$$$ ★★★   Smooth and off dry, lovely spice and floral qualities, aromatic and lush.

Jacopo Poli Stagione de Pere, *Italy*

$$$ ★★★★   Smooth and mellow with dry but lush pear and a long, spiced finish.

Jacopo Poli Stagione di Lamponi, *Italy*

$$$ ★★★★   Explosive raspberry nose and a lush, smooth, spiced flavor with thick, creamy texture and a long, mellow finish.

Laird's Rare Apple Brandy 12 Years Old, *USA*

$$$ ★★★   Medium orange/amber color; spicy nose; fresh and racy with dry, edgy flavors of apple and spice; clean and toasty.

Maschio Prime Arance Orange Flavored Brandy, *Italy*

$$$ ★★   Dazzling orange fruit and a long, exotic finish.

Maschio Prime Uve Cru Moscato Giallo, *Italy*

$$$ ★★   Brandy from whole yellow Muscat grapes; intense, charming, and full of terroir.

Valentin Tomato Viski, *Croatia*

$$ ★★★   A unique tomato eau-de-vie with silky texture and spicy green-tomato flavors; unusual and delightful.

Zwack Pecsetes Pear Brandy, *Hungary*

$ ★★★   Vivid pear fruit with ripe, mouth-filling flavors; very nice.

GRAPPA, MARC, AND PISCO

Aqua Perfecta Grappa of Zinfandel, *USA*

$$ ★★★   Smooth and intense with distinct pomace character; long and dense, with smooth, mellow, complex finish.

Bonny Doon Vineyard Marc, *USA*

$$$ ★★   Hot, spicy, and peppery with racy flavors.

Bonollo Grappa of Amarone Barrique, *Italy*

$$$ ★★★   Medium amber in color; aromatic, lush, and smooth with mellow, sweet flavors; long and lush, lovely.

Capel Pisco, *Peru*

$ ★   Fresh, tropical fruit and vanilla nose; dense and organic with meaty, coarse flavors.

Capel Pisco Alto del Carmen, *Peru*

$ ★★   Smooth and creamy with fruit and mellow vanilla; clean and lush, long and balanced.

Ca' del Solo Grappa di Fragolino, *USA*

$$ ★★★   Spicy, forward, and floral with spice, grape, and vanilla; long and mellow.

Charbay Single Barrel Grappa di Marko, *USA*

$$$ ★★   Smooth and spicy, clean and fleshy, herbal, long, and rich; Merlot-based.

Classick Cabernet Briarstone Vineyards Grappa, *USA*

$$ ★★   Fiery and alive with classic barnyardlike grappa flavors; quite nice.

Classick Cabernet Stags Leap 2001 Grappa, *USA*

$$ ★★   Layered and multidimensional grappa with a lengthy finish.

Clear Creek Distillery Grappa of Pinot Grigio, *USA*

$$ ★★   Clean and smooth with spice, pepper, and leafy flavors; long and mellow.

Clear Creek Distillery Grappa of Muscat, *USA*

$$ ★★   Floral and smooth with clean, spicy finish; grassy, lush, and perfumed.

Clear Creek Distillery Marc, *USA*

$$ ★★★   Smooth and creamy, lush and mellow, long and balanced with vanilla and spice.

Coppo Grappa 1994, *Italy*

$$$ ★★★   Intense and racy; straw and herbal flavors and a hot finish.

Germain-Robin Merlot, *USA*

$$$ ★★★   Smooth, pretty, and spicy with creamy, vanilla flavors and a long, mellow finish.

Germain-Robin Syrah Grappa, *USA*

$$$ ★★   Smooth and lush, ripe and dense; thick and spicy.

Germain-Robin Viognier Grappa, *USA*

$$$ ★★★   Peppery, smooth, and dry with vanilla, spice, and long, lush finish.

Jacopo Poli Sarpa da Poli Cabernet and Merlot, *Italy*

$$ ★★★   Lush chocolate, coffee, and spice; smooth and elegant, lovely, mild.

Jacopo Poli Amarosa di Torcolato, *Italy*

$$$ ★★★   Smooth and lush with spice and lovely length; moderately dry, earthy, and herbal.

Jacopo Poli 1998 Amorosa di Vespaiolo, *Italy*

$$$ ★★★★   Elegant and smooth with refined, pure flavors of spice and white flowers; long and fine.

Luce Grappa, *Italy*

$$$ ★★★   Smooth, sweet, and mellow with grass, spice, and sweet vanilla finish.

Michele Chiarlo Grappa di Barolo, *Italy*

$$ ★★★   Smooth and creamy with spice, pepper, grass, and lovely vanilla; long and mellow.

Monovitigno Cru Picolit, *Italy*

$$$ ★★   Intense pomace nose and explosive grapey flavors with a hot finish.

Nonino Grappa di Merlot Monovitigno, *Italy*

$$ ★★   Composty nose; smooth, spicy, and dry with herbs and long, earthy finish.

Nonino Grappa di Chardonnay Monvitigno, *Italy*

$$ ★★   Amber color; smooth and spicy with grassy flavors and earthy notes.

Nonino Grappa Cru Monovitigno Picolit, *Italy*

$$$ ★★★   Smooth and spicy with elegant, lively flavors; racy, peppery, and complex; vanilla and butterscotch notes.

liqueur and bitters

A DRINK OF PHAROAHS, ✳ EMPERORS, AND KINGS ✳

L iqueurs are the most diverse of spirits, and they also are among the oldest. Over the centuries liqueurs have held a prominent role in folk medicine. These potent spirits have been used medicinally to cure a bad stomach or protect against fainting. Cordials or liqueurs have also been put to work on bigger issues such as finding a mate or mending a broken heart.

✳ DISTILLING LIQUEURS ✳

The Base Spirit

When distillation was first discovered, alchemists felt they had literally trapped life-giving spirits in their elixirs of life. In every country the words for these elixirs were different but the meanings were the same: the water of life. In France there was aqua vitae, which is now eau-de-vie. In Ireland the Gaelic term *uisage beatha* gives us the word "whiskey." In Russian the stuff was called vodka. In Scandinavia, it's aquavit (or akvavit), and in Spanish it's *aguardiente.*

Distilling the spirits is a process in which a liquid turns into a vapor by heating and is then brought back to liquid form by condensation, drop by drop. In a pot still, alcohol is distilled at a low proof (around 130 to 140 percent alcohol or 65 to 70 proof). The resulting liquid is rectified then purified by renewed or continuous distillation. Once the 190 proof (95 percent pure) spirit is odorless and flavorless it can be used in the blending of other spirits and as a base for liqueurs. Spirit bases must be carefully chosen spirits and brandies of high quality. Purity is essential to create a high-end liqueur. Neutral spirits (from potatoes or beets, for example), neutral grain spirit, whisky or whiskey, rum, cognac, Armagnac or grape brandy, fruit spirit, rice spirit—all can be used as a base for liqueurs.

The quality of the spirit is based on the origin and nature of the material, the manner of distillation, and the degree of rectification. Unless a liqueur specifies a type of spirit, such as Baileys Irish Cream or Drambuie, which are whiskey-based, neutral or grain spirit is the assumed base.

Lacing: Making It Sweet

Dates and figs were used to sweeten ancient liqueurs. The date palm was plentiful along the banks of the Tigris, Euphrates, and Nile rivers, the heart of early civilizations. Throughout the Middle Ages and early Renaissance, honey was abundant in Europe and became the preferred source of sweetener. Cane sugar was introduced first by the Arabs who conquered Spain, and was a rarity in Europe. It wasn't until the sixteenth century, when sugarcane production took off in the New World, that the supply became abundant. In a short time sugar replaced honey as the main product for lacing liqueurs. Sugar is turned into syrup by the addition of small quantities of water; in the kitchen, this mixture is called simple syrup. The syrup is added to the alcohol and flavor base. The minimum sugar content for liqueurs is 20 percent (or two hundred grams of sugar per liter). Many liqueurs have up to 35 percent sugar, and "crèmes" must contain 40 percent or four hundred grams of sugar per liter. Sugar accomplishes several things in the liquor; it moderates the acidity of certain fruits (such as citrus), softens the bitterness of some herbs and plants, and allows the perfume aroma to be heightened. The blend of sweet and tart is one of the most pleasurable treats for the palate and certainly one very strong reason for the appeal of liqueurs.

Flavorings

With everything in the world at their fingertips, distillers can allow their imaginations to run wild in the creation of liqueurs. Some manufacturers, such as Marie Brizard, have lines of up to thirty-five flavors. Since every house has its own recipe and no two recipes are alike, you will find numerous crèmes de menthe, cherry kirsches, and coffee liqueurs offered in the marketplace. Other houses, such as Cointreau, make only a single proprietary product. It's important to keep in mind the distinction between various generic types of liqueurs on the one hand and proprietary names on the other. There are many brands of curaçao, for example, a type of liqueur flavored with exotic oranges. Grand Marnier, however, is a proprietary name for a specific orange liqueur that is made exclusively with cognac.

Many of the recipes used by the older manufacturers have been passed down for generations, often with very little alteration of the original. It's reported, for example, that only four people in the world have the recipe for the popular herbal liqueur Chartreuse, and the formula is passed to a new generation only at death. When you gaze at the liqueurs on any back bar in America, you are taking a look at world history on a shelf.

Chemical extracts or essences are not prohibited in the production of liqueurs, but it is very rare that a distiller will stoop to artificial flavorings, a practice used for only the lowest quality products on the market. When used in the manufacturing of a product, the term "artificial" or "imitation" must be on the label in the United States, while in France the term *fantaisie* is designated. In regard to coloring, the colors are generally based on vegetable substance or other naturally occurring food colorings unless otherwise noted.

From the Source to the Bottle: The Art of Flavoring and Manufacturing Liqueurs

The first major step in the process is the selection and preparation of raw ingredients. All plants, fruits, or other natural ingredients to be used in the recipe at hand must be picked at the height of maturation, inspected, cleaned, cut, pitted, crushed, stemmed, peeled, or sorted prior to the extraction of the flavor.

There are three methods of extracting aroma and flavor from

these ingredients: maceration (which includes infusion or digestion), percolation, and distillation. The operations can be separate
or combined. The method of extraction depends on the nature of
the aromatic substance being used, as the goal is to achieve the
greatest intensity of flavor in the process. The results of the
process will be aromatized spirits, infusions, or distillates.

Maceration

This is the simplest of the processes and consists of soaking delicate ingredients in tanks of high-proof alcohol for a sufficient
period of time so the alcohol can absorb the character of the substance. Maceration is used in the case of most tender fruits such
as strawberries, raspberries, peaches, and bananas. The heat of
distillation could burn and alter the taste of these fruits. The
length of time required for the perfume to be absorbed and for
complete infusion with the spirit can be anywhere from several
weeks to several months.

Another form of maceration is infusion (also called digestion). It
is used mainly when the ingredients are dry leaves and plants.
This process is very similar to steeping tea. The leaves or plants
are moistened until they get soft. Following this they are covered
with a heated spirit. The spirit gradually takes on the flavor of this
"tea."

Percolation

As the name implies, this process is much like brewing a pot of
coffee. Spirits are put in the bottom of a tank, heated, and then
pumped up and sprayed over the aromatic ingredients at the top.
The spirit becomes infused with flavor as it drips back down to the
bottom. The process is done over and over again until as much flavor as possible has been extracted. Vanilla beans and cocoa pods
are processed in this method.

Distillation

Only pot stills are used for this method. The purpose is to extract
and concentrate aromatic elements rather than produce alcohol.
Pot stills ensure that vapor waters can be easily collected. When
the flavoring agents—flowers, plants, seed, or rinds—have been
dried beforehand, distillation is the preferred method to gather
their flavors. Once the distillation process is run the heads and
tails (the first impure spirits and the last) are removed and the
process is run again. This second distillation removes the impurities that can result in a morning-after headache.

Creating the "House Blend"

Once ingredients have been extracted as infusions and distillates in one of the three processes, they are combined to create the "house blend" for the final product. A macerated substance can be distilled before it is finally blended or the distillate may be redistilled several times, perhaps with the addition of other herbs and spices in the subsequent runs. All this is done to enhance flavor and aroma before the final blending.

When the formula demands it, liqueurs are aged in old wooden vats or casks in temperature-controlled warehouses. Those liqueurs that aren't aged usually contain ingredients that were previously macerated. Time is essential for the mellowing and maturing of the liqueur and for achieving the perfect fusion of ingredients. Over the past decades some distillers have attempted to introduce ways to shorten the process—heat, ozonization, light waves, even electrolysis—but none of the methods has produced a liqueur of acceptable quality. There is no substitute for the tried and true process of aging in wood. As the man said, "If it ain't broke, don't fix it."

Following aging, if the liqueur contains colloidal materials that cannot be removed by simple filtration, the liqueur is put through a "fining" process. Substances commonly used for this final filtering process can include albumen, milk, bentonite, or isinglass. This will improve the "shine" and brilliance of the liqueur.

After filtration, simple syrup or honey is added and the recipe is adjusted with water or alcohol to reach the desired alcohol content—generally 25 to 40 percent. Some herbal and fruit brands have an alcohol content of 55 percent, such as Chartreuse and some curaçaos. Aged brandy may be added at this point to give the liqueur greater complexity. The addition of color to excite the imagination comes next. Infusions of plants and fruits—brown from tea and coffee or cocoa, green from leaves, yellow from saffron, red from cherries, and red-violet from black currants—enhance the aesthetic of the liqueur. A final filtration removes any suspended particles. The finished liqueur is now ready for bottling and sale. A few liqueurs (anisette, kümmel, and curaçaos) are cold stabilized before final filtration so certain oil may be removed. This is done to prevent clouding.

Liqueurs, like other spirituous beverages, should always be stored in an upright position so that the cork will not deteriorate from prolonged exposure to alcohol. Even bottles sealed with screwcaps have been known to leak over months of storage on their sides. Liqueurs that have been opened will not deteriorate provided they are kept tightly sealed, though after several years there might be some perceptible difference in the product.

Classifications: Types of Liqueurs

The original modern distillers who set up standards to ensure quality and consistency applied terms to their finished products that are still used today, but only partly. Originally there were four main groups of liqueurs, all of which were products of distillation or infusion, and they were classified according to sweetness and alcoholic strength. Liqueurs were classified by quality as ordinaire (lowest quality), demi-fine, fine, or surfine. The terms "crème," "oil," or "balm" referred to a thick and oily consistency, while "water," "extract," or "elixir" indicated a lighter texture. Ordinaires included waters and oils, while fines and surfines included oils, balms, crèmes, and elixirs.

Today these distinctions are not made. Instead, spirits are usually classified as crèmes (such as crème de menthe), liqueurs, fruit-flavored brandies, and creams (which include real dairy cream). Crèmes are sweeter, heavier, and denser, with usually twice as much sugar as other liqueurs. The term "crème" also implies that the spirit's flavor is attributable to a single ingredient. Crème de menthe, for example, is a mint liqueur; crème d'ananas is a pineapple liqueur, and so on. Creams, on the other hand, are liqueurs made with stabilized cream. They are thick, mild, and dangerously easy to drink. They keep best in the refrigerator after opening. A few favorite cream liqueurs are Baileys Original Irish Cream, Godiva Cream, Vermeer Chocolate Cream from Holland, and the dashing new Bushmills Cream from Ireland.

Drinks designated simply as liqueurs are made with neutral grain or cane spirits, and can be of any desired proof. Liqueurs are blended at a proof that brings out the qualities of the fruit, while the proof of a fruit-flavored brandy is regulated by law. Fruit brandies (discussed further in the brandy section of this book) are specially classified to denote their brandy base; they must be at least 70 proof.

The general term "eau-de-vie" is a French expression for an unsweetened fruit brandy and has also come to mean any unsweetened liqueur. Schnapps, as it's known to consumers in the United States, is a sticky, sweetened, flavored liqueur. True German schnapps and the Scandinavian snaps are actually flavored eaux-de-vie with no added sweetener.

With myriad liqueurs on the market, sorting out the differences among these types can be daunting. If you like the taste of peaches, for example, you could look for a peach brandy (distilled directly from peaches, with no added sugar); a peach liqueur (a grain spirit, laced with sugar and flavored with peaches); a peach-flavored brandy (grape-based brandy, flavored with peaches), or a true peach schnapps (grain spirit flavored with peaches, with no added sugar). The best way to discover the differences is through tasting.

✳ LIQUEURS: A HISTORY ✳

Liqueurs can trace their ancestry back to at least 800 B.C., to a drink composed of anise berries and palm wine. This early incarnation pleasured the taste buds of sybaritic Arabian kings, Egyptian pharaohs, and Roman emperors, who relished the unique, concentrated flavor of this exotic beverage. Throughout the ages, liqueurs or sweetened wines were used also by pagan priests in religious rituals and festivals. It was thought that drinking the "nectar of the gods" would ensure a good harvest, an heir to the throne, or a victory in battle.

While we may never know exactly how the process of fermentation began or who to credit for its invention, once discovered, fermented beverages became an important part of every great civilization's social and cultural life. In the Eastern Mediterranean the first liqueurs were produced from grapes, dates, rice, or beer. Date wines were the most abundant liqueur in Mesopotamia (now known as Iraq) and Egypt, since the date was the most plentiful food in the region. Babylonians drank a rose-petal water and fennel drink, while the ancient Greeks made a liqueur containing honey and herbs, which would eventually evolve into the beloved ouzo. In Asia, the Chinese distilled a rice and sugar wine, while Vikings and German tribes drank a version of honey liqueur called mead.

On the Italian peninsula, the Romans inherited a taste for liqueurs from the Greeks. Great inventors that they were, the Romans expanded on the Greek recipes, striving for new combinations of herbs and sweeteners, which were then added to wine. Apothecaries already knew that certain plants had cleansing and medicinal properties, so the practice of making "flavored wine" became an important part of hygienic and therapeutic life. Later, when Moors from the Middle East conquered Spain, the practice of making sweet "wines" spread into Western Europe. The Vikings introduced these early liqueurs to Northern Europe.

In the eleventh and twelfth centuries the important medical

schools at Salerno in Italy and at Montpellier in France began studying the writings of Hippocrates and his works on nectars. These medieval scholar-physicians worked to perfect the alchemy of distillation, making discoveries important to the development of liqueurs as we know them today. In the late 1200s Arnold de Vila Nova, a Catalan alchemist, wrote the first book on the subject of flavored alcohol, later translated into English as *The Boke of Wine*. Arnold described the process of distilling wine into aqua vitae and the process of flavoring the resulting spirits with spices and herbs. This medieval mix-master claimed that these elixirs could restore the body and cure many ailments. The word "distillation" comes from the Latin word *distillare,* meaning to trickle down or drop. Distillation refers to the process whereby a heated liquid containing alcohol and water boils and vaporizes. Since alcohol evaporates at a lower temperature than water, the alcohol vapor rises first and is separated from the water vapor. As the alcohol vapor cools below boiling, it returns to a liquid state. The result is an alcoholic spirit. The breakthrough technique of distillation would eventually expand the production of liqueurs, taking it from the religious to the commercial world.

In the Middle Ages aqua vitae, the "water of life," was thought to be divinely inspired, and it became the special province of the monasteries. Monks became masters of the early distillation techniques. It would be these medieval religious orders that would create hundreds of early liqueurs—a practice that continues today. The monasteries subscribed to Roman and Greek theories concerning the curative power of the herbal drinks and set about diligently trying to create their own elixirs of life. (And it certainly didn't hurt if they tasted good as well!) The cloistered life was ideal for experimentation. There was plenty of land, time, and money to ensure an almost uninterrupted process of discovery. From the 1400s through the early 1600s monastic orders created a considerable number of liqueurs, some of which remain popular today. Bénédictine was created by the Benedictine monk Dom Vincelli in 1510. The recipe for Chartreuse, originally known as "Elixir de longue vie," was a gift given to the Carthusian monastery near Paris in 1605 from François d' Estrées Hannibal, the marshal of artillery under Henry IV. Other monastic liqueurs, such as La Senancole, Carmeline, and Trappastine, were all created at this time. As interest in liqueurs grew, it became apparent that these new spirits were not destined to stay behind cloistered walls.

As exploration expanded, travelers, Crusaders, and pilgrims crossed Europe, bringing with them new plants and herbs. The introduction of spices, herbs, and raw sugar from the New World helped to further commercialize the craft of liqueurs. The monks took advantage of these new discoveries, but it was the alchemists in the growing cities of Europe who really got into the act. They began to practice the art of distilling magical liquids from plants and herbs. This possibly profitable venture vastly outweighed the risks of being accused of sorcery and witchcraft, though in those superstitious times, the practice of magic could lead to a death sentence.

Alchemists used hundreds of the new herbs and plants, attributing specific curative qualities to each. Lily was thought to calm the fire of love, while sage was good for maintaining health and improving memory. Monk's-hood could be used to fight off colds or control fever. According to physician Andrew Boorde, who wrote *A Dyetary of Health* in 1542, the beautifully named grains of paradise were "good for the stomake and the head" and purslane "dothe extynct the ardor of lassyvyousnes, and doth mytygate great heate in all the inwarde partes of man."

By the sixteenth century the local alchemist had been transformed into the neighborhood apothecary. These precursors to modern-day pharmacists prescribed various potions guaranteed to cure a panoply of maladies including baldness, madness, a neglectful love, and even the plague. The treatise on alchemy written in 1651 by the philosopher and scientist John French, in London, was the first serious modern study on the medicinal use of liqueurs. Included in the six-part series were numerous fascinating recipes, including one for a concoction called Aqua Celestis, which called for a whopping sixty-four ingredients, including gold, Oriental pearls, and pure amber. This pricy drink was thought to prevent fainting and infection. Though they would continue to be touted for their medicinal benefits, liqueurs would soon become something more—a social drink for the upper class.

From Medicine to Medici

The Italian aristocrat Catherine de Medici introduced social liqueurs to the (at the time) undercivilized Parisians in 1536, when she married the French king Henri II. Think what you may about Catherine's politics, her enlightenment of the French in matters of food and drink changed the course of culinary history. A Renaissance "hostess with the mostest," Catherine introduced aristocratic society to liqueurs and fine dining and had a direct role in the increasing popularity of digestifs. With court dinners often lasting for upward of six hours with sixty-five courses or more to digest, the tasty elixirs were soon in high demand.

By this time monasteries were competing with both local and royal apothecaries to concoct new liqueur creations. Because kings and queens lived in continual (and well-founded) fear of being poisoned, royal gardens were soon expanded to include great collections of medicinal and remedial herbs and flowers. These carefully monitored plants were also used by the royal apothecary to create drinks for the court. The ever-inventive Catherine had her own private garden and apothecary lab, where her doctors would concoct poisoned "gift" liqueurs that guaranteed her enemies a speedy demise. Meanwhile, apothecaries, witches, and fortune-tellers began making potions to comfort and (supposedly) heal the populace. The most popular tonics were, of course, those that were thought to guarantee love. These were given names such as Oil of Venus, Perfect Love, and Lover's Delight, and were probably about as effective as Love Potion No. 9. The use of liqueurs as tonics, as well as their popularity as alcoholic drinks, created such a demand that the monks could no longer keep up sufficient levels of production. As a result, apothecaries were able to leave the fringes of society and become legitimized as professionals.

While Catherine was introducing delicious and sometimes deadly liqueurs to the French, the Dutch and Germans were creating their own versions of sweetened alcohol. These tonics were, at the outset, more restorative than the new delicate French concoctions. In 1575 Lucas Bols founded what would eventually become Bols Distilleries, an immense international liqueur production company. In what amounted to a little shed (t' Lootsje) on the edge of Amsterdam, Bols began to produce Dutch bitters from imported oranges, as well as kümmel, a drink made from caraway, which aided digestion. Not long afterward, in 1598, the Danzig, Germany, distiller Der Lachs began producing a related caraway and aniseed liqueur. The original sweet liqueur was clear and flavored with aniseed and caraway. Gold was added to the concoction when it became known that gold was valuable in the treatment of certain diseases. (The modern-day Goldschläger is a contemporary descendant of this liqueur.)

Despite its Dutch origins and German name, kümmel is now also associated with Russia. The liqueur traveled from west to east in a most unusual manner. In 1696 Peter the Great of Russia visited Amsterdam to learn shipbuilding firsthand. He worked as a laborer and kept his identity a secret. During the eighteen months he lived in Amsterdam he discovered kümmel. Peter loved the liqueur so much that he visited the Bols distillery to see how it was made. Returning to Russia he introduced it to his court, where it became a must-have commodity. In 1823 the Allasch distillery was established in Livoura on the estate of Baron von Blanckenhagen to make the family's version of this liqueur for export as Mentzendorff Kümmel.

With royal attention focusing on these sweet drinks, liqueurs swiftly became the most fashionable of beverages. When Louis XIV ascended to the French throne, he particularly liked a liqueur called rossolis, from the French "Roi Soleil" (the Sun King) and probably related to the Italian liqueur rosolio. The king's blend contained orange flowers, musk roses, lilies, jasmine, cinnamon, and cloves. One of Louis's mistresses, Madame de Montespan, used to have witches make love potions to arouse the king's passion. (Viagra was still a long way off.) When her potions were discovered, the infamous paramour was accused of attempting to poison Louis, and Madame de Montespan came very close to losing her head—literally—over her royal lover. This so-called *affaire des poisons* created a change in the regulation of manufacturing liqueurs, cordials, and tonics. Professional liqueur makers, trying to distance and protect themselves from common charlatans, created a distillers union. With new guild regulations implemented, liqueurs gained a legitimacy they had never enjoyed before.

In Paris in 1755 the brilliant female distiller Marie Brizard and her nephew, Jean Baptiste Roger, created the first anisette, the now famous anise seed liqueur. Marie had inherited the secret formula from a West Indian she had successfully nursed back to health from a horrible illness. So convinced was she that the drink would be popular, she decided to make it commercially. Anisette was an overnight sensation. It, along with several other liqueurs, rapidly became a staple in public coffeehouses. Ironically, it was still unheard of for polite women to drink in public; these cafés catered to a primarily male clientele who spent the afternoons discussing politics and consuming glass after glass of the colorful, sweet liqueur. As you might imagine, the more anisette that was consumed, the more impassioned their discussion.

The art of making liqueurs was further legitimized by the 1757 publication of A. Cooper's *The Complete Distiller.* Cooper, a scientist and distiller, issued the four rules for making compound cordials and liqueurs: (1) Use neutral spirits. (2) Be sure to leave the fruits and plants to "digest" for a length of time. (3) Pay attention to the heat of the fire, lest the plants stop up the still head and "throw boiling Liquor about the Still-house, so as to do a great deal of Mischief." (4) Use only the "heart" of the distillate (not the heads and tails, which contain impure compounds). Cooper's book became the bible for distillation and was plagiarized worldwide for over a century.

In the beginning liqueurs were predominantly flavored with herbs, but the distillers, ever on the lookout for new flavors, eventually turned to fruit. These new concoctions were grouped under the general term "ratafias," which was derived from the custom of drinking a toast to "ratify" a treaty. To create these tasty spirits, cherries, gooseberries, strawberries, and raspberries were macerated in alcohol with a distillate of spices, herbs, and sugar. The Loire Valley of France and the Po region of Italy supplied most of the fruit used in production.

The onset of the French Revolution in 1787 ended the pleasant days of sipping fruit liqueurs on the streets of Paris. The country was thrown into chaos, and the long afternoons of pontificating in local cafés came to a grinding halt. Those who were lucky fled the country; the less fortunate succumbed to the insanity that gripped France. No one was safe from suspicion of treason, not even the cloistered monks. Monasteries were destroyed and closed. The palace gardens and libraries were looted by the angry working-class *sans-culottes.* All luxury items were discarded, lest the user be labeled an enemy of France. The recipes for many liqueurs, including Chartreuse and Bénédictine, were lost during this time.

Throughout the reign of Napoleon, order gradually returned to France and the rest of Europe. However, it wouldn't be until war subsided on the continent and Napoleon was exiled that distillers and inventors would prosper again, in the emerging Industrial Age. For liqueur manufacturers, exportation became as important as servicing their domestic markets, and in some cases more so. Many of the liqueur firms that are still known today were founded in the postrevolutionary period: Cointreau and Marnier-Lapostolle in France, De Kuyper in Holland, Luxardo in Yugoslavia, Stock in Italy, and Drambuie in Scotland.

The Victorian era saw a steady growth in the appreciation of liqueurs around the world, but it was not until the elegant and carefree age of the Belle Epoque at the turn of the century that liqueur distillers again hit their stride. Every country had its own take on the sweet drinks. Women celebrated the liberating *fin de siècle* by hitting the cafés and, as a result, the majority of new proprietary liqueurs were designed with the tastes of the gentler sex in mind. America created the violet-laced Crème Yvette. The French concocted Liqueur des Belles, Maiden's Cream, and the rather dubious Old Woman's Milk. The Dutch whipped up the suave Rose Without Thorns and the naughty Illicit Love.

The best-known drink reintroduced in France at this time was the strongly intoxicating anise-flavored absinthe. Made from a base of alcohol and wormwood, this drink became a favorite with sophisticates from the 1840s on. The French referred to it as La

Fée Verte, or the Green Fairy. Traditionally diluted with icewater poured over a sugar cube, absinthe found a place in the hearts and glasses of many artists and poets, including Oscar Wilde, Baudelaire, Toulouse-Lautrec, Van Gogh, Manet, Picasso, and Anaïs Nin. Even Sigmund Freud and the always-sociable Joseph Stalin were fans of absinthe. Though wormwood was eventually condemned as a dangerous hallucinatory agent, the hallucinations were more likely due to the fact that absinthe was 72 proof. Absinthe was banned in 1915 and disappeared from the market as concerns about its addictive and even lethal qualities increased.

From the Belle Epoque through World War II, liqueurs held a steady place on American liquor shelves, but it was the arrival of the Italian spirit Galliano in the late 1960s that created a true shock wave. The addition of Galliano to vodka and orange juice sent the traditional screwdriver packing: The Harvey Wallbanger was born. This new cocktail with the funny name appealed to the American sweet tooth, tasting of Galliano's anise, honey, and vanilla. It became a fixture in popular culture. Due to a savvy marketing campaign featuring a hapless surfer named Harvey Wallbanger, sales of Galliano skyrocketed. Other distillers took note, and soon marketing became almost as important as manufacturing. Distillers began to create flavors geared to contemporary trends. This practice continues today.

After several failed attempts at creating a stable emulsion of cream and spirits, most notably Heublein's Cows, Baileys Irish Cream was introduced in 1979. This revolutionary product blends the luscious tastes of cream, chocolate, coffee, and whiskey. It's a bit like having a liquid hot fudge sundae. Sweet and creamy liqueurs made a nice addition to coffee and found their way into other new and imaginative concoctions. Complicated cocktails gradually replaced simpler mixed drinks and straight whiskey, and a new generation embraced liqueurs.

✳ LIQUEURS TODAY ✳

Today's distillers are creating an exciting and wide variety of liqueurs for all taste buds. New flavors seem to come out almost weekly. For the chocolate cookie fanatic, there's Just Desserts Chocolate Chip Cookie Liqueur. For lovers of exotic fruit, there's Alizé Wild Passion, made with passionfruit, mango, grapefruit, and cognac. Hpnotiq, from France, comes from a generations-old recipe from the distiller's family. This blue drink is a combination of cognac, premium French vodka, and natural tropical fruit juices. While new to America, the tradition of adding fruit and tropical juices to cognac is a centuries-old practice in the Cognac region. Adding vodka to the mix is an example of how distillers are creating new takes on old favorites. While many distillers are issuing branded versions of the ever-popular Italian artisanal liqueur called limoncello, they often add artificial colorings and flavors. Make certain to check that you're getting an all-natural limoncello to truly enjoy this delectable Italian liqueur. Even the traditional Mexican spirit tequila is being turned into a liqueur. Patrón XO Café combines coffee and tequila, while Agavero offers the addition of caramel.

Liqueurs are now produced all over the world from well-established distilling houses in France, Italy, Germany, and the Netherlands, to such locations as Jamaica, Israel, and Ireland. As the number of micro-distillers in the United States grows, so does the production of American liqueurs. One of several domestic products worth noting is Crater Lakes Hazelnut Espresso Vodka, from Oregon—a savory addition to a chocolate milk shake. Liqueurs such as Amarula Cream from South Africa, the lychee-flavored liqueur Soho, and Graf's Fränkische Pflaume, a German plum liqueur, are essential ingredients in some of the sexy new cocktails on the urban club scene. Drinks with such catchy names as Watermelon Squeeze, Trummer's Plum, and the evocative

What's in a Name: Liqueur or Cordial?

The word "liqueur" comes from the Latin *liquefacere*, meaning to melt or dissolve. It aptly describes the basic process of creating a drink wherein substances are dissolved in alcohol. The name implies a harmonious blending of several ingredients to create a unique character rich with flavor and aroma. The base of the word "cordial" comes from the Latin word *cor*, which means heart. Many of these potions were originally prescribed by apothecaries and monks to cure, or at least warm, the heart. Until the mid-seventies Europeans tended to use the word "liqueur" while Americans preferred the word "cordial." Today, however, the word "liqueur" dominates the drinking scene on both sides of the Atlantic.

Please, Honey are being concocted in trendy upscale bars and restaurants. These newcomers are giving serious competition to standard cosmopolitans and martinis, while favorite liqueurs such as Kahlúa, Baileys, and Amaretto Disaronno continue to sell well. This popularity is reflected in the statistics. Both here and abroad, liqueur sales have been growing steadily around 5 to 10 percent a year since the early seventies.

✳ WHAT ARE LIQUEURS? ✳

To be labeled a liqueur, a product has to fulfill three conditions. It must have a spirit base, it must be flavored, and it must be sweetened. Sweetening was originally referred to as "lacing" which described the process of "threading or weaving" the sweetener into the liquor. Since each distiller has its own secret techniques and recipes, and most now enjoy scouring the entire world for flavorings and bases, there are thousands of possible combinations. The variety of liqueurs is nearly endless.

HOW SWEET IT IS:
✳ DRINKING AND TASTING LIQUEURS ✳

Chilling a liqueur slightly, in the refrigerator or with the addition of ice, will enhance the spirit's flavor. Cooling the liqueur cuts the impression of sweetness and alcohol, and increases the aroma by bringing out subtle nuances that are not as perceptible when liqueur is served at room temperature. Freezing is not recommended, since extreme cold will dull the complexity of the flavors.

When pouring liqueurs, I suggest that you refrain from using those tiny "liqueur glasses" that seem to grace every household breakfront. These glasses, while often quite lovely to look at, are nearly impossible to drink from, and they look slightly ridiculous in the large hands of most grown-ups. Instead, opt for a larger glass with a chimney-shaped opening that will concentrate the subtle perfume of the liqueur. The glass should have a stem so as to avoid being overwarmed by the touch of your hand, and it should be clear to accentuate the glorious color of the spirit. Of course, a nice Waterford, Baccarat, or Riedel crystal glass is always a wonderful way to enhance the experience of drinking liqueurs, but even the most inexpensive of glasses, if properly shaped, will contribute to your enjoyment and appreciation.

Drinking Liqueurs

When making drinks with liqueurs, it's a good idea to frost the glasses in the freezer before your guests arrive. If you're making sweet drinks, try coating the rim of the glass with lemon juice and sugar before freezing for a lovely addition. When using twists, rub the lemon or orange along the rim of the glass, then twist once over the drink before serving. Place the liqueurs you plan to use in the refrigerator (not the freezer) anywhere up to twenty-four hours before serving.

Glasses to Have on Hand

Snifter of around four to six ounces.
Coupe champagne glass or frappé for cocktails served on
    shaved or crushed ice.
Old-fashioned glasses for drinks served on the rocks.
Tall glasses for long drinks.

When consumed without ice or water, liqueurs can be served neat at just below room temperature. Or you might want to try one of these other ways of serving your favorite.

Frappé. A liqueur served in a champagne saucer or cocktail glass full of crushed or chipped ice and traditionally sipped through a short straw.

Flambé. A flaming drink. Setting drinks aflame is a daring and romantic ritual, but should be done cautiously. It's best to practice first so the mood you set is dramatic, not terrifying. Use a long match to warm the liqueur before flaming, but not in the glass you'll drink from. If the liqueur is low proof, add a dash of brandy, bourbon, Scotch, or vodka so the liqueur will flame. To flambé an iced drink, cut a slice of orange, lemon, or lime peel from room-temperature fruit (cut only the outer zest and avoid the white pulp). Pat the peel dry. Now hold the peel between your thumb and forefinger and bring it close to the flame of a long match. A quick squeeze of the peel will release flammable citrus oils and a brilliant burst of flame will flare up. Now drop the peel into the spirits, stir twice, and enjoy.

Pousse-café. A showpiece drink that consists of several liqueurs floating on top of one another to achieve a rainbow effect in the serving glass. This after-dinner treat is achieved by carefully pouring liqueurs into a tall cordial glass one at a time. Start with the heaviest liqueur first. Density may be hard to determine and may require some experimentation before perfecting the order. To visualize the drink's unique presentation, here is one suggested combination (out of hundreds).

From Bottom to Top

¼ ounce green crème de menthe
¼ ounce yellow Chartreuse
¼ ounce Peter Heering cherry liqueur
¼ ounce brandy

Tasting Liqueurs

Especially when tasting liqueurs, it is important not to overload your taste buds. These spirits are intense and wildly different from one another. To fully enjoy each flavor, try to keep the number of liqueurs you taste to half a dozen. Unlike flights of other spirits, such as vodka, where food is a nice accompaniment, liqueurs are best appreciated on their own. If you must nibble, use a bit of plain bread to cleanse your palate, but I would recommend simply a sip of water between tastes.

Use a clear, clean glass that will hold a reasonable amount of liqueur. A chimney or tulip shape will best permit concentration of the aroma. A stem prevents liqueur from being warmed by the hand, which can affect the flavor and aroma. A brandy balloon is an easily available glass shape that will allow the bouquet to expand. Clear glass permits proper appreciation of the color of the spirit.

Before you even taste the liqueur, hold the glass up to the light and admire the color, then enjoy the "nose" or aroma of the liqueur. Note whether it is delicate or somewhat overbearing. Does it smell like an authentic concentrated version of the spirit's ingredients, or like a synthetic bubblegum version? Now sip. Roll it over the tongue and consider the flavor, the sweetness, and the heat of the spirit. A younger spirit will be "hotter" or sharper than one that is aged. Rinse your palate with cool water. Now sip the liqueur again and savor the flavor in your mouth. See whether you pick up secondary flavors. When you swallow, feel the warmth of the spirit and enjoy the aftertaste, or finish.

✳ THE FLAVORS OF THE WORLD IN A BOTTLE ✳

Liqueurs are lusciously sweet drinks that are meant to be savored. Capturing the essence of some of the world's unique and beautiful flavors, these potions provide an ideal endnote to a wonderful meal. Explore the world of liqueurs and you'll taste oranges from the Orient, herbs from western France and the Po Valley of Italy, coffee beans from Mexico, and cream from Ireland. There is also a group of potions called bitters that, for want of a better place, are also described here.

These are some of the most popular concoctions, grouped by flavor. Specific brand name liqueurs are in bold type.

Nut, Bean, and Seed Liqueurs

While many liqueurs have a slight undertone of almond, some use this nut and other nutlike flavors as their primary ingredient. The stones and kernels of apricots, sloeberries, and cherries and nuts are primarily used to produce the taste.

Almond

Amaretto Disaronno (Italy). The most popular nut liqueur is not really made from nuts at all. It's actually flavored with the almond-like pits of apricots grown in orchards northwest of Milan. These pits have a nutty but slightly bitter flavor, which explains why the liqueur is called amaretto, Italian for "a little bitter." Another reason many people think this lush liqueur is made from almonds is that the very popular almond cookies made in the region are called *amaretti*.

A lovely story is associated with the invention of Amaretto Disaronno. It may be just a legend, but it is widely accepted as truth. The year 1525 was a horrendous one for Lombardy. Famine and war had ravaged the land, and the people were destitute. An obscure young artist, Bernardino Luini, a disciple of Leonardo da Vinci, was painting a fresco in the sanctuary of Santa Maria della Grazie in Saronno, a small village north of Milan near Lake Como. He chose as the model for the Madonna in his painting the proprietress of the small inn in which he was staying. The poor young innkeeper was a beautiful widow raising two small children. She wanted to express her gratitude to the talented artist, but she had no money to spend on a gift. Instead she invented a special drink made from the apricot pits that her daughter gathered in nearby orchards. She combined the pits with herbs and alcohol, and the rest is history. The drink, a true love potion, was the beginning of an ardent romance, and Luini went on to become a celebrated artist. While the young widow's name is lost to us, her image hangs to this day in the fresco Luini painted in the church in Saronno.

The formula for the drink was passed down from innkeeper to innkeeper until 1807 when Carlo Dominico Reina obtained the recipe and began selling it in his apothecary shop. His signature encircles the neck of the product to this day. Since 1939, Amaretto Disaronno (with the original "di Saronno" contracted into a single word and used as a trademark) has been produced commercially by Illva, the Industria Lombarda Liquori Vini Affini, in Saronno. It's sold in a distinctive square antique bottle with a gold label.

Amaretto Disaronno is deep amber in color and has a unique almond and herb flavor with hints of mint, cinnamon, and vanilla. The liqueur is fairly thick in texture. Its intense sweetness is nicely balanced by the gentle bitterness of the apricot pits. The spirit is not aged, but passes a few months of "marrying" time in stainless steel tanks.

Successfully marketed in the United States, Amaretto Disaronno is consumed by itself after dinner or on the rocks, and is an ingredient in several mixed drinks. It has joined a precious few other liqueurs—Cointreau, Grand Marnier, Chartreuse—as a frequently used ingredient in pastries and other desserts. The success of the original amaretto has, of course, brought forth a stream of imitators, some made in Italy and some made domestically. Other Italian amarettos include Lazzaroni, Galliano, Patrician, Trave, Stock, and Amaretto di Torani. Domestic versions include Amaretto di Amore, De Kuyper Amaretto di Cupera, Gaetano, Boston, Bols, Arrow, Hiram Walker, and Dubouchett. These versions are quite pleasant, if not as complex as the original. Most of them, particularly those made in this country, are considerably less expensive.

Crème de noyaux. Domestic and foreign producers make a cordial flavored with bitter almonds, mace, nutmeg, and other spices. This product is not as strongly almond-flavored as amaretto. It is consumed straight, on the rocks, mixed with vodka, or combined with crème de cacao. Some call this liqueur "crème de noyaux," some call it "crème de noya." Some American liqueur producers make crème de almond, a clear red cordial usually based on almond oil or, occasionally, apricot pits. Typically it has a snappy flavor reminiscent of cinnamon and is a colorful addition to mixed drinks.

Hazelnut

Frangelico (Italy). Frangelico is a relative newcomer from northern Italy that has had a significant recent sales success in the United States. Its main flavoring ingredient is hazelnut. A light amber liqueur, Frangelico is crisp and fairly dry with a lush texture and the taste of toasty hazelnuts. There are hints of vanilla and white chocolate in the complex herbal flavors. The Frangelico legend centers on a seventeenth-century hermit-monk named (what else?) Frangelico, who created this liqueur out of woodland nuts and herbs. It is now made commercially in Barbero in Piedmont, not far from Torino. The bottle is in the shape of a pious, robed cleric. Frangelico is a lovely after-dinner drink, straight, in a snifter, and it is also quite good on the rocks. For a refreshing cocktail, blend it half and half with vodka.

Crème de noisette. Based on the lovely and rich hazelnut, these liqueurs are often blended with lemon peel, mace, and all-spice. Fairly sweet with a pale amber color, noisette may resemble a light crème de cacao. There is also a macadamia nut liqueur from Hawaii, which has slight coffee undertones.

There are a few domestic cordials that use a hazelnut base. As with the amaretto reproductions, these are less complex, less expensive, but usually quite pleasant. Gaetano and De Kuyper make widely distributed versions.

Pisa Nut Liqueur (Italy). A recent addition to the roster of nut-flavored liqueurs, Pisa offers a complex blend of several nut essences with a definite slant toward almond and hazelnut. It has a smooth, sweet taste and a pleasing bitter-almond finish. The ingenious slanted bottle is modeled after the Leaning Tower of Pisa. The liqueur is delicious on its own and also makes a nice addition to coffee or cappuccino and other mixed drinks.

Chocolate and Cocoa

Crème de cacao. Before the Spanish conquered South America, Indians had cultivated cocoa trees for hundreds of years. Montezuma, king of the Aztecs, introduced the Spanish explorer Cortés to chocolate in a drink. Once Spain controlled Mexico, Cortés and his men began planting cocoa trees throughout the new Spanish territories. Eventually he brought cocoa back with him to Spain. When the brother of the ruthless French cardinal de Richelieu brought cocoa to France in the seventeenth century, chocolate became a luxury item and a French obsession (and it still is). The other ingredient used in crème de cacao is vanilla. Like its counterpart, cocoa, the vanilla bean was originally grown in South America. Vanilla pods grow on a climbing vine plant that is a member of the orchid family. The best vanilla comes from the island of Réunion, near Madagascar, where French colonial planters first planted the bean.

Crème de cacao is a liqueur made from cacao and vanilla beans. All major liqueur manufacturers produce it. It is produced in either white or brown color, and there is generally no discernable flavor difference between the two. Some manufacturers of chocolate liqueurs infuse the blends with vanilla, mint, cherries, coconut, or oranges.

Vermeer Dutch Chocolate Cream (Netherlands). Real Dutch chocolate combined with vodka and dairy cream make for a delectably smooth and chocolatey experience. This grown-up version of chocolate milk is quite nice on the rocks, but mixes easily into chocolate martinis, White Russians, and other coffee drinks.

Other chocolate liqueurs include Cheri Suisse from Switzerland, Godiva from Belgium, Marie Brizard's Cacao from France, Royal Mint-Chocolate from France, and Vandermint from Holland.

Coffee

The coffee bean has had a long voyage from obscurity to its present position on most of the world's breakfast tables. While it has been a Western drink for only three hundred years, coffee was first written about around 800 B.C. The Greek poet Homer mentions a mysterious black and bitter beverage that could awaken the weariest of travelers. There is also evidence that four thousand years ago warriors from northern Africa went off to battle with apple-sized balls of ground coffee beans mixed with fat as rations. The coffee plant was born in Africa in the Ethiopian region of Kaffa. By the beginning of the fifth century, coffee had made its way to Arabia and, not too long afterward, to Turkey. Yemeni Arabs actually made wine from coffee beans.

By the sixteenth century the first coffeehouse was established in Constantinople. As the trade routes to the mysterious East opened, coffee was introduced into Europe. By 1763 there were 218 coffeehouses in Venice. The caffeine craze spread to Vienna, London, and other great cities, where coffeehouses became centers of social, political, and literary activities. At about the same time coffee was introduced into the Americas.

Coffee was cultivated on plantations in the Caribbean and West Indies, and later in the mountains of Mexico, Brazil, and Hawaii, where climate and soil were ideal for the proliferation of this tropical crop. The production of coffee shifted away from the Middle East as the Dutch and English colonies became the centers for coffee growth.

At some point during this process of world proliferation, probably toward the end of the last century, someone got the bright idea to blend coffee with distilled spirits to make a drink that combined the unique, toasty flavor of coffee with the smoothness and sweetness of a liqueur. The results of this alchemy included the big two coffee liqueurs, Kahlúa and Tia Maria.

Kahlúa (Mexico). Introduced to the United States in 1962, this mahogany-colored, smooth, and syrupy liqueur in the distinctive high-neck bottle with the yellow label has dominated the liqueur market. Kahlúa, the industry standard among coffee liqueurs, has a smoky, toasty coffee flavor with a background of vanilla. It is bright and clean-flavored with a snappy finish and attractive coffee candy sweetness.

Tia Maria (Jamaica). Although still fairly sweet, Tia Maria is dryer and lighter than Kahlúa. It is a product of the Caribbean island of Jamaica and claims to derive from a formula that has been handed down since 1655. In that year the English stormed this then-Spanish island, causing the family that had developed the recipe for the liqueur to flee their plantation. Tia Maria, a courageous housekeeper, saved the family's youngest daughter and the recipe. The daughter kept the formula and passed it on to her eldest daughter on her wedding day. In this way the family tradition continued for nearly three hundred years. In the late 1940s Dr. Kenneth Lee Evans, a Jamaican physician, was served the liqueur at a friend's home. He immediately asked for and got permission to produce the liqueur commercially.

Tia Maria is made from Blue Mountain coffee grown north of Kingston. The amber-colored liqueur has a smoky, roasted aroma and a crisp, tangy coffee and herb flavor with a silky café-au-lait smoothness.

The success of these two coffee liqueurs has spawned a squad of wannabes. Many compete solely on the basis of price, but there are actually some very lovely ones as well. Most of the large quantity of coffee liqueur sold in America is not consumed straight up or even on the rocks. The bulk of it goes into mixed drinks, the most popular of which is the Black Russian. A search will turn up several hundred other cocktail recipes that call for coffee liqueur.

Fruit Liqueurs

Americans love fruit, and fruit liqueurs offer a virtual orchard of captivating natural flavors. Although many of the world's most aromatic fruit liqueurs are made abroad, several domestic companies also offer complete lines. Bols, De Kuyper, Marie Brizard, Old Mr. Boston, and Hiram Walker all offer excellent examples.

Here are some of the fruit liqueurs you might encounter at your favorite spirits merchant.

Banana
Crème de banane (foreign and domestic). Many producers make this white or gold liqueur. It is generally very sweet and syrupy. Banana liqueurs are used in desserts and a few mixed drinks.

Black Currant
Crème de cassis (France and United States). A deep red, low-alcohol, syrupy, sweet concoction, this liqueur was of little use until someone mixed it with Aligoté, the extremely tart white Burgundy. The resulting aperitif, called Kir after the wartime mayor of Dijon, showcases the good qualities of both ingredients, and became a fixture at parties in the 1980s. It can be made with any crisp, dry white wine. The combination of crème de cassis and champagne, called a Kir Royale, is another nice use for this liqueur. I particularly like the Double Crème de Cassis de Dijon liqueur from Lejay-Lagoute.

Black Raspberry
Chambord (France). This thick, sweet, low-alcohol liqueur is flavored mainly with French black raspberries, but other fruits and herbs are used as well. The mixture is sweetened with honey. It is deep amber, tinged with ruby, and its appealing flavor suggests candy fruit. Chambord is made by La Maison Delan in France and packaged in the United States. The bottle is squat and round, with a gold crown. Chambord is particularly delicious poured over vanilla ice cream, and a tablespoon or so in a glass of champagne makes a charming aperitif.

Several domestic producers sell blackberry liqueurs. These are mostly 60 proof and purplish red. They are quite sweet, dense, and are attractive when poured over fruit or ice cream.

Cherry
Cherry Marnier (France). Like Grand Marnier, this spirit uses brandy as a base. It is medium sweet and slightly thick.

Maraschino (Italy and United States). These clear, relatively dry liqueurs are made from the spicy Marasca cherries of Italy and Dalmatia (in the former Yugoslavia). The cherry pits are distilled separately and contribute to a charming bitter-almond nuance. Maraschino is used frequently in mixed drinks.

Cherry Heering (Denmark). One of the best-known cherry brandies has been made from the same method for 165 years. Back in 1818 Peter Heering created his special cherry brandy flavored with Zeeland or Stevns cherries. They are crushed with their stones and then the liqueur is steeped in huge oak casks. The company is still family-owned.

Lemon

Limoncello (Italy).This is a sweet liqueur made of lemons, sugar, and alcohol. Originally made by the farmers along the Gulf of Naples, it is one of Italy's most popular drinks. I particularly enjoy Villa Massa (Italy) 60 proof. Made exclusively from the peels of Sorrento lemons, this fresh-tasting liqueur is a little like sunshine in a bottle. It's lovely chilled or over ice and makes a nice addition to mixed drinks and desserts.

Melon

Midori (Japan). This bright green liqueur, a recent addition to the bar, is made by the giant Japanese distiller Suntory. Midori is fairly sweet but its muskmelon flavor is delicious and quite charming.

Maple

Sortilège (Canada). An unusual recent entry, this Canadian distilled spirit is a blend of premium Canadian whisky and maple syrup. Delicate and not too sweet, this liqueur is delightful when served on its own and is actually quite pleasant when drizzled over ice cream or baked apples. If you let your imagination wander, you might even find a place for it on the weekend breakfast table next to a tall stack of buttermilk pancakes.

Orange

One of the most popular fruits used in liqueurs is the orange. In Greek mythology they were called golden apples and were a sacred fruit that was the centerpiece of stories involving Hercules and Atlas. Sweet oranges, Confucius tells us, grew in the Chinese provinces of Chekiang and Kantung in 500 B.C. However, they did not appear in Europe until the fifteenth century. The first oranges in Europe were the bitter variety brought to Spain by the Arabs. It would take the advent of faster trade ships and more modern modes of transportation for the sweet oranges to make their way to Europe. The divine fruit symbolized fidelity, love, and purity in early Christian times, and in medieval France the orange tree was the tree of kings. So great was the reverence for the rare fruit that Louis XIV ordered an orangerie constructed to house the first orange tree brought to France. At the time the tree was already one hundred years old. With so much history behind it, the orange seemed destined to become the flavor of one of the most popular of all fruit liqueurs.

Cointreau (France). Cointreau sells nearly two million cases in 217 different countries annually. The Cointreau distillery was founded in the town of Angers in the Loire Valley after the French

Revolution. They first made guignolet, a cherry liqueur, but in the 1800s Edouard Cointreau, the founder's son, traveled to the English colonies in the Caribbean and discovered small, bitter wild oranges. The fruit would never last the long voyage, so he shipped dried peels to Angers. His father, Edouard Cointreau, Sr., experimented with the peels and mixed them with other types of oranges. He eventually came upon the secret formula that created a double-distilled orange liqueur that was dry. He was the first to make such a dry liqueur—three times drier than most liqueurs of the time. The drink was so popular that imitations proliferated under the name "triple sec" (three times as dry). Frustrated at the imitators, Cointreau named his creation after himself.

Three generations and 142 years later, the same secret formula is still in use by the family. Cointreau is bittersweet with a delicate orange flavor derived from the peels of oranges from Europe, the Caribbean, North Africa, and the Middle East. It has a silky texture and, although sweet, leaves a decidedly dry impression on the palate. Since its American introduction at the 1893 International Exhibition in Chicago, Cointreau has had a devoted following here. To handle the demand, a marketing subsidiary was recently established in New York. Cointreau can be used in any mixed drinks that call for triple sec (especially the margarita), but this elegant liqueur is best served on the rocks or on its own.

Grand Marnier (France). Marnier-Lapostolle was founded by Jean-Baptiste Lapostolle in 1827. At first the company bottled a number of liqueurs, but by the turn of the century its orange version had taken center stage. Grand Marnier is based on cognac and the peels of bitter oranges from Haiti. It is amber in color, and its dry citrus component combines congenially with the rich toastiness it receives from cognac. Grand Marnier has become indispensable in dessert making and is used in many pastries and soufflés. It's also delicious over ice or served neat in a cordial glass or snifter. As a stand-alone drink, Grand Marnier, because of its cognac base, has more depth and complexity than Cointreau.

Curaçao. Curaçao is a generic name referring to the island that produces some of the Caribbean's best bitter oranges. The peel was brought in the seventeenth century to Holland, where the Dutch created the first orange liqueur. In the nineteenth century it was considered a drink for ladies. Today there are many curaçaos on the market. Most are produced in the United States but are made with imported peels. These liqueurs are usually amber and sweet, with a charming bitterness. Curaçaos are about 60 proof, and some use a brandy base. A number of distillers make one that has been tinted blue. There is no significant difference in flavor or proof between this product and the regular variety, or between amber and the few clear curaçaos available.

Sloe

Sloe gin (England and United States). The sloe is a small wild American plum. The liqueur made from it is misnamed, because it is not a gin, although early versions were made by macerating the fruit in gin. Bright red and medium sweet, it has an intriguing flavor of wild cherry and bitter almond. Sloe gin is almost never consumed alone; it is used in mixed drinks such as sloe gin fizzes.

Herbal Liqueurs

Absente (France). Not to be confused with absinthe, the now illegal drink of decadent Parisian poets, Absente is a very recent creation by spirits marketer Michel Roux. It packs all the licorice flavor of its predecessor, but the possibly harmful wormwood extract is "absent." Even without the wormwood, all that alcohol may have you recklessly reciting Baudelaire, so it's a good idea to dilute Absente with four parts water as was done with absinthe. Traditionally, this was done by pouring the water through a slotted spoon holding a sugar cube. The drink will turn milky like an anisette and lose a bit of its kick.

    Bénédictine (France). The closely guarded formula for Bénédictine was first produced in 1510 in the Bénédictine abbey cf Fécamp in France by Dom Bernardo Vincelli. It is said that an angel appeared to the monk in a vision and urged him to use angelica as a remedy against the plague. He set out to create a mixture of herbs and spices that would not only prevent the plague but cure other ills as well. During the French Revolution, the formula was lost until a distinguished merchant from Fecamp, Alexandre Legrand, rediscovered the recipe in 1863 among some long-hidden manuscripts. The Legrand family has been producing Bénédictine ever since, and today it is still made in the same location. DOM Bénédictine herbal liqueur is made on a cognac brandy base. After several separate distillations, Bénédictine is aged for four years before it is bottled. DOM, which is printed on every label, stands for *Dio Optimo Maximo,* Latin for "To God, Most Good, Most Great." Hundreds of imitations have been tried, but the original formula still stands alone.

    Chartreuse (France). Chartreuse dates from the beginning of the seventeenth century when the recipe for an "elixir de longue vie" (elixir of long life) was given to a Carthusian monastery outside

Paris by Henri IV's marshal of artillery. For more than 150 years the monks tinkered with the formula. In 1764, at the Carthusian monastery in the Massif de la Chartreuse in southeastern France, Frère Maubec was in charge of the study that settled on a blend made from 130 different plants and herbs. Two Chartreuse liqueurs were produced, an Elixir de Santé and an Elixir de Table. The latter version was the green drink that is still popular today. As in the case of Bénédictine, the recipe was almost lost during the French Revolution. A monk charged with preserving the copy of the recipe was left in the monastery. He was eventually arrested and imprisoned, but not searched. The brave monk secretly passed on the manuscript to a sympathizer who got the recipe back to Chartreuse.

Green Chartreuse has a minty, spicy flavor. It is crisp, peppery, and very high in alcohol—55 percent to be exact. In 1838 a yellow version of Chartreuse was created. It is sweeter and mellower than the green, and its hue was so intriguing that the liqueur gave its name to a color. Honey was added to the mix and the alcoholic content was dropped to 43 percent. In addition, small lots of both green and yellow Chartreuse are specially aged in oak for twelve years and labeled VEP (Vieillissement Exceptionnellement Prolongé, or exceptionally prolonged aging). These aged liqueurs develop a softer more complex flavor. The green VEP is 54 percent alcohol and the yellow is 42 percent. In the early 1920s the production and marketing of Chartreuse was sold into nonchurch hands. The formula and the direction of production, however, remain under the control of Carthusian monks who work every day at the present Chartreuse distillery in Voiron, a small city in the foothills of the Alps not far from Grenoble.

Elisir du Dr. Roux (France). A gorgeous green liqueur concocted by spirits marketer Michel Roux, this elixir is filled with fourteen different herbs and aromatics. Many of the ingredients are derived from energy-enhancing plants common to the landscape of Provence. Taken straight it's an acquired taste, but it adds a wonderful herbaceous flavor to mixed drinks.

Galliano (Italy). The most popular of Italian herbal liqueurs, Galliano was named after the Italian war hero Giuseppe Galliano. It is lush and moderately syrupy in texture with a smooth herbal-vanilla flavor that finishes with a pleasant twinge of bitterness. This liqueur is less complex than its French cousins, but at the same time its flavors may be easier for many consumers to like. Galliano was first made around the turn of this century in Livorno, on the Tuscan coast. It is now produced in a modern plant near Milan. Unlike its French counterparts, this Italian liqueur is given very little age. After several separate distillations, the various lots are blended and then held for three months while their flavors marry. Then, after being adjusted to 40 percent alcohol, Galliano is bottled. In the United States it had a tremendous upsurge in popularity when the Harvey Wallbanger became a fashionable cocktail in the 1960s. In Trieste, near the Austrian border, Stock, one of Italy's biggest distillers, makes an attractive Galliano clone called Roiano.

Jägermeister (Germany). Jägermeister is an herbal concoction made since 1878 by the Mast family in Wulfenbüttel, Germany. It tastes at first like a liqueur, but finishes like a bitters, with spicy, peppery, and decidedly bittersweet flavors. It is classed here as an herb liqueur along with Bénédictine and Chartreuse, but its flavors would also make it welcome in the bitters category. Made from fifty-six different herbs, Jägermeister has its share of medicinal herbs such as rhubarb roots from the Himalayas, gentian roots from the Alps, valerian roots from Japan, and chamomile blossoms from Egypt. In addition, there are plenty of barks, seeds, and resins. It is reddish brown in color. The recommended way to drink Jägermeister is to down it, chilled, in a short, single shot. Some like to follow it with a beer. Seen as a shortcut to extreme inebriation, Jägermeiser shots became very popular with the college set in the 1980s.

Pernod (France). Henri-Louis Pernod opened his distillery in 1805 to manufacture commercially a liqueur created by his father-in-law. The liqueur was an absinthe, a heady concoction of 65 to 75 percent alcohol flavored with anise and the supposedly hallucinogenic wormwood. Pernod's absinthe was a huge hit, especially among the bohemian set in Paris. Fearing corruption of public morals, government authorities decided to ban absinthe in 1915. Pernod was forced to close down. But he reformulated his recipe, minus the offending wormword, and reopened his distillery five years later. Since that time Pernod has been an unqualified success both in France and abroad. Pernod is a true anisette produced by distillation and using only aniseed. The similar-tasting liqueur type known as pastis (such as the Ricard brand) is made by maceration using a combination of aniseed and licorice.

Tuaca Liquore (Italy). This handsomely packaged Italian liqueur is a relative newcomer to the marketplace. It is light amber in color and has an attractive, moderately sweet herbal-vanilla flavor.

Sambuca Romana (Italy). Flavored with anise, elderberries, sugar, and a secret combination of herbs and spices giving a licoricelike taste, Sambuca Romana is the most popular of the Italian sambucas produced. The name comes from the Latin name for the elderbush, *Sambucus.* Galliano and Luxardo are other distillers of sambuca.

Licor 43 (Spain). "Cuarenta y Tres" gets its name from the forty-three ingredients that are its components. This is the most popular liqueur in Spain. The product has been made since 1924 by Diego Zamora, but its roots go back several hundred years to artisanal products made by locals.

Schnapps

Not to be confused with snaps or schnaps (the popular Scandinavian and German terms for aquavits), schnapps are white brandies distilled from fermented fruits. These spirits keep some of the congeners that are removed in the production of vodka. Clear and sweetened, these spirits are flavored with everything from cinnamon to something called "cheriberi." Often the aromas call to mind a well-stocked candy counter.

It is apple schnapps that plays such a strong role in the very popular apple martini, and peppermint schnapps adds the sting to the vodka stinger. These very popular spirits are excellent for mixed drinks and will appeal to the most imaginative mixologists. One of the main differences between schnapps and flavored vodkas is that vodkas will be flavored with natural fruit essences, while any flavoring, including artificial compounds, are permitted in schnapps. It is worth noting that American commercial brands are heavily sweetened and often contain glycerin, while the true German schnapps are unsweetened and contain no glycerin.

Cream Liqueurs

Cream liqueurs are the hottest thing to hit the liquor business in years. It all started in 1979 when a company called International Distillers and Vintners (IDV) brought a totally new product to market, Baileys Irish Cream. This "cream liqueur" was the result of a technological breakthrough that allowed fresh cream and alcohol to be combined in such a way that they were completely homogenized and remained so indefinitely. Made in Ireland, this smooth blend was mixed with sweeteners and flavorings to make something unique. The total effect was reminiscent of the classic brandy Alexander; the big difference was that this drink would never separate.

Cream liqueurs are very nice at the end of a meal, served either chilled or at room temperature, neat or on the rocks. They also are delicious poured over ice cream or mixed with brandy to create a less sweet, more potent drink.

Baileys Original Irish Cream (Ireland). It its first year Baileys sold only a scant seventeen thousand cases. The next, more than ten times as much was consumed. In 1983 more than one million cases were purchased. It was the most dramatic product introduction in the history of the wine and spirits industry. Today sales are even greater and are still growing. (It appears that cream liqueurs have a bit more staying power than wine coolers did.) As might be expected, this impressive success prompted a number of variations from other companies. Some were flavored with rum or coffee, while others were very much like Baileys, only less expensive. So far, none of them has been able to slow the phenomenal sales of the leader.

Baileys Irish Cream is light brown in color and contains fresh dairy cream (which the company claims is not more than two hours old at the time of production), Irish whiskey, and natural flavorings such as vanilla and chocolate. The mixture is then homogenized to ensure uniformity in every bottle, pasteurized to preserve freshness, and then cooled and bottled. Baileys has medium viscosity and is smooth and creamy without being cloying. It has a fresh and appealing milk chocolate flavor.

Amarula Wild Fruit Cream (South Africa). Obtained from the amarula tree, this liqueur was first introduced in 1995. The legend goes that locals began noticing that elephants were gorging themselves on the fermenting fruit of the tree. Instead of being aggressive and hostile, the elephants were happy. The tree developed a mystical cachet, which has carried over to the liqueur made of its fruit.

Bitters

Bitters are the essences of bark, roots, fruits, plants, stems, seeds, and other botanicals incorporated into an alcohol base. This type of distillate is a relatively modern development, having come along in the nineteenth century, but it is really descended directly from the original medicinal elixirs that were the forerunners of today's liqueurs. Actually, the line of demarcation between bitters and liqueurs is a bit fuzzy. A number of bitters fit the definition of liqueur and vice versa. The characteristic that sets bitters apart, besides their obvious bitterness, is their original use as a medicine, usually as a stomachic or digestive aid.

Amer Picon (France). Amer Picon is a reddish-brown bitter liqueur that has been made in France since 1837. It contains gentian and cinchona bark, which yields quinine, but the most prominent flavor is bitter orange. Aficionados like to drink Amer Picon on the rocks with soda.

Angostura Bitters (Trinidad). The formula for Angostura was developed in 1824 by Dr. Johann Siegert, who was the surgeon-general in the army of the South American hero Simón Bolívar. The introduction of the tonic came after Dr. Siegert spent four years trying to find a potion that would improve the health and appetite of his troops. The name derives from the fact that the good doctor was headquartered in the port of Angostura, Venezuela, which is now known as Ciudad Bolívar.

Angostura contains herbs and spices, but the formula is still kept secret by the Siegert family. The only herb actually named on the label is gentian. Angostura is presently manufactured in Trinidad in the West Indies. Angostura is a powerful 90 proof, which explains why it is only dispensed in drops and dashes. It does have a unique ability to enhance and intensify the flavors of other ingredients in drinks as well as in foods.

Cynar (Italy). Artichokes? That's right, this Italian bitter *aperitivo* is made from a maceration of several herbs, but the main flavor comes from artichoke leaves. Cynar (pronounced "chee-nahr") is sipped before dinner in Italy, often on the rocks with a slice of orange. It is also frequently used in mixed drinks.

Campari (Italy). The world's most popular bitters was created by Gaspare Campari in 1860, the year Italy was united into a single nation. His idea was to offer a new drink to the patrons of his elegant Milan café, and it became an immediate success. By the turn of the century, thanks to the marketing savvy of his son Davide, Campari had become a national fixture, and soon after that it grew into an international triumph. Today this bright red, spirit-based *aperitivo* is available in 169 countries. Over five million cases are sold worldwide. The Campari company still uses Gaspare's original formula, which includes herbs and fruits from four continents. These ingredients are blended and then aged in oak. Campari's flavor is soft, sweet, and pleasantly bitter.

In Italy Campari is so popular mixed with soda that premixed Campari-Soda sells more than four hundred million bottles each year. In addition, two world famous cocktails are made from Campari: the Americano and the Negroni. The Americano is equal parts of Campari and sweet vermouth, and the Negroni is equal parts of Campari, sweet vermouth, and gin.

Fernet Branca (Italy). I first tasted this strange brown liquid in Gascony when it was proffered as a certain cure for extreme gastric distress. It worked. This elixir was originally introduced in 1845 by a young Milanese woman named Maria Scala, who subsequently married into the Branca family. The mysterious "bitters liqueur" is made from a secret formula that contains some forty herbs and spices—including rhubarb, chamomile, anise, cardamom, clove, gentian, and myrrh. Many of these ingredients come from the Alpine foothills not far from Milan, but others are imported from remote parts of the world. Each component is carefully tested for quality before being used in production. The word "fernet" translates as "hot iron," which refers to a pokerlike tool that was used to stir the mixture in the early days of Fernet Branca's production. Since the beginning, this popular brand of bitters has been made in Milan exclusively by the Branca family. The secret formula has been carefully passed down from generation to generation, and today the ingredients are put through a computerized measuring program to ensure consistency in the product. Europe's most popular digestif, Fernet Branca sells more than a million cases a year in Italy alone. Most Italians drink this elixir straight or on the rocks. In Argentina it is often taken as an aperitif, while in Germany it is sometimes followed by beer. Some people like to add it to their coffee after a meal.

Gammel Dansk (Denmark). Over four hundred thousand cases of Gammel Dansk are sold in tiny Denmark every year. This bitters is made from an age-old recipe that includes twenty different herbs and fruits. The dark amber drink is peppery, assertively herbal, and completely dry. Its flavor is one of the liveliest and bitterest among bitters.

Peychaud's Bitters (United States). Antoine Amedie Peychaud was a New Orleans apothecary who, in 1793, concocted a tonic that was supposed to cure virtually every disease known to man. Although its curative powers may have been somewhat overstated, Peychaud's tonic became a local favorite as a flavoring for mixed drinks. Peychaud's is usually dispensed a few drops at a time. It is also used in a number of Creole recipes.

Punt e Mes (Italy). The Carpano company has been producing vermouth in the Piemonte region of northern Italy since 1786. At the café on Turin's Piazza Castello the bartender's specialty was mixing various flavorings into vermouth. The addition of bitter quinine was particularly fashionable. It was so popular, in fact, that the Carpano company decided to bottle this particular combination so that it could reach a wider audience. The result was a bitter vermouth. Punt e Mes was named inadvertently by a member of the Turin Stock Exchange who was so preoccupied by his work that he mistakenly asked for a "point and a half" instead of a bitter vermouth. Punt e Mes is always served chilled, straight up in a chilled shot glass or over ice with a splash of soda water and an orange slice. It also works very well in the Americano and Negroni mentioned above.

Making Liqueurs at Home: Two Recipes

Limoncello

6 lemons (not too ripe and grown
    without chemical treatment)
4½ cups vodka
2 cups sugar
4½ cups water
2 two-liter glass bottles

Peel the lemon, being careful to avoid the white part of the peel. Put the skins in a bottle with a wide neck. Add the vodka. Close firmly and let it rest for twenty days in a dark room. After twenty days put the sugar and water in a pot and warm the concoction until the sugar dissolves. Pour the alcohol/lemon mix through a strainer covered with cheesecloth into the sugar and water syrup. Stir for a few minutes. Fill the two bottles quickly and close. Let the concoction rest for another twenty days in a dark room. Chill and drink.

Banana Liqueur

1 large, just-ripe banana, peeled
4 cups vodka or light rum
1¼ cups granulated sugar
½ cup water
1 two-inch piece of vanilla bean

Mash the banana. Add the banana to the vodka or rum. Using a wooden spoon, submerge the banana mash. Steep for two weeks in a dark room. Put the sugar and water into a pot and warm the concoction until the sugar dissolves. Slit open the vanilla bean. Pour the banana/alcohol mixture through a cheesecloth-covered strainer into the water and sugar syrup. Add the vanilla bean. Stir for a few minutes. Pour into two bottles and close quickly. Let the flavorings rest in a dark room for thirty days. Remove the vanilla bean. Strain again and put the spirit back into the bottle. Age for another thirty days. Now the bottles can go into the fridge or on your shelf until you want to serve the liqueur.

tasting notes

NUT, BEAN, AND SEED LIQUEURS

Amaretto

Amaretto di Amore, *USA*
$ ★★   Luscious nutlike flavors and a slightly bitter finish.

Amaretto Disaronno, *Italy*
$ ★★★   Medium amber color; smooth, creamy, dense with almond, marzipan flavors; long and lush.

Paolo Lazzaroni & Figli Amaretto di Saronno, *Italy*
$ ★★   Caramel and marzipanlike flavors with a lengthy finish.

Nuts

Frangelico, *Italy*
$$ ★★★   Light amber color; sweet, creamy with lovely hazelnut and vanilla flavors; balanced and long.

Pisa Nut Liqueur, *Italy*
$$ ★★   Medium dark amber; lovely aroma of sweet hazelnuts and spice; smooth and sweet with nuts and cinnamon.

Charbay Nostalgie Black Walnut Liqueur
$$$ ★★   Dark amber color; sweet and lush with bitter walnut and spice.

Chocolate

Just Desserts Chocolate Chip Cookie Liqueur, *USA*
$$ ★★★   Rich dark-chocolate flavors in a cream.

Just Desserts Thin Mint Chocolate Cookie Liqueur, *USA*
$$ ★★   Unappealing color but creamy mint flavors.

Vandermint Minted Chocolate, *Holland*

$$ ★★★   Deep, dark amber color; smooth and lush with lovely flavors of mint and chocolate; long and nicely balanced.

Coffee

Crater Lake Hazelnut Espresso Liqueur, *USA*

$$ ★★★   Dark amber color; toasted coffee and lush hazelnuts, moderately sweet with rich, fresh flavors.

Illy Café Liqueur, *Italy*

$$ ★★   Lush and creamy with lots of sweetness and intense coffee flavors; toasty, rich, and long.

Kahlúa Coffee Liqueur, *Mexico*

$ ★★   Intense espresso-bean character with a thick, rich mouth feel.

Kahlúa Especial, *Mexico*

$$ ★★   The high-octane version of Kahlua (70 proof instead of 54 proof); luscious texture and bursting with roasted coffee-bean flavors.

Patrón XO Café, *Mexico*

$$ ★★★   Dark brown color; roasted coffee nose, thick and dense with sweet coffee flavors; rich, dense, and long; capitalizes on the popularity of its sibling tequila brand.

Rumba Coffee Liqueur, *Mexico*

$ ★★★   Dark amber with lovely sweet, pure espresso flavor and long, smooth finish; good, clean spirits and lovely long flavors.

Sabra Coffee Liqueur, *Israel*

$$ ★   Dark amber color; thick coffee flavors, very sweet and showing some cherry fruit with a bitter aftertaste.

Strega Sambuca, *Italy*

$$ ★★   Spicy and dense with coffee and licorice tones.

Tia Maria Coffee Liqueur, *Jamaica*

$$ ★★   Dark and sexy with deep, pungent rum and coffee flavors.

FRUIT LIQUEURS

Cherry

Amour en Cage Ground Cherry Liqueur, *Canada*

$$ ★★★   Intense and concentrated with deep, earthy, cherry flavors.

Heering Cherry Liqueur, *Denmark*

$$ ★★   Ruby color; sweet and lush with jammy, dense cherry fruit.

Pear

Aqua Perfecta Poire Pear Liqueur, *USA*

$$ ★★★   Orangy-amber in color; creamy and lush with the essence of pear with notes of orange peel and a sweet, creamy texture; long and balanced.

Belle de Brillet Poire Williams Liqueur, *France*

$$ ★★   Supple pear flavors with a rich mouth feel.

Douce Provence Poire Williams & Cognac Liqueur, *France*

$$ ★★★   Apple and smoke; toasty, lush, rich, and long.

Mathilde Liqueur Poires, *France*

$ ★★   Light golden in color; creamy and very sweet (almost too much sugar) but with lovely pear fruit and smooth vanilla.

Raspberry

Aqua Perfecta Framboise Raspberry Liqueur, *USA*

$$ ★★★   Dark ruby color; explosive raspberry fruit with tangy acidity, aromatic notes, and exquisite flavors; thick and lush with smooth texture and gorgeous fruit.

Chambord Raspberry Liqueur, *France*

$$ ★★★   Dark ruby color; lush, sweet, jammy black raspberry fruit and smooth texture.

Lemon

Caravella Limoncello Originale, *Italy*

$$ ★★★   Cloudy yellow; thick and sweet with true lemon flavor and lemon rind bitterness with spice and zesty spirits.

Giori Limoncello, *Italy*

$ ★★   Lemon chiffon flavors; lush, ripe, and fat.

Limoncé Liquore di Limoni, *Italy*

$$ ★★★   Cloudy yellow; creamy and smooth with sweet lemon fruit and a nice twist of spicy lemon oil.

Marchesa Limoncello Anna Maria Toscano, *USA*

$ ★★★   Cloudy lemon yellow; sweet and lush with ripe lemon-drop flavor and a long, racy finish.

Villa Massa Liquore di Limoni, *Italy*

$$ ★   Clear and bright with a light greenish yellow tint; sweet and viscous with snappy, penetrating flavors.

Orange

Bauchant Liqueur Napoléon, *France*

$$ ★★★   Medium amber; lovely bouquet of fresh Valencia oranges; silky and viscous with bright orange flavors and some hot, spicy cognac flavors.

Caravella Orangecello Originale, *Italy*

$$ ★★★   Cloudy orange color; smooth citrus flavors with notes of orange peels; sweet and creamy with snappy spirits.

Citronge Extra Fine Orange Liqueur, *Mexico*

$$ ★★   Smooth and spicy with soft orange flavors and creamy texture; sweet and lush with some heat on the finish.

Cointreau Orange Liqueur, *France*

$$ ★★★   Smooth and sweet with fragrant orange, orange peel, and spice flavors; long and showing some heat; the first triple sec and still the definitive version.

Dobbé "O" Orange Liqueur with Cognac, *France*

$$ ★★   Pale gold color; lush orange flavors and notes of zest; sweet and smooth with thick texture and a spicy finish.

Extase XO Liqueur d'Orange, *France*

$$$ ★★★   Smooth and ripe with vanilla, honey, and lovely orange flavor with spicy cognac and an alcohol burn at the end.

Grand Marnier Liqueur, *France*

$$ ★★★   Burnished orange and cognac flavors with beautiful balance; this is the original Grand Marnier recipe and it's a classic.

Grand Marnier Cuvée du Centenaire, *France*

$$$ ★★★★   A special version created in 1927 to mark the company's centennial; sublime essence-of-orange flavors and a silky, exquisite finish; uses rare cognacs aged up to twenty-five years.

Grand Marnier Cuvée Spéciale Cent Cinquantenaire, *France*

$$$$ ★★★★   The 150th anniversary edition of Grand Marnier, with fifty-year-old reserve cognacs; rich amber color, lovely toasted orange nose, smooth and creamy with lush orange and orange rind flavors and complex cognac highlights with spice and a nice alcohol bite. Possibly the world's greatest liqueur.

GranGala Triple Orange Liqueur, *Italy*

$ ★★★   Creamy, orange peel and spice; sweet, hot, and balanced; long and rich.

Sabra Chocolate Orange Liqueur, *Israel*

$$ ★★   Dark ruby amber color; sweet and lush with chocolate and candied orange.

Santa Teresa Orange Liqueur, *Venezuela*

$$ ★★   Rum based; lush and sweet with orange flavors and rich caramel; long and sticky.

Miscellaneous Fruit

Alizé Gold Passion, *France*

$ ★★   Sexy and enticing; fresh, vibrant fruit with oak undertones; contains passion fruit and cognac.

Alizé Wild Passion, *France*

$S   ★★★   Citrusy and exotic with appealing tropical fruit flavors; a blend of passion fruit, mango, grape-fruit, and cognac.

Envy, *France*

$$ ★★   Deep electric blue in color; bright fruit punch fla-vors with elements of orange, passion fruit, and guava; fresh and intense with sweet, tangy flavors.

Fruja Mango Liqueur, *USA*

$ ★★   Exotic tropical fruit tones with a moderate finish.

Hpnotiq, *France*

$$ ★★★   Cloudy blue color; juicy, tangy tropical fruit fla-vors (pineapple, passion fruit, orange) with racy acidity and a long, snappy finish.

Marie Brizard Kiwi Strawberry Liqueur, *France*

$ ★★   Greenish chartreuse color; spicy and fresh with kiwi and strawberry flavors and lots of sugar.

Marie Brizard Orange Banana Liqueur, *France*

$ ★   Orange-gold in color; decent flavors of orange and sweet banana; not wholly authentic and very sweet and cloying.

HERBAL LIQUEURS

Anisette and Pastis

Absente, *France*

$$ ★★★   Light green color; intense, mostly dry and intense licorice flavors; bright and spicy, pep-pery and long.

Charbay California Pastis

$$$ ★★   Smooth and creamy with soft, sweet licorice; mellow, lush, and balanced with mild flavors.

La Muse Verte Pastis, *France*

$$ ★   Immediate anise-licorice flavors backed with herbaceous notes.

Nectar Aguardiente, *Colombia*

$ ★★   Smooth anise nose; clean, vanilla, and anise flavors, spicy, long, and fresh.

Pernod Pastis, *France*

$$ ★★★   Bright lemon yellow; smooth and complex with smooth anise and licorice, balanced herbs and spice, long and complex.

Ricard Pastis de Marseilles, *France*

$$ ★★★   Medium amber color; silky anise, licorice, and Provençal herbs; complex, spicy, intense, and classic.

Other Herbal Liqueurs

Bénédictine D. O. M., *France*

$$ ★★★   Amber hued with striking herb flavors wound with citrus.

Chartreuse Liqueur (Green), *France*

$$ ★★★   Light green color; intense bitter herbs, moderately sweet and complex with mint, green herbs, and spice.

Chartreuse Liqueur (Yellow), *France*

$$ ★★★   Intense acid yellow hue; milder (80 proof as opposed to 110 proof) and sweeter than its green sibling, with similar mountain-herb flavors and a lingering finish.

Elisir du Dr. Roux, *France*

$$ ★★★   Greenish, chartreuse color; strong, thick, sweet, and bitter with herbs, mint, and spice; a newfangled liqueur dressed up as a classic, but quite nice.

Jägermeister, *Germany*
$ ★★★   Dark brown color; smooth and lush with clean, mellow spices and lively licorice; long and balanced; intended as a digestif but popular as shots.

Licor 43, *Spain*
$$ ★★★   Lush, sweet, and complex with herbal and vanilla tones.

Liquore Strega, *Italy*
$$ ★★★   Lemon yellow color; smooth and lush with sweet, herbal flavors highlighted with mint, bitters, and long, complex finish.

Tuaca Liqueur, *Italy*
$$ ★★   Dark amber color; smooth and creamy with sweet honey-vanilla flavors and some fruit and herbal notes; long and rich.

Oro di Mazzetti Liqueur, *Italy*
$$ ★★   Smooth and sweet with grappa flavors and a rich candied finish; contains flakes of 23-karat gold.

SCHNAPPS

De Kuyper Peachtree Schnapps, *USA*
$ ★   Moderate peach flavors with a sweet aftertaste.

De Kuyper Sour Apple Schnapps, *USA*
$ ★   Zippy and puckery; flavors of Granny Smith apple and a tart finish.

Dr. McGillicuddy's Mentholmint Schnapps, *Canada*
$ ★   Refreshing breath-mint flavors; may be an acquired taste.

De Kuyper Peppermint Schnapps, *USA*
$ ★   Hot, sweet, and thick with tangy, minty flavors.

Dr. McGillicuddy's Vanilla Schnapps, *Canada*
$ ★★   Creamy, lush, and lovely with nice exotic vanilla.

CREAM LIQUEURS

Irish Cream Liqueurs

Baileys Irish Cream, *Ireland*
$ ★★★   Rich, café-au-lait flavors; lush and ripe on the finish.

Bushmills Irish Cream Liqueur, *Ireland*
$ ★★★   Smooth and creamy with milk chocolate and rich, smooth flavors; lovely balance with racy spirits and long, smooth finish.

Carolan's Irish Cream Liqueur, *Ireland*
$ ★★   Thick, creamy, dense, and lush.

Old Whiskey River Bourbon Cream, *USA*
$$ ★★★   Smooth and creamy with lovely mocha and chocolate flavors and a zingy hit of whiskey on the finish.

O'Leary's Irish Cream Liqueur, *Ireland*
$ ★★   Lush and creamy with caramel notes; spicy and long on the finish.

O'Mara's Irish Country Cream Liqueur, *Ireland*
$ ★★★   Racy with vanilla and lovely caramel notes.

Rum Cream Liqueurs

Angostura Caribbean Rum Cream, *USA*
$ ★★   Café-au-lait color, smooth, thick, and creamy with spice, caramel, and rum flavors; sweet and lush with a nice, hot lift at the finish.

Sangsters Rum Cream Liqueur, *Jamaica*
$ ★★★   Creamy rum and spice flavors; racy spirits notes.

Sylk Cream Liqueur, *Scotland*
$$ ★★★   Creamy and rich with viscous, honey-cream texture and a long finish.

Brandy Cream Liqueurs

Boulard Crème Boulard, *France*
$ ★★   Creamy apple flavors with a Calvados-like finish.

Christian Brothers Amber Cream Liqueur, *USA*
$ ★   Creamy and thick with a velvety mouth feel and a long finish.

E. & J. Cask & Cream Liqueur, *USA*
$ ★★★   Pure and lush; smooth, ripe, and rich with bright vanilla, caramel, and spice; long, creamy, and balanced.

Chocolate Cream Liqueurs

Paul Masson Mocha Caramel Cream Liqueur, *USA*
$ ★★   Smoky and dense; ripe and lush.

Paul Masson Chocolate Hazelnut Cream Liqueur, *USA*
$ ★★   Toasty and malty; lush and ripe.

Vermeer Dutch Chocolate Cream, *Netherlands*
$$ ★★★   Smooth and creamy with lovely chocolate and lively spirits; balanced and long.

Miscellaneous Cream Liqueurs

Amarula Marula Fruit Cream Liqueur, *South Africa*
$ ★★★   Made from the fruit of the African marula tree; smooth and creamy with lovely, rich flavors of vanilla, milk chocolate, and exotic spice; long, lush, and with a nice hit of racy alcohol on the finish.

Just Desserts Crème Brûlée Liqueur, *USA*
$$ ★★★   Velvety and luscious with creamy flavors and a persistent finish.

1921 Crema con Tequila, *Mexico*
$$ ★   Cloying and spicy with thick, sweet flavors.

Del Maguey Crema de Mezcal, *Mexico*
$$ ★★★   Sweet, lush, and creamy with lovely spice and vanilla.

BITTERS

Campari Aperitivo, *Italy*
$ ★★★   Bright red color; smooth and bitter with sweet, lush herbs and spice.

Cynar, *Italy*
$ ★★★   Dark amber brown color; smooth and sweet with a charming bitterness from artichoke; rich, long, and nicely balanced.

MISCELLANEOUS LIQUEURS

Agavero Tequila Liqueur, *Mexico*
$$ ★   Clean flavors of agave and spice.

Bärenjäger Honey Liqueur, *Germany*
$$ ★★   Clear, light amber; sweet and lush with honey and caramel flavors; toasty and long.

Metaxa, *Greece*
$$ ★★   Made from muscat wine and aromatics; smooth and perfumed with gentle, lush flavors of toasty brown sugar; quite unique.

Dr. McGillicuddy's Cinnamon Flavored Whiskey, *Canada*
$ ★★★   Cinnamon on the nose with sweet, hot, lively flavors; spicy and clean on the finish.

Sortilège Liqueur with Canadian Whisky and Maple Syrup, *Canada*
$$ ★★   Surprisingly refreshing, with toasty tones of vanilla, malt, and oak underlying silky, maple flavors.

Southern Comfort, *USA*
$ ★★   Medium amber color; peach and vanilla with underlying bourbon flavors; long and balanced.

Celtic Crossing Original Celtic Liqueur, *Ireland*

$$ ★★★   Amber colored; thick, smooth, and unctuous with caramel, spice, and honey; long and mellow, lush and rich but not too sweet.

Irish Mist Liqueur, *Ireland*

$$ ★★   Lush and velvety; nice cereal-like flavors with a long finish.

CHAPTER TEN

the well-stocked bar

very spirit has its own history and mystique, and each evokes a different time and place. A smoky single-malt Scotch is a walk across a foggy moor with a hunting dog by your side. A snifter of cognac is a well-worn leather armchair beside a roaring fire in the library of a French château. A gin and tonic is a rest on the veranda at the end of a long hot day in the British Raj. Tequila is a roisterous mariachi band and enchiladas. Mixed drinks bring to mind American movies from the mid-twentieth century: Bette Davis in an off-the-shoulder cocktail dress, the Rat Pack clowning around in a Vegas nightclub, Nick and Nora Charles ordering dueling martinis.

To share the romance and ritual of fine spirits with friends, you'll need a well-stocked bar. Entertaining is all about providing your guests with exactly what they want in a seemingly effortless way. You don't need to be able to whip up complex creations such as a pisco sour or an Alaskan Polar-Bear Heater on short notice, but with a little planning you can serve fine spirits in the right glasses or concoct just about any standard cocktail your friends request.

✳ GLASSWARE ✳

It's the epitome of luxury to savor your favorite bourbon on the rocks in a handsome, sturdy highball glass that feels just right in your hand, or to sip a rare Armagnac from a crystal snifter specifically designed to hold it.

When it comes to serving spirits, either in a cocktail or straight up, the modern bartender has many more options than Bette Davis did. Several firms that make glasses for different types of wine also make spirits glasses. Riedel, a pioneering Austrian crystal firm, produces a glass for nearly every imaginable spirit: old or young cognac, blended or single-malt Scotch, vodka and aquavit, even *reposado* tequila. Real aficionados may want to spring for such specialized glassware. But there's really no need to invest a fortune in glasses: A few well-chosen designs will get you through any cocktail party. Be sure to buy as many glasses as you will have guests, to avoid the embarrassment of having to serve someone his or her Manhattan in plastic.

The finest glassware has traditionally been lead crystal. There are some health concerns associated with lead crystal, however. A small amount of lead does leach into liquids, especially over time. That antique decanter may look elegant, but use it for serving only. Don't store spirits in it or in any lead crystal vessel, even overnight. Minimize leaching by soaking new lead crystal in vinegar for twenty-four hours before using it. Also, putting it in the dishwasher increases the amount of lead it releases, so wash your lead crystal by hand.

It's not necessary to buy lead crystal to stock a bar elegantly. Several manufacturers—including Orrefors, Ravenscroft, Spiegelau, and Riedel—now make lead-free crystal stemware, both hand- and machine-blown, and a few producers, such as Oneida, iittala, and Anchor Hocking, make an assortment of lead-free crystal cocktail glasses as well. The Tritan brand, available exclusively from the Wine Enthusiast, is made with titanium; these glasses are not only lead-free but also stronger than most crystal stemware.

Whether you opt for leaded or nonleaded, here are the essential glasses for a well-stocked bar.

Snifters, especially those the size of basketballs, are passé; for dark spirits drunk neat, look for smaller modern glasses. Riedel's cognac glasses hold roughly half what its white wineglasses hold, and a similar glass will serve for Armagnac, cognac, Calvados, California alambic brandy, even single-malt Scotch and artisanal bourbon. Eschew gimmicky devices such as brandy pipes or brandy warmers; these will make you look silly and actually impair your enjoyment of the spirit.

White spirits, usually served cold, take an even smaller glass than dark spirits when served neat. Riedel's glass for vodka, gin, and aquavit looks like a small wineglass with a wide mouth. Another option for white or dark spirits is a straight-sided shot glass that holds one and a half to two ounces.

The versatile stemmed cocktail glass can be used for martinis, cosmopolitans, Manhattans, and many other cocktails served straight up. For most other mixed drinks and for straight spirits on the rocks, you'll need an assortment of plain, straight-sided glasses: old-fashioned or highball (eight to ten ounces) and a taller collins (ten to fourteen ounces).

Always keep red and white wineglasses, champagne flutes, and beer glasses on hand for those who don't drink cocktails. Teetotalers or designated drivers can sip ginger ale or mineral water from collins glasses.

Specialty glasses are for those who have a serious interest in a specific spirit. If aged tequila is your passion, or if you're crazy about cordials, by all means invest in a set of Riedel glasses designed for your spirit. If you have a favorite mixed drink that you make often, buy a set of margarita, Irish coffee, or whiskey sour glasses.

✳ EQUIPMENT ✳

Blender. This will be the priciest tool in your bar. The Waring two-speed bar blender is a dependable classic. Cuisinart, Hamilton Beach, and KitchenAid all make bar blenders that are powerful enough to process ice. Their professional versions can be expensive, but most make a standard version priced at less than $100. The most powerful and hardy all-purpose blender is made by Vita-Mix and will cost in the neighborhood of $300. Important safety tip: Don't try to crush ice in a food processor.

Cocktail shaker. There are two basic types. The Boston shaker is a metal base with a slightly smaller glass shaped like a pint beer glass, used by most professional bartenders because it's fast. The classic cocktail shaker is a metal or glass base, a lid with a built-in strainer, and a small cap that fits over the lid. You can even use two beer glasses in a pinch, but why not make a statement? Nothing else sets the style of a home bar like the right shaker. Classic shakers come in myriad shapes and sizes, from ultramodern stainless steel bullets to antique frosted glass to retro reproductions. You can even find shakers shaped like trains, lighthouses, or penguins.

New shakers range in price from a few dollars for an acrylic shaker to $500 for a hand-blown glass and sterling silver Deco model called the Glass Slipper. Most hold sixteen to twenty-four ounces, but there are mini shakers available too. Don't fill the shaker completely; the drink inside must have room to move.

Strainer. This small metal paddle with a spring curved around the edge is used to strain the ice from stirred drinks and drinks made in a Boston shaker.

Long-handled spoon. Use a spoon for muddling and stirring. You can also purchase a miniature mortar and pestle for muddling.

Glass pitcher. Great for serving large quantities of blended or stirred drinks.

Bottle and can openers. The spirits industry, unlike the wine industry, long ago gave up corks and wax seals and embraced screw caps or easily removable stoppers, which makes opening most spirits easy. You'll still need a church key or kitchen can opener to get at some mixers.

Corkscrew. Buy your favorite type—the classic waiter's lever-style model, the original patented Screwpull in heavy-duty plastic, or the double-pronged "Ah-So." If you open lots of wine in addition to occasional bottles, you can invest in one of the more heavy-duty models, such as the Screwpull Lever Model or the popular Metrokane Rabbit. Again, avoid gimmicks such as electric wine openers and also avoid those annoying rabbit-eared openers.

Jigger. A simple measuring tool that is indispensable for making good cocktails. The larger side is a jigger, or one and a half ounces. The smaller side is one ounce, a pony.

Measuring cup and spoons. Choose a standard glass measuring cup and a set of metal spoons. Cocktail recipes are not scientific formulas, but measuring accurately is essential for consistent results, especially for beginning bartenders. Once you've gotten the hang of mixology, you can give up recipes and create your cocktails freestyle.

Ice bucket and tongs. A good-looking glass or lined metal bucket puts ice where you need it. For a stylish presentation, make sure the ice bucket coordinates with your cocktail shaker. Most ice cubes are too big for bar use. The low-tech solution is to put the cubes in a clean cloth bag or towel and crush them with a wooden mallet. This works surprisingly well, and fractures the ice to provide more surface area. If this sounds like too much work, Metrokane makes a very efficient 1950s-style manual ice crusher, or if you're truly lazy buy an electric ice crusher.

Champagne stopper. Keep a couple of these on hand to store unfinished bottles of sparkling wine. Make sure the stopper snaps down over the lip of the bottle; a regular cork will pop out eventually from the pressure of carbonation. Accidents like this have wreaked havoc in my refrigerator on more than one occasion. My favorite of these stoppers is made by Screwpull.

Citrus juicer. Any type will do. A simple and effective cast-aluminum citrus squeezer that resembles an oversized garlic press is available inexpensively from Williams-Sonoma and Crate & Barrel. Mechanical citrus juicers by Metrokane and OrangeX are easy to use and attractive. If you routinely prepare margaritas for thirty, you might want to invest in an electric juicer, such as those by Waring, Juiceman, and L'Equip. Look for a model that handles both citrus and other fruits.

Paring knife. A small sharp knife is needed for cutting up citrus or other fruits. It can also be used to cut strips of citrus peel, or zest, when you want to give a drink a hint of citrus oil without the sharp juice flavor. An inexpensive citrus stripper or zester will make uniform strips without cutting into the bitter white pith.

Plastic cutting board. Ideal for cutting up the aforementioned citrus and other garnishes, a plastic cutting board is easier to keep clean than a wooden board.

Soda siphon. This is an optional piece of equipment, since you can buy many types of seltzer or mineral water, but using a soda siphon adds a certain touch of 1930s glamour to the proceedings. The most expensive ones are stainless steel with brass heads, but less expensive glass or brushed aluminum models work too. A single charger, which is filled with the compressed carbon dioxide that provides the fizz, will carbonate a liter of water.

Drink recipes. Every good bartender has a favorite recipe book. If you're new at the cocktail game, find a book that provides definitions and explains techniques, such as my *Complete Book of Mixed Drinks* (HarperCollins), which offers more than one thousand drink recipes.

Have plenty of clean dishtowels on hand for cleaning up spills and condensation. Other bar essentials include cocktail napkins, glass swizzle sticks to stir drinks, straws, toothpicks for spearing olives, and of course small paper umbrellas to adorn tropical drinks.

✳ MIXERS ✳

If you're going to use fine spirits, don't scrimp on mixers. Nothing ruins a good cocktail like cut-rate ingredients. Avoid diet mixers; they have a too-sweet, artificial taste that'll spoil any drink. Schweppes makes very good and widely available tonic and ginger ale, two bar staples that you should always have on hand. If they're sold in your area, try the new gourmet "microsodas" instead of commercial sodas such as Coke or Seven-Up.

You'll need both sweet red and dry white vermouth (although those who prefer their martinis bone dry may simply want to stare at the vermouth bottle while pouring their gin or vodka). Look for good-quality French or Italian varieties such as Martini & Rossi, Noilly-Prat, or Cinzano. Or seek out new versions made by California winemakers, such as Quady's Vya sweet red vermouth and Duckhorn's King Eider dry white vermouth. These small-batch spirits will add flavor and complexity to your usual cocktails.

Squeeze fresh orange juice, and use fresh lemons and limes with superfine sugar or simple syrup instead of frozen or bottled drink mixes. It's a little more work, but your screwdrivers, mojitos, and margaritas will taste much fresher and more vibrant. If you're making several sweet drinks, prepare your own simple syrup by boiling equal parts water and granulated sugar until the sugar dissolves.

Buy bottled still water for both mixing and ice cubes unless you have great-tasting tap water. A soda siphon or bottled seltzer is a necessity.

Also good to have on hand are cranberry juice, tomato juice, Rose's lime juice (but try to use fresh-squeezed lime juice whenever possible), grenadine, Tabasco, Angostura bitters, Worcestershire sauce, black and green olives, cocktail onions, Maraschino cherries, fresh mint, and salt.

✳ BAR LAYOUT ✳

A home bar can be anything from a full wet bar with its own refrigerator and sink to a corner of the kitchen in a studio apartment. It's easy to designate an area of the kitchen as a permanent or temporary bar; the aim is to collect your ingredients and equipment in one place so you can assemble cocktails without dashing about.

If you're limited by a small space and a small budget, find a work surface in your kitchen with room for blender, cutting board, and ice bucket. Put your corkscrew, openers, and other tools in a nearby drawer. Bottles of spirits and assorted glassware can go in the cupboard above your head.

Clear some space in your kitchen fridge. Spirits needn't be refrigerated, but make room in the freezer for vodka and aquavit. Keep vermouth and other mixers in the refrigerator, but leave fruit out; you'll get more juice from citrus if it's not cold when you squeeze it. For cold mixed drinks, chill the glasses ahead of time. Make or buy lots of ice.

If you have more room to dedicate to cocktails, look for half-size portable bars in furniture stores or online. Hideaway bars, which fold down to look like dressers or cabinets, are especially retro. You can sometimes find vintage bars in secondhand stores, and several manufacturers make very chic reproductions harking back to the 1930s (Deco wood and leather) or fifties (kitschy fake bamboo and Jetson fabrics). Many of these portable bars can be moved outside in good weather—just add tiki torches.

✳ THE BOTTOM LINE ✳

Spirits and cocktails should be about fun. Don't get too hung up on formalities. Once you're a seasoned tequila aficionado or Scotch noser, you can get as serious as you like about your favorite spirits. Keep in mind, though, that even professional spirits connoisseurs think of their work as pleasurable. With a world of spirits waiting to be discovered, the bottom line is: Enjoy!

bibliography

Behrendt, Axel, and Bibiana Behrendt. *Grappa*. New York: Abbeville Press, 1999.

Blue, Anthony Dias. *The Complete Book of Mixed Drinks*. Rev. ed. New York: HarperCollins, 2003.

Brander, Michael. *Brander's Guide to Scotch Whisky*. New York: Lyons & Burford, 1996.

Broom, Dave. *Handbook of Whisky*. London: Hamlyn, 2000.

————. *New American Bartender's Handbook*. San Diego: Thunder Bay Press, 2003.

Calabrese, Salvatore. *Classic Cocktails*. New York: Sterling Publishing, 1997.

————. *Cognac: A Liquid History*. London: Cassell & Co., 2001.

Conrad, Barnaby III. *Absinthe: History in a Bottle*. San Francisco: Chronicle Books, 1988.

Cutler, Lance. *The Tequila Lover's Guide to Mexico*. 2d ed. Vineburg, Calif.: Wine Patrol Press, 2000.

DeWulf, Lucienne M. L., and Marie-Françoise Fourestier. *Adventures with Liqueurs.* New York: Books in Focus, 1979.

Emmons, Bob. *The Book of Gins & Vodkas.* Chicago: Open Court, 2000.

Faith, Nicolas. *The Simon and Schuster Pocket Guide to Cognac and Other Brandies.* New York: Simon and Schuster, 1987.

Firth, Grace. *Secrets of the Still.* McLean, Va.: EPM Publications, 1983.

Grimes, William. *Straight Up or On the Rocks: The Story of the American Cocktail.* New York: North Point Press, 2001.

Grossman, Harold J. *Grossman's Guide to Wines, Beers, and Spirits.* Rev. 7th ed. New York: Charles Scribner's Sons, 1983.

Hallgarten, Peter. *Spirits & Liqueurs.* London: Faber and Faber, 1983.

Hamilton, Edward. *The Complete Guide to Rum.* Chicago: Triumph Books, 1997.

Herbst, Sharon Tyler, and Ron Herbst. *The Ultimate A-to-Z Bar Guide.* New York: Broadway Books, 1998.

Jackson, Michael. *Michael Jackson's Complete Guide to Single Malt Scotch.* Philadelphia: Running Press, 1990.

Kretchmer, Laurence. *Mesa Grill Guide to Tequila.* New York: Black Dog & Leventhal, 1998.

Lembeck, Harriet. *Grossman's Cyclopedia: The Concise Guide to Wines, Beers, and Spirits.* Philadelphia: Running Press, 2002.

Milroy, Wallace. *Wallace Milroy's Malt Whisky Almanac: A Taster's Guide.* Fully updated 4th ed. New York: St. Martin's Press, 1991.

Murray, Jim. *The Complete Guide to Whiskey.* Chicago: Triumph Books, 1997.

———. *Jim Murray's Irish Whiskey Almanac.* Glasgow: Neil Wilson Publishing, 1994.

Neal, Charles. *Armagnac: The Definitive Guide to France's Premier Brandy.* San Francisco: Flame Grape Press, 1998.

Pacult, F. Paul. *American Still Life: The Jim Beam Story and the Making of the World's #1 Bourbon.* Hoboken, N.J.: John Wiley & Sons, 2003.

———. *Kindred Spirits: The Spirits Journal Guide to the World's Distilled Spirits and Fortified Wines.* New York: Hyperion, 1997.

Regan, Gary, and Mardee Haidin Regan. *The Bourbon Companion: A Connoisseur's Guide.* Philadelphia: Running Press, 1998.

———. *The Joy of Mixology.* New York: Clarkson Potter, 2003.

Smith, Gavin D. *Scotch Whisky.* Stroud, U.K.: Sutton Publishing Limited, 1999.

Steadman, Ralph. *Still Life with Bottle: Whisky According to Ralph Steadman.* New York: Harcourt Brace & Company, 1994.

Tucek, Robin, and John Lamond. *The Malt Whisky File.* 2d ed. New York: Lyons Press, 1997.

Waymack, Mark H., and James F. Harris. *The Book of Classic American Whiskeys.* Chicago: Open Court, 1995.

Wittels, Betina J., and Robert Hermesch. *Absinthe: Sip of Seduction.* Denver: Corvus Publishing, 2003.

index

Aalborg Akvavit, 44
Aalborg Jubilaeums, 44
abatangas, 126
absente, 281
absinthe, 267–68, 283
Absolut Vodka, 20, 22, 25, 28, 44
*Absolut Vodka Advertising Story,
The,* 25
echolado pisco, 235
Act for Encouraging the
Consumption of Malted Corn
and for the Better Preventing of
French and Foreign Brandy
(1689), 53
Act for the Encouraging of the
Distillation of Brandy and
Spirits from Corn (1690), 51
agave, 3, 104, 105–7, 109, 110, 112,
113, 115, 116, 118–19, 123,
124–25
agua miel, 105, 107, 108
aguardiente, 87, 111, 112, 257
alambic, word origin of, 3
alambic continuous still, 224

alchemists, 1, 3, 263, 264
alcohol, word origin of, 3
Aleksey I, czar of Russia, 14–15
Alexander I, czar of Russia, 15
Alexander III, czar of Russia, 15–16
Alexander III (the Great), king of
Macedonia, 73
Allied Domecq, 202
Almaden Vineyards, 236
Alvarez, Claudio, 92
Alvarez, Evaristo, 92
Alvarez LeFebre, Claudio, 92
Alvarez Soriano, Claudio, 92
Amaretto Disaronno, 273–74
Amarula Wild Fruit Cream, 285
American dry gin, 51
Americano, 286, 287
American Temperance Society, 188
Amer Picon, 285
Anchor Junipero Gin, 58
Ancient Age Distillery, 189, 195
Anderson, Olof Peter, 44
Andrew Usher and Company, 150
Angostura Bitters, 286

anisette, 266, 283
Anne, Queen of England, 53
Anti-Saloon League, 55
Appellation d'Origine Contrôlée
    (AOC), 83, 116, 118, 221, 228
applejack, 229
aquavit, 3, 11, 42–46, 146, 257
gin compared with, 48–49
aqua vitae, 3, 146, 164, 256, 263
Arango, Doroteo, 113
Archand, Franz Karl, 76
Ardbeg, 145
Aristotle, distillation discovered by, 2
Armagnac, 5, 211, 222–26
aging of, 212, 225
tasting notes for, 246–48
Arnold de Vila Nova, 263
aromatico pisco, 235
Auchentoshan, 144, 154
Augier, 214
Austin, Nichols & Company, 194

Bacardi, 81, 89–90, 91
Bacardi, Emilio, 89–90
Bacardi, Facundito, 90
Bacardi Massó, Facundo, 89
Baikal, Lake, 26–27
Baileys Irish Cream, 268, 284, 285
Baker's Bourbon, 193
Ballantine's, 143, 150
Balvenie, 145
banana liqueur, 288
bar, well-stocked, 301–7
    equipment for, 303–5
    glassware for, 302–3
    layout of, 306–7
    mixers for, 305–6
barley, barley malt, 138–39, 142,
    158
Basil Hayden's, 193
Batista, Fulgencio, 92
Beam, Baker, 192, 193
Beam, Carl, 192
Beam, David, 192
Beam, James Beauregard, 192
Beam, John, 192
Beam & Hart Old Tub Distillery, 192
Beam's Black Label, 192
Beam's Choice, 192
Becher, Johann Joachim, 17–18
Bedford, Jimmy, 198
Beefeater Distillery, 51
Beefeater London Dry Gin, 54, 61,
    65
beets, 76

Belvedere Vodka, 11, 25, 28
Bénédictine, 267, 281
Ben Nevis Distillery, 145
Bergeron, Vic, 79, 86–87
Berry, Francis, 160
Berry Brothers & Rudd, 160–61
bitters, 285–87, 299
Black & White, 150
Blackfriars Distillery, 65
Black Russian, 277
Blanche d'Armagnac, 226
Blanton Distillery, 195
blenders, 303
Bloody Mary, 18–19, 20, 45
blue agave, see agave
Blum, Harry, 192
Bodegas Osborne, 231
Boehm, Jacob, 192
Boke of Wine, The (Arnold de Vila
    Nova), 263
Bols, 52, 61, 265, 277
Bols, Lucas, 265
Bombay Dry Sapphire Gin, 58
Bombay Sapphire Gin, 58, 59, 61,
    62
Bonny Doon, 235, 237
Boodles British Gin, 54, 61
Booker's Bourbon, 184, 191, 193
Boone, Wattie, 187
Boorde, Andrew, 264
Booth's Gin, 54, 61, 62
bootlegging, 15, 16, 55–56, 152
Boru Original Irish Vodka, 11, 28
bourbon, 5, 181–84
    aging of, 4, 182, 183–84
    definition of, 181
    drinks containing, 191–92
    history of, 182, 184–90
    major Kentucky distillers of,
        192–96
    tasting of, 190–92
    types of, 184, 189
Bowmore brand, 5, 145, 154,
    162–63
Bowmore Distillery Company, 163
Boyd, Samuel, 166
Braeval Distillery, 162
brandewijn, 210, 214
brandy, 1, 3, 210–55
    aging of, 212
    basic process for, 211–12
    definition of, 210
    fruit-based, 237–38, 251–53
    from Mendocino, 5
    name origin of, 210

tasting notes for, 239–55
tasting of, 238–39
ypes of, 211
Brandy de Jerez, 211, 230–31,
    250–51
Brilliant Vodka, 11, 28
British dry gin, 47–48
British Empire:
    and gin and tonic, 54–55
    and history of rum, 74–76, 77–78
British Navy, rum and, 77–78
British Virgin Islands, 78
Brizard, Marie, 266
Bronfman, Samuel, 199–200, 202
Brown, Creel, 196
Brown-Forman, 187, 198
brum, 72, 73
Buchanan, James, 150, 151
Buchanan's, 152
Buffalo Trace Distillery, 195
Buffalo Trace Kentucky Straight
    Bourbon Whiskey, 195
Buñuel, Luis, 59
Burns, Robert, 148–49, 161
Burroughs, James, 51, 65
Bushmills, 5, 163, 165, 166–67
Bushmills Black Bush, 167
Bushmills Old Distillery Company,
    166

Cabo Wabo, 121
cachaça (caxaça), 83–84, 85–86
Caipirinha, 85–86
California brandy, 212, 236–37,
    249–50
Call, Dan, 197
Calvados, 211, 227–30
    tasting notes for, 248–49
Calvino, Italo, 231
Cameronbridge Distillery, 150
Camp, Benjamin, 92
Camp, Eduardo, 92
Campari, 286
Campari, Davide, 286
Campari, Gaspare, 286
Campbeltown, Scotland, 144
Camus Distillery, 219
Canada:
    and Prohibition, 55, 80, 160, 189,
        199–200
    and whiskey industry, 153
Canada-Chile FTA, 82
Canadian Club Whisky, 201–2
Captain Morgan Rum, 81
Cardhu Distillery, 159

Carlyle Hotel, 59
Casa Noble brand, 121
Castro, Fidel, 90, 92
Catherine de Medicis, 264–65
Catherine II (the Great), Empress of
    Russia, 15
century plant, 110
Chambord, 278
Charles II, King of England, 164
Charles III, King of Spain, 111
Charodei Vodka, 11, 22
Chartreuse, 258, 260, 267, 274,
    281–82
Chateau Laubade, 226
Cheery Cherry, 157
Cheever, John, 57
Cherry Heering, 278
Cherry Marnier, 278
Chinaco Añejo, 124
Chinaco brand, 124
Chivas brand, 150, 153
Chivas Regal, 143
chocolate, 275–76
Chopin Vodka, 11, 22
Christian III, King of Denmark, 44
Chudov Monastery, Russia, 13
Churchill, Jenny, 191
Citadelle Gin, 61, 67
Clear Creek Distillery, 236, 237
Cles des Ducs, 226
Coale, Ansley, 236–37
Coal Isla Distillery, 152
Cock 'n' Bull restaurant, 20
Cocktail Hour, The (Gurney), 57
cocktail shakers, 303–4
coffee, 276–77
Coffey, Aeneas, 54, 150, 165, 167
Coffey still, 71, 142, 143, 150
cogeners, 15, 211
cognac, 5, 151, 164, 211, 212–22,
    280
    aging of, 212, 214–15, 219–20
    blending of, 220–21
    distillation of, 218–19
    grapes for, 217–18
    invention of, 214
    labeling of, 221–22
    official districts for, 216–17
    tasting notes for, 239–46
Cognac region, 212–14
Cointreau, 258, 267, 274, 279–80
Cointreau, Edouard, Jr., 280
Cointreau, Edouard, Sr., 280
cold compounding, 4
Columbus, Christopher, 73

column still, 65, 142, 143, 218
Complete Distiller, The (Cooper), 266
congeners, 4
Connemara, 166
Consejo Regulador del Tequila
    (CRT), 117, 118
continuous column still, 54, 71, 218
Cooley Distillery, 166
Cooper, A., 266
Copacabana, 56
Cor, John, 138, 146
coriander seed, 51
Cork Distillers, 165
cosmopolitan, 20
Cotton Club, 56
Cox, Jennings S., 84
Craig, Elijah, 187
Craigellachie Distillery, 152
Creekside, 235
crème de banane, 278
crème de cacao, 275–76
crème de cassis, 278
crème de noisette, 275
crème de noyaux, 274
Cristall Vodka, 22, 29
Crosby, Bing, 113
Crow, James, 182
Crowley, Martin, 124, 125
Crown Royal, 203
Cuba, and rum industry, 77, 78–80,
    84–85, 87, 89–90, 92
Cuba Libre, recipe for, 79
Cuervo, José Antonio, 121–22
Cuervo, José Maria Guadalupe de,
    111, 121, 122
Cuervo Labastida, José, 122
Cuff and Buttons, 201
curaçao, 258, 260, 280–81
Cutty Sark, 161
Cutty Sark brand, 143, 156, 160–61
Cynar, 286

daiquiri, 84–85
Dalwhinnie Distillery, 152
Damrak Amsterdam Original Gin, 67
Damrak Gin, 61
Danaka Vodka, 11
Daniel Jasper "Jack" Newton, 197–98
Danish Distillers, 44
Danish Mary, 45
Danzka Vodka, 11
Dartigalongue, 226
De Kuyper, 267, 277
Delamain Reserve de la Famille, 221
Denmark, 3, 44

Depression, Great, 57, 113, 152
Der Lachs Distillery, 265
Desert Juniper Hand Crafted
    American Gin, 67
Dewar, Tommy, 150
Dewar's brand, 143, 150, 152
Diageo, 81, 154, 160
Diaz, Porfirio, 112–13
Diego Zamora, 284
distillation, 1–4, 50
    history of, 2–3, 13, 263
    process of, 2, 257, 263
    see also specific spirits
distillers, 4, 5
Distiller's Company, 53
Distillers Company Limited (DCL),
    152, 154, 160
Distiller's Corporation-Seagram's,
    Ltd., 199, 202–3
Doig, Charles, 139
Don Q Rum, 91
Doxat, John, 59
Drambuie, 267
Dufour, Vital, 226
Dutch gin, 48, 51
Dyetary of Health, A (Boorde), 264

Eagle Rare, 195
Early Times Distillery, 192
East India Company, 214
Eaton, Alfred, 197
eau-de-vie, 3, 214–15, 226, 227,
    230, 232, 235, 237–38, 251–53,
    257, 261
eggnog, 74
Egypt, 2
El Floridita, 85
Elisir du Dr. Roux, 282
Elizabeth II, Queen of England, 203
Elmer T. Lee, 195
El Tesoro, 121
England:
    gin consumption in, 53, 54
    history of gin in, 52–55
    Scottish union with, 147
    see also British empire
essential oils distillation, 50
Estrées Hannibal, François d', 263
Evans, Kenneth Lee, 277
Excise Act (1779), 164–65
Excise Act (1823), 149, 161, 165

Famous Grouse, 143
Ferdinand IV, King of Spain, 111,
    121

Fernet Branca, 286–87
Fields, W. C., 60
filtration, 4
Finlandia Vodka, 21
Finnegans Wake (Joyce), 167
Fitzgerald, F. Scott, 56
flambé, 271
flavoring, 4
Floc d'Armagnac, 226
Flores, Jesús, 122
Four Roses Distillery, 196
Four Roses Kentucky Bourbon,
    195–96
France, 3, 48, 154
    and history of rum, 74, 75–76, 77,
    82–83
    vodka in, 11, 18, 27
François I, King of France, 213,
    214
Frangelico, 274–75
frappé, 271
Free Trade Area of the Americas
    (FTAA), 82
French, John, 264
French Martini, 24
Frïs Vodka, 11

Galliano, 268, 282–83
Galliano, Giuseppe, 282
Gammel Dansk, 287
genever, 48, 52
"Gentle Grafter, The" (O. Henry), 60
Gentleman Jack, 198
George VI, King of England, 161,
    203
George Dickel Distillery, 197
George T. Stagg, 195
George T. Stagg Distillery, 189
Germain-Robin, 235, 236–37
Germain-Robin, Hubert, 236–37
German gin, 48
Gilbey's Gin, 54, 61, 62
gimlet, 58
gin, 3, 5, 11, 47–68
    aquavit compared with, 48–49
    brand profiles of, 64–66
    cold compounding process for, 49
    distillation of, 48–50
    drinks containing, 58, 59–61, 64
    essential oil process for, 50
    first premium, 54–55
    flavoring of, 4, 48, 51
    food with, 62
    gin head distillation of, 50
    grains and botanicals for, 50–51

history of, 52–58, 188
    invention of, 52
    mastikha compared with, 49
    name origin of, 53
    newest brands of, 58
    recipe for, 52
    tasting notes for, 66–68
    tasting of, 61–64
    types of, 47–48
    vodka compared with, 58, 59
Gin Act (1736), 54
gin and tonic, 54–55
gin head distillation, 50
gin martini, 59–61
gin palaces, 54
glassware, 302–3
    for gin, 62, 303
    for liqueurs, 270–71
    for scotch, 155
    for tequila, 126, 303
    for vodka, 22, 303
Glenfiddich brand, 145, 153
Glen Garioch, 154
Glengoyne Distillery, 144–45
Glen Grant Distillery, 162
Glenkinchie Distillery, 144
Glenlivet, The, 145, 149, 153,
    161–62
Glenlivet and Glen Grant
    Distilleries, Ltd., 162
Glenrothes brand, 145
glogg, 45
Goldschläger, 265
Gonzales, Lucrecia, 124
Gonzalez, Guillermo, 124
Gordon, George, Fifth Duke of, 149,
    161, 162
Gordon, James, 141
Gordon & MacPhail, 141
Gordon's London Dry Gin, 54, 62,
    67
gorzalka, 17
Gothenburg (Göteborg) Exposition,
    44
Gouberville, Gilles de, 227
Graham, William, 186
Grand Marnier, 258, 274, 280
Grand Metropolitan, 154
Grant, George Smith, 162
grappa, 5, 211, 231–35, 253–55
Great Tavern Revolt (1648), 14
Great Universal Stores, 166
Greece, 2
Grey Goose Vodka, 11
grog, 77, 78

guarapo, 87
Guinness, 154
Gurney, A. R., 57

Hacienda Cuisillos Distillery, 111
Hagar, Sammy, 121
Haig family, 150, 167
Hamilton, Alexander, 185
Hamptons Gin, 67
Harris, Phil, 113
Harvey Wallbanger, 268, 283
Havana Club Rum, 90
Hayden, Basil, 193
Heaven Hill Distillery, 183
Heering, Peter, 278
Hemingway, Ernest, 85
Hendrick's Gin, 67
Hendrick's Vodka, 11
Hennessy, Richard, 164, 215
Hennessy Paradis, 221
Henry, O., 60
Henry II, King of France, 264
Henry IV, King of France, 223
Herradura brands, 121, 123
Herradura Distillery, 113
Herradura Selección Suprema, 123
Herrera, Danny, 114
Herron, Louis, 201
Hertzberg, Peder Harboe, 43
Heublein Corporation, 18, 19, 122
Highland Refresher, 157
Highlands, Scottish, 144–45,
    148–49, 153
Hilton, Tommy, 114
Hine, Thomas, 215
Hinky Dinks, 86
Hiram Walker & Sons, 153, 194, 277
Holland, *see* Netherlands
Holland gin, 48, 51

Industria Lombarda Liquori Vini
    Affini (Illva), 274
International Distillers and Vintners
    (IDV), 284
Invergordon Distillery, 143
Ireland, 3, 48
    distilleries in, 4, 163
    and history of whisky, 146–47
Irish Distillers, 165, 166, 167
Irish whiskey, 137, 163–67
    history of, 152, 164–67
    tasting notes for, 179–80
    see also Scotch whisky
Isidor the Greek, 13
Islay, Scotland, 145, 162–63

Ivan III, czar of Russia, 14
Ivan IV (the Terrible), czar of Russia,
    14

Jack Daniel Distillery, 197–98
Jack Daniel's Old No. 7 Tennessee
    Sour Mash Whiskey, 197, 198
Jack Daniel's Single Barrel, 198
Jacopo Poli grappas, 234–35
Jägermeister, 283
James B. Distilling Company, 189
James I, King of England, 166
Jameson, 165, 167
Jameson, John, 167
J&B, 143, 156
Janneau, 226
Jefferson, Thomas, 187–88
Jerez Brandy Regulating Council,
    230
Jim Beam, 192
Jim Beam Black, 192
Jim Beam Brands, 189
Jim Beam Distilleries, 183, 184,
    187, 191, 192–93
John Jameson & Sons, 167
Johnnie Walker, 143, 150, 152,
    159–60
Johnnie Walker Black Label, 159
Johnnie Walker Blue Label, 160
Johnnie Walker Extra Special Old
    Highlands, 159
Johnnie Walker Gold Label, 160
Johnnie Walker Green Label Pure
    Malt, 160
Johnnie Walker Old Highlands, 159
Johnnie Walker Red Label, 159
Johnnie Walker Special Old
    Highlands, 159
Johnnie Walker White Label, 159
Jones, Paul, 196
José Cuervo brands, 114, 119,
    121–22
José Cuervo Distillery, 106, 111,
    112, 123
    see also La Rojeña Distillery
José Cuervo Tradicional, 122
Joseph Seagram and Sons, Ltd., 196
Josselyn, 73
Joyce, James, 167
juniper berries, 48, 51, 52
Junipero Gin, 67
J. Wray Nephew Rum, 86

kabaks, 14–15
Kahlúa, 277

Kanbar, Maurice, 26
Kentucky Derby, 191
Ketel One Citroen, 26
Ketel One Vodka, 25–26
Kilbeggan, 166
King, Marjorie, 114
Kir, 278
Kirin Brewery, 196
Knickerbocker Hotel, 59
Knob Creek, 191, 193
Knockdhu Distillery, 152
kohl, 3
kümmel, 265–66
Kunnett, Rudolph, 18
Lafontan, 226
Lagavulin Distillery, 145, 152
La Gonzaleña Distillery, 124
Laird and Company, 229
Laphroaig brand, 145
Lapostolle, Jean-Baptiste, 280
La Rojeña Distillery, 122
    see also José Cuervo Distillery
Larresingle, 226
Leestown Distillery, 195
Legrand, Alexandre, 281
Leyden Dry Gin, 58, 62, 67
Licor 43, 284
Limoncello, 279, 288
Lincoln, Abraham, 188, 193
Linie Aquavit, 44
liqueurs, 256–85
    base spirit for, 256–57
    bitters types of, 285–87, 299
    cordials vs., 269
    cream-containing, 268, 284–85,
        297–98
    definition of, 270
    drinks containing, 268, 277, 278,
        280, 283, 286, 287
    flavoring of, 258–59
    fruit types of, 277–81, 291–94
    herbal types of, 281–84, 294–96
    history of, 262–68
    house blends of, 260–61
    nut, bean, and seed types of,
        273–77, 289–91
    processes for making, 259
    recipes for, 288
    sweetening of, 257–58
    tasting and drinking of, 270–72
    tasting notes for, 289–300
    types of, 261–62
    variety of modern, 268–70
London dry gin, 47–48
Los Arango Tequila Distillery, 113

Los maestros del Ron, 89
Louisiana Purchase (1803), 187
Louis XIV, King of France, 266,
    279
Lowlands, Scottish, 144, 148–49,
    150, 165
Luini, Bernardino, 273
Lully, Raymond, 3, 13
Luxardo, 267
Lysholm family, 44

Macallan, 145, 156
McBey, James, 160–61
McCarthy, Steve, 237
McCarthy, Thomas, 193–94
Mackie, Peter, 150
MacPhail, John Alexander, 141
Madero, Francisco, 113
Magellan Gin, 67
maguey, 110, 111, 112
mai tai, 79, 86–87
Majorca, 3, 13
Maker's Mark Distillery, 183, 187,
    194–95
malt, 138–39, 142, 158
Manhattan, 191
Manhattan Club, 191
Maraschino, 278
marc, 211, 235, 253–55
margarita, 110, 114–15, 118, 126,
    280
Marie Brizard, 258, 277
Marnier-Lapostolle, 267, 280
Marquis de Montesquieu, 226
Marrero, Ramon "Monchito," 88
Martell, 219, 237
Martell, Jean, 215
Martell Extra, 221
Martin, John G., 18, 20
martini, 11, 20, 24, 57, 58, 59–61
Martinique, 77, 82–83
Martin Miller's London Dry Gin, 67
mashing process, 139
mastikha, 49
Matusalem brand, 92
Maubec, Frère, 282
mead, 262
Mendeleyev, Dmitry, 16
mescaline, 120
Mexico:
    and blue agave, 106, 124
    and history of tequila, 110–16,
        118, 119, 121–25
mezcal, 110–11, 112
    tasting notes for, 135–36

mezcal *(cont.)*
    tequila compared with, 119–20
    see also tequila
Midori, 279
Miller Brewing Company, 26
mint julep, 191
mixto tequila, 108, 109, 110, 113,
    115–16, 122
mojito, 87–88
molasses, 69, 70, 75, 82
Molasses Act (1733), 75, 76, 199
Montespan, Marquise de, 266
Morales, Pancho, 114
Moreau, Amalia Lucía Victoria, 89
Morgan, Jack, 20
Morrison Bowmore, 154
Morrison Bowmore Distilleries, Inc.,
    163
Mor Vodka, 11
Moscow Mule, 20
Motlow, Clifford, 198
Motlow, Daniel, 198
Motlow, Lem, 198
Motlow, Reagor, 198
Motlow, Robert, 198
Mount Gay, 91–92
Mutter, James, 163
Mutter, William, 163
My Last Sigh (Buñuel), 59
my precious, 64

National Distillers Products
    Company, 189
Negroni, 286, 287
Nelson, Horatio, Viscount, 78
Nelson, Willie, 187
Nelson's Blood, 78
Netherlands, 3, 48
    and cognac, 214, 215
    gin's invention in, 52
    and history of rum, 72–73, 75
Nicholas II, Czar of Russia, 16
Nikon, Russian prelate, 14
Noe, Booker, 192, 193
Nolet, Carl, Sr., 26
Nolet, Joannes, 25
Nonino, Elizabeth, 233
Nonino grappas, 233–34
Norma Oficial Mexicana Tequila,
    116, 117
North American Free Trade
    Association (NAFTA), 82
North American whiskey, 181–209
    blended, 198–203
    bourbon type of, 181–96, 204–7

    Canadian, 199–200, 201–3, 208–9
    and Civil War, 188
    corn content of, 181, 183
    history of, 182, 184–90, 198–200
    and Prohibition, 188–89, 197,
        199–200
    rye type of, 183, 207–8
    sour-mash process for, 182–83,
        203
    tasting notes for, 204–9
    taxation of, 185–86, 187, 188
    Tennessee type of, 196–98, 207
    and Whiskey Rebellion, 185–86
    see also bourbon; Irish whiskey;
        Scotch whisky

Oban Distillery, 145, 152
Occidental Hotel, 59
Olbracht, Jan, King of Poland, 17
Old Bushmills Distillery Company,
    166
Old Crow, 182, 189
old-fashioned, 192
Old Forester, 183
Old Grand-Dad, 189
Old Grand-Dad Distillery, 193
Old Jameson Distillery, 167
Old Joe Distillery, 196
Old Moore Distillery, 193
Old Mr. Boston, 277
Old Overholt, 189, 200
Old Pepper, 182
Old Prentice Distillery, 196
Old Rip Van Winkle, 195
Old Taylor, 189
Old Tom, 53, 60
Old Tub, 192
Old Vatted Glenlivet Whisky, 150
O. P. Anderson Aquavit, 44
orange blossom, 64
ouzo, 262
Overholt Distillery, 189
Oxford University, 191

Pagliuchi, 84
Parra, 231
patent still, 142, 143, 150, 165
Patrón, 121, 124–25
Pepper, James E., 192
Pernod, 283
Pernod, Henri-Louis, 283
Pernod-Ricard group, 5, 162, 165,
    166, 167, 194
Peter I (the Great), Czar of Russia,
    13, 15, 265–66

Petiot, Fernand "Pete," 18–19
Peychaud, Antoine Amedie, 287
Peychaud's Bitters, 287
Phillips, Thomas, 166
phylloxera vine louse, 151, 215, 217
piña colada, 80, 88
Pisa Nut Liqueur, 275
pisco, 235–36, 253–55
Plymouth Gin, 48, 58, 59, 61, 65–66
Poli, Jacopo, 234
Pomace brandies, 231–36
Ponce de León, Juan, 90
potatoes, 17–18, 22, 43
pot still, 71, 140, 158, 165, 218, 259
pousse-café, 271–72
Powers and Cork Distilleries, 167
Powers Distillery, 165
Prohibition, 19
    and gin, 50, 55–57, 188
    and rum industry, 78, 80, 90
    and Scotch industry, 152, 160
    and tequila industry, 113
    and whiskey industry, 165, 188–89, 193, 197, 199–200
Puerto Rico, 77, 88, 89, 90
pulque, 104, 110
Punt a Mes, 287
puro pisco, 235
pusser's rum, 78

Rain Vodka, 195
ratafias, 267
Reina, Carlo Dominico, 274
Rémy Cointreau Group, 91
Rémy Martin Louis VIII, 221
rhum agricole, 83
rhum industriel, 83
Riedel, 155
Ripy, Thomas B., 193
Rob Roy, 155
Rockefeller, John D., 59
Roger, Jean Baptiste, 266
Rojas, Vincente Albino, 122
Ron Rico (Ronrico) brand, 90–91
Roosevelt, Franklin D., 57
Rosebank Distillery, 144
Roux, Michel, 25, 281, 282
rum, 3, 5, 69–103
    aging of, 71–72
    blending of, 72
    brand profiles of, 89–93
    description of, 69–70
    distillation of, 70–71
    drinks containing, 84–88

flavored, 94, 100–103
history of, 70, 72–80, 189, 199
name origin of, 72–73
popularity of, 80–81
regulations and guidelines for, 81–82
storage of, 94
tasting notes for, 94–103
tasting of, 93
rum and coca-cola, 79
rumbarricoes, 77
rum punch, 75
Rum-Verschnitt, 82
Russell, Jimmy, 194
Russia, 3
    bootlegging in, 15, 16
    history of vodka in, 11, 13–17, 19, 26, 27
rye whiskey, 5

St. George Spirits, 235, 237
St. Maarten's Spirits, 124
Sake to Me, 24
Sambuca Romana, 283–84
Sames, Margarita, 114
Samuels, Bill, Jr., 194
Samuels, Leslie, 194
Samuels, Margie, 195
Samuels, Robert, 194
Samuels, T. William, 194
Samuels, William, 194
Sanchez Romate, 231
Sandiford, William, 91
San Francisco World Spirits Competition, 5, 65
sangrita, 126
Sauza, Cenobio, 112, 122–23
Sauza, Eladio, 123
Sauza, Javier, 123
Sauza brands, 121, 122–23
Sauza Distillery, 106, 112
Savoy Cocktail Book, 65
Sazerac Company, 195
Scala, Maria, 286
Scheidam Holland Gin, 51
schnapps, 261, 262, 284, 296
Scotch and soda, 155
Scotch Malt Whisky Society, 141, 142
Scotch sour, 155
Scotch whisky, 137–63
    aging of, 4, 140–41
    blended, 142, 143, 150, 151, 153, 156, 157, 177–78
    brand profiles of, 159–63

Scotch whisky *(cont.)*
  distillation of, 140
  drinks containing, 155, 157
  fermentation of, 139, 142
  future of, 154–55
  grain type of, 138, 142–43
  history of, 146–54
  independent bottlers of, 141, 142
  major markets for, 154
  malting process for, 138–39
  malt type of, 5, 138–42, 153–54
  mashing process for, 139
  and Prohibition, 152, 160
  regions for making of, 143–46
  single-malt, 5, 141–42, 153–54,
    168–77
  tasting notes for, 168–78
  tasting of, 155–57
  taxation of, 147–49, 153
  terminology lexicon for, 157–59
Scotland, 3, 4, 48, 146–54
Scottish Malt Distillers Association,
  151
screwdriver, 20
scuttlebutts, 77
Seagram, 153, 162
Seagram, Joseph, 203
Seagram's, 202–3
Seagram's Five Crown, 202–3
Seagram's Seven Crown, 202–3
Seagram's VO, 203
Sea Wynde brand, 92–93
Sempé, 226
Serrallés, Juan, 90–91
Serrallés, Sebastian, 90
Serrallés Distillery, 91
Shafter, William R., 84–85
Siegert, Johann, 286
Siete Leguas Distillery, 124
Siete Leguas Tequila, 113
Simon, André, 226–27
Singapore sling, 58
Skal (Swedish toast), 46
Skyy Blue, 26
Skyy Cosmo Mix, 26
Skyy Vodka, 22, 26
slaves, slave trade, 75, 76, 83, 87,
  199
sloe gin, 281
Small Stills Act (1816), 149
Smirnoff Vodka, 18, 21, 27
Smirnov, Piotr Arsenyevitch, 15, 27
Smirnov, Vladimir, 17, 18, 27
Smith, George, 149, 161–62
Smith, John Gordon, 162

snaps, 261
Sober, Cumberbatch, 91
Sober, John, 91
solera brandy, *see* Brandy de Jerez
Sorrows of Gin, The (Cheever), 57
Sortilège, 279
sotol, 121, 136
Sotol Hacienda de Chihuahua, 121
Southern Comfort, 200–201
Spain, 3, 48, 154
  and history of rum, 73–74, 75, 90,
    116–17
  and history of tequila, 110–11
Spanish-American War, 79, 84–85
sparge, 139, 158
speakeasies, 55, 56
Speyside, Scotland, 145, 153, 159,
  161–62
spirits, 1–7
  and well-stocked bar, 301–7
  see also specific types of spirits
spirits still, 140
Springbank Distillery, 144
Spudka Potato Vodka, 22
Stanley P. Morrison, 163
Star Hill Distillery, 195
Steadman, Ralph, 147
Stein, John, 167
Stein, Robert, 54, 150, 167
Steinhäger gin, 48
Stewart, Thomas, 59
*Stewart's Fancy Drinks and How to
  Mix Them* (Stewart), 59
Still Life with Bottle (Steadman), 147
Stock, 267, 283
Stolichnaya Vodka, 11, 21, 26–27
Stoli Limon Vodka, 11
Stön Vodka, 11
Strathisla brand, 153
sugar, sugar industry, 70, 73, 75,
  76, 83, 87, 257
Sugar Act (1764), 75
Sugarplum Cherry, 45
Suntory, 5, 163
Sutter, John, 236
Sylvius, Franciscus De Le Boë, 52

tafia, 82
Taggia, Martini di Arma di, 59, 61
Tagle, Pedro Sanchez, 110
"Tam O'Shanter" (Burns), 161
Tanqueray, 48, 54, 58, 64–65
Tanqueray, Charles, 64–65
Tanqueray Malacca, 65
Tanqueray No. 10 Gin, 58, 61, 65

Tapatio Distillery, 107
tastings, 5–6
taverns, 14–15
Teacher's, 150
temperance movement, 55, 188, 199
    see also Prohibition
tequila, 3, 4–5, 104–36, 198
    and agave plant, 3, 104, 105–7,
        109, 110, 112, 113, 115, 116,
        118–19, 123, 124–25
    aging of, 108–10
    brand profiles of, 121–25
    classifications of, 108–9, 115,
        116
    distillation of, 108
    drinks containing, 110, 114–15,
        126
    fermentation of, 107–8
    food with, 126
    history of, 110–16
    mezcal compared with, 119–20
    mixto type of, 108, 109, 110, 113,
        115–16, 117, 122
    oxygenation of, 127
    popularity of, 117–19
    and Prohibition, 113
    regulation of, 115, 116–17
    tasting notes for, 128–35
    tasting of, 125–27
tequila sunrise, 110, 118
Teton Glacier Potato Vodka, 11
Thomas, Jerry, 59
Tia Maria, 277
Tippling Act (1750), 54
Tito's Handmade Vodka, 11
Tobias, Charles, 78
Tommy's Bar, 114
Trader Vic's, 79, 86–87
Trapier, William Heyward, 191
Triangle Trade, 75, 76, 199
triple sec, 280
Tru Blue Martini, 59
Tru restaurant, 59
Tuaca Liquore, 283
Tuillière, Monsieur, 224
T. W. Samuels Distillery, 194
Tyrconnell, 166

uisige beatha, 3, 147, 257
Under, Vern, 114
United Distillers, 154
United Distillers and Vintners
    (UDV), 154
United Kingdom Distillers'
    Association, 151

United States, 48, 154
    brandies of, 212, 236–37, 249–50
    history of gin in, 50, 55–58
    history of rum in, 76, 78–80
    history of tequila in, 112,
        113–14
    history of vodka in, 18–21, 22,
        25–26, 27, 57–58
    history of whiskey in, 76,
        152–53
    and Prohibition, 19, 50, 55–57,
        78, 80, 90, 113, 152, 160, 165,
        188–89, 193, 197, 199–200

Van Gogh Gin, 58
Vassily III, Czar of Russia, 13
Vermeer Dutch Chocolate Cream,
    276
vermouth, 59, 60
Vernon, Edward, 77
Vert, Constantino Ribalaigua, 85
Viatka Monastery, Russia, 13
Vignes, Jean Louis, 236
Villa, Pancho, 113, 124
Vin & Sprit AB, 44
Vincelli, Bernardo, 281
Vincent Van Gogh Dutch Chocolate
    Vodka, 41
vino mescal, 110
Vinomex, 121
Voda Blueberry Infused Vodka, 34
vodka, 4, 5, 9–41
    bootlegging of, 15, 16
    brand profiles of, 25–28
    distillation of, 16, 18, 27
    drinks containing, 18–19, 20, 24,
        268
    filtration of, 4, 10, 15, 27
    flavored, 11, 12, 34–41, 58
    food with, 22–23
    gin compared with, 58, 59
    history of, 11, 13–21
    ingredients of, 10–11, 17–18, 22,
        25–26, 27
    name origin of, 3, 9, 13
    spice, herb, and miscellaneous
        flavors of, 41
    subgroups of, 22
    tasting notes for, 28–41
    tasting of, 22–23
vodka gimlet, 11
vodka martini (vodkatini), 11, 20,
    58, 60
Volstead, Andrew J., 199
Volstead Act (1920), 55, 57, 199

Walker, Alexander, 159
Walker, Alexander, Jr., 159, 160
Walker, Hiram, 201–2
Walker, James, 202
Walker, John, 159, 160
Walker's Kilmarnock Whisky, 159
Walpole, Robert, 148
Ward, Aubrey, 91
wash, 139, 140, 142, 158
Wash Act (1784), 148
Washington, George, 74–75, 185, 186
Wathen Distillery, 189
Weber, Dr., 105
whiskey, 1, 5
    ndustry consolidation and, 4, 152, 153, 154, 165–66
    name origin of, 3, 147
    see also Irish whiskey; North American whiskey; Scotch whisky
Whiskey Rebellion, 185–86
Whiskey River Bourbon, 187

Whisky Parliament, 151
White Horse, 150, 152
Wild Turkey 12 Years Old, 194
Wild Turkey Bourbon, 183, 194
Wild Turkey Distillery, 193–94
Wild Turkey Kentucky Spirit, 194
Wild Turkey Old No. 8 Brand, 194
Wild Turkey Rare Breed, 194
Wilkinson, James, 187
William Grant & Sons, 153
William Grant's, 143
William III, King of England, 53
Williams, Evan, 187
Wilson, Woodrow, 199
W. L. Weller, 195
Women's Christian Temperance Union, 55
Women's Crusade, 55
Wooten, Ed, 19
wort, 139, 159
Wyborowa Vodka, 22

Zyr Vodka, 11